P9-ECT-089

WITHDRAWN

Wonder
of Wonders

Wonder
of Wonders

A Cultural History of
Fiddler on the Roof

Alisa Solomon

METROPOLITAN BOOKS

HENRY HOLT AND COMPANY

NEW YORK

Metropolitan Books
Henry Holt and Company, LLC
Publishers since 1866
175 Fifth Avenue
New York, New York 10010
www.henryholt.com

Metropolitan Books® and ® are registered trademarks of Henry Holt and Company, LLC.

Library of Congress Cataloging-in-Publication data

Solomon, Alisa, 1956–
    Wonder of wonders : a cultural history of Fiddler on the roof / Alisa Solomon.—First edition.
        pages cm
    Includes bibliographical references and index.
    ISBN 978-0-8050-9260-8
    1. Bock, Jerry. Fiddler on the roof.   2. Stein, Joseph. Fiddler on the roof.   3. Sholem Aleichem,
1859–1916.   4. Musicals—New York (State)—New York—20th century—History and criticism.
5. Theater, Yiddish—New York (State)—New York—History—20th century.   6. Jewish theater—
New York (State)—New York—History—20th century.   I. Title.
    ML410.B661S65 2013
    782.14—dc23

                                                                                    2013003900

Henry Holt books are available for special promotions and premiums. For details contact:
Director, Special Markets.

First Edition 2013
Designed by Meryl Sussman Levavi
Printed in the United States of America

1   3   5   7   9   10   8   6   4   2

For Marilyn,
miracle of miracles

Contents

———

A Note on Spelling

———

Transliterating from Yiddish can be tricky when different sources take different approaches to Yiddish orthography. I follow the transliteration system of the YIVO Institute for Jewish Research unless the words are quoted from a source that spells them differently. This goes for the names of characters despite some potential confusion: Tevye (according to YIVO and most recent translations and as used in *Fiddler on the Roof*), Tevya (used in the play by Arnold Perl, discussed in chapter 2), and Tevyeh (as quoted from some press reviews of the earliest translations into English); Tsaytl and Tzeitel; Khave and Chava; Motl and Motel; Hodl, Huddel, and Hodel; and so on.

More complicated is the name Sholem-Aleichem. I use this common spelling, along with initial capital letters (which don't exist in Yiddish), for its widespread familiarity. (The YIVO standard "Sholem-aleykhem" looks distractingly strange.) I include the hyphen as current scholarly convention—and the writer's own signature—dictates, more accurately signaling that the pseudonym is an ordinary compound phrase used by Yiddish speakers all the time. It is a common, if slightly formal, greeting that literally means "Peace unto you" but colloquially best translates as "How do you do?" That is why one never refers to the writer simply as "Aleichem" or "Mr. Aleichem." To do so would be as weird as calling Howdy Doody "Mr. Doody."

WONDER
OF WONDERS

A Little Bit of This,
A Little Bit of That

Glenn Beck was welling up as he neared the conclusion of his Restoring Courage rally in Jerusalem in August 2011. The conservative, conspiracy-mongering talk show host choked back tears as he bade his audience farewell. As he left the stage, exit music swelled: "Sabbath Prayer" from *Fiddler on the Roof*.

A few weeks later, Occupy Judaism was planning an outdoor radical Yom Kippur service as an extension of the demonstrations taking place in Lower Manhattan that fall. To get the word out, one of the organizers made a poster that adapted one of the Occupy Wall Street logos. He took the original image—a ballerina balancing on the back of the bronze *Charging Bull* statue that lurches in a park in New York's financial district—and Photoshopped the dancer out. In her place, he substituted the silhouette of a tottering violinist: another invocation of *Fiddler on the Roof*.

There could hardly be more clashing sensibilities than those of Glenn Beck and Occupy activists—Beck condemned the movement as "worse than Robespierre"—yet both staked a claim to the Broadway musical about the affable dairyman Tevye and his three marriageable daughters living in the Jewish Pale of Settlement in 1905. Beck's use of the song from the show was naive and even kitschy, while Occupy's appropriation of the image winked with postmodern irony, but both operated from the assumption that *Fiddler* bears talismanic power to endow an event or object with a warm glow of Jewish authenticity.

The show—created by Jerry Bock (music), Sheldon Harnick (lyrics), Joseph Stein (book), and Jerome Robbins (direction and choreography)—was an instant blockbuster success when it opened in 1964, smashing all box office records in its day. The initial production played 3,242 performances—the longest-running show on Broadway for years. It won Tony Awards in nine categories in 1965. National Public Radio featured *Fiddler* as one of the "100 most important American musical works of the 20th century." The American Film Institute named Norman Jewison's movie version among the "100 most inspiring films of all time." There have been four Broadway revivals, countless national tours, and probably more local productions than the licensing agency can count—more than it even knows about. Some two hundred schools across the country put it on each year. The show has survived censorious dictators, bad productions, and highbrow scolds.

As the first work of American popular culture to recall life in a shtetl—the Eastern European market towns with large Jewish populations—*Fiddler* felt tender, elegiac, even holy. It arrived just ahead of (and helped to instigate) the American roots movement. It was added to multicultural curricula and studied by students across the country in Jewish history units, as if *Fiddler* were an artifact unearthed from a destroyed world rather than a big-story musical assembled by showbiz professionals.

Beyond its continuing vibrant life in the theater, *Fiddler*, like no other musical before or since, has seeped into the culture more widely, functioning in sometimes contradictory ways—which makes sense, since the show's essential gesture is dialectical: it looks backward and forward, favors both community and individual needs, honors the particular and the universal, struggles between stasis and change, bewails and celebrates. Tevye seems to be constantly caught in these opposing forces and, before our eyes, weighs the arguments of every dilemma—on the one hand, on the other hand . . .

Fiddler has served as a Jewish signifier: "Now, I know I haven't been the best Jew," Homer tells a rabbi from whom he is trying to borrow money in an episode of *The Simpsons*, "but I have rented *Fiddler on the Roof* and I intend to watch it." And Tevye or the Fiddler can often be found sharing a rooftop with Santa Claus on interfaith winter holiday cards.

The show has operated as a barometer of Jewish political status: In 1974, Augusto Pinochet banned *Fiddler* in Chile as a "Marxist inspired"

DAN SIERADSKI

Occupy Judaism's Fiddler on the Bull.

work containing "disruptive elements harmful to the nation." Thirty-five years later, in 2009 in Venezuela, Hugo Chavez defunded the orchestra for a theater presenting *Fiddler* because it wasn't Marxist enough. *Fiddler* has been a powerful intertextual work, commenting from within in Joseph Cedar's movie *Footnote* (a family torn by generational conflict goes to see a performance), David Bezmozgis's novel *The Free World* (a Soviet émigré family with a Stalinist patriarch sees the movie while stuck in Rome, waiting for visas), and Nadia Kalman's novel *The Cosmopolitans* (*Fiddler* as a structuring device), to name just a few cases.

Fiddler has become ritual: kids at summer camps sing "Sabbath Prayer" on Friday evening as they light candles in place of the Hebrew blessing, and for decades weddings didn't feel complete without a rendition of "Sunrise, Sunset."

And more. The show is a global touchstone for an astonishing range of concerns: Jewish identity, American immigrant narratives, generational conflict, communal cohesion, ethnic authenticity, and interracial bridge building, among them. It also solidified the origin story of American Jews as flight from persecution in Eastern European shtetls—never mind the actual origins of those from urban centers or from Sephardic and Middle Eastern backgrounds.

How could a commercial entertainment do all this? The answer lies in large part in where *Fiddler* came from and how it was made. *Wonder of Wonders* sets out to tell that tale: to look at what prepared the way for the musical historically, culturally, and aesthetically, how it turned into a show with such abiding power, and where it has been a catalyst for cultural shifts. It is a story about ethnic assertion and cultural adaptation and about the exigencies and outsize personalities of showbiz. Tracing the surprising, enduring, shape-shifting utility of the beloved musical, *Wonder of Wonders* explores how a work of popular culture can glow with a radiant afterlife, illuminating for different audiences the pressing issues of their times.

Specifically, it is a story about theater, the making of it and the meanings that come from the messy and marvelous collaborations that are its essence—interactions among artists, between artists and audiences, between a show and the world.

The story begins at the source: Sholem-Aleichem, the great Yiddish writer who created Tevye in a short story in 1894 and, over the next two decades, occasionally put a new chapter about his tragicomic hero into the world. Best beloved as a story writer, Sholem-Aleichem also created novels and plays and he was eager to break into New York's Yiddish theater scene.

His first major foray into the theater, with his first full-length play, was a smash. Called *Tsezeyt un tseshpreyt* (*Scattered and Dispersed*), the play, which dealt with intergenerational conflict, triumphed at the Elysium Theater in Warsaw in the spring of 1905. It was performed in Polish (because of the Russian Empire's standing, if erratically enforced, ban on performances in Yiddish) and the house was packed. At the urging and expense of the producer and translator, Mark Arenshteyn, Sholem-Aleichem traveled from his home in Kiev to Warsaw to see for himself.

"What shall I write you about yesterday's triumph?" Sholem-Aleichem asked his daughter in a letter the day after he saw the show. In ecstatic detail, he described how the audience "literally covered me with flowers" after the first act and how after every act that followed they called him to the stage repeatedly. In the fourth act, he reported, "the public simply went crazy, applauding every phrase that had any connection to the play's theme. At the end, hats started flying in the air and some kind of wild, elemental force tried to gobble me up. For a moment I thought the theater might cave in."

He wondered, with a little false modesty, as to the cause: was it the popularity of the folk writer, the Jewish public's yearning for a Yiddish theater, or simply the mob's lack of restraint? In any case, Sholem-Aleichem evaded the "thousand-headed mass that awaited its prey" at the theater's exit only because a police officer hid him away in a locked loge for half an hour and then slipped him out a back door. "My God! What would happen if it were possible to play in Yiddish?"

With more prescience than he could have guessed, Sholem-Aleichem concluded, "My fate and your future (I mean that of my successors) are tightly bound up with the Jewish theater. Write it down in your calendar."

She would have done well to mark a date more than half a century later that would not only forever tie Sholem-Aleichem's fate to the theater but also shape the future of remembered Jewish history: September 22, 1964, the opening night of *Fiddler on the Roof.*

PART I

WHEN AMERICA
COMMANDS

CHAPTER I

Tevye's Long Journey
to the New York Stage

SHOLEM-ALEICHEM SAT IN KIEV AND THOUGHT ABOUT THE New York theater. He was exhausted from a reading tour that autumn of 1905, through a land sputtering with aftershocks of the failed revolution. Train strikes had delayed his travel and he was depressed by the hunger and hopelessness he had seen among the adoring crowds who poured out to hear his wry stories of the Jewish folk. At forty-six, he was uncertain about his own future as well. Though he was the most famous Yiddish author in the world, beloved by readers from Berdichev to Brod, Boston to Buenos Aires, he had no idea where his next kopek would come from. With a wife and five children to support (his eldest of six was already on her own and engaged to be married) and unrest still rumbling through the Russian Empire, he dreamed—like millions of other Jews in the region—of finding deliverance in America.

Specifically, he expected to make a killing in the flashy Yiddish theater scene. Surely, the great actor-managers in New York would clamor for a play from the celebrated writer and pay handsomely for it, too. What's more, he believed, his work would raise the level of theirs. In place of the sensational melodramas and trivial operettas that dominated the Yiddish repertoire, Sholem-Aleichem would offer an honest charm. Instead of the flamboyant figures who pranced and declaimed, his characters would be true-to-life Jews. His plays would be funny, yes; touching, sure. But not by dint of the cheap gags and sentimental exaggerations that were the yeast of the plays that hacks "baked"—as the critics said—by the dozen. Rather, the comic humanity and the pathos of his famous fiction would shine forth from a nobler, more sincere form of drama. Sholem-Aleichem was convinced: New York's Yiddish theater would save him. And he would return the favor.

A good place to start would be with a stage adaptation of *Stempenyu*, a highly successful novella about a dazzling, philandering violinist who woos Rokhele, a beautiful young woman tied to an inattentive husband. When he published it in 1888, the author had been writing for five years under the Yiddish pen name Sholem-Aleichem—literally "Peace be unto you" but the conversational equivalent of "How do you do?" In the late nineteenth century, serious Jewish writers such as the young Sholem Rabinowitz aspired to be could be proud to identify themselves with works penned in Hebrew or Russian—but not in Yiddish. Intellectuals and proponents of the Jewish

AVRAHAM NOVERSHTERN, AT BEIT SHOLEM-ALEICHEM AND JOSEPH DORMAN

Sholem-Aleichem, urbane businessman and beloved *folkshrayber*.

Enlightenment, the *Haskalah*, scorned the vernacular "jargon" that made its way into print only for the degraded texts that appealed to women—prayer books for those unlearned in the holy tongue, formulaic romance novels. Rabinowitz had long left the shtetl of his boyhood and, after standard study in a religious *kheyder*, had been educated in a Russian high school; as the tutor to the daughter of a wealthy estate owner near Kiev for three years, he'd had a taste of the high life (he was fired for courting his pupil); at twenty-one, he was pursuing a writing career and asserting his place in the intelligentsia. Hebrew, therefore, formal and flowery, was the language he used when he wrote essays on Jewish pedagogy during the longueurs of his day job as a Jewish community record keeper and liaison (a *rabiner*) in a provincial town government in the Ukraine.

In 1881, the editor of the Hebrew journal Rabinowitz wrote for also started putting out a Yiddish weekly and the imprimatur such a publication granted the derided language tapped open an old desire. Rabinowitz had determined as a child that he'd become a writer one Saturday evening as he listened in on his grandfather reading to guests from a thin, yellowed book (or so his self-mythologizing autobiography maintains). The boy could not make out the words or even the general subject of the Yiddish his grandfather recited, but he could hear the visitors laughing. Someday, Rabinowitz decided, he too would bring such delight to the common people. With the publication of the Yiddish supplement to the Hebrew paper, he now had the chance.

The Yiddish language's standing had been rising with the growth of Jewish nationalism, spurred on by a wave of pogroms that began after the assassination of Alexander II in March 1881 and then spread through the southwestern swath of the empire over the next several years. The violence tearing up Jewish towns and urban neighborhoods shocked Jews who had believed they could gain full emancipation and equality in the Russian Empire; cosmopolitanism looked less promising in the face of antisemitic attacks. With the model of earlier modern national movements that emphasized the distinctness of peoples through their languages, the Jewish intelligentsia began to valorize the "folk" and their lingua franca. Hard-core Yiddishists, insisting on the language itself as the binding agent for Jews, represented only a single faction of competing nationalist visions. But whether making the case for the glory of the proletariat, the promise of Zionism, the redemption of Hasidic devotion, or the utility of cultural autonomy within Russia, Jews were hashing out these arguments in one vernacular.

Still, to be on the safe side, following a convention of the period, Sholem Rabinowitz opted for a pseudonym when, in 1883, he published a satirical sketch in the weekly about crooked elections for a *rabiner* in a town just like the one where he lived. In May of that year, he had wed his former pupil, Olga Loyev. Now there was even more of a reputation to protect. His new father-in-law, a secular intellectual, would hardly have welcomed Rabinowitz's stooping to that "unmanly" tongue any more than his father back in Pereyaslav, a poor Talmudic scholar and ardent Hebraist, would support it. (The pseudonym also had the advantage of protecting the author from the wrath of thinly veiled people he ridiculed in the feuilleton.) "Sholem-Aleichem" soon went on to publish a series of humorous epistolary stories. The very choice of moniker conveyed the waggish tone of the work. Essentially, it is a joke of the who's-on-first variety. ("What's your name?" "How do you do." "Yes, how do you do. And what's your name?") Within the short space of a few years—first writing full-time with his father-in-law's financial support (after a brief stint as the inspector on a sugar estate) and then, after Olga's father's sudden death in early 1885, liquidating the estate and playing the Kiev stock market—he began to produce a distinctive body of work while also laboring to advance Yiddish literature as a form. And he did so without ever discarding the pseudonym, even long after it was necessary. On the contrary, the persona took on a peculiar life of its own as Sholem-Aleichem fashioned himself into a *folkshrayber*, a folk writer. The multilingual, urbane businessman, in his tightly buttoned vests and wire-frame spectacles, who spoke Russian at home with his family, took stage as the Yiddish voice of the people. And readers—those who remained in the shtetls and those who had left them behind—embraced him as their own. They invoked his name every time they said hello.

But there was nothing simple or artless about his extraordinary output. Coming into his own, especially at the turn of the twentieth century, Sholem-Aleichem brought to life enduring characters who appeared in Yiddish periodicals from time to time, as he conjured them into new episodes: the clueless financial speculator Menakhem-Mendl and his long-suffering wife, Sheyne-Sheyndl; the downtrodden yet lighthearted "little people" of Kasrilevke; and his supreme creation, the irrepressible Tevye.

From Tevye's first appearance in 1894, the stories take the shape of dialogues between the hero and his silent interlocutor, the author Sholem-Aleichem, whom Tevye addresses; they read like monologues but are framed as tales told to a specific listener, lending them complex layers of irony that allow readers to see the limits of Tevye's self-consciousness as he narrates his experiences retrospectively. The first story, "Tevye Strikes It Rich," uncoils tightly, introducing the garrulous, pious patriarch and painting Tevye's social place in the isolating outskirts of a village (he does not live in a shtetl) where he barely ekes out a living for his wife and seven daughters as a drayman. When he delivers some wealthy women lost in the woods back to their dacha, he is rewarded with the astonishing sum of thirty-seven rubles and a cow, and he becomes Tevye *der milkhiker*—milkman or dairyman in the usual translations but more literally, in Sholem-Aleichem's neologistic application, "the milky one" (as distinct, as any reader familiar with kosher dietary rules would know, from being *fleyshik*, or meaty). It's a feminizing descriptor, signaling Tevye's warmth and nurturing nature and, later, the challenge to his paternal authority that will come from his daughters as the eight tragicomic stories unfold over the next two decades. Tevye opens the first episode telling Sholem-Aleichem what he learned from his good fortune: "Just like it says in the Bible . . . as long as a Jew lives and breathes in this world and hasn't more than one leg in the grave, he mustn't lose faith."

The world begins to challenge that faith in the second story, "Tevye Blows a Small Fortune" (1899), in which his distant relative Menakhem-Mendl persuades him to invest in a disastrous financial scheme. By the third story, "Modern Children" (1899), modernity begins to push from within the family, as Tsaytl persuades her father to forgo the marriage deal he arranged for her with the butcher Lazar Wolf and to let her marry her poor, beloved tailor, Motl. The pressure intensifies in the fourth story, "Hodl" (1904), written in the midst of the fervor that produced men like Perchik, the revolutionary, whom Hodl follows when he is imprisoned in Siberia. Bereft, Tevye ends this chronicle by asking Sholem-Aleichem to discuss something more cheerful with him: "Have you heard any news about the cholera in Odessa?"

In the early years of his career, before finding the mature literary voice that would produce Tevye, Sholem-Aleichem struck the tone of the *maskilim*—proponents of the *Haskalah*—by calling for a world-class

Yiddish literature that would rise above the *shund*, or shameful trash, of the pulp novels that had dominated Yiddish fiction in the nineteenth century (though many of the *maskilim* never let go of their distrust of Yiddish and, as Sholem-Aleichem developed his own work, ended up dismissing him, in the literary scholar Dan Miron's words, "as a vulgar comedian who pandered to the uneducated plebs"). To further the cause, he edited what he hoped would be a yearly anthology, modeled on Russian literary annuals and their Hebrew imitators, highlighting the finer Yiddish writers. The first edition of *Di yidishe folks-bibliotek: a bukh fir literatur, kritik un vissenshaft* (*A Jewish Popular Library: A Book of Literature, Criticism, and Scholarship*), published in 1888, ran some six hundred pages and included works by Mendele Mocher-Sforim and I. L. Peretz (the literary giant's first publication in Yiddish); it also featured Sholem-Aleichem's own novella *Stempenyu*. (When he lost his enormous inheritance in the stock market in 1890, abandoning volume 3 was the least of his worries; he had to flee Kiev for two years to escape his creditors.) In that same period, he wrote a pamphlet attacking the leading proponent of *shund*, Nokhum Meyer Sheikevitch, who cranked out preposterously plotted romances under the name Shomer. Five years before George Bernard Shaw famously coined the term "Sardoodledom" to ridicule the vacuous star vehicles scribbled by the French playwright Victorien Sardou, Sholem-Aleichem delivered a similar verdict against Yiddish prose potboilers in his essay "*Shomers mishpet*" ("Shomer's Trial"). *Stempenyu* was meant to demonstrate how real Yiddish books should be written. In case the example of the novella wasn't enough of a clue, Sholem-Aleichem included a pompous preface written in the form of a letter to Mendele Mocher-Sforim, whom he greatly admired.

Addressing Mendele as the "grandfather" of Yiddish literature, Sholem-Aleichem explained that what distinguished a Jewish novel was its expression of the national characteristics of Jews, which differed from those of other people and, in fact, could not be conveyed in a standard romance. In a Jewish novel, the thwarted lovers had to put their values above their happiness, or, rather, find their happiness in the fulfillment of their values. As in Jewish life, he argued, in a Jewish novel duty should prevail—and pay off. Rokhele does fall in love with Stempenyu—his sublime fiddle playing transports her, his mystifying musician's slang excites her (Sholem-Aleichem included a glossary), and he is gorgeous and solicitous, to boot. She sneaks away from home, heart aflutter, to meet him for walks and conversations. In the end, however, she not only stays faithful to her husband but awakens his devotion and lives happily ever after. Stempenyu gets his just deserts: he is left pining for Rokhele in his miserable marriage.

When he thought of adapting *Stempenyu* for the Yiddish stage some half a dozen years after its publication, Sholem-Aleichem expected it to offer the same chastening lessons to the theater that it had tendered to Yiddish fiction. Besides, the main characters seemed made to order for a dashing male actor and a pretty ingenue. And music was absolutely essential to the plot, so songs wouldn't have to be interspersed at random, as was so common on the Yiddish stage; they could be fully integrated in an artistic way.

Thus, with great self-assurance, in that fall of 1905, he sent the script from Kiev to an acquaintance in New York, a physician and anthropologist named Morris Fishberg, who had offered to represent him when they'd met in Warsaw some six months earlier at the rapturously received premiere of *Tsezeyt un tseshpreyt*. He asked Fishberg to bring this surefire hit to America's two leading actor-managers of the Yiddish theater, the grand and graceful impresario Jacob P. Adler and the heartthrob of the ghetto Boris Thomashefsky. Having received no reply after a few weeks and ever more eager for a cash advance, Sholem-Aleichem followed up with a second letter on October 8. He reminded Fishberg that he should already have received *Stempenyu, or the Jewish Paganini*, and told him that a second script was on its way. He added a portentous postscript. Admitting he "should have told you this before," he noted that his work possessed no spectacular effects. "I will never permit myself to give in to American taste and lower the standards of art," Sholem-Aleichem vowed.

Then his world turned upside down. Reactionary resistance to Russia's October Manifesto took the violent form of attacks on students, workers, and Jews. Some five hundred Jews were murdered by mobs in Odessa as police stood by. And in Kiev, Sholem-Aleichem and his family had to flee their apartment in a building most of whose occupants were Jewish—a likely target—and take shelter in the Imperial Hotel.

From there, Sholem-Aleichem wrote to Fishberg "with trembling hands." At first he took heart in seeing armed soldiers on the streets, who would surely help. "And they really did help," he reported, "but not us.

They helped loot, beat, plunder, steal. Before our eyes, before the whole world's eyes, they helped smash windows, crash through doors, and break locks, and they lined their own pockets. In front of our children, they beat Jews to death—women and children—and shouted, 'Money! Give us your money!'" He decided he should come immediately to America with his family to "sit out these evil times."

Two days later, still holed up in the Imperial Hotel, he wrote to Fishberg once more. "I send you the fifth act of *Stempenyu*," he said. "A new act instead of the earlier one." In the rewrite, Sholem-Aleichem made a drastic change: he killed off his protagonist, even though, he told Fishberg, "a Jewish heroine seldom poisons herself on account of love." But what choice did he have if he wanted to satisfy American tastes? From the confines of a hotel room in a city full of shattered glass, its streets strewn with a hundred dead bodies, the lofty standards of art seemed a lot less urgent than only three weeks before. "What can one do," Sholem-Aleichem asked Fishberg, "when America commands?" It wouldn't be the last time that the works of Sholem-Aleichem were adapted with an eye toward New York showbiz.

Willing as Sholem-Aleichem was to "give in to American taste" after all, there wasn't any follow-up from the impresarios in New York. Fishberg managed to secure a commission for him from the daily paper the *Yidishes tageblat* for a series of dispatches on the situation in Russia— some forty "pogrom letters" that ran between November 1905 and January 1906—but Fishberg sent not a word about the prospects for Sholem-Aleichem's scripts.

In this fraught period—the rhetorical pogrom letters reveal the author as bitter and traumatized—he wrote a fifth Tevye story, as if the hopeful hero's confrontation with the harrowing world were now necessary, a compressed means of chronicling a foreboding new chapter in the history of the Jewish Pale. In "Khave," published in the spring of 1906, Tevye is as chatty as ever, but the story of the apostate daughter who abandons her home, her faith, and her people to marry the Ukrainian, Fyedka, adds a new, almost overwhelming current of anguish. Sholem-Aleichem shows Tevye heartbroken, bewildered, and at loose ends; he follows the precepts of his faith but finds no solace in them. By story's end, he wants to make himself disappear. He implores Sholem-Aleichem, "Don't make a book out of this, and if it should happen that you do, write like it's someone else, not me."

The *Yidishes tageblat* had promised Sholem-Aleichem $600 for the pogrom reports but turned over only $250, so Sholem-Aleichem embarked on yet another reading tour to make ends meet. The highlight of the trip was a stop in London in July 1906, not only because of the ardor of the fans who greeted him but also because he had a chance to see Jacob Adler onstage and even to meet "the king of the Yiddish actors," as he put it, when Adler called on him "to pay his respects" and to ask whether Sholem-Aleichem "with his golden pen would write for the Yiddish stage in New York."

Adler was performing in Yankev Gordin's *Der meteref* (*The Madman*), a four-act drama about a man with noble ideals—that factory workers should labor in decent conditions, that wives should not be beaten by husbands—that make him an outcast from a cynical, hidebound community. According to Adler, Gordin, the literary "reformer" held up by the champions of a "higher" Yiddish theater for such plays as his versions of *King Lear* and *Faust* (*Got, mentsh, un tayvl*), was no longer writing for him, and he invited Sholem-Aleichem to turn out several plays he could star in. The author did some quick calculations: "Reb Yankev Gordin, he who translates and improves Shakespeare and Goethe earned in one year, for two original dramas and for two improved dramas by others, not less and not more than five thousand dollars," he recounted to his son-in-law the aspiring writer Y. D. Berkowitz, hastening to explain that that was "around ten thousand rubles to us." So he asked Adler: "How many plays do you need?"

"Not fewer than ten dramas," the impresario answered. "Five original and five improved from others."

"Well, then," Sholem-Aleichem told Berkowitz, "I instantly rolled up my sleeves."

In his letters to Berkowitz and when he described the meeting further after returning to his family, now in Geneva, Sholem-Aleichem sounded giddy, as if he'd fallen under the actor's spell. His "new hopes and high spirits" were in no way dampened by Adler's suggestion that he learn a little about constructing dramatic action by studying plays by none other than Gordin himself. And if he was troubled by Adler's failure even to acknowledge the plays he had sent to him the previous autumn, he made no mention of it.

Back home in Geneva, he drafted *David ben David* within three weeks. The hero, a gentle millionaire whose parents have died, fixes on the idea for a Jewish national homeland in historic Palestine, which serves as an excuse for his uncle to declare him mentally unstable and thus seize the inheritance due to him. Sholem-Aleichem was so sure of the script's prospects he went out and bought a hectograph machine so that he and Berkowitz could print up some thirty copies. How much better it was than Gordin's work, Sholem-Aleichem thought. He had despised *Der meturef* in London. Adler dazzled, of course, but the script enraged him. He regarded the whole thing as a lie. No real Jews speak or act as Gordin depicted them, Sholem-Aleichem railed. His writing was "imitative of the great *goyim* [Gentiles]." Sholem-Aleichem condemned the play in terms that have long since been used by one Jew to discredit the work of another—including versions of his own: he challenged its authenticity. "It is false," Sholem-Aleichem insisted, "through and through false." With Berkowitz's assistance, he bound all thirty copies of *David ben David* in thick red covers. He planned to take them to America.

He would not, however, take his whole family. Short of funds for the fares, he and his wife would bring their youngest child, Numa, then five, and leave the older children behind. First, he'd tour England again to make some money, and then the three would sail from Southampton. Adler was still performing at the Pavilion Theatre in London, and on the afternoon of August 14, Sholem-Aleichem assembled a few friends in his room at the Three Nuns Hotel to listen along as he read his new play for the impresario. The small audience followed the tragic action with tension, which was relieved now and then by humor, according to the writer Israel Cohen, who was in attendance. The author gestured and altered the inflections of his voice to bring the characters to life. As for Adler, he "fidgeted and nodded his head occasionally, and when the reading was over he made some criticism, which the author readily agreed to consider." After that August day, there's no record that Sholem-Aleichem ever said a word about *David ben David* again. Adler certainly never produced it. All but one of the thirty bound copies—the one Berkowitz had kept—disappeared, presumably burned by their author.

Two months later, on October 13, in a grim mood, Sholem-Aleichem boarded the American Line's SS *St. Louis*, along with Olga and Numa and some 3,500 other passengers. Happy as he was to leave London, where he had few friends and everything felt cold and foreign, he was losing confidence in his prospects overseas. The *Yidishes tageblat*, still owing him money for his pogrom reports, paid even less for some short stories he'd sent on ahead. Why, they insisted, should a New York publication pay him anything at all when the pieces had already been published in Russia and could easily be reprinted for nothing? Abandoning faith in the Yiddish press as his savior, Sholem-Aleichem decided that everything would depend on the theater. But Adler's indifferent response to *David ben David*—not to mention his silence on the earlier scripts— dulled those prospects, too. Like the vast majority of the other travelers, Sholem-Aleichem was headed to America without really knowing what he would do once he got there. From his second-class cabin, as the voyage neared its end, he heard choral singing from the deck below. But, he wrote to his family, "nothing can dispel the despondency and the gnawing in the heart. Like a fog settling upon the soul."

Arriving in New York Harbor on the gray and rainy afternoon of October 20 brightened his outlook. A telegram announcing the birth of his first grandchild, a girl, greeted him at the pier, along with his brother, Bernard Roberts (born Baruch Rabinowitz), who had immigrated years earlier and done well as a luggage manufacturer. The crowd of some two hundred well-wishers who shouted "hurrah" and threw their hats in the air for Sholem-Aleichem had been organized by fledgling local Zionist groups; they sang "Hatikvah" as their most earnest gesture of welcome. Fishberg was there. So was the editor of the *Yidishes tageblat* (despite the quarrel Sholem-Aleichem had with him) as well as the editor of the other major Orthodox paper, the *Morgn zhurnal*. Fans hoisted the writer onto their shoulders and carried him around, cheering (which made Numa burst into tears). Jacob Adler, accompanied by his wife, the actor Sara Adler, and their children, presented him with a bouquet of flowers. "The occasion could not be more exultant," Sholem-Aleichem wrote home. The next day found him no less buoyant: everyone was promising business deals and mountains of gold. Never mind that he still had no clue "from where the gold will pour"; on his first day in America, "it seems a new era is dawning on our horizon, full of success, luck, and happiness."

As he held court at his brother's apartment in the Bronx, surrounded by flowers sent by admirers, Sholem-Aleichem told interviewers from both the Yiddish- and English-language press that, among other things, he planned to write for the Yiddish stage—after studying it for a while. One magazine—the *Menorah*, an English-language Jewish monthly—had announced in its September issue that Adler had acquired some of his plays for the coming season; they'd have to rely on their humor, it predicted, to "make up for [Sholem-Aleichem's] lack of ability as a dramatist."

Adler had expressed the same anxiety and perhaps Thomashefsky hesitated to put on the plays he'd received earlier, for similar reasons. But at the same time, these consummate theater men understood the commodity value of Sholem-Aleichem's very name. He was widely beloved by readers in America who had enjoyed his stories in newspapers back home as well as in New York. Recreational amateur groups put on his one-act plays in private little productions; social groups across the political spectrum read his stories aloud together, as did individual families. He was, the actor-managers figured, a bankable icon of the old home. And their theaters were hurting. Nickelodeons were springing up downtown, luring audiences away with their five-cent miracles of moving pictures. Meanwhile, the music halls—popular in both Yiddish and English on the Lower East Side—offered spectators a variety of entertainments that also competed with the theaters. Not for the last time, theater producers figured they could rely on Sholem-Aleichem to draw a warm bath of nostalgia for their audiences. His plays might not be so great, but his brand seemed like a sure bet.

Perhaps as part of an early marketing strategy, Adler and Thomashefsky threw a benefit evening of tribute befitting a superstar on October 31. It began at Adler's Grand Theater, where fans packed all three tiers and saluted Sholem-Aleichem with an ovation lasting several minutes. Jewish community luminaries delivered laudatory speeches. Sholem-Aleichem offered a humorous reading. Eventually some three hundred members of the crowd repaired to a banquet, where Adler and Thomashefsky and their wives shared the head table with the honored guest. The absence of one faction of the community may have been lost on Sholem-Aleichem, but not on the English-language Jewish weekly the *Chronicler*, which laced its coverage of the festivities with a telling complaint:

> The Jewish quarter might have shown some unity. All Jewish writers should have participated in the reception. Why did the Jewish Socialists and other radicals stay away? . . . Must we know to what party he belongs before we can honor him! Are they not all Jews who write for the Yiddish stage? Why did they not come? And why was the affair

made so much of an advertisement for several Yiddish actors? Why was the dinner at such an ungodly hour, and why, oh why, will some people insist on delivering lectures after dinner held at two o'clock in the morning?

Another reception followed a few days later, this time at the Educational Alliance, a community center founded by Jacob Schiff and others in 1893 whose scope, its charter proclaimed, had "an Americanizing, educational, social and humanizing character." The German Jewish elite regarded the folk writer as sharing their goal—moral sanitizing of the unwashed masses—and sought to claim him as an emblem of that effort. A legend quickly sprang up, telling how a special guest at the reception drove home the applicability of Sholem-Aleichem to the American context: Mark Twain. Indeed, newspapers that covered the author's arrival in America translated him to local readers as "the Yiddish Mark Twain." At the Educational Alliance reception, the American writer is said to have responded, "I am the American Sholem-Aleichem."

For some two weeks, the New York press, in English and in Yiddish (with the conspicuous exception of the anarchist paper the *Fraye arbeter shtime*), ballyhooed the "great literary personality," as the local English-language press called him. But, as Sholem-Aleichem recognized, the front pages would quickly give over to the arrival of new celebrities, and anyway, acclaim didn't pay the rent. The benefit evening had raised $1,000 for the author, but the proceeds remained in the hands of a "treasurer" and Sholem-Aleichem felt humiliated and angry that a couple of weeks after the event he had to go see the imperious man to request the money; the treasurer handed over a check with a dismissive flick of the wrist, never even looking the beneficiary in the eye.

The funds didn't last long: half went to Geneva and the rest to the renting of a furnished apartment in the Bronx, near Bernard. Under exclusive contracts with the *Tageblat* and the *Morgn zhurnal*, Sholem-Aleichem earned $40 per week for his regular contributions—hardly enough to support Olga and Numa in New York, much less the brood back in Switzerland. So off he went, as he had so many times in Europe, on a reading tour of the provinces. The American circuit was neither as heartening nor as lucrative as the ones back home. Arranged by Zionist organizations, which had slim followings in those years, the events—where

Sholem-Aleichem served essentially as the warm-up act for Zvi Hirsch Masliansky's fiery orations—deflated his spirits further. The winter tour left him, as Berkowitz recounted, "with only a hard chill that later drove him to his lung disease, and a pack of . . . stories from American country Jews."

At last, however, the theater was coming through. Early in the new year of 1907, Thomashefsky paid the handsome sum of $1,000—nearly two years' wages for a local presser in the garment trade—for the rights to *Stempenyu*. The role of the philandering musician seemed perfect for a man so handsome and adored that—as the influential writer and editor of the *Forverts*, Abe Cahan, put it—"When girls objected to the grooms their parents encouraged, their mothers would say, 'What? You expect a Thomashefsky?'" He had no doubt that the multitudes would come to swoon at him as the irresistible musical romantic. The turmoil of a young woman chafing at the strictures of shtetl life would also speak to many spectators who, not so long ago, left just such a world behind. Rokhele's ambivalence would allow them both to indulge their nostalgia and to affirm their break with the old home.

Then, just as Thomashefsky was beginning rehearsals in mid-January, and much to his surprise (or so he claimed years later), announcements appeared in the *Forverts*, *Tageblat*, and other papers boasting of "the first play by the famous literary author Sholem-Aleichem for the first time." They were advertisements for *Shmuel Pasternak oder Der oysvurf* (*Samuel Pasternak, or The Scoundrel*), produced by and starring Jacob Adler. He was counting on his audience of sweatshop workers to embrace a farce that traces the downfall of a crooked small-town stockbroker. Ridiculing a speculator in over his head and revealing finance capitalism to be thoroughly corrupting—what could be better for drawing proletarian ticket buyers, many of them roused by the growing labor movement?

If nothing else, the two directors, old friends and bitter rivals, knew how to fan a conflict for publicity—and they were desperate to boost ticket sales. Thomashefsky stepped up the pace of his rehearsals and took out his own ads: "Sholem-Aleichem for the first time as a playwright! Sholem-Aleichem's greatest masterpiece, *Stempenyu*, which has amazed the whole world, been translated into every language, and has now been dramatized by Sholem-Aleichem exclusively for the People's Theater!" The race—and hyperbole—was on as the impresarios vied for the premiere of the brand-name author. A friend of Sholem-Aleichem's persuaded the showmen to declare a draw: they would open on the same night, February 8, leaving both companies little time to get ready.

A couple of nights before the opening, a storm dumped eight inches of snow on New York. Six horses died after slipping and falling on the ice. Streetcars came to a standstill—a Twenty-third Street crosstown car remained stuck for a full night. Shops stayed closed for days. But the twenty-nine-mile-per-hour winds did nothing to cool the feverish preparations and flaming tempers in the Yiddish theaters. Both directors rushed their companies through rehearsals; Sholem-Aleichem dashed from one to the other, apparently unable to prevent the hasty "improvements" the two directors were making to his scripts. Thomashefsky added in some rhyming couplets; Adler embellished his part with jokes that lay "like poor patches on a rich garment," as far as Sholem-Aleichem's son-in-law, Berkowitz, was concerned.

When opening night came, fans traipsed through slush to fill both the two thousand seats at Adler's Grand at the corner of Chrystie and Grand and, three blocks away, the 2,500 seats at the People's Theater on the Bowery near Delancey. Sholem-Aleichem himself slid up and down the streets to spend two acts in one theater and two acts in the other. In both, spectators called him to the stage for several lengthy ovations. "The audiences seemed happy to me," he wrote to his family the next day. He noted that the partisan press could not be counted on, but as long as audiences were responding so enthusiastically, he added, the critics hardly mattered. He was half right: the press did, in fact, divide right down Yiddish New York's ideological fault lines. And Sholem-Aleichem himself widened the rift—and then walked right over the cliff—by delivering a curtain speech during the intermission of *Pasternak*. Though not given to grandiloquence, the author got caught up in the opening-night excitement and seized his minutes in the spotlight to hold forth about the "new page in Yiddish theater" that his play was turning over. Implying that he himself was the theater's redeemer, propelled onto the stage by "new winds blowing" that would blast away *shund*, he ranted not against cheap entertainments but against Yankev Gordin, dramatic hero of the progressive elite. The *Forverts*, and the left more generally, championed Gordin as a leader of a literary theater of ideas, a realist in the mode of such serious modern dramatists as Ibsen and Gorky. The Orthodox press reviled Gordin for the very reasons the left-wing press embraced him: his eagerness to show the dark sides of life—poverty, family discord, social pressure, moral failure (though he didn't hesitate to crank out some pot-boilers under a pseudonym when he needed ready cash).

In contrast, Sholem-Aleichem's characters displayed foibles, not tragic flaws; their mishaps tore at the audience's heartstrings, triggered laughter, or both; they didn't offer an object lesson in the social questions of the day. In short, these characters were Jews as Sholem-Aleichem knew and loved them, not—like Gordin's dramatis personae, in his opinion—generic people dressed up in beards or *shaytls* (the wigs worn by observant married women). In making the point from the stage at Adler's Grand, Sholem-Aleichem unwittingly cemented his alliance with the Orthodox element of New York's Jewish community, and they reinforced the bond with their unreserved praise for his comedy.

In the *Morgn zhurnal*, for example, an unsigned review proclaimed that *Pasternak* heralded "a new epoch for Yiddish drama in America . . . full of authentic Yiddish humor." Best of all, the critic asserted, "there was no dirt" in Sholem-Aleichem's play, none of the "outrages that filled the Yiddish plays of the realist period." The same day, the *Tageblat* review concurred that until Sholem-Aleichem came along there was "no true Yiddish theater before now. The dramas were not dramas, and the comedies were no comedies either. All the roles were stolen, false." Worst of all, of course, was realism "with its dirt, its shame" and its "stifling" of Jewish life and humor on the stage. With the production of Sholem-Aleichem's work, the paper declared with relief, "a new world opens for Jewish theatergoers." (A second review in the *Tageblat*, a day later, focused on *Stempenyu* and condemned its third-act curtain falling, with heavy implication, on a bedroom scene. "This is simply scandalous," the critic maintained. "Even the realists didn't dare present such scenes. It's an insult to everyone. Especially the women.")

The insult, from the point of view of the progressive papers, was Sholem-Aleichem's curtain speech. In the *Varhayt*, the nicest thing Louis Miller could say about *Stempenyu* was that "whenever a flash of Sholem-Aleichem's talent as a novelist sparkles, Sholem-Aleichem the dramatist snatches it away like a thief." Regarding *Pasternak*, the reviewer reported that he "exercised the privilege of ordinary mortals" by leaving in the middle. He wondered how Sholem-Aleichem could have come from

Russia untouched by either Tolstoy's brooding play of seduction and murder, *Power of Darkness*, or Gogol's piercing satire about political corruption, *The Inspector General*.

In the *Yidisher kempfer*, Joel Entin called *Pasternak* "a stillborn monster, a broken piece of calamity that any wind could blow away." In the balcony, where Sholem-Aleichem had heard spectators laughing their heads off, Entin heard a silence like that of "a hospital wing filled with chloroformed patients."

Within a couple of short weeks, both plays closed. And that, declared B. Goren in his 1917 history of the Yiddish theater, "brought to an end Sholem-Aleichem's career as a playwright" in New York.

Abe Cahan summed up the problem best in the *Forverts*. True, New York's self-appointed Yiddish cultural czar didn't care much for the work itself—"the figures have no more life than a clay golem whose forehead bears a sign: 'miser' or 'scoundrel' or 'good contemporary daughter,'" Cahan wrote of *Pasternak*. But more significantly, he announced in his column that it was time for a new judgment of the Jewish folk writer: "Once Sholem-Aleichem played a great role in Yiddish literature, but now that we have talents like Sholem Asch [the modernist playwright and novelist some twenty years Sholem-Aleichem's junior], his place is not as great or important." As far as Cahan was concerned, Sholem-Aleichem belonged to a different world, a world across the sea, best left behind. And, from a theatrical standpoint at least, the public seemed to agree. Adler and Thomashefsky had miscalculated. The more they appealed to the idea of Sholem-Aleichem as culture hero of the homeland—and the more the progressive press hammered on the point as a drawback—the less marketable he was on their stages.

The problem wasn't the quality of the works so much as a clash between the function of the theater and the function of Sholem-Aleichem in that moment. It was one thing to enjoy his stories in the private sphere of the home or amid the gatherings of hometown organizations or even amateur dramatic clubs. But the boisterous commercial realm of the theater was a site for forging a new collective identity, a place where Jews constituted themselves as an American public—largely proletarian, urbanized, and concerned with the new and pressing demands of cultural adaptation. To the extent that the Yiddish theater in New York invited spectators to dwell nostalgically on the customs, characters, and convictions of life in Eastern Europe, it was held in taut tension with the promises (fulfilled or broken) and the exigencies of life in America. Both sides of that equation—the old life and the new—could be held up on the stage for ridicule or for affection, for wistfulness or wrath. The point isn't that the Yiddish theater in New York always made fun of or rejected the past or that it always extolled the American present. But the here and there, the then and now existed in relationship to each other. Though World War I would disrupt the emotional nature of that balance, in 1907 the carefully constructed persona of the *folkshrayber* of the Pale could find no footing on the lower Bowery, where Jews were becoming a different kind of folk, a modern urban audience and American ethnic group. Some four months after his plays flopped, Sholem-Aleichem, along with Olga and Numa, made the return voyage to Europe. Friends lent him money for the fare.

* * *

Sholem-Aleichem returned to Geneva, overjoyed to reunite with his family but still uncertain of how he'd keep afloat. Some income trickled in from two Yiddish newspapers in America, where, before leaving, he had begun two serial novels, and he kept sending them installments: *Motl peysi dem khazns* (*Motl, Peysi the Cantor's Son*), a bildungsroman told by a boy who moves from a shtetl to New York after his father dies, a masterpiece of comic irony, and *Der mabl* (*The Flood*), a melodrama set in Russia against the failed revolution of 1905 and the subsequent pogroms, a critical failure to this day. Because these serials were written for an audience of immigrants, the emphasis on the precariousness of the Jewish future in the Old Country comes as no surprise, but more generally Sholem-Aleichem's work was striking a tone of dejection.

A new Tevye story written shortly after his return to Europe reflected a profound sinking of spirit—a story much too sad (and at odds with the theme of generational conflict) to make its way into a Broadway musical some sixty years later, the only one of the Tevye tales in which the dairyman explicitly compares himself to Job: Shprintze, daughter number four, faces trouble with her suitor, like her sisters before her. But unlike her older siblings, she does not defy her father's wishes. The man she falls for, the son of a wealthy customer of Tevye's, enters her orbit when Tevye invites him home for blintzes, and the handsome, blithely idealistic and spoiled youth keeps coming back to see the girl whose name rhymes with the holiday dish. The romance ends abruptly when his family hastily moves to a faraway town, separating the boy from this beloved beneath his station. "Do you think she complained? Do you think she cried even once?" Tevye asks. "If you do, you don't know Tevye's daughters! She just flickered out like a candle." And then Shprintze drowns herself in the river. Tevye inches toward the recognition of his own culpability in promoting the doomed affair but stops just short of tragic self-knowledge, making his resolve to get on with life all the more agonizing to witness.

Meanwhile, amazingly, Sholem-Aleichem did not give up on the New York theater. He had parted from Adler and Thomashefsky on cordial terms, the actor-managers seeming to have responded with a them's-the-breaks shrug at enduring one more failure on their stages. (Indeed, the entire 1906–07 season bombed at the People's and Kalish theaters; only Adler's Grand scored some hits that year.) As for his own plays' shortcomings, Sholem-Aleichem quickly shook off any responsibility he may have felt and placed all the blame on the low level of the Yiddish theater and its ill-trained audience. As far as he was concerned, the New York stage had done him a terrible injustice, and he would have to rectify it.

Within months of returning to Europe, Sholem-Aleichem was writing a new script, *Der oytser* (*The Treasure*), in which he pits American opportunity against the backwardness of the shtetl—and neither world comes off well. The plot follows Benny, a self-made American, on a visit back to the shtetl where he was born. His symbolic—but statistically unlikely—occupation as a farmer highlights the contrast between his productive labor in the new land and the pie-in-the-sky dreaming of the *luftmentshn* in his hometown, who believe that if only they could locate a legendary buried fortune all their problems would be solved. The cost of Benny's success is his Jewish connection: he lacks all knowledge of the texts, customs, and commitments that bind the members of the community to one another and to Jewish history. In this play, and in other works written after his first, frustrating efforts in New York, Sholem-Aleichem figures the journey to America as a process of dissolution. (He strikes the same note in *Wandering Stars*, his sprawling, satirical 1909 novel about a Yiddish theater troupe that eventually makes its way to New York.) The author, still not reading the American scene accurately, reckoned that

The Treasure, a "genuinely Jewish comedy," as he described it, would hit home with an immigrant audience still adjusting to their breach with their old homes. In February 1908, he sent *The Treasure* to Berkowitz, who was then living in New York, and instructed him to take it to Adler right away. "Watch the impression it makes on him," he told his son-in-law. "If it is very good, request an immediate advance of $2,000. If it is more moderate (which I doubt), take $1,500. Obviously, it would be better to leave with the play and wait a few days for him to come begging. But alas, we sit here with hardly a penny—God should have pity—so don't leave empty-handed." For good measure, Sholom-Aleichem included a letter for Berkowitz to deliver with the play: "My good friend and great artist Adler! I give you my most recent work, *The Treasure* . . ."

Though Berkowitz thought the reading had made a good enough impression, Adler complained that the play piled up speeches in place of a plot and offered a meager two hundred dollars for it. Berkowitz recounts that he dutifully tried shopping it to Thomashefsky and to the third great actor-manager in the New York triumvirate, David Kessler. Those negotiations did not go anywhere, either.

Back in Geneva, Sholem-Aleichem despaired of his son-in-law's reports and with no income in sight, set out one more time on a reading tour of the Pale; there, at least, he was still a superstar. He sold out one of the biggest halls in Warsaw for five nights running. As the grueling weeks of one-night stands in towns large and small wore on, Sholem-Aleichem wore out; in August, in a town called Baronovici, he collapsed with acute pulmonary tuberculosis and spent the next several months recuperating.

New York's Yiddish theater hadn't been faring much better. In a dismal season, no play was going to gain the attention of the theater managers unless it could promise a treasure calculable in box office receipts. If Sholem-Aleichem had ventured naively into the New York theater scene on the downward side of its peak in 1906–07, he was clueless that by the following year the playhouses were hurtling ever faster down that slope. The stock market crashed in the fall of 1907, kicking off a yearlong depression that threw more than a quarter of the Lower East Side's labor force out of work. Community organizations such as hometown societies (*landsmanshaftn*) pitched in to help, thus emptying their coffers of the monies they might have put up for their usual theater benefits:

the ticket base collapsed. More and more, cheap and escapist moving pictures—shown in storefront movie houses that were sprouting up all over the city's most densely populated neighborhoods—siphoned spectators away from theaters and even supplanted most music halls; a seat at the movies cost only one-fifth the price of a gallery seat in the theater and they quickly became the preferred amusement of the strapped Yiddish masses.

In the fall of 1908, when Sholem-Aleichem had hoped *The Treasure* would premiere on Adler's stage, the impresario leased the Grand Theater to an English-language producer who brought in American blood-and-thunder melodramas during the week (with ten-cent seats in the gallery). Reserving only Sundays for himself, Adler presented "serious" plays in afternoon and evening performances, but by March he gave up and set out on a tour of the provinces.

The two other Yiddish theaters in the neighborhood tried to outdo their newfangled competitors with spectacle and shmaltz. They mounted mawkish musical melodramas that took up the same dilemmas as Sholem-Aleichem's *Treasure*, but from an entirely opposite point of view: they assured audiences, in song and with lavish staging, of their Jewish integrity. Joseph Lateiner's *Dos yidishe harts* (*The Jewish Heart*)—whose convoluted plot involves a Jewish man finding his long-lost mother and feuding with her antisemitic Christian son—broke box office records at Kessler's Thalia Theater, running thirty-two weeks in 1908–09. Thomashefsky took the cue and quickly put on *Di yidishe neshome* (*The Jewish Soul*), whose young heroes also stand up against antisemitism and assimilation—and also announce they will be moving to America.

Thomashefsky kept a good thing going by opening the fall 1909 season with another nationalistic melodrama, *Dos pintele yid*, typically translated with the far less pithy or pungent phrase *The Quintessence of Jewishness* or *The Essential Spark of Jewishness* (a *pintele* being a tiny point or speck). It, too, features the repentance of a parent—this time, an antisemitic father—confronted by his proud (and illegitimate) Jewish son.

These runaway hits allayed the anxieties of their audiences—while *The Treasure* would have stoked them—at a time when the children of the first big wave of Yiddish-speaking immigrants were coming of age. In these plays, the young heroes not only lay claim to their quintessential spark and reignite it in a fallen elder; they also extol America as the place it will have enough oxygen to stay lit. Sholem-Aleichem would never succeed on the American stage until his work acknowledged that point.

Where *The Treasure* laments Benny's neglect of Judaism and his loss of connection, the *shund* sensations reflect and celebrate a new, still vibrant Jewish identity, commensurate with American success. For the young adults attending movies and popular English-language entertainments that played cheek by jowl with the Yiddish theaters, the *harts*, *neshome*, and *pintele* plays presented no rebuke. And for their parents, the plays offered reassurance that the age-old question gaining new urgency in America—what does it mean to be Jewish here?—could find a satisfactory answer. (Outside the cultural realm, this question was being taken up by Jewish activists building a communal political muscle: they were pressing to have "Hebrew" removed as a racial category from the upcoming 1910 U.S. Census.) The notion of a Jewish ethnicity was beginning to emerge in the streets, sweatshops, and schoolrooms of neighborhoods like the Lower East Side and Brownsville. The Yiddish theater was giving it form—and, thanks to Thomashefsky (and the playwright Moyshe Zeifert), who revivified an old phrase, a name: the *pintele*—that inexplicable, irrepressible nugget of identity.

At the same moment, on the English-language stage some three and a half miles away, a popular melodrama posed an audacious new question: Why should that nugget last? The play was Israel Zangwill's *The Melting Pot*—the title popularized the phrase for decades to come—and it made its New York debut at the Comedy Theater on West Forty-first Street on September 6, 1909, just two weeks before *Dos pintele yid* opened. The plot hinges on the romance between David, a Russian Jewish émigré, and Vera, a non-Jewish social worker, also from Russia, and on David's grand plans for composing a musical work that will exalt America as the "great new continent that could melt up all race differences and vendettas, that could purge and re-create." All his hopes nearly crumble when he learns that Vera's father was the czarist officer back home who ordered the pogrom in which David lost his family and was forever traumatized. But the couple overcomes this contrived catastrophe through faith in their new country, where they can create a baggage-free future. Making heavy use of alchemy metaphors, the play suggests, happily, that ethnic identities—including, presumably, a Jew's defining *pintele*—can dissolve into "the glory of America, where all races and nations come to labor and look forward!" The play had premiered in Washington, D.C., a year earlier (with President Theodore Roosevelt in attendance) and then moved to Chicago, where it unleashed a national debate on the question of intermarriage (which occurred at the negligible rate of a few percent at the time). In New York, it enjoyed a modest success, running for about four months.

If English-speaking audiences (many Jews among them) were applauding David's curtain speech in midtown, heartened perhaps by the ideal of harmonious homogeneity in which they all could participate regardless of background, the mass Yiddish-speaking audience streaming in to see *Dos pintele yid* downtown were cheering for a different vision of Americanization: one that did not cost their distinctiveness.

Despite the record ticket sales—the *Forverts* estimated that some 55,000 people saw *Dos pintele yid*—the show could not pull Thomashefsky's theater out of the red. As for Adler, with no similar extravaganza to offer he didn't have a chance of surviving the 1909 season. That fall, he infamously sold his lease for the Grand Theater to the budding movie moguls Marcus Loew and Adolph Zukor. (Thomashefsky and Kessler participated behind the scenes, each paying Adler $5,000 to abandon New York for the year and ease up the competition.)

Back in Europe, Sholem-Aleichem remained thoroughly ignorant of the economic distress of New York's Yiddish theater, and almost as ignorant of the mind-set of its audience. But for a time, at least, he could stop chasing after Adler and Thomashefsky. If he still dreamed of conquering the American stage, his survival no longer depended on it: a Russian-language edition of his works, as well as a settlement on proper royalties for his Yiddish publications (secured by Olga), finally provided a comfortable income. For the next several years, Sholem-Aleichem and his family moved according to the climate best for his health: winters on the northwest coast of Italy, springs on a Swiss lake, summers in the Black Forest resorts of Germany. While Adler and Thomashefsky were scrambling in New York, Sholem-Aleichem, despite weakness from the TB and other ailments, was entering one of the most productive periods of his writing life.

In addition to work on *Wandering Stars*, 1909–10 saw the publication of his *Railroad Stories*, a series of twenty dark monologues—tales told to a traveling salesman (who in turn tells them to the reader) by a wide range of Jews riding in a third-class train car as it trundles through

Russia. Both contained by the train's compartment and set loose into the modern world by its speed and reach, the passengers occupy a spate of contradictions: a father with a gravely ill son is the happiest in his town because he persuades a renowned medical professor to examine the child; a husband goes along with his wife's strenuous efforts to get their son into a Russian high school only to see the son join a student strike; a pimp from Argentina makes a rare trip back to his shtetl to grab himself, so he claims, a "hometown girl" for a wife.

A chief accomplishment of this period was the completion of the Tevye cycle—though Sholem-Aleichem added a new ending later—with the seventh story, "Tevye Leaves for the Land of Israel" (1909). The daughter at the center this time, Beylke, attaches herself to a man her father approves. Golde, his wife, has died, sending Tevye into a fit of nihilism— "What's the point of the whole circus, this whole big yackety racket of a world on wheels? Why, it's nothing but vanity, one big zero with a hole in it!" Hoping to prevent further troubles for her father, Beylke weds the nouveau riche boor suggested by the local matchmaker, even though Tevye sees she cannot bear him. The new son-in-law schemes to send the embarrassingly low-class Tevye away, if not to America (which does not interest Tevye), then to Palestine, "where all the old Jews like you go to die." The story ends with Tevye recognizing his part in obedient Beylke's unhappiness—"To tell you the truth, when I think the matter over, the real guilty party may be me"—and selling off his belongings, even his horse, as he prepares to leave for the Land of Israel. Two years later, in 1911, Sholem-Aleichem published the entire series of stories, written over seventeen tumultuous years, in a single volume, *Tevye der milkhiker*. It seemed he was shutting the book on his voluble hero, as if, remarkably, there were nothing more he could say, as if just when Tevye stood on the brink of "going up" (the literal translation of the verb for moving to the Land of Israel), there was no lower point to which Sholem-Aleichem could bring him.

But things got worse for the people Tevye had come to embody. In March 1911, as Sholem-Aleichem was publishing the complete Tevye cycle, a thirteen-year-old Ukrainian boy disappeared on his way to school in Kiev. When his mutilated body was found a week later, the local right-wing movement seized the misfortune to inflame opposition to liberals in the Duma who had considered abolishing the Pale—elections were coming up—by distributing leaflets at the boy's funeral claiming he'd been slain by Jews who needed his blood to bake matza and calling for pogroms to avenge the death of the "martyr." Though local police linked the murder to a criminal gang, the Kiev district attorney dismissed their findings and prosecuted the case as a ritual murder. In July, authorities arrested Menachem Mendel Beilis, an unassuming clerk in a brick factory located near the scene of the crime. He languished in prison for two years as the case ground forward.

When the trial finally came to pass in the fall of 1913, it riveted the worldwide press as well as Sholem-Aleichem, who eventually linked Beilis's fate to Tevye's. High-profile writers and intellectuals, Jewish and Gentile, spoke out against the obvious scapegoating. In New York and in other cities around the globe where Yiddish theater scraped by, a spate of Beilis plays rushed onto local stages, provoking denunciations of the theaters' shameless exploitation of a national tragedy for commercial ends—in newspapers that did not fail to advertise the plays. In New York, even Jacob Adler threw a *tsaytbild*—or "picture of the times"—onto the boards. And soon so did Kessler and Thomashefsky.

Sholem-Aleichem, too, could not help but respond to the trouble riling up the city where he once lived and cowered as pogromists rampaged through the streets. He wrote a novel called *Der blutiger shpas* (*The Bloody Hoax*), whose plot centers on a high-stakes prince-and-the-pauper reversal (perhaps influenced by his association with Mark Twain): as they graduate from high school, two friends, Hersh Rabinowitz and Grigori Popov, agree secretly to trade places for a year so Popov, a wealthy Gentile, can learn what life is like for the Jews in czarist Russia. Starting out as a standard comedy of inversion, the novel takes a bitter turn when Popov is accused of a blood libel. (Sholem-Aleichem adapted the novel into a play a few years later, giving it a more comic twist and a new title, *Shver tzu zayn a yid*—Hard to Be a Jew.)

Sholem-Aleichem followed the Beilis case obsessively and as he pondered the deadly farce onstage in the Russian courtroom, Tevye marched back into his imagination. He pulled from his drawer a dramatic adaptation he had tinkered with some years earlier at the suggestion of a friend, and, predicting that the new medium of cinema would supplant the stage, and even literature, he wrote two screenplays based on his Tevye cycle. One, drawn from the first story, in which Tevye returns the lost ladies to

their dacha, uses film's unique capacity to show fantasy sequences—
Tevye could imagine his passengers as witches with a dissolve; spectators
could visually enter his dreams of becoming a miller, a store owner, even
a banker doing business with Rothschild as he contemplated his reward.
The adaptation of "Khave" relies on flashbacks—Tevye visibly recalling
his daughter's image as he bewails her shattering choice. (In this version,
she drowns herself in a well at the end.)

Visiting Berkowitz and his family in Berlin in the fall of 1913, Sholem-
Aleichem tried to peddle these screenplays to local filmmakers, along
with one adapted from *The Bloody Hoax*. But the directors passed on the
material—they didn't want to show Russia in a bad light at a time when
German-Russian relations were strained—and, according to Berkowitz,
his father-in-law stashed the scripts for better times, perhaps in America.
At least there was the good news of Beilis's acquittal, which made
Sholem-Aleichem break into "a hysterical shaking." He sent Beilis a
congratulatory gift: a set of his collected works.

When Sholem-Aleichem returned to his family in Lausanne, Tevye
was still tugging on his psyche. He went back to work on the dramatization, and he kept revising it when—unable to bear the cold winter—he
moved on by himself to the Italian Riviera. He didn't seem to worry that
a change from the original genre would alter the way his protagonist
frames his own experiences as stories—onstage, Tevye would speak
directly to spectators instead of to the unseen yet mediating Sholem-
Aleichem persona. Rather, he was thrilled with the outcome, as he told
his wife in a letter the day he finished a completely new dramatic version,
in four acts with seven scenes. In the last scene—the most touching, he
told her—Tevye takes leave of his home, kissing the naked walls and bidding a sad farewell to the cat that is about to be abandoned.

The story he put at the center was Khave's—the daughter who marries a Ukrainian man and is mourned as though dead—but this time he
gave it a happy ending: in the play, Khave leaves her husband and returns
to the family fold when she hears that Jews are to be expelled from their
homes. Sholem-Aleichem was responding directly to edicts that followed
the Beilis affair (and, in an early draft of the play, he even had Khave's
husband believing the blood libel). Writing the play forced him to revisit
the set of stories he thought he'd completed in 1911: if Tevye was going to
be kicked out by czarist edict, he couldn't already have left for the Land

of Israel. So he opened the new story, "Lekh Lekho" ("Get Thee Out"), with Tevye telling the author, who must be surprised to see him still clamoring around the village, that just as he was getting ready to leave, his son-in-law Motl suddenly died and he had to stay behind to take care of his daughter Tzaytl and her children. That set up the plot possibility (which would prove crucial to *Fiddler*) for the local officer to come and throw him out. And in the story, as in the play, Khave returns to accompany her father and sister into the wilderness.

The title—recognizable to Sholem-Aleichem's readers—hints ironically at some possibility of redemption: it quotes God's words to Avram in Genesis, telling him to leave his home for a land where God would make of him a great nation. Tevye's prospects may be more humble and uncertain. Nevertheless, he tells Tsaytl, "We ought to be counting our blessings. Even if we didn't have a penny to our names, we'd still be better off than Mendel Beilis."

When Sholem-Aleichem first thought about dramatizing the Tevye stories, he knew that the role—"the crown of my creation," as he called him—would require an extraordinary actor, one who could combine grandeur and humbleness, draw equal measures of tears (but not too sentimental) and laughter (but without ridicule). It would take an artist of great skill, sensitivity, and charisma. As the play progresses, he predicted, "the audience loves him all the more." He'd thought originally of Rudolph Schildkraut, when the legendary actor was still in his heyday, but now he had that grand old shark Jacob Adler in mind. "Although a hard man to do business with," Sholem-Aleichem admitted in a letter to a friend in New York whose help he was requesting, Adler was "truly an artist, and I realized that Tevye was made for him."

Even before he finished his script, Sholem-Aleichem drafted a letter—a mash note, really—to Adler. The address at the top of the page alone slathered on the flattery: to "the great artist and master of the Yiddish stage, Mr. Jacob P. Adler, New York." It went on to insist, "only an artist like you is able of creating and revealing the soul of this character." Sholem-Aleichem spared no praise for his own work. He elaborated its merits at length:

Great master of the stage! In my play you will not find any of the effects for which the Yiddish theater public has been cultivated for so many years. No heartrending, teary scenes of little corpses in cribs, of crazy women, disheveled maidens who scream as if in a madhouse and make the whole Bowery cry. No saccharine songs that pander to (and overestimate) "Moyshe's" cheap fandom; also no love-'em-and-leave-'em boarders to whom modest maidens give up their chastity, before shooting themselves right in front of the audience. Also, no vulgar jokes and no tickling the audience's armpit with the fingertip in hopes of making a buck. No. Don't look for any of those tricks. You won't find them from me. Instead, you will find a Jew, a father of five daughters, a simple man but a whole one, honest, devout, suffering. His life is full of tragedy, but he will make the audience laugh from beginning to end, not with derision but with the happy laughter of sympathy and fellow-feeling for all his great anguish and little troubles. . . . I like to think that this will become the crown role of your long artistic path before you bid your profession farewell—God grant you endless days, amen!

> One of your most fervent admirers,
> Sholem-Aleichem

In a postscript, Sholem-Aleichem distributed the other roles to Adler's wife and daughters. "In short," he concluded his lengthy appeal, "this is your family play."

The Adler family never did play those parts (though Jacob Adler's son Luther would take over for Zero Mostel as Tevye in the original production of *Fiddler* half a century later). Indeed, the author never even sent the letter he had taken such pains to compose. A friend from New York leveled with him, reporting that the directors there no longer believed in the potential of his works, so Sholem-Aleichem spared himself yet one more humiliation and completed the play for eventual publication just in case, maybe someday, Tevye would make his way onto a stage.

By that time, New York's Yiddish theatrical epicenter had shifted from the ever-seedier Bowery to Second Avenue. In 1911, David Kessler opened the 2,000-seat Second Avenue Theater at Second Street. Thomashefsky, in a loose partnership with Adler, followed a little over a year later when the real estate developer (and father of burlesque impresarios) Louis Minsky built them an Italian Renaissance theater a couple of blocks down, with gold and rose interiors, for $1 million—the National

Theater, also seating 2,000 people. Music halls along the same avenue—differentiating themselves from the nickelodeons that offered a vaudeville act or two while movie reels were being changed—began presenting three- and four-act melodramas.

"Second Avenue" became the name for New York's theatrical *Yiddishkayt* (Jewishness) itself: flagrant tearjerkers, full-blown tragedies, ditty-filled romantic comedies, cautionary issue drama: all might play on a single night along the fourteen-block avenue for rapt and raucous spectators. The critics would never entirely abandon the sharp distinction between venerable artistry and shameless pandering—no more than English-language theater discourse would do without such binary standards—but increasingly both ends coexisted under the rubric of "Yiddish theater." Often, within a single play.

The recession of 1913–14 pinched the theaters and the auxiliary businesses that had sprung up along Second Avenue—sheet music shops, photography studios, cafés for stars and their devotees to congregate and argue. But when war broke out in Europe, demand for American armaments and other exportable goods surged and, with it, the economy. In the years following, the Yiddish theater, like its English-language counterpart, enjoyed a spurt of growth and stability.

Not soon enough for Sholem-Aleichem. In any event, the great master Jacob P. Adler and his ilk lost their hold on his imagination in the summer of 1914. Only one thing mattered then: getting out of Europe as it was going up in flames.

Sholem-Aleichem and his family were vacationing on Germany's Baltic coast when the war erupted that July. One day they were beach resort layabouts, the next they were enemies of the state. Germany had declared war on the land of their birth; as Russian nationals (though they hadn't lived in Russia for nearly a decade), they had to get out. Along with other tourists, the family scrambled for a spot on one of the overcrowded trains heading toward Berlin, hoping, somehow, to get a train crossing out of the country from there. With borders closing and foreigners at the Berlin station fighting desperately to push their way onto trains heading north, Berkowitz and Sholem-Aleichem made their way onto one and, after a harrowing day, onto a boat for Sweden, and then on to Copenhagen. The five women and two little girls left behind in Berlin had to wait two days to find room on a train that then took three days to make the journey to

Denmark, where they reunited with the family and tried, once more, to set up a new life.

Sholem-Aleichem fell into a depression as he learned that Russia's Yiddish press and publishing industry had been shut down in an instant. He spent four listless months in Copenhagen and then, on November 19, 1914, wearily and warily, he and most of his family boarded the *Frederick VIII*, bound for America.

When they pulled into the harbor at Hoboken, New Jersey, on December 2, the greeting for the author was more modest than it had been eight years earlier: just a couple of friends and some Hebrew school kids waving blue-and-white flags—no prominent Jews or Yiddish writers. The journalists who showed up peddled the same old story about the Jewish Mark Twain who called himself "Peace be with you." Sholem-Aleichem burst out with a bitter laugh the next day when he saw that one paper referred to him as "Sholem Yankev Abramovitch"—the given name of another author altogether, his literary "grandfather," Mendele. Astonished by how much New York had grown and speeded up since he'd left, and by how strong and self-assured the new generation of Jewish Americans seemed, Sholem-Aleichem felt more alienated than ever, as though he'd arrived too late into a world that had created itself without him and then flown off, far beyond his orbit.

For all the changes Sholem-Aleichem noticed in the city, one thing remained constant: it would not cut him a break. The Yiddish daily, *Der tog*, had contracted with him to write two pieces a week for $100, but he complained that the editors lacked enthusiasm for his work. Weaker than ever, he once again embarked on provincial reading tours to pump up his bank account and his ego—with mixed success on both counts. And he tried, yet again, to write for the stage. Over the summer of 1915, he worked on *Dos groyse gevins* (*The Grand Prize*), a jolly four-act comedy about a tailor whose simple happiness is spoiled when he wins a fortune in a lottery, and he felt certain that this time he himself would win big. In a July letter to his children Misha and Emma, who had stayed in Copenhagen (Emma looking after her ailing brother), he wrote with no diminishment of his stagestruck enthusiasm: "I hope to have it produced in the fall by Adler or Thomashefsky. I think its success is a sure thing." Or maybe he knew better and was putting on a cheery front for his children.

Either way, *The Grand Prize* was not even produced. Thomashefsky told him the play was weak. Sholem-Aleichem turned to David Kessler with yet one more new play. When he read it for the esteemed actor, Kessler nodded off.

That insult was nothing compared with the horrendous news that was to come: in September Misha died. Word arrived by telegram the day after Yom Kippur, and in that instant Berkowitz saw his father-in-law disintegrate before his eyes. Soon thereafter, *Der tog*—operating at a loss—told Sholem-Aleichem they would not be renewing his contract for a second year. All he could do to console himself, as he told his older daughter in a letter to Odessa, was to remember that in Europe things were even worse.

Sholem-Aleichem picked up a regular assignment from another daily newspaper, the *Varhayt,* but by January he took to his bed with influenza and was too sick to enjoy the splashy debut of his Motl stories in English in the Sunday magazine of the *New York World.* Ever more frail, he continued to write and to give readings through the spring, but his fire had gone out. On May 13, 1916, at the age of fifty-seven, surrounded by his family and some friends, Sholem-Aleichem died.

* * *

In this single sad instance, Sholem-Aleichem's theatrical timing was superb. His funeral—including a stately procession from his home in the Bronx through the full length of Manhattan, across the Lower East Side, and into the cemetery in Brooklyn—brought out as many as 250,000 mourners (nearly a sixth of New York's 1.5 million Jews) and involved dignitaries from every faction of New York Jewish life.

As New York's Yiddish press had been reporting, and as high-profile relief benefits in Manhattan had been emphasizing, among the vast destruction in the region for all residents, the war brought violent upheaval to the more than four million Jews of the Russian Pale and Habsburg Poland, who lived right in the pathways of the armies traipsing over the eastern front. More than half a million had been driven from their homes by czarist edict. Tens of thousands starved to death. Elsewhere, hundreds of thousands more, who were not forcibly expelled, fled the fighting in their towns and teemed into cities like Warsaw and Vilna. In response to the catastrophe, American Jews came together in an unprecedented union—not only Orthodox and socialists but also the uptown German elite linking up with representatives of the Yiddish-speaking masses—to form the American Jewish Joint Distribution Committee, which raised funds for war refugees. So, too, they united in grieving the death of Sholem-Aleichem, the icon of that ravaged world, the self-styled Jewish *folkshrayber*. His funeral gave stage to the community's need for collective mourning.

Public funerals for prominent figures had taken place from time to time before on the Lower East Side, but none had been so big or covered as much territory as Sholem-Aleichem's. And none had been so brilliantly orchestrated to address all the factions of Jewish New York, employing the traditional rituals of Jewish burial to make an emphatic assertion of Jewish unity.

Those who "guarded" the body before burial by staying close by and reciting psalms, as Jewish law requires, comprised more than a hundred Yiddish writers, arriving in shifts at Sholem-Aleichem's home—among them young modernist poets, Zionist orators, and socialist journalists. (One was Joel Entin, the critic who had slammed *Pasternak* as "a broken piece of calamity" less than a decade earlier.) The procession on the day of the funeral, a Monday, paused at religious, secular, German, and Eastern European institutions, acknowledging the communal role of all. The memorial prayer, "*El mole rakhamim*," was sung along the way by a Reform cantor and by the Orthodox superstar Yossele Rosenblatt. A dozen eulogists—and the men flanking them on the dais—represented the gamut of cultural and political Jewish life in New York.

That made sense, in the writer Yehoash's estimation. "Sholem-Aleichem was from beginning to end a microcosm of the Jewish people," he said in his eulogy. And such a symbol provided the community with exactly what it needed in an emotionally complex period in which the immigrant generation sensed it was losing, in Europe's violence, what it had already rejected. If Sholem-Aleichem could not be fully embraced in the New York Yiddish theater—the boisterous arena for the forging of a go-getting Jewish Americanness—because he was perceived as representing the suffering of Jews in Europe, he could now be earnestly celebrated in that very role in the theater of the streets. As the departed symbol of the lost Old World, Sholem-Aleichem was nothing less than the community's collective *pintele yid*.

That function required flattening into literalness the artistic persona he had cultivated in the early part of his career, and myriad commentators lent their sincere weight to the project. In an "appreciation" after his death, the Hebrew writer Yosef Haim Brenner, for one, declared Sholem-Aleichem "not a 'folk writer,' not even '*the* folk writer,' but rather . . . a living essence of the folk itself. . . . What we have [in his work] is the life of the people in its authentic form, a true, vibrant cross-section of their lives. . . . The great Sholem-Aleichem had no style—he had no need of style."

There could not be a more usable Eastern European Jewish past than that. And therefore Sholem-Aleichem—and before long that "crown of my creation" Tevye, with whom the author was increasingly (if erroneously) identified—became a font for signifying, and even for conferring, "authentic" *Yiddishkayt.* Which is to say, every competing Jewish faction, cause, or campaign claimed him as its own. And molded him to serve its agenda.

* * *

Three years after his death, more than a decade after his double debut in that ill-fated February of 1907, Sholem-Aleichem finally found success on the New York stage. The new prince of Yiddish theater, Maurice Schwartz, opened his second season as a director on August 29, 1919, with a Sholem-Aleichem play and had a colossal creative and commercial triumph. Not only did it fuel Schwartz's Yiddish Art Theater with income and with the inspiration to produce epic family dramas over the several decades the theater lasted in one form or another, it also demonstrated the enduring stage-worthiness of a family story about Jewish steadfastness and adaptation amid a world of change: it was the premiere production of *Tevye der milkhiker.* (A few months before, Zion films made a silent feature adapted from "Khave" that invented the characters of Fyedka's parents; it disappeared in obscurity.)

Schwartz's script was essentially the one Sholem-Aleichem had almost sent to Adler in 1914; the author had tinkered with it some once he had come back to America, and, as a condition for granting Schwartz license to produce it, Olga Rabinowitz insisted that their son-in-law, Berkowitz, supervise any text revision. (Berkowitz added the village priest from the "Khave" story to the dramatis personae, though Sholem-Aleichem had not included him.) At last, Sholem-Aleichem had his smash hit—the show sold out for sixteen straight weeks—despite a few reviews that insisted that great prose, with its openness to ambiguity and its potent narrative viewpoint, loses its dynamism when translated to the specificity required of the stage: no performance can ever match the ideal in a reader's imagination, the argument goes. "What more can the stage say about Tevye that the book has not already said?" asked M. Grim in the most cantankerous review that peddled this line. Grim—like future guardians of Yiddish literature who would rail against *Fiddler*—maintained that Schwartz (and presumably the author himself, though Grim does not mention his role in the adaptation) had "wiped out" the "brilliance, the Sholem-Aleichem-ness." Others mocked Schwartz's penchant for animals onstage (real chickens, doves, a cow, and a horse crowded Tevye's yard) and a clunky lighting effect (a moon that rose in the west but seemed to illuminate the house from the east). Still, Olga Rabinowitz was pleased enough with *Tevye*'s success that she granted Schwartz the rights to the entire Sholem-Aleichem canon—and he made good use of it over the next several decades, presenting, with irregular success, productions of such plays as *The Grand Prize, Wandering Stars* (adapted by Schwartz from the novel), and *Hard to Be a Jew* (featuring as Popov a promising young actor named Muni Weisenfreund—later known as Paul Muni). In 1931, Schwartz brought Sholem-Aleichem to Broadway in an English-language version of *Hard to Be a Jew,* running for seventy-seven performances under the producer-approved title of *If I Were You.*

It is as Tevye, though, that Schwartz reigned supreme. Even critics who found fault with the staging more generally lauded him for his effective new approach to acting. Though not quite thirty at the time, Schwartz was larger than life and brought a surprising sense of wisdom as well as playful charm to the part. His commitment to toning down the stamps and shouts, the broad gestures and center-stage speechifying of the popular theater in favor of a quieter, more contemplative acting style paid off with Tevye. Schwartz won high praise, for example, for a first-act scene in which, sensing with a glance that Khave's suitor, Fyedka, has been in the house to visit her, Tevye seems to feel the foundations of his poor but happy Jewish home shake. Or when he silently rebukes his eldest daughter, Tzaytl, when she tries to awaken some sympathy in him for her sister. The influential Abe Cahan extolled Schwartz's "wholehearted" and "realistic" performance, most remarkable, in Cahan's reckoning, for steering clear of "*shund* effects" and "tricks to draw unearned applause." Schwartz did, however (as several critics noted), elicit genuine tears.

Maurice Schwartz in his film of *Teyve der milkhiker*, bringing realism and restraint to the role.

After the first sixteen weeks, the play held the stage at the Irving Place on weekends for almost the entire season. Schwartz put Tevye in rotation when the troupe toured to such cities as Boston, Los Angeles, London, Paris, and Vienna, contributing to the worldwide popularity of the play. And he kept it in the repertoire for years, continuing to play Tevye with "an unstrained style which approaches suaveness itself" and moving with agility "from stark tragedy to downright slapstick." Perhaps Bertha Gersten, who played Khave (to reviews lamenting her lack of fire), captured Schwartz's achievement best in her memoir: "It was hard to tell if Schwartz created Tevye or Tevye created Schwartz."

But Schwartz's performance alone can't account for the success of *Tevye der milkhiker*. The new realism of the acting meshed with the play's ability to speak to a community in the throes of cultural transition (just as *Fiddler* would do two generations later). With the Great War over and the scope of its destruction known, and with pogroms erupting in Russia's civil war, *Tevye der milkhiker* gave audiences a new occasion for coming together to focus their thoughts and emotions: a tempered presentation of one traditional man's recognition that his way of life is going under.

Centered, as it is, on the Khave story, the play sounded a question that had rushed to the surface of communal consciousness with the war—an implicating question that the popular audience, perhaps, didn't have breath to ask directly. Khave's marriage raises it obliquely as it conflates the threats of antisemitism and intermarriage: Would Jews survive?

Reviewing the production for the *Forverts* in 1919, B. Vladek was exactly right when he noted how the play touched the public's nerve at a time when "the whole Jewish people is in danger of being wiped out, when no day goes by without news about Jewish misfortune." The audience broke out in thunderous applause, he reported, "when Khave comes back and Tevye turns out to be the conqueror in spirit and in belief." Vladek suggested that their ovation conveyed their own steadfast conviction that "no one can break the Jews."

In that instance—and in the myriad forms *Tevye der milkhiker* has taken over nearly a century since then—the play served as a touchstone for communal pride and commitment to continuity in times of turmoil, no matter how extensively or fractiously that community may revise, or internally dispute, its essence. As a drama about cultural adaptation that itself has been adapted repeatedly for shifting cultural circumstances, *Tevye* has grappled with the anxieties and the promises of constancy and change in form as well as content.

* * *

Maurice Schwartz's regular revivals and world tours helped bring *Tevye der milkhiker* into the international Yiddish repertoire—as did Jewish history itself. Artists around the world created versions of the drama that responded to their own local upheavals.

In Warsaw, amid the interwar groundswell of Jewish culture, the actor Rudolf Zaslavsky staged an adaptation of the story "Tevye Goes to the Land of Israel" in 1928. Polish Jews, who had not gone through the kind of rupture from the homeland that American immigrants had experienced, received the production as a touching rendering of a revered classic, but in that time and place the play could not help but feel like a bit of a throwback. Eight years earlier, the Vilna Troupe (which had moved to Warsaw in 1917) revolutionized the Yiddish theater with its production of *The Dybbuk: Between Two Worlds*, the mystical play by S. Ansky based on his ethnographic expedition through western Russia just before World War I. The expressionistic staging (directed by Dovid Herman in Warsaw and then, in 1922, by the avant-garde pioneer Evgeny Vakhtangov in a Hebrew-language production in Moscow, while Maurice Schwartz's production in New York in 1921 took a less stylized approach) challenged the folksy realism of plays like *Tevye*. In another two decades or so, the village milkman would acquire tragic new resonance on the killing fields of Poland, of course, but while Yiddish modernism flourished in Warsaw *Tevye* laid a claim for Yiddish classicism—the pleasing standard against which a new aesthetic could define itself.

The Tevye material seems to call for at least a measure of theatrical realism. Apart from the story's demand for empathy with its characters, which abstract stage styles typically spurn, the breaking down of the Old World has an emotional impact only if that world is established through the experiences of engaging characters. Post–World War I modernism, after all, rejected everything Tevye stood for: convention, tradition, belief in an all-powerful God. If a Tevye play has already disassembled such values in its very form, there is no place for the play to go, no means by which the action can unfold a process of dissolution. So the artists of the Soviet Yiddish stage understood. A five-hour adaptation of the Tevye stories was a triumph at the Moscow State Yiddish Theater (or GOSET, the Russian acronym by which it's usually known) only after the regime officially repudiated avant-garde approaches.

GOSET belonged to the sweeping Soviet program for spreading the revolutionary gospel to the masses in the languages to which they'd most readily respond. Recognizing Jews as a "national minority" (along with such groups as Uzbeks, Tatars, and Ukrainians), the state subsidized Yiddish-language schools, newspapers, publishers, and theaters; GOSET's charge was to produce work that was, as the regime sloganeered, "national in form and socialist in content." The theater, which opened in 1921, managed to walk the tightrope of that seeming contradiction for some three decades, producing some of the greatest productions in the USSR in any language. The state often pointed to GOSET as a shining jewel of cultural achievement. And Sholem-Aleichem was one key to its success. Reviled by early Soviet critics for "romanticizing" prerevolutionary Jewish life, Sholem-Aleichem was quickly rehabilitated, heralded as a sly satirist of czarist oppression. GOSET's debut production, in 1921, was an evening of Sholem-Aleichem one-act plays adapted from the Menakhem-Mendl stories notable, among other things, for set designs by Marc Chagall, who decorated the entire theater with murals as a means of erasing the boundary between audience and stage. Across the walls and ceiling, multisized figures danced, leaped, and rolled in a carnivalesque pageant featuring the theater's artists, proletarian spectators, an emerald cow, and repurposed folkloric motifs. An acrobat wearing tefillin cartwheels as though overturning religion; a Torah scribe writes "once upon a time" onto a scroll, thereby secularizing a sacred text; and a green-faced violinist wearing a striped tallis that juts properly across his cubistically rendered clothing stands astride the rooftops of two little houses.

The staging was also emphatically antirealistic. Chagall "hated real objects as illegitimate disturbers of his cosmos and furiously threw them off the stage," the art critic and GOSET dramaturg Avrom Efros recounted. In costumes and makeup also designed by Chagall, actors moved in an angular, mechanical choreography and their faces were painted with brash geometric designs—half green, half yellow for Solomon Mikhoels, who played Menakhem-Mendl with one eyebrow raised two inches higher than its natural position. The production, Efros wrote, looked like "Chagall paintings come to life." Chagall was long gone from the USSR by the time GOSET got around to staging *Tevye*, but his work would eventually be identified with Tevye's story.

About a decade into GOSET's history, the Soviet regime demanded adherence to "socialist realism," and the theater had to change gears; the original director, Alexander Granovsky, defected to Germany, leaving the theater's reins in the hands of Mikhoels, reportedly one of the nation's greatest actors in any language. In 1939, he directed and performed in GOSET's version of *Tevye der milkhiker*. As *Tevye* had been at the Yiddish Art Theater in New York, its Soviet cousin became one of GOSET's greatest hits. And as in America, the version in Moscow swayed with the local prevailing winds. Mikhoels, a small man but a sturdy presence onstage, played Tevye as a sympathetic relic of what he deemed a "fossilized patriarchal life of the Jewish family," whose Scripture quoting showed how inadequate the "dead dogma" of Judaism was for explaining "the contradictions that develop with changed social relations." Luckily, Perchik comes along not only to woo Hodl but also to teach Tevye the merits of dialectical materialism.

That same year, Maurice Schwartz made a movie version of *Tevye der milkhiker*, using for exteriors a wheat and potato field near Jericho, Long Island—Schwartz said it looked just like the Ukrainian countryside near his birthplace. While filming, the company heard the shocking news that Hitler and Stalin had signed a nonaggression pact. It wasn't just the planes blaring into and out of nearby Mitchel airfield that disrupted the filming. Political discord strained life on the set. Like any other Yiddish cultural project of the period, *Tevye*'s company comprised participants with conflicting commitments—Depression-era Communists, anti-Stalinist socialists, unaffiliated lefties, apolitical artistes. What united them was dread: as the filming fell behind schedule and work was extended past the end of August, the worst news broke—the Nazis had invaded Poland, where many had relatives. And now the story of Tevye's perseverance and Khave's return to her people took on an almost sacred temper. It is certainly the most somber of the *Tevye* adaptations. "There sits upon Tevya's shoulders the great resignation which is the birthright of his people," declared a reviewer for the English-language *Chicago Daily Tribune* when the film was released in December.

For audiences, it expressed the anxiety and horror that gripped American Jews reading helplessly of Hitler's advance across Europe. Schwartz stressed the antisemitism of Tevye's neighbors. He created an opening scene in which Khave is taunted by a gang of Jew-baiting Ukrainian youths. In general, the film paints Ukrainians in coarse strokes, as violent, gruff, drunk, and brutish. Meanwhile, Schwartz slathered on the pathos. He filmed the sequence in which Tevye tells the local priest he'd rather see his children "perish" than marry outside their faith. (Overhearing the conversation, Khave faints.) And he created another in which Tevye not only confronts the priest in an effort to retrieve Khave (as in the original story) but also throws himself at the priest's feet (while Khave whimpers upstairs, as if locked away from the home she already pines for). In a drawn-out sequence filled with precise ritual detail, Tevye and Golde sit shiva as if their daughter were dead. Golde soon dies in earnest. Tevye is evicted and Khave pleads to come back because the marriage has turned out a disaster. In what the film critic J. Hoberman calls "a triumphant rebuke" to the typical assimilationist fables proffered by most popular Yiddish movies, the closing shot tracks Tevye's wagon setting off for Palestine.

The film may have captured the Jewish mood at the beginning of the war, offering some vague hope in the wish fulfillment of Tevye's defiant survival. But even as critics praised Schwartz's virtuosity and the film's unusually high production values, they upbraided him for not representing the real Sholem-Aleichem. Foreshadowing the objections some Jewish critics would level at *Fiddler on the Roof* some twenty-five years later (and indeed at every dramatic and cinematic version of the material), the Communist *Morgn frayhayt* critic said the film "does not at all agree with the spirit and essence of Sholem-Aleichem's writing." Schwartz plays "with deep understanding" for the hero, he concluded. "But it is not *Tevye der milkhiker*, it's something else and something worse." The *Forverts* concurred: "Merely a shadow of Sholem-Aleichem remains." But today's corruption is frequently tomorrow's fidelity: what comes to be considered "authentic" is often simply the most recent precedent from which a new interpretation departs. In time, Schwartz's film would seem like sterling.

Dramatizing the tension between tradition and progress, *Tevye* would cycle through many rounds of such charges in the years to come, serving as Jewish culture's always shifting constant. Still, it was no straight line from the Yiddish Art Theater to *Fiddler on the Roof*. The cultural sphere had to absorb Sholem-Aleichem into English after the Second World War. As he had become for the Yiddish-speaking generation after the first war, Sholem-Aleichem became available to their English-speaking children as an icon of the past, employed for cementing a new mode of Jewish American memory making. Cahan and the Yiddish theatergoing public had dismissed him as too outdated to be relevant in 1907. Four decades later, his oldness was useful in a new way. His work would speak powerfully to postwar exigencies—but only when adapted as America commanded.

CHAPTER 2

BETWEEN TWO WORLDS
OF SHOLEM-ALEICHEM

A HANDFUL OF TRANSLATORS, WRITERS, AND ARTISTS ESTABLISHED
the ground on which *Fiddler* could eventually stand. In works produced
between 1943 and 1957, they made Sholem-Aleichem accessible to non-
Yiddish readers, painted in words and pictures the milieu he represented, and proved his stage-worthiness for the American mainstream.
In the complicated postwar period—a time of both exuberance and
trauma for American Jews—they taught Tevye to speak English and laid
his path to the stage.

These projects came in various genres and styles and from disparate
directions, some with the express, urgent purpose of recovering a civilization that had just been extinguished, some propelled by the ideals of a
lingering left, some dictated by the personal exigencies of an artist's
imagination. In the aggregate, they performed a crucial cultural task at a
devastating time: they created the East European Jewish past for non-
Yiddish-speaking Americans. They provided the language, imagery, and
conceptual framework through which Americans encountered that world
that was no more. For second- and third-generation Jews especially, they
sutured a rupture with a legacy that might not have been acknowledged
had it not burst.

Two different works titled *The World of Sholom Aleichem* nearly book-
end this period of proliferating popular representations of East European Jewry. The first, an elegiac book by the Jewish nationalist Maurice

Samuel, published in 1943, set the parameters for much of what follows; the second, a play by the leftist internationalist Arnold Perl, produced in 1953, was the first to bring Sholem-Aleichem (in English) to theatergoers around the country, and did so as a defiant rebuke to the anti-Communist blacklist. And centrally, in between, came two volumes of Sholem-Aleichem stories translated by Frances and Julius Butwin, inspired in part by Samuel's book and utterly necessary to Perl, and the popular ethnography of the shtetl *Life Is with People*. If in the popular imagination *Fiddler* eventually cemented the image of the shtetl as a metonym for all of East European Jewish culture and fixed Tevye permanently within it, these various works made and mixed the mortar.

* * *

Samuel, a rising star of the Jewish intelligentsia, was well placed to blaze the English-language trail through Sholem-Aleichem (though he could not predict or, in the end, condone the Broadway musical to which it led). Having come back to *Yiddishkayt* as an adult after an indifferent youth, he burned with the zeal of a convert. Born in Romania in 1895 and raised in the Jewish immigrant quarter of Manchester, England, he showed little sign that he would become, as the Yiddish scholar Emanuel S. Goldsmith dubbed him, "the leading spokesman of Jewish rejuvenation and creative survival in America for half a century." By his bar mitzvah, he had declared himself an atheist and a socialist, identities he sustained into his young adulthood. But when he dropped out of Manchester University after his three-year scholarship came to an end and migrated to the Lower East Side of New York in late 1914, a few months shy of his twentieth birthday, he had already grown weary of the "dogma" and "intellectual bullying" of party politics.

In New York, Samuel fell under the spell of the commanding intellectual oratory of the Zionist leader Shmarya Levin. Samuel stalked Levin's public appearances, at first struggling to keep up with his rich, allusive Yiddish but always sitting transfixed in the front row. (Samuel would go on to translate Levin's three-volume autobiography.) The Yiddish and Hebrew he had disregarded as a boy he now reached back for, the better to participate in the cultural and political disputations tearing up the intellectual world he wished to join. Samuel frequented the Yiddish theater—Jacob Adler, even in his waning days, impressed Samuel most—and swallowed up the competing daily papers and the new Yiddish poetry of every faction. His uncle Berel, a tailor eking out a living by mending and pressing clothes in a grimy shop on East Fifteenth Street, served as Samuel's unwitting tutor, simply by shooting the breeze in his pungent Yiddish. The language itself, Samuel later reflected, was his "gateway into Jewish life."

His experience in Europe after the First World War stoked his Jewish nationalism. In 1917, Samuel was drafted into the United States Army and, because of his fluent French, put to work in counterespionage in Bordeaux. From there, he took a seven-week stint as a secretary and interpreter for the Morgenthau Commission to investigate pogroms in Poland at the end of the war. Samuel found that the speeches he was called on to translate for Henry Morgenthau Sr., a German Jew and a staunch assimilationist, stuck in his craw. In researching the outbreaks of antisemitic violence, Morgenthau operated, in Samuel's view, with unctuous consideration of Polish authorities and their chauvinism, "as if the pogroms had been two-sided"; the resulting report, issued in October 1919, implied to Samuel's dismay that "it was natural for the Poles to have regarded the Jewish minority as a hateful obstacle to Polish national liberation," that if the Jews had just kept their heads down and blended in better, they wouldn't have brought such trouble upon themselves. Samuel returned to New York in 1921 ready to dedicate his life to the Jewish cause.

He worked for a number of years as spokesperson for the Zionist Organization of America, before setting out as a freelance essayist, translator, and speaker—in short, as a public Jewish intellectual, or, more aptly, as an intellectual Jew, for while the members of a younger generation of literary and political commentators from Jewish backgrounds were just beginning to argue the world with radical fervor at City College in the 1930s, they "defined themselves Jewishly by their alienation from their Jewishness." Samuel had long left Marxism behind; writing in journals like *Menorah* and *Jewish Frontier*—not in *Partisan Review* and *Commentary*—he had as his driving purpose "to help Jews acquire an interest in Jewish knowledge with the hope that they will transmit it to their children."

To reel the second and third generations back from the brink of assimilation so as to share a stake in Jewish continuity, Samuel declared Judaism part and parcel of America's noblest heritage. Never mind the grimy ghetto melodramas and the shmaltzy songs that embarrassed their audiences' children. In stentorian tones and perfect tweeds, a pipe perched on his lip, a dreamy glint in his dark, myopic eyes, Samuel held forth about the great achievements and contributions of Jewish literature. Among his twenty-six books (plus another two dozen books he translated), Samuel took Arnold Toynbee to task for Christian bias, assembled a history of the Beilis blood libel case, examined antisemitism as a disease of the Western mind, chronicled the emergence of Israel (three different times as the story evolved), and translated into English I. J. Singer, Sholem Asch, and Haim Nachman Bialik, among others. The years 1953 to 1971 featured his radio (and, in the later years, TV) conversations about the Hebrew Bible with the thoroughly genteel and Gentile Mark Van Doren. Samuel promoted the Bible's literary importance, making it relevant—and justifiable—to even the most secular of listeners. "The man who does not see in the prophets, in the Moses narrative, in the Ruth story, in Job, in the Song of Songs, the highest type of individual genius," Samuel wrote, "should apply his literary faculties exclusively to the study of crossword puzzles." Sholem-Aleichem, he analogized, was to Yiddish culture as Dickens was to Victorian England, Balzac to nineteenth-century France, and Shakespeare to Elizabethan England.

Sholem-Aleichem was something more even than they: he was "the mirror of Russian Jewry." Samuel could see him no other way in the dire moment of his reflection: he was working on his pathbreaking translation of Sholem-Aleichem under the pall of emerging news of the Nazi genocide. In Samuel's circle, details trickling in about the "final solution" were a constant and urgent matter, even as the organizational Jewish establishment hesitated to press for a direct American response and the news media failed to cover it adequately. *The World of Sholom Aleichem*, published by Knopf in 1943, would have to be more than a collection of stories. It was a literary call to arms (not only by dint of the advertisement for war bonds on its jacket flap). As Ben Hecht asserted that his widely performed and radio-broadcast pageant *We Will Never Die*, featuring scenes of murdered Jews recounting their demise, functioned as "the first American newspaper reports on the Jewish massacre in Europe," so Samuel maintained that Sholem-Aleichem could rouse readers with a different sort of summons. Tracing a bitter line from Sholem-Aleichem's world to the peril of the moment, Samuel writes, "It was a principle of Russian law that everything was forbidden to Jews unless specifically permitted. But by an oversight which Germany has since corrected, the right to remain alive was not challenged." Rather than tell how Europe's Jews were suffering atrocities and dying, he could tell how they had lived.

Samuel didn't simply render Sholem-Aleichem's stories in English—he considered that impossible, given the intricacies, idioms, and allusions in the original. So he "transmitted rather than translated" them. He interjected his descriptions of the cultural realm in which the plots unfolded. "Every other sentence cries out for a paragraph of explanation," Samuel asserts, by way of self-pardon for his free hand with the material. "I wrote round him and about him."

The resulting work is as compelling as it is bizarre. Samuel renarrates selected pieces of Sholem-Aleichem's fiction into an amalgamation of storytelling, biography, criticism, and contemporary commentary. In part the book resembles the condensed, simplified *Tales from Shakespeare* by Mary and Charles Lamb; in part it contrives a new form of literary ethnography, drawing sociological conclusions from Sholem-Aleichem's creations and presenting him not so much as a deliberating writer but as "the common people in utterance . . . the 'anonymous' of Jewish self-expression." It's as if in handing Sholem-Aleichem over to the English-reading audience at such a precarious moment, Samuel had to deliver an authentic, unassailable record. His offering couldn't be a concoction, not even the concoction of a great literary genius. With this book Samuel was erecting a cenotaph, marking the loss of a civilization that was being annihilated even as he wrote—"an exercise in necromancy." He needed what he depicted to be real, worthy of lamentation, untainted by artifice.

He declares as much. Referring to anthropological case studies from the late 1920s and 1930s of a small, presumably average American city, Samuel asserts, "We could write a Middletown of the Russian-Jewish Pale basing ourselves solely on the novels and stories and sketches of Sholom Aleichem, and it would be as reliable a scientific document as any 'factual' study; more so, indeed, for we should get, in addition to the material of a straightforward social inquiry, the intangible spirit which informs the material and gives it its living significance."

No one carries that spirit more fully than Tevye, "the best known and best loved figure in the world of Sholom Aleichem." The Tevye Samuel gave to English readers was "[a] little Jew wandering in a big, dark forest, symbol of a little people wandering in the big dark jungle of history," a Tevye stripped of irony and refinished in sentimentality. He emerges from Samuel's pages as the dominant exemplar, even the spokesperson, for the murdered Jews of Eastern Europe—as if the world of Sholem-Aleichem were so static that the distance between 1915 and 1945 had collapsed into a day, and his characters so real that they could stand in for the millions who perished.

Samuel is also the first to make Golde a shrew. Exaggerating Sholem-Aleichem's portrait of Tevye's no-nonsense wife and channeling Tevye's sexism, Samuel—who confessed in a letter to a friend his "very real hatred" of women—baselessly renders Golde "without equal at handing out a dinner of curses and a supper of slaps." The misogynist tinge clings to the character in many later versions, often mitigated onstage, at least, by the warmth and likability of the actors who came to play her.

* * *

The "world" of Samuel's title is the shtetl (though the word he uses is "townlet"). "Arguably the greatest single invention of Yiddish literature," as David Roskies puts it, the shtetl was now reinvented in the decade or so after the war, for American use. *The World of Sholom Aleichem* was first to establish the image of the shtetl as a Jewish pastoral, a self-contained, albeit beset, domain where Jews of all classes endured through time marked out in Sabbaths and holy days. Though Samuel notes that in the original stories Tevye resides on the edge of a rural village among Gentiles, his book so thoroughly associates the dairyman with the "little people" of Kasrilevke it's easy to conclude, reading *The World of Sholom Aleichem*, that Tevye lived in the shtetl among them. And that is where he explicitly is placed in a radio play based on Samuel's book that aired on a new radio program sponsored by the Jewish Theological Seminary, *The Eternal Light*, in early 1945. There in Kasrilevke Tevye remains when, two years later, *The Eternal Light* presents *The Daughters of Tevye*. This first English-language dramatization of the Tevye stories, made for the midcentury ecumenical program that aimed to promote harmony among Jews and Christians, turns them into saccharine; here, Perchik goes off not to Siberia but, happily, to finish university in Petrograd, and a daughter called Rachel heads to Seattle to marry a hometown boy who made good in America. From here on, Tevye (in English) is a man—a spokesman—of the shtetl.

Writing in the face of its final demise, Samuel can't help but present the shtetl romantically as "a remarkable civilization, with values which the world cannot spare." He selects carefully from Sholem-Aleichem's oeuvre to keep him bound by the shtetl, claiming that the author paid little mind to characters who entered the wider world stage: he ignores novels like *The Flood*, *Wandering Stars*, and *The Bloody Hoax*. Thus he sets in motion the American image that grows and persists in the works that came after. As they followed, they reiterated his assertion of the most enduring and endearing shtetl ideal: that its "prosperity was spiritual rather than material." This became the overriding trope of American remembrances of Eastern European Jewry—what Lucy Dawidowicz impatiently describes as an image of people "forever frozen in utter piety and utter poverty."

This false but strangely reassuring image found eager audiences among American Jews who were trying to reconcile news of European Jewry's slaughter with their own dash to assimilate. It appealed to them as the antisuburb, notes the historian Edward S. Shapiro, its simple dignity and sense of community contrasting with the bland conformity and acquisitiveness of suburbia: the shtetl conferred an admirable patrimony. In addition to helping to send *The World of Sholom Aleichem* into a tenth printing, American Jews flocked to the blockbuster Chagall retrospective opening at the Museum of Modern Art in New York in the summer of 1946, then mounted at the Art Institute of Chicago in the fall. The next year, they purchased the volumes of photographs of Jews in interwar Poland by Roman Vishniac—*kheyder* boys at desks, wizened men with vacant eyes, barefoot girls with smudged cheeks. One of the books featured an introduction by the theologian Rabbi Abraham Joshua Heschel that practically lifted Samuel's summation: Vishniac's albums presented "one great portrait of a life abjectly poor in its material condition, and in its spiritual condition exaltedly religious." Heschel's line was quoted on the book's dustcover. (He elaborated the idea further in his own book, *The Earth Is the Lord's: The Inner World of the Jew in Eastern Europe*.)

Myth building makes quick riddance of inconvenient facts. That Chagall's hometown of Vitebsk was a burgeoning cultural center and no primitive backwater did not stand in the way of his reputation as an authentic,

if fanciful, chronicler of Old World spirituality; that his wife, Bella Chagall, came from a well-to-do family and studied at Moscow University was
no impediment to her whimsical memoir of girlhood Sabbath and holiday
observances in *Burning Lights*, another popular book of the period, being
absorbed into the dominant narrative. Vishniac's project—commissioned
by the American Jewish Joint Distribution Committee in the late 1930s
with the fund-raising aim of awakening American consciences to the
plight of European Jewry as Hitler rose to power—was designed to show
the most vulnerable segments of the community and thus to leave out the
diverse and sizable population of Jews who carried on modern, cosmo-
politan lives in major cities; that did not prevent his images from visually
coming to define the entirety of the destroyed Jewish culture.

No work advanced the idea of the shtetl as the single, uniform, self-
contained memory site for Ashkenazi Jews more than *Life Is with People:
The Jewish Little-Town of Eastern Europe* (1952), Mark Zborowski and
Elizabeth Herzog's work of "salvage ethnography." (The paperback edition was given a new subtitle—*The Culture of the Shtetl*—and featured a
cover drawing by Chagall, *House in Vitebsk*.) The authors based their
study on interviews with émigrés to America from all over Eastern
Europe, most of whom had left as children (some of them originally from
large cities)—and whose memories had been shaped and amended by
their reading of Sholem-Aleichem and other Yiddish writers. Zborowski
and Herzog's work was also informed by their reading of Bella Chagall,
Heschel, and Samuel. Touted as an authoritative, even scientific account,
in truth the book presented "a composite portrait of a virtual town, not
an empirical description of an actual one," Barbara Kirshenblatt-
Gimblett notes. But it was widely and enthusiastically received (despite a
few reviews pointing out discrepancies and errors) as a reliable record
put down in the nick of time. It is still in print.

* * *

All these background resources notwithstanding, there could of course be
no *Fiddler* without the Sholem-Aleichem stories themselves. When the
first major volume in English—*The Old Country*—was released in June
1946, it entered the already entrenched mind-set that saw Sholem-Aleichem
as representing a "world" and speaking from the grave for its murdered
Jews. The volume of twenty-seven stories, translated by Frances and Julius

Butwin and published by Crown, was "more than a book," wrote none other than Ben Hecht, invoking this discourse in his review for the *New York Times*. It appeared just two months before he would stage his Zionist pageant *A Flag Is Born*, in which his Old World protagonist, a Holocaust survivor (played by Paul Muni), is called Tevya. Of the Butwin volume, Hecht said: "It is the epitaph of a vanished world and an almost vanished people. . . . All the Tevyas whose souls and sayings, whose bizarre and tender antics Sholom Aleichem immortalized in the richest Yiddish prose ever written—were massacred, six million strong, by the Germans. . . . In Sholom Aleichem's books you can see all the ghosts, . . . not merely the report of a people. They are their historical farewell to a civilization that wiped them out." The review was illustrated with an image from a Chagall lithograph: in front of a crooked line of pointy-roofed houses, a horse draws a cart into the frame and a fiddler rushes along, violin in hand, looking like he's about to take a tumble. The *Times* gave the picture a caption: "The Vanished World of Sholem Aleichem." (Crown's advertisements made a less lachrymose appeal, promising plenty of "fine, juicy humor.")

With a spate of ecstatic reviews—many of them singling out the special charm of "Tevye Wins a Fortune," the one dairyman story in the collection—the book climbed quickly onto the *New York Times* bestseller list and stayed there some three months. Right away, Crown signed Frances Butwin to a new Sholem-Aleichem project (her husband, Julius, had died while *The Old Country* was in galleys): a volume highlighting the Tevye cycle. Published in 1949, *Tevye's Daughters* presents seven of his adventures, "scattered" among pieces from other Sholem-Aleichem series, Butwin explains, to "indicate the lapse of time between the stories" as they had been printed, over decades, in newspapers. (A few years later, she translated *Wandering Star*.)

Almost right away, the Tevye volume was picked up for adaptation into a Broadway musical. In February 1949—less than a month after *Tevye's Daughters* came out—a playwright approached Crown for the rights to create a dramatization and his libretto soon caught the attention of a successful composer-lyricist team, who secured an eleven-month option on the material later that year.

But Richard Rodgers and Oscar Hammerstein II were busy adapting *Anna and the King of Siam*, among other projects, and they felt the Tevye script needed a huge amount of work, so the months whizzed past and by the summer of 1950 they had released their claim. The world never found out how the leading musical-comedy duo, both from German Jewish backgrounds, would have conjured Tevye's world, a realm as foreign to them as *South Pacific*'s Bali Ha'i, *The King and I*'s Siam, and, for that matter, Oklahoma.

Right after Rodgers and Hammerstein let their option go, the illustrious producer Michael Todd scooped it up. Born Avrom Goldbogen to parents who had emigrated from Poland—his father a rabbi, no less— Todd may have had more affinity for the material and he reportedly raised the $100,000 budgeted for the show. But a production did not materialize. Todd was best known for staging slightly upscale burlesques whose gaudy sets were more dressed than the women gallivanting on them, so perhaps he couldn't win the confidence of further backers and artists. Who could say how the showman who was represented on Broadway at the time with *Peep Show* and *The Live Wire* would treat the dairyman's marriageable daughters? The plans went nowhere.

The playwright, one Irving Elman, did not give up. For several years, he and his agent, the formidable Edmond Pauker, sent the script to actors, producers, and directors, hoping to bring the "folk play with music" to the stage. (The music, for which Elman took credit, was an assemblage of well-known Yiddish tunes such as "Rozhinkes mit mandlen" ["Raisins with Almonds"], Avrum Goldfadn's lullaby from his 1880 operetta, *Shulamis*.) Many who read the script declared enthusiasm for its warmth and humor, but almost all expressed reservations, too: "you need to take out all the animals," "it feels so unwieldy as to be almost unmanageable," it's "sprawling, undramatic," "too Jewish and too folkish for the general public," not "commercial enough." Leading Jewish actors— Menashe Skulnik, Joseph Buloff, Sam Jaffe, and Jacob Ben-Ami—would have been glad to star as Tevye, if changes they recommended were made to the script and if a producer could raise the funds.

Could be, the Broadway stage was not yet hospitable to Tevye in the early 1950s. The Jewish characters who trod the musical boards in the several years Elman tried to get his adaptation produced included the vaguely implied Jews cavorting in an upstate New York summer camp for adults in Harold Rome's *Wish You Were Here* (implied only by virtue of the setting), and the Yinglish revues *Bagels and Yox* and *Borschtcapades*, proffering skits, songs, and vulgar comics scoring laughs based on the old scheme of playing in-jokes (the bits of kitchen Yiddish) for audiences who, in the dominant culture, anxiously regarded themselves as outsiders. One might also count Nathan Detroit in *Guys and Dolls* if you take his lyric—"I'm just a no-goodnik. All right already. It's true. So nu?"—to clinch his Jewish connection. But generally, Broadway's musical makers, though most were Jewish, were not yet putting overt Jewish characters front and center. The Great White Way had no room for puffed-up patriarchs of the Old World, with chickens in their yards and prayers on their lips. Such images could be embraced in books and records—objects brought into the private sphere (and part of the midcentury rise of consumer objects as confirmers and even conferrers of identity). Jewish radio shows could accommodate Tevye, too, as they were also enjoyed in the domestic realm. But in the more diverse, public arena of Broadway, Tevye may have been too risky a commodity.

The leaders of the Jewish establishment, at least, were not ready for such a prominent production: the tercentenary celebration of Jewish life in America that they organized in 1954 unfolded under the slogan "Man's Opportunities and Responsibilities under Freedom." Their aim, the initiating statement said, was to pay homage to the "American heritage of religious and civil liberty" and demonstrate "the strength of the American people's commitment to the principles of democracy in our struggle against communism and other forms of totalitarianism of our day." Aghast, the pioneering cultural pluralist Horace Kallen complained that this Jewish celebration didn't have very much that was Jewish to distinguish it. That, in fact, was the point. The tercentenary celebrated how well Jews could blend into America, not the ways in which they stood out. And in popular culture of the period, Jews remained coded, cutesy, crazily comic, or downright "de-Semitized," as Henry Popkin charged in a famous 1952 essay in *Commentary*. Tevye had to cool his heels in the assimilating wings for another decade before striding onto the Broadway stage. Besides, Elman's play (lost to posterity) was by most accounts simply not so good.

* * *

One precinct of Jewish American life, however, was ready to share Sholem-Aleichem's characters on a public stage: the left. Communists, ex-Communists, socialists, and fellow travelers made their own claim on the *folkshrayber* as the Cold War began. If one stream flows toward *Fiddler* in this period from the source of Maurice Samuel and the invention of the sentimental shtetl, another equally strong current finds its wellspring in radical culture.

Frances and Julius Butwin led the way. Both child immigrants from Eastern Europe, they found their impulse to translate Sholem-Aleichem "not in a postwar effort to salvage the 'vanished world' of eastern European Jewry," according to their son, Joseph Butwin, but as progressives stirred by the Popular Front's promotion of proletarian and folk literature. (For Frances Butwin, an additional catalyst was her upbringing in Charleston, South Carolina, amid the community's self-conscious cultural renaissance, one of America's "remarkable acts of memory and invention.") Though by the mid-1940s, the alliance of Communists, socialists, industrial unionists, and bourgeois liberals in the fight against Fascism had long collapsed, the impact of the "cultural front" had not dissipated. Far beyond the party-line agitprop with which Popular Front art is commonly dismissed, much excellent work was ignited by the radical fervor of the 1930s and it shaped American culture well into the Cold War. Thanks to the Butwins, Sholem-Aleichem was part of this transformation.

Living in St. Paul, Minnesota, the Butwins found a "great friend, mentor, and comrade" in Meridel Le Sueur, author of the acclaimed people's history of the upper Midwest *North Star Country* (1945). *The Old Country* emerged from the same Popular Front exigencies—a valorization of "the folk" and the promotion of regional roots—after the Butwins had read Samuel's *The World of Sholom Aleichem* and recognized some parallels. Their volume and Le Sueur's, Joseph Butwin notes, were just two of numerous "country" books published in the 1940s in a vogue for American folkways. (*Desert Country*, *Palmetto Country*, and *Deep Delta Country* appeared in a series published by Duell, Sloan and Pearce. Crown, meanwhile, was getting in on the boom with *A Treasury of American Folklore* and *A Treasury of Jewish Folklore*. The radio and recording industries also developed folk departments, which featured Yiddish songs among their vernacular regional musics.) The Jews, too, were (once) a folk.

The Butwins' selection and translation of Sholem-Aleichem stories hardly pressed any of them toward an ideological doctrine; it was enough that the "little people" of Kasrilevke were a hardworking common folk, "lacking food, clothing, money and indeed everything but courage, faith and humor," as the *Chicago Daily Tribune* reviewer put it.

The books inspired leftists to create stage and radio performances. The dancer and choreographer Sophie Maslow, known for her *Dust Bowl Ballads* and *Folksay*, turned to Sholem-Aleichem to explore her Jewish heritage in a similar idiom, in what became her most famous dance, *The Village I Knew* (1950). In a series of seven scenes, it abstractly depicts rituals of shtetl life and events from stories in *The Old Country*. (She also drew on the visual imagery of Marc Chagall.) Maslow was from Brooklyn (with secular, socialist immigrant parents), so *The Village* was not in fact a place she "knew" firsthand; laying claim to it, the performance introduced a mode of identification that would characterize shtetl stagings to come, right up to *Fiddler*: it evoked nostalgia for a place one had never actually been.

When the writer Arnold Perl and the actor Howard Da Silva teamed up two years later to stage *The World of Sholom Aleichem*, their work, too, appealed to the sentimentality of a general audience, even as the two men were drawn to the material for its depiction of Jews scraping by under the boot of the czar. In Sholem-Aleichem's stories, they saw the imperative for Jews, having experienced oppression, to proclaim solidarity with anyone facing injustice. More than that, they were fighting injustice by virtue of doing the play: both were blacklisted and out of work and they hired a company that was blacklisted, too. Sholem-Aleichem didn't just provide some of their material; he was their red flag. At a time when mainstream Jewish organizations were purging leftists from their staffs, opening their files to HUAC, and, in the case of the American Jewish Committee, advocating the execution of the Rosenbergs, a team of unemployable, unrepentant leftists, at least some of them Party members (or former members), produced a surprise Jewish smash hit. While *Fiddler* was not drawn directly from Perl's *World of Sholom Aleichem* or from the *Tevya and His Daughters* that he presented later, the Perl productions demonstrated that old Yiddish stories could find a sizable contemporary audience and make it happy.

* * *

Da Silva and Perl made an unlikely pair. The actor, ten years older, was a big, brash personality, not particularly tall, but imposing, built like a bulldog and sometimes snapping like one, too. Perl was short and wiry and, if not classically handsome with his round glasses and receding hairline, intensely charismatic—a charmer who dressed nattily and whose flinty, flirty eyes journalists noted as "piercing." Where Da Silva sometimes came off as a blowhard, Perl captured everyone's attention with his persuasive discourse. Where Da Silva often worked from gut feeling, Perl reasoned everything through. But the two men shared political convictions, a newfound love of *Yiddishkayt*, and ferocious levels of energy, and they forged a theatrical partnership through which they could not only ride out but just about beat the blacklist.

Until 1951, Da Silva (born Silverblatt to immigrant parents in Cleveland) was enjoying stupendous success as an actor. From the 1930s, including a stint with the Federal Theater Project, he appeared frequently on the New York stage—the Butwins saw his magnetic performance as the menacing outsider, Jud Fry, in the original Broadway production of *Oklahoma!* when they came to New York to sign their deal with Crown for *The Old Country*—and by the mid-1940s, he had a thriving career in Hollywood, cast in feature roles in several films a year by the end of the decade. Then the friendly witness Robert Taylor named him before HUAC, declaring Da Silva suspicious because "he always seems to have something to say at the wrong time." Indeed he did, when he himself was called before HUAC in Los Angeles in March 1951. The moment Da Silva was sworn in, he began lambasting the committee as "a smoke screen" for "forces seeking to drop the atom bomb," shouting in his sonorous actor's voice over the chairman's pounding gavel. For every question about his affiliations, he offered a retort about the committee's attack on free thought, its labeling as subversive anyone who declares himself for peace, its general illegality. The first uncooperative witness to plead the Fifth Amendment, he would not answer their questions about his Communist activities. And he refused to say whether he would support the United States if it were invaded by Soviet Russia.

Soon after Da Silva's appearance, RKO Pictures edited him out of the just completed film *Slaughter Trail*, in which he'd played the lead role, and spliced in new footage of a different actor (Brian Donlevy). Da Silva took the hint. Along with some comrades from the Actors Lab—a West Coast offshoot of the Group Theater—Da Silva went to New York to look for work. Unlike the Screen Actors Guild, Actors' Equity, the union of theater performers, had voted to defy any political blacklist and even included a clause in every hiring contract to that effect.

Arnold Perl was never called before HUAC, though the FBI listed him on its "security index" for years and kept tabs on his participation in meetings, rallies, and workshops, most of them focused on labor rights and racial equality. Raised in a middle-class, liberal home, he turned leftward as a student at City College in the 1930s and stayed active as he pursued a career as a writer. His work took off in the army, of all places, where he was assigned to write anti-Fascist scripts. "I have gotten radio detectives in and out of trouble, scared children and fought straw men on so-called adult programs," he said of the entertainments he'd scripted professionally, "but it took a draft board to give me my first chance to write something for radio I didn't mind having my name connected with."

It was also in the army—specifically when he entered Dachau with his unit at the end of the war—that Perl felt a sudden, shocking surge of connection to the Jewish people. He spoke no Yiddish and never practiced any ritual observance growing up. But he was by nature curious about everything, a nondenominational intellectual who read voraciously for several hours late into every night. When he came back to New York, he started soaking up whatever he could find about Jewish culture. His career was flourishing. He was writing for the new, surprisingly progressive documentary units on the radio networks (his harrowing, detailed account of Nazi crimes in *The Empty Noose*, broadcast on the eve of the executions at Nuremberg, was heard by more than five million Americans); he also started freelancing for *The Eternal Light*. He stretched his script consultations with Rabbi Moshe Davis at the Jewish Theological Seminary (which produced the program) into informal tutorials.

Then, in June 1950—the month that saw the arrest of the Rosenbergs and the outbreak of the Korean War—three retired FBI agents calling themselves American Business Consultants published *Red Channels*, the booklet that listed 151 people working in broadcast and their alleged associations with Communist causes. Little surprise that Perl's name was among them—and that his commissions dried up. Though he kept banging out scripts on his small manual Royal typewriter and managed to sell them through a front (earning only a fraction of the amount the front took home), he plummeted from a bright career that had enabled him to purchase a home in the swanky Westchester suburb of Mamaroneck and support his wife and three children to a state of economic uncertainty that, within a couple of years, also included alimony and child support payments.

He and Da Silva joined forces to create their own theater company, knowing they could be their own bosses. They had encountered each other years before in Popular Front activities—back in 1946 Da Silva had acted in a one-night presentation of a twenty-minute Perl script by the left-wing troupe Stage for Action. Before banding together, each had adapted Sholem-Aleichem on his own—a double coincidence, since both had chosen one of the same stories. Da Silva recorded several tales from the Butwins' *Old Country* on an album for Decca Records of the same name, in 1948. In a slightly nasal, animated voice, he narrates and plays all the roles in "The Fiddle," "A Yom Kippur Scandal," and "Dreyfus in Kasrilevka"; intricately scored music by Serge Hovey works almost in dialogue with him. Meanwhile, among his radio dramatizations of Sholem-Aleichem for *The Eternal Light*, Perl also adapted "The Fiddle," the story of a boy obsessed with learning to play the violin despite being forbidden by his father. When Perl and Da Silva established Rachel Productions (they both had daughters named Rachel) and began to hatch a repertoire, the Butwin volumes and Maurice Samuel were the obvious place to start. The drawing by their comrade Ben Shahn that became their logo—a man in a cap and thick beard playing a violin—added to the association between Sholem-Aleichem and a fiddling Jew. (Shahn's association with Sholem-Aleichem continued, too, as he went on to illustrate collections of Yiddish stories, including reissues of the Butwin volumes.)

Perl and Da Silva liked to tell people that they were motivated by the "mutual impulse" to share this culture with audiences who might not have been familiar with it and thereby disprove the snub they were tired of hearing—that if they didn't know Yiddish they couldn't understand their heritage. But there was more to it than that. As a reporter who interviewed them at the time understood, they wanted to highlight "Sholom-Aleichem's gentle but firm plea for tolerance and humanism."

The casting itself made such a plea. Phoebe Brand, Morris Carnovsky, Sarah Cunningham, Jack Gilford, Gilbert Green, Will Lee, Marjorie Nelson: almost all the actors were blacklisted. More than giving them jobs (which paid barely over minimum wage), the production was displaying the talent America was missing when it shunted good artists aside. (Da Silva was also making an integrationist point by casting Ruby Dee, whom he had met shortly before rehearsals were to begin, at a rally for the Rosenbergs; her husband, Ossie Davis, served as stage manager.)

In putting characters from the Yiddish classics onstage, Perl was "reminding people of where they come from" and also "telling them that people are enormously and richly flexible in the face of difficulties." He was talking about the resilient residents of the Pale. But he could have been talking about himself and the company presenting *The World of Sholom Aleichem*.

* * *

The play opened on May Day of 1953 at the Barbizon Plaza Hotel in Manhattan. In the theatrical climate of the period, everything about it seemed strange. The Barbizon? Sholem-Aleichem? Was it in Yiddish? The press agent, Merle Debuskey, had to insist that ads and announcements note that it was in English. But Perl and Da Silva had good reasons for their choices. The title might strike a friendly chord with people who remembered Maurice Samuel's book, which was still in print a decade after its publication and, in any case, it would indicate that the production (like the book) intended to bring to life not just a story but an entire milieu. (Some of the material in the play was also drawn from Mendele Mocher-Sforim, I. L. Peretz, and the folk stories of Chelm.) As for the venue, the thirty-eight-story modern classical hotel that dominated Central Park South between Sixth and Seventh Avenues had been originally designed in the 1920s as a residence for artists and musicians, so it included small halls for recitals and dramatic performances. Despite having changed hands and clientele during the Depression, the building retained a small auditorium with about 500 fixed seats and a small proscenium stage (albeit with no wing space). *The World of Sholom Aleichem* had to play on an irregular schedule, clearing out on nights that conventions were booked. But for the price, Rachel Productions couldn't do better.

Besides, they wanted an intimate relationship between the actors and the audience and a spareness of style that a small house afforded. Spectacle and razzle-dazzle hardly belonged in the world of Sholem-Aleichem. If not by design, certainly to good effect, the work joined the nascent Off-Broadway challenge to the gimmicky effects of Broadway entertainments (the swimming pool center stage in *Wish You Were Here* being only one much-mocked example of the moment).

But it meant they'd garner little attention from the press. Weekly magazines covered only Broadway in those years, and the major daily papers, which had at least noticed the excitement over Geraldine Page's performance in *Summer and Smoke* at the newly founded Circle in the Square, saw no compelling reason to spend any of the precious real estate in their arts pages on a show by an untested playwright based on quaint ethnic folk stories and performed in a bizarre location. Nonetheless, audiences came—hordes of them. At first, fellow progressives and liberal artists (some of them too fearful of guilt by association to go backstage to greet the company after the show). Then, responding to word of mouth, a wider audience. After forty sold-out performances, *The World* had to relinquish the Barbizon for events already scheduled there over the summer. When it reopened in September—for what turned out to be nine more months, making it the longest-running play of the season—it was a phenomenon. The producers marked the occasion by selling a fifteen-page souvenir booklet featuring drawings by Ben Shahn inspired by the show: in quick, sputtering lines—a seemingly naive style in keeping with the play's—some twenty figures populate the pamphlet, among them a wide-eyed fellow cradling a goat, a man with a trim beard reclining on his side, holding his head in his hand, a woman with a handbag staring out from the page.

Now all the mainstream reviewers clamored for seats. The *New York Times* critic, Brooks Atkinson, threw his support behind the production (after some cajoling by Debuskey), first acclaiming it as "fine theater and splendid humanity" in his review, then piling on more accolades in a Sunday essay: "It is pure art with no shortcomings." The other dailies followed suit: "Human warmth, generosity and affecting simplicity have carried the day," "shows how theater-wise imagination with long experience can make so much out of so little." Even Eleanor Roosevelt weighed in, praising the production in her syndicated newspaper column and assuring readers, "Don't think because it's about Jews you won't like it."

In large measure, audiences responded to the novelty—and aptness—of the bare-bones, congenial style. Hokey as it may seem today, the opening scene was received in 1953 as a charming innovation: Mendele the Bookseller (played by Da Silva, who also directed the show) entered through the house, maneuvering a battered baby carriage bulging with books as he made his way to the stage. He spoke directly to the audience, familiarly: "I apologize. I don't mean to stare. Just looking, trying to figure what in all these treasures would interest you the most." He rummaged through the carriage and pulled out "The Enchanted Tailor" by Sholem-Aleichem and introduced the first of the three playlets. Presented as a folk tale from Chelm, the fictional town of fools (though Perl also used elements from Sholem-Aleichem's own treatment of the story), it follows the *melamed* (it means "teacher") as he goes to a nearby town to buy a milk goat but is tricked into bringing home a male goat—and tricked again when he takes it back to complain. The drama captivated audiences with its rustic appeal to the imagination: the *melamed* (Will Lee) danced in skipping steps from town to town, the goat—whether male or female—indicated merely by the stiff rope leash he carried. Music by Serge Hovey and simple lighting established scene and mood: distinct pools delineated the *melamed*'s home, the goat seller's, and the inn between them where the goat was switched. A wash of light tinged with green created the forest the *melamed* scampered through from one locale to another.

In contrast, act 2, "Bontche Schweig" ("Bontche the Silent") projected a tattered majesty, underscored by the ethereal pomp of music by a composer who went uncredited (because as a visiting Israeli he was not authorized to work in the United States). It was based on the story by I. L. Peretz (featured in Maurice Samuel's *Prince of the Ghetto*). Bontche (Jack Gilford) is a humble, life-worn man who arrives in heaven—the stage bathed in pale lavender light. Dressed in rags and burlap assembled from fabric the designer, Aline Bernstein, had torn from a packing crate, he is judged to be worthy of great reward and is invited to name his grandest wish. All he can think to ask for—and that, meekly—is a hot roll with butter. The angels turn away in shame. Da Silva arrayed the actors in formal groupings, and while their performances did not cross over into abstraction, he insisted that they avoid "over-detailed naturalism."

The evening closed with an adaptation of a Sholem-Aleichem work, "The High School" ("Gymnasia"), the piece in the collection *Railroad Stories* that chronicles a talented boy's effort to gain admittance to a school closed to Jews—and that coincided with abiding quotas for Jews in some universities and with debates in the press and the courts over racial segregation in America's public schools. (The Supreme Court had heard a first round of arguments in *Brown v. Board of Education* some five months earlier, though its ruling was still a year away.) This act presented yet another theatrical style: fourth-wall realism with characters in period dress but, still, minimal scenery—some bare tables and chairs—and no special effects. Robert de Cormier—a highly sought-after arranger who had worked with Paul Robeson and was directing the left-wing Young Jewish Folksingers (the first group to record "We Shall Overcome")— fashioned the traditionally Ashkenazi score, working from the doleful Yiddish folk song "The Golden Peacock."

Perl built a deliberate progression into the move from cute folktale to moral parable to modern predicament, from storybook theater to stately presentation to realism. Creating that trajectory is likely the reason Perl presented the first act as a folktale; in material promoting the show and in the program, he never mentioned the Sholem-Aleichem version of the story, though he name-checks it in the script. That story sits in the center of the Butwins' *Old Country* and, running some forty-five pages, is the longest in the volume. Titled "The Enchanted Tailor," it enters darker territory than the playlet Perl presented. Sholem-Aleichem tells how the tailor (not a *melamed*, or teacher, in his rendering) is driven mad with confusion over the trick the innkeeper plays on him and hovers on the precipice of death; his neighbors become so incensed they prepare to wage battle against the town the goat came from. In writing the story relatively early in his career and putting it out as if derived from "an obscure chapbook" written some decades earlier, Sholem-Aleichem deliberately aimed to mimic the style of a folk narrative, and to push that form in a tragic direction.

But that mood fit neither Perl's thrust nor the already calcifying convictions about those Old Country Jews (and about Sholem-Aleichem): sentimentality can't abide tragedy. So Perl leaned more heavily on a lighter version published in the 1948 anthology *A Treasury of Jewish Folklore*, edited by Nathan Ausubel (a comrade who had left the Communist Party by the time Perl's play was presented). It was Ausubel who placed the story under the Chelm rubric, and Perl used it to open the play with some funny examples of the nincompoops reasoning their way through life's vexing questions. (Why is the ocean salty? Because of the thousands of herrings who live there.) The Chelm approach to the gender-queer goat tale allowed Perl to begin the show with naiveté, then progress to passive acceptance, and finally to end with Jews who stand up and fight for justice. Da Silva's "Production Notes" in the script were explicit: "If we have succeeded in moving from fantasy to mild criticism to statement in the three pieces, the audience will move with us." The statement? The student's father sums it up in act 3, once the boy has triumphed: "This is the dawn of a new day. No more pogroms, no ghettos, no quotas. . . . In this fine new world, there will be no Jews, no gentiles, no rich, no poor, no underdogs, no undercats. . . . You don't have enough to eat, strike! The draft is taking your sons, strike! You don't like the ghetto, strike!"

The company's political comrades loved this rousing finale, while some Jewish-identified fans who wrote to congratulate Perl and Da Silva singled out the "Bontche" scene as the one that moved them most. Critiques in the left and Jewish press split the same way. Both groups— sometimes overlapping but organizationally distinct—latched onto *The World of Sholom Aleichem* as their own champion. The show went on from New York to tour the country, traveling on both these tracks. When arranging a San Francisco engagement, for instance, Perl happily reported "very real interest on the part of the left (California Labor School, the Rosenberg Committee, etc.)," which had pledged to buy 2,000 seats, as well as from "a limited group on the right (Hadassah, the Oakland Jewish Community Center)," the latter of which also committed to 2,000 seats.

While some on the left objected to the "continuous emphasis on the most negative virtues, Bontche's silence and humility" (as a friend wrote to Perl to say, unwittingly echoing Peretz's originally intended critique of passivity), the blacklisted screenwriter Ring Lardner Jr. was able to appreciate "Bontche," he told Da Silva, as he became "increasingly aware that simply presenting the culture of an oppressed people in a revealing and stimulating way constituted genuine progressive content." Then, as the third act unfolded, Lardner realized that the parents in "The High School" are "true heroes of the irrepressible masses, and their development from one level of struggle to another makes for people's theater at its best."

The publishers of *Counterattack* drew the same conclusion. The weekly four-page compendium of "Facts to Combat Communism," published by the authors of *Red Channels*, devoted almost all of its September 25, 1953, issue to denouncing "the people who are cashing in on" *The World of Sholom Aleichem*. Aghast, the writers listed short bios of the company members such as might appear in a playbill, except that instead of past productions they'd appeared in, *Counterattack* detailed incriminating associations with "the Communist-controlled" United Electrical Workers Union, International Fur and Leather Workers Union, Jefferson School of

Social Science, Joint Anti-Fascist Refugee Committee, Civil Rights Congress, Committee for the Negro in the Arts, as well as the Party itself. Egregiously, the newsletter charged, the theater troupe had misappropriated Sholem-Aleichem: "He was anti-Communist." Having thus abducted the Yiddish author, Rachel Productions was mendaciously trying "to give the impression that it is 'Jewish theater' and thus win the support of unsuspecting Jewish individuals and groups." The proof of the ruse? That "not one person in the cast is a member of the Hebrew Actors Union"—never mind that this was a union only for those performing in Yiddish.

Counterattack obsessively chased the play all over the country as it was presented over the next several years, in newly mounted productions in Chicago and Los Angeles and in a scaled-down version for six cast members who piled into a station wagon in the late fall of 1955 and drove to gigs in some dozens of cities, often performing for only a night or two in Jewish community centers, high school auditoriums, and, occasionally, well-appointed theaters. Perl boasted, with no small measure of amazement, that the touring company played forty-nine engagements in nine weeks. (The show was also mounted in London and in South Africa, where the director expected it to "stir up, however gently, the social consciences, the sensitivity of Jew and Gentile alike, to the cruelty of racial prejudice and persecution in our country." With a cast led by Jacob Ben-Ami, it also played in Buenos Aires, where performances had to take a hiatus while a coup overthrew Juan Perón.) *Counterattack* urged readers to alert Jewish leaders in their communities of the subterfuge of the production, dramatized by Perl "in a manner designed to promote Moscow's line." Couldn't audiences see that "Perl has twisted the entire theme of the story . . . to give it social and political protest preachment, to make it an appeal for strikes"?

Despite its plodding approach to dramatic criticism, *Counterattack* was not wrong that Perl had "cooked up a closing speech by the father" that changed Sholem-Aleichem's original ending to "The High School." But its dire warnings had no impact on Jewish leaders. For all its liberties with Sholem-Aleichem, the play was no Trojan horse sneaking Communist propaganda into the Jewish community centers of America. First, Perl, a man who took his vodka straight-up and his Pall Malls without filters, was not given to subtlety: the writing was too blunt to be sneaky. And the messages Perl drew from the Yiddish material meshed well enough with the liberal sentiments of the communities eager to see the work. Even the Jewish Welfare Board, which had joined the panicky Cold War effort to dissociate Jews from any link to Communism by urging JCCs around the country not to allow radicals to speak in their facilities, helped to arrange a tour.

If there was any Marxism behind the project, it was in Perl's and Da Silva's understanding the relationship among production, distribution, and consumption: they had not only tapped a market of second- and third-generation Jews eager for positive public portrayals of their heritage but also may have helped to invent it by creating a product the community hadn't yet known it needed.

Jewish fans and reviewers alike found relief from the tinselly Yinglish trifles holding out on Second Avenue and from the revues that had recently moved onto Broadway. Specifically drawing a contrast with *The World of Sholom Aleichem*, Jewish critics lashed out at "the lox and bagel rash" whose "humor smelt of dead herring," at works that "slanted toward the lowest human denominator of vulgarity, banality, slime, and treacle" and gave stage to "Goebbels-like mockery" and "Streicher-like 'escapades.'" *The World* portrayed "the finest and best in Jewish culture." At the Barbizon, where it was "surprising to see European Jewish life so completely and directly understood in so antithetical an environment," the long-maligned Jews could find "delicate sensitivity" and the achievement of "what had hitherto been termed unachievable—they have reclothed the old world and its culture in English garb without doing violence to its essential being."

With such Manichean options, some of these guardians of Jewish culture were even ready to abandon Yiddish: "Let's have Jewish plays in English, and let us do it with the same artistic integrity as the marvelous troupe at the Barbizon is doing it." Rabbis endorsed the play in synagogue newsletters and from their pulpits; even the Zionist Organization of America found in it "particular meaning to us as Zionists, deeply concerned with the perpetuation and advancement of positive Jewish cultural values." When, in a lone plaint, Midge Decter wrote to the *New York Times* to defend the Yiddish classics against "that frou-frou" that made the original work "comfortable" instead of conveying its "beautiful tension or agony," she was not the first intellectual—nor the last—trying to snatch Sholem-Aleichem back from the grubby adjustments of showbiz. (She wrote at greater length against the play in *Commentary*.) In a way, she was right: Perl cutesified "The Enchanted Tailor"; he sapped the tart irony from "The High School." But high-minded as such defenses may be, they are also too high-handed. Some sixty years after its premiere, the play's failings as dramatic art glare like floodlights, but in its moment it spoke to an exigent desire. Writing in Chicago's English-language Jewish weekly the *Sentinel*, the longtime editor, J. I. Fishbein, summed things up best. "May this herald a new era in American Jewish life," he exhorted, "wherein Jews will be able to be proud of their contributions rather than being ashamed of them."

The JCCs asked for more and Perl set out to oblige. First, he assembled a show he called *Holiday*, drawing primarily from Sholem-Aleichem's Kasrilevke stories set on Purim, Hanukkah, Passover, and the Sabbath—some of which he'd adapted for *The Eternal Light* nearly a decade earlier. Perl had no intention of bringing the work to an Off-Broadway public but wrote only "with the limited Center audiences in mind"—the newly emerging nostalgia market eager to link its current aspirations to its past forbearance. The promotional materials for *Holiday* appealed brazenly to that sentiment. "These are people of the Old Country and the New World," the advertising copy promised. "They are stories 5,000 years old and stories of tomorrow; this is a celebration of our parents, for ourselves and for our children. This is our HOLIDAY." Apart from a little trouble with the time line (Sholem-Aleichem's Kasrilevke did not exactly go back five millennia), Perl took some liberties in the playlets themselves. "I have violated a lot of so-called orthodox canon," he admitted at the time, "but I think the performance should be a delight and so the beards can be ripped off the holidays and fun had by all."

Perl may have read the eagerness for more Sholem-Aleichem correctly, but the show found few takers. Perhaps the directors who booked such programs, beardless as the men among them may have been, found it a bit too loose with the observances of the Jewish calendar as it offered "all the holidays of the Jewish year—rolled into one great holiday." But it provided the basis for a professional production in Los Angeles that Perl devised about a year later: *Sholom Aleichem's Old Country*, as he called it, combined three stories, this time all of them originally by the eponymous author, and once again Mendele (played by Herschel Bernardi, who also directed) connected them with his narration. Two stories were pieces Perl had already dramatized—"The Purim Scandal" (part of *Holiday*) and "The Fiddle" (*The Eternal Light*)—and, most significant, the third was drawn from *Tevye the Dairyman*, the story of Tsaytl, the eldest daughter, who marries her beloved tailor instead of the rich butcher.

Reviewers, drawn by the warm memory of *The World of Sholom Aleichem*, were kind in their dismissal—"Here are the beginnings, but only the beginnings, of something that could be of great value to the theater," said one. They singled out the Tevye story as "the most substantial," adding that its "rather rambling structure is almost completely redeemed by professionalism and charm." That was encouragement enough. Perl adapted several more of the Tevye stories and within a few months announced the New York premiere of *Tevya and His Daughters*, slated to open in September 1957. Sholem-Aleichem's dairyman was about to have his major English-language stage debut.

By then, Da Silva and Perl had brought in two more producing partners for a much more ambitious endeavor, Banner Productions. They leased the 299-seat Carnegie Hall Playhouse with plans to create "a new and vital theatre center with diverse entertainment appealing to the wide variety of tastes." More than five years into their banishment from broadcast media, they were casting their lot ever more ardently with the stage. The theater would operate every day of the week and nearly around the clock, with programming for children in the afternoon, a midnight cabaret on weekends, a Monday night work-in-progress staged reading series, and, at the center, a full production on a standard eight-shows-a-week schedule. As their premier offering, Banner Productions would proudly present a play whose hero, they announced, had been variously described: "he is Don Quixote (and Sancho Panza); he is Chaplin's Tramp; he is Job with a sense of humor. He is the Eternal Jew, his shadow as long as the Jewish Exile, his laughter as warm as the sun. He is the obstinate, indestructible, individualist, Tevya the Unextinguishable."

Promoted as taking the "same care for music and costuming, for staging and design that made *The World of Sholom Aleichem* a memorable theater evening," *Tevya and His Daughters* broke Off-Broadway records for advance ticket sales. Before the lights went up on Mike Kellin in the title role, appealing to God in an opening monologue, the show had taken in $28,000, well clearing the budgeted production costs of $19,644. Columbia Records had produced an LP version before opening, too—another first for Off-Broadway. Four years after Perl's and Da Silva's initial triumph, a Sholem-Aleichem sequel seemed like a sure bet.

Once again Da Silva directed with a homey style, relying on music by Serge Hovey to underscore the action and simple scenery (a painted backdrop by the artist Jack Levine featured rustic thick-brush images of shtetl houses receding into the distance). Kellin's partner in the role of Golde was Anna Vita Berger, and the two made a quaint, somewhat low-key pair. Berger was determined to avoid any shred of shrewishness, aiming for the hardscrabble practicality that contrasted with Tevye's spiritual nature. As for Tevye, New York hadn't seen him onstage since Maurice Schwartz had played him—in Yiddish—as an older, broken man held together and aloft by the wisdom and unyielding practice of Judaism. Now, for the first time in English, newly encountered by myriad audience members, Tevye was younger and lighter—warm, sweet, almost as easygoing as the all-accepting dad of the *Eternal Light* radio version a decade before.

Da Silva coached the actors to avoid exaggeration in their Jewish characterizations: he explicitly wanted the "music" of Jewish inflection without any singsong shtick, that is, the familiar, warm feeling of Jewishness with any traces of nasty old stereotypes washed away. Perl provided some occasional phrasing to help create the effect: he has Tevye saying, "Rich she'll be" and "Fed she'll be." He gave Golde lines like, "My enemies should have such luck." Drawing language from both the Butwin volume of Tevye stories and Maurice Samuel's creative portrayal, Perl fashioned Tevye as a kindhearted naif who could be steered away from his hidebound beliefs by sound reasoning and appeals for justice. In each of the three stories he dramatized—Tevye's rise from drayman to dairyman and the marriage tales of Tsaytl and Hodl—Perl paints Tevye as eager to make his daughters happy as he is receptive to their newfangled values. Often Perl secularizes Tevye's constant quotations—sometimes they sound more like a rustic's trite proverbs than a religious man's inventive references to Scripture. ("A woman is like a melon. Who knows what's inside?" "Work is noble, but money is more comfortable.")

In the episode focused on Hodel's romance with the revolutionary Perchik, Perl's version of the paterfamilias ends up resembling the protagonist of Bertolt Brecht's early Leninist play *The Mother* (based on a Gorky story) in which a working-class parent learns to see her personal travails within the larger framework of mass political struggle. Perl doesn't go nearly as far as Mikhoels did in his Soviet portrayal of Tevye, but he does nudge his Tevye toward revolutionary enlightenment. His guide is Perchik, who challenges Tevye's fatalism—"this is the way God made the world"—with passionate speeches that need not embellish much on the rhetoric Sholem-Aleichem gave him. (However, Perl does co-opt Theodor Herzl's famous phrase about the prospect of a Jewish state—"If you will it, it is no dream"—for Perchik's promise of postczar paradise in Russia.) The difference is his Tevya's response.

By play's end, Tevya is encouraging a reluctant Hodel to go join Perchik in Siberia and reassuring her: "He'll serve his time; you'll wait. Meanwhile the pot is boiling as they say. Then one day (When? One day)—it happens and the sun will rise and everything will be bright and shining. Then he'll be free with all the others like him and together you'll roll up your sleeves and turn the Little Father [the czar] upside down." Hodel goes off to pack. As soon as that's settled, Tevya winds up the play

Mike Kellin and Anna Vita Berger in Perl's *Tevya and His Daughters*

with a brief monologue, telling the audience what he has to look forward
to now that he has concluded happy marriages for two of his daughters:
"My Chava, my next, has begun with a writer: a second Gorki, she tells
me. Although who the first Gorki is I never heard. How they live, these
writers, I haven't yet discovered. Maybe they eat pages. The name of this
writer is—Fedka Galaghan: not exactly a Jewish name. So what will happen there, I leave to your tender mercies. My little ones are too young to
be problems; but they'll grow into it. (*He laughs.*)"

In short, Perl's was a Tevya without tension. Nothing was at stake for
him or the play because he made no effort to hold fast to his religious
practice in the face of change. That was a dramaturgical problem the
mainstream reviewers could not excuse—despite charm and humor, "it
is theater that is missing," Brooks Atkinson summed up in the *New
York Times*—and it also was the reason the show found no traction with
Jewish audiences. As a total pushover, Tevya had little to say to them
about the preciousness of the lost world or the confrontation of their
forebears with modernity. He was pleasant enough but hollow. The *Forverts* was not being academic or snobbish when it declared, simply, "This
is not *our* Tevya."

As a good Marxist (who had left the Party by this point), Perl engaged
in some public self-criticism, writing to the letters section of the *New
York Times* drama pages to promise that the "cast, director, playwright,
composer and producers have used the period since 'Tevya's' opening to
assess our mutual weaknesses and to seek solutions in the light of published reviews. Audience response during the past few days has been our
barometer. We have been led to believe that some of the failings of opening night have been overcome."

But not enough to keep the show going. It closed in mid-November,
after a six-week run. A touring version for half a dozen actors in a van
once again set out for some JCCs, but *Tevya and His Daughters* did not
thrill the provinces, as *The World of Sholom Aleichem* had done. When
the hero shrugged everything off, he gave spectators little reason to care
about his fate.

Besides, artistic taste among theatergoers was challenged and was
changing in the four short years since *The World* had charmed spectators
with its storybook simplicity. Off-Broadway was exploding. Jean Genet's
The Maids had its shattering New York debut in a rinky-dink space in

the neighborhood not yet known as the East Village; Joseph Papp was directing modern-dress Shakespeare with young, multiracial casts; the Living Theatre had already been kicked out of two buildings by city authorities; and a blacklisted fat comedian named Zero Mostel was about to astonish the theater community with his shaded portrayal of Leopold Bloom in *Ulysses in Nighttown*. Broadway, too, was finding new forms that made Perl's plays seem quaint in more than subject matter. *Waiting for Godot* held out on West Forty-fifth Street for two months in the spring of 1956. And not even two weeks after *Tevya and His Daughters* opened at the Carnegie, two rival groups of hoodlums burst onto the stage at the Winter Garden and changed the Broadway musical forever: *West Side Story*—"conceived, directed, and choreographed by Jerome Robbins," as he insisted his credits read—was an operatic tragedy in the idiom of a musical, mixing vernacular movement and ballet, Latin-inflected jazz and twentieth-century classical music, street slang and lyrical dialogue. The modernist, urban, liberal sensibility of its four Jewish and gay creators was expressed most of all in the "plea for racial tolerance" that the story, in the composer Leonard Bernstein's phrase, could make. And in contrast to "Sholom Aleichem's gentle but firm plea for tolerance and humanism" in *The World*, *West Side Story* was making it through an edgy contemporary story in a groundbreaking form devised by some of the greatest talents the American theater has known.

Spectators of all stripes embraced *West Side Story*, of course, but for Jews—who still made up some 70 percent of Broadway audiences by some counts—the show spoke especially to a growing postwar objection to bigotry, which was starting to project outward now that Jews themselves were no longer primary victims of intolerance (this is why the original concept for the show, pitting Jews against Catholics, couldn't work). In his influential and best-selling 1955 book, *Protestant, Catholic, Jew*, the sociologist Will Herberg had declared that American Jews were no longer a fringe, foreign-seeming minority but regular citizens who simply practiced one of the three religions that expressed the American way of life: they were as normal as their Gentile neighbors. As the 1950s drew to a close—at least according to the organizations that claimed to represent them—Jews worried less and less about antisemitism and extended their sympathy to the current victims of racial and ethnic prejudice. In addition to being no match for the thrilling experiments taking place on New York's not-for-profit and commercial stages, *Tevya and His Daughters*—"all syrup," "too sweet," and "languid" as reviews put it—was not balanced by any moral seriousness that midcentury American Jews could grab hold of.

And at last, between *The World of Sholom Aleichem* and *Tevya*, the blacklist started to fade. Perl, ever optimistic, was feeling "a beginning of a thaw" in the summer of 1955—some six months after the Senate had voted to censure Senator Joseph McCarthy—and he was hired to write for what he deemed a "worthless" television program. He even began to hope that his passport might be restored and he would be able to travel to Europe. Even as what he called the "assault on the theater"—HUAC's Foley Square hearings investigating Broadway—opened that same summer, Perl saw better times on the near horizon. "And yet, my friend, the world grows ever more hopeful," he wrote to Jacob Ben-Ami, then on tour with *The World of Sholom Aleichem* in Buenos Aires. "I think we may all still be allowed to work to the best of our ability—some day and soon."

Perl's comrade in the left-wing faction of the American Federation of Television and Radio Artists, the radio host John Henry Faulk, had filed suit against AWARE (a private organization that monitored the industry for subversives, cofounded by the author of *Red Channels*). Roy Cohn and the other lawyers defending the publishers of *Counterattack* and *Red Channels* managed to drag the case out for several years, but in the meantime—before 1962, when a jury would award Faulk the largest sum in a libel judgment to date—Hollywood had started to crack open the door to artists it had recently shunned. As Tevye trod the boards in New York, on the West Coast Alfred Hitchcock hired the blacklisted actor Norman Lloyd as associate producer for his new TV series. Bit by bit, others would be finding work again.

Once again, Sholem-Aleichem helped. In 1959, the producers of the acclaimed new television program *Play of the Week*, airing in syndication on New York's independent Channel 13 (later to become part of the public broadcasting network) and on some one hundred affiliated stations around the country, decided to present Perl's *World of Sholom Aleichem* among its offerings of videotaped stage dramas drawn from the canonical and contemporary repertory. It was the program's tenth show, following plays by Euripides, Turgenev, John Steinbeck, Graham

Greene, Jean Anouilh, Jean-Paul Sartre, and Langston Hughes, among others. The producer Henry Weinstein, who had loved the play and thought it deserved a wider audience, pushed the production forward over the objections of his bosses, executive producer David Susskind and station owner Ely Landau, who derided the work as "too Jewish." To direct, Weinstein hired an experienced television man, Don Richardson (born Melvin Schwartz), and he insisted on casting many of the original blacklisted actors and a few more, despite Susskind's anxiety. If he'd get in any kind of trouble for hiring one shunned actor, he figured, how much more trouble could he attract for hiring a bunch? Enfeebled *Counterattack* threatened a campaign against the program, but the independent station did not rely on sponsors, so there was no target for their attacks.

Morris Carnovsky (who had already appeared in a *Play of the Week* show) reprised his role as the father in "The High School," and Jack Gilford returned as Bontche; new additions from the rolls of the spurned included Lee Grant (Defending Angel) and Sam Levene (Mendele, the bookseller). The leading roles were completed with Nancy Walker (the Melamed's wife) and Gertrude Berg (the mother in "The High School"), plus one more actor, Zero Mostel, who had once been Richardson's acting student and whose stage career was taking off, even as he was barred from the movies. Some months earlier, he'd won an Off-Broadway Obie Award for his lead performance in *Ulysses in Nighttown*. He was the only actor cast in all three of the playlets that make up *The World of Sholom Aleichem*, playing the Melamed in "A Tale from Chelm," an angel in "Bontche Schweig," and a relative (with a spry dance at the celebration of the boy's admission) in "The High School."

Even if Weinstein had considered asking Da Silva to re-create the part of Mendele, the actor would have had to decline; Da Silva was tied up on Broadway, having just opened in a costarring role as the political machine boss Ben Marino in *Fiorello!*, a musical by a young songwriting duo making a splashy showing: Jerry Bock and Sheldon Harnick.

Richardson rehearsed the company for catch-as-catch-can chunks of time over two weeks in a grotty room of the Polish National Hall on Manhattan's Lower East Side. Enthusiastic as he was about working with Mostel, Richardson soon excluded his former student from rehearsals—Mostel kept changing his blocking, timing, and even his lines, throwing the rest of the cast off-balance. Even without rehearsing, Mostel would deliver when it came time to tape, Richardson felt sure, despite his having to shoot in long takes, as in a live show with no stops, because the new type of tape they were using was too difficult and expensive to edit. In a tiny studio, Richardson manned a camera and called the shots; he put the program in the can in two days.

Richardson was right about Mostel: he performed brilliantly. *Variety* called him the "highlight of the show" and singled out his "remarkable pantomime talents," especially in the twinkle-toed dance he performed as the Melamed, pulled from village to village by the invisible goat, his wrists twirling upward and his bulky body circling after, light as a balloon. In general, critics lauded the "stunning production" of "three one-acters of beauty, compassion and protest." Not a single review mentioned that the broadcast occasioned the return to the airwaves of artists who'd been banned for years. Even to some of the actors, the small-scale event

PHOTOFEST

Perl's *The World of Sholom Aleichem* helps break the blacklist on TV with Zero Mostel, Morris Carnovsky, and Nancy Walker.

didn't seem momentous. Lee Grant, for one, allowing that it was "a victory just to get something on in that period," remembered the production merely as "one of those things that snuck by" without having much of an impact. After all, despite all the affiliated stations around the country, early public television drew small audiences. Nonetheless, a taboo had been broken and any first breach makes the next one easier. Perl credited *World*'s success on *Play of the Week* with opening the way, at least for him, back to regular employment in television. (By 1963, he was a lead writer for *East Side, West Side,* the high-quality weekly series about a New York City social worker played by George C. Scott; taking on urban issues like prostitution and poverty from a decidedly liberal point of view, it was produced by David Susskind.)

The first air date of December 14, 1959, preceded by a couple of weeks an event often credited as a fatal blow to the blacklist: the director Otto Preminger's announcement that he was engaging Dalton Trumbo, one of the Hollywood Ten, as the screenwriter for his adaptation of Leon Uris's blockbuster novel *Exodus*. Trumbo had been writing under a pseudonym for some time, as *Counterattack* had repeatedly reported—aghast, as usual—but now Preminger insisted on trumpeting his name in the credit roll.

By the time *Exodus* debuted on December 15, 1960—almost exactly a year to the day of the broadcast of *The World of Sholom Aleichem*—America was entering a new phase. The Cold War still raged, but the domestic Red hunt had finally ended. A young, appealing new president was about to take office (thanks, in part, to television's new role in electoral politics). The Federal Drug Administration had approved the Pill in the spring of that year and nearly 2.5 million women were taking it. African American students had begun sitting in at segregated lunch counters in the South, escalating the direct action of the civil rights movement. "The sixties" hadn't quite started, but they were coming.

For Jews—who had voted for John F. Kennedy by a greater margin than Irish Catholic Americans—the new decade opened on enormous changes. Antisemitism was evaporating into the atmosphere of postwar sympathy for Jews and of national optimism. Where one American in five told pollsters in 1948 they wouldn't want a Jew as a neighbor, by 1959 such antipathy was expressed by only one in fifty. The new problem preoccupying Jewish organizations was assimilation: now that a majority of

Jews had moved out of urban enclaves into the suburbs, where they built and joined synagogues in droves but rarely attended worship services, what would make them—and keep them—Jewish? In the generation since the war, in the historian Arthur A. Goren's words, "the transcendent place of the 'destruction and renewal' theme in the group consciousness of American Jews" was set. Jews, as all-American exemplars of a shmattes-to-riches trajectory, were themselves part of the regeneration. And so, increasingly, was Israel.

Exodus played no small part in building and shaping Jewish America's self-image and politics and the culture Jews would embrace in the new era. Published in 1958, Uris's potboiler, loosely based on the shipload of Holocaust survivors turned away from Palestine in 1947, stayed on the best-seller list for more than a year, holding the number-one spot for nineteen weeks. When the film opened, it boasted an advance sale of $1.6 million—the largest of any movie to date. Paul Newman starred as the brave and sexy sabra Ari Ben Canaan, "the fighting Jew who won't take shit from nobody," as Uris characterized him. Infusing Jews with a strong dose of empowerment, the movie borrowed the sweeping visuals and providential sensibility of popular biblical epics like Cecil B. DeMille's *Ten Commandments* (1956) and *Ben Hur* (1959). It echoed, too, the morally unambiguous, adventuresome arrogance of the Western, with Arabs figured as Indians, unaccountably hostile enemies who must be driven from the land. Before *Exodus*, postwar pop culture versions of recent Jewish experience presented victims who simply couldn't stay hidden forever—*The Diary of Anne Frank* was published in the United States in 1952, played on Broadway from 1955 to 1957, and was released as a film just five months before *Exodus*—or heroes, like those of the Warsaw Ghetto Uprising, who went down fighting valiantly, as commemorated in John Hersey's popular novel *The Wall* (adapted by Millard Lampell for a modest Broadway run in 1960). But now, here were Jews taking up arms and winning. Even *Jewish Currents*—the left-wing magazine that was Communist until its 1956 break with the Party—couldn't contain its excitement over *Exodus*'s plucky personae: "They are Jews who fight, who die, who live and who triumph," it gushed. Historians of Jewish America writing about the period point repeatedly to *Exodus* as the cultural phenomenon that, more than any other, produced Israel as an answer to the Holocaust. With these heroics, the invented memory of the shtetl brought forth by Maurice Samuel's *World of Sholom Aleichem, Life Is with People*, Chagall's paintings, and representations of Sholem-Aleichem's works in the late 1940s and 1950s became one endpoint of a teleological arc that bent toward Israel. And that gave depictions of the people of the shtetl a newly, and nostalgically, noble purpose—not as passive victims but as preservers of a great culture that would be redeemed.

For what, after all, made Ari Ben Canaan, the very negation of the Diaspora Yid, a Jew? In part, self-assertion. In the climactic moment of *Exodus*'s central romance—the affair between Ari and Kitty Fremont (Eva Marie Saint), the Gentile nurse from Indiana (and surrogate for American viewers)—Ari looks over the Jezreel Valley and reminds her, "I just wanted you to know that I'm a Jew. This is my country." But when Kitty objects ("All these differences between people are made up. People are the same, no matter what they're called."), Ari makes a speech that goes further, happily rejecting the long-held ground rule of American assimilation: "Don't ever believe it. People are different. They have a right to be different. They like to be different. It's no good pretending the differences don't exist. They do. They have to be recognized and respected."

This was a stunning statement of Jewish uniqueness at the height of Jewish absorption into the American middle class—made by a sandy-haired, blue-eyed, hunky movie star, in the name of the "normalization" of the Zionist project. So what, exactly, was the difference—for thoroughly secular Ari Ben Canaan and for those who eagerly watched and cheered him on in suburban movie theaters? There was only one answer: the past. The culture they came from and the catastrophe it suffered. America's new Jewish utopianism, Zionism, unlike the Israeli version, gave Jewish history in Europe a meaningful role as glorious legacy. Brave and brawny Ari Ben Canaan made mainstream culture safe for Tevye the Dairyman.

That the TV broadcast of *The World of Sholom Aleichem* and the movie version of *Exodus* played such significant roles in signaling the end of the blacklist spoke not only to the immense impact the Red hunting had had on Jewish artists (as well as teachers, union activists, and others). The two works, coming from such contrasting points of view and telling such disparate stories, also pointed the way toward popular Jewish culture that could incorporate both the trope of an idealized vanished world and the assertion of Jewish particularism, of both an empathy for other oppressed groups and an unabashed pride in Jewish achievement.

Reviewing *Tevya and His Daughters* in 1957 for the *New York Times*, Brooks Atkinson took pity on Sholem-Aleichem's genial hero. "Since Tevya had the worst of everything in Old Russia," Atkinson wrote, "he deserves the best of Broadway now." In a new period of Jewish communal optimism and liberal consensus—and with the right team of artists coming along—Broadway could soon give Sholem-Aleichem's milkman a proper welcome.

PART II

——

Tevye Strikes It Rich

CHAPTER 3

TEVYE LEAVES FOR THE
LAND OF BROADWAY

IN THE SUMMER AND FALL OF 1959, WHILE BLACKLISTED ARNOLD Perl was preparing *The World of Sholom Aleichem* for television, Jerome Robbins was traveling the world with his troupe, Ballets: USA, on an official tour sponsored by the U.S. State Department. *West Side Story* was just completing a game-changing two-and-a-half-year Broadway run and the next show he directed and choreographed, *Gypsy*, had just opened to ecstatic reviews. Six years after his appearance as a friendly witness before the House Un-American Activities Committee, Robbins had been selected to represent his country in its Cold War project of cultural diplomacy. At a cost of nearly $250,000 (some of the bill footed by the hosting countries), the program sent Robbins's ethnically diverse company of twenty young dancers to perform, over nearly five months, in eighteen cities, among them Tel Aviv, Barcelona, Reykjavik, Istanbul, Belgrade, and even Soviet-dominated Warsaw.

The government could not have been more pleased with the result. In one city after another, the company triumphed with its ambitious and varied program. They presented Robbins's contemporary version of *Afternoon of a Faun*, his satiric ballet *The Concert*, the cool sensation *N.Y. Export: Opus Jazz*, and a brand-new piece, *Moves*, in which dancers confronted audiences without music, scenery, or costumes. Their bodies in relationship to one another—whether in dances for the full company, a harsh pas de deux, a combative quintet for men, or a languid quartet for women—were all that Robbins needed to stir emotion and create a sense of unfolding drama. "There have been brilliant successes before and since—symphony orchestras, choral groups, jazz ensembles, other dance companies and so on," wrote the anonymous reporter providing the official "tour analysis" for the program's administrators. "But only 'Ballets: USA' was hailed everywhere as something new, fresh, original, and inherently American, growing out of and depicting the vitality of American life and art, and more, acclaim for an American creative genius."

From Robbins's explosive debut as a choreographer in 1944 with *Fancy Free* (the playful ballet following three sailors on shore leave in New York, with music by Leonard Bernstein), *American* was the word critics most commonly used to describe his innovative choreography, heralding its urban themes, high and tense energies, and admixture of the vernacular and balletic—combining homegrown invention with European patrimony, jitterbug with grand jeté. And American is what Robbins himself wanted his dances to be. "Sir, all my works have been acclaimed for its [*sic*] American quality particularly," he told HUAC chair Clyde Doyle in 1953, after explaining that he had lost all romance with Communism when a comrade asked him to comment on the role dialectical materialism played in his creation of *Fancy Free*. Artists require freedom, he explained. "The minute they become subject to any dictums they're being false." And without a trace of irony, but with a good dose of condescension, Doyle urged him "to even put more" of that American quality into his work.

Being recognized as American—and now, being a celebrated symbol of "American creative genius"—was not a matter of patriotism for Robbins so much as a means of evasion. The proud national identity, he hoped, would cancel out another one he'd been given by virtue of birth. "I didn't want to be a Jew," he stated simply (and repeatedly) in notes toward an autobiography that he never completed. "I didn't want to be like my father the Jew. . . . I wanted to be *safe*, protected, assimilated, hidden in among the boys, the majority." That desire—bound up with his early shame as a gay man—shaped many of Robbins's choices when he was young. His name change—from Rabinowitz (his parents joined him in 1944, even as Robbins himself was beginning to think he was established enough to risk reclaiming his original patronymic)—is only the most ordinary and obvious. Later, Robbins scrawled some notes in which he contemplated his early attraction to the ballet as a means of distancing himself from his heritage: "I affect a discipline over my body & take on another language—the language of court & Christianity—church & state—a completely artificial convention of movement—one that deforms and reforms the body & imposes a set of artificial conventions of beauty—a language *not* universal—one foreign to East & 3rd world." And then he pondered: "In what wondrous and monstrous ways would I move if I would dig down to my Jew self?"

Even the decision to name names before HUAC, Robbins rebuked himself two decades after the fact, oiled the wheels for his getaway: "I betrayed them to HUAC. It was not communism i betrayed, it was my mother and father—for I surrendered to the 'American' committee my ethnic religious and cultural background, saying to them here—kill them—I rat on them and with my stoolie words I buy being on the other side—see—you can tell I'm not one of them—I'll feed them to you. And I did." (Robbins himself never confirmed the conventional wisdom that he appeared as a friendly witness in response to threats that his homosexuality would be exposed if he didn't cooperate; but the two identities, Jewish and gay, merged in the conflated stereotype of weak and wimpy manhood that he loathed.)

And yet, on tour in Europe, at the very moment his work was hailed as "a display of 100 per cent Americana of 1959," Robbins sensed that his transformation could never be complete and even, perhaps, that he didn't want it to be. In half-restored Warsaw, where the troupe performed at the towering Soviet-built Palace of Culture and Sciences, the *pintele yid* poked at his psyche.

How could it not? Warsaw still bore wounds of the war. By some historians' reckoning, 90 percent of the city's buildings had been demolished in a deliberate Nazi plan to lay waste the capital of Polish and Jewish cultures. Amid the hastily erected Soviet boxes that crammed the skyline, the painstaking reconstruction of the Old Market Square, and the barren main thoroughfare of Marszałkowska Street, a visitor could hardly miss the lingering signs of devastation. What's more, though the name Auschwitz had not yet become a worldwide synecdoche for the Holocaust (itself a word not yet in wide circulation), the death camp was already lodged in American popular culture as the most notorious of the six sites for the mass gassing of Jews and other "undesirables" that the Nazis had established on Polish soil: it was the extermination camp described on the astonishing 1953 episode of *This Is Your Life* that reunited the survivor Hanna Bloch Kohner with people from her past—her father, mother, and first husband had perished at Auschwitz, TV viewers were told. And in Uris's *Exodus* Auschwitz is singled out among all the camps as the most horrific: "Auschwitz with its three million dead! Auschwitz with its warehouses crammed with eyeglasses. Auschwitz with its warehouses crammed with boots and clothing and pitiful rag dolls. Auschwitz with its warehouse of human hair for the manufacture of mattresses!" Robbins and his troupe would not have seen posters around Warsaw advertising full-day train tours to the death camp, as they could today, but they could not have escaped the knowledge that in Poland—despite everything else that also defined the squeezed and struggling country— they were standing in a graveyard. Robbins hated it and couldn't wait to leave. The grueling itinerary gave him four full days in town. He impulsively decided to spend one of them looking for the shtetl where his father, Harry, had been born.

Several decades premature for the Jewish heritage tourist industry, Robbins hired a chauffeur—the watchful Intourist system would not have permitted him to rent a car and go exploring on his own—and asked the driver to take him (and one of his dancers, Jamie Bauer, whom he'd invited along for the day) to Rozhanka. On a chilly morning, they headed east out of Warsaw, driving for hours over the flat, farm-dotted terrain, toward a misty memory.

Robbins had spent a summer in Rozhanka some thirty-five years earlier. When he was almost six years old, his mother took him and his sister to meet their widowed grandfather, Nathan Meyer Rabinowitz. Along with one of Harry's cousins and her child, they sailed to England and then traveled to London, Paris, Berlin, Warsaw, and across Poland by train. A horse-drawn wagon carried them over unpaved roads and, finally, turned down the shtetl's main street. Robbins's grandfather, a baker, still lived in the thatch-roofed house that Harry had left in 1904, fleeing from conscription into the czar's army and following his two older brothers to America. His parents had to buy a cemetery plot, bury an empty coffin, and bribe a clerk for a death certificate to cover his disappearance.

In the interwar period, unlike much of Poland, Rozhanka was neglected by most of the factions vying for support among the country's 3.3 million Jews. Communists, Bundists, and Hasidim lacked inroads there; only the Zionists were organizing amid the 120 Jewish families—about six hundred people—who populated the town (along with forty Christian families). The Zionist youth group established a drama club the year of young Jerry's visit and presented a range of Yiddish plays—*Moyshe the Tailor*, *The Way to Buenos Aires*, and *King Lear*, among them.

But what captured his heart in the "tiny town with dirt streets and kerosene lamps" was a sense of being carefree and thoroughly content— never mind the lack of electricity or indoor plumbing. Playing outdoors all day with the local children, catching fish from the brook, making mud houses: all of it might have seemed idyllic to any urban American boy. But Jerry's happiness ran deeper. In Rozhanka, he felt no shame about being a Jew. He sat on his grandfather's lap, cuddled against his chest, and this "figure with a long white beard . . . who I loved a lot and who I knew loved me" sang Yiddish songs to him, and he joined in. "It was a time of soft and beautiful loveliness" for him. "It was my home, that I belonged to." Robbins recalled those days with a wistfulness not found in any of his other reminiscences of childhood. He recorded these memories some five decades later. On the tape, he chokes back a sob as he claims his belonging. By then, he had seen with his own eyes that Rozhanka was no more.

The shtetl's demise began with a German incursion in January 1942—parachutists, a tank, some motorcycles with machine guns. The Russian army retook the town, then lost it again, and by mid-September Nazis seized total control. Before the end of the year, they sent all of Rozhanka's Jews to the ghetto in nearby Szczuczyn. The following April, the ghetto was liquidated, its captives sent to the slaughter.

Meanwhile, Poles settled into some of the homes that Rozhanka's Jews left behind; other houses were dismantled. The Jewish study house was converted into a stable and the cemetery into a pasture for cows to graze in; gravestones were removed and used for buildings and pavement.

When he went looking for Jewish Rozhanka in 1959, Robbins found nothing.

But he likely found it in the wrong place.

In 1904, when Harry Rabinowitz, his father, stole away from Rozhanka, the shtetl belonged to the vast czarist empire. Two decades later, when Jerry sang Yiddish songs on his grandfather's knee, the post–World War I borders enclosed Rozhanka within the Republic of Poland. But by the time the celebrated choreographer felt a sudden urge in Warsaw to see what had become of his ancestral home, the border had been dragged westward and he would have needed a Soviet visa to go there—not something available on a whim to an American in 1959, even, or maybe especially, to an American on an official U.S. tour, and his passport from the period bears no trace of a Soviet stamp. Even if his Polish driver had been brash enough to dare it, a wink and some hard currency at the border crossing would have presented a striking scene after several hours of driving across flat countryside and Robbins's companion didn't recall one. Where, then, did they go? Could the driver, in all innocence, have taken Robbins to a Polish village called Różanka that lies just west of Belarus and north of Lublin? Or to either of the other two Polish towns with that name (though one of them lies west of Warsaw and the other considerably south)?

In some sad sense, it doesn't matter. If there once had been Jews in any of them, their traces would have been gone. Just about every Polish shtetl suffered some version of Rozhanka's tale of invasions and round-ups and deportations. In 1959—half a century before a new generation of Poles would seek to learn about and commemorate the once-vibrant Jewish culture in their land—"everything was a void," as one survivor put it upon returning to his hometown after the war. Before, the hundreds of shtetls that were scattered through Poland were astonishingly diverse, as different from one another as industrial production is from ox-driven agriculture, a Hasidic community from a Misnagdic, or anti-Hasidic, one. But in destruction they looked alike; ruination felt the same whether it was a textile factory or a barn, a bathhouse or a tavern that was appropriated by Poles or reduced to rubble. That's one reason the extraordinary *yizkerbikher*—the collectively created post-Holocaust memorial books of maps, anecdotes, town histories, and martyrologies that retrieve a community for history—take a similar form and tone no matter which of the hundreds of shtetls is memorialized. Rozhanka's *yizkerbukh* ends with a poem:

Oh, Rozhanka, my shtetl, so prized
I see you now more vivid than ever
Oh, when into my thoughts you arise
You awaken longings without measure. . . .

It strikes the same melancholic chord as many a *yizkerbukh*'s elegy as it makes, essentially, Robbins's choked-up assertion: "It was my home, that I belonged to."

Survivors who assembled the *yizkerbikher* from municipal records, oral histories, and their own urgent memories and storehouse of literary tropes understood that their towns, though separate and distinct, became parts of a whole through obliteration. Each was specific and each was also representative. A contributor to one *yizkerbukh* captured this consciousness by describing his town as "The 'Anatevka' of our youth and childhood dreams." Though actually from Rudki, which lies twenty-five miles west of Lviv, in what is now Ukraine, he was invoking the name of the fictional setting in stories by Sholem-Aleichem as a way of marking the way each ruined town now stood for them all through their common fate.

Robbins would help give Anatevka that same meaning for a vast, worldwide audience. But in 1959 the name meant nothing to him. Still, he now knew how the shtetl had become a figment of memory and imagination. On the long ride back to Warsaw for an evening performance at the looming Palace of Culture, the seeds of *Fiddler* were planted within him. It would take an outside impetus, though, before he could promise to give the shtetl "a new life on the stage." It came two and a half years later in the form of a draft script for a musical.

* * *

A few weeks after Robbins returned to the United States in the fall of 1959, the new musical *Fiorello!* scored a dizzying success on Broadway. Winner of that season's Best Musical Tony Award (which it shared with *The Sound of Music*), it traces the political rise of Fiorello La Guardia—the World War I hero, champion of the poor, and slayer of Tammany Hall corruption—as he toils through the years of the Depression and Second World War, on his way to becoming the beloved three-term mayor of New York City. Directed by George Abbott, who also shared book credits with Jerome Weidman, the show was distinguished by its clever and jaunty songs by Jerry Bock (music) and Sheldon Harnick (lyrics).

As a form, the musical was flourishing in those years. This was the peak of the much-touted "golden age" of the "integrated book musical," the sort of show that employed song and dance not as entertaining diversions but to establish the scene, advance the story, develop the characters, intensify the emotion, and deepen the serious themes. The oft-told teleology—Rodgers and Hammerstein's *Oklahoma!* climbed out of the primordial swamp of revues, follies, and frivolous operettas in 1943 to signal the evolution to this upright genre—may oversimplify both the range of musical shows produced on Broadway from the 1940s to the 1960s and the variety among integrated book musicals themselves, but it is true that Bock and Harnick entered the field at just the moment their talents and interests could be put to best use.

Bock, born in New Haven in 1928 and raised in Queens, studied music at the University of Wisconsin and from early on displayed a playful capacity for capturing the essence of different musical styles within a popular idiom. When he impulsively decided to audition for the music school at Wisconsin in the fall of 1945—he had planned to study journalism—he had no prepared piano piece to perform for the panel of skeptical professors. So he offered one of his favorite party tricks: he played the simple bugle call "Reveille" as if it had been composed by Bach, then, in turn, as if it had been written by Chopin, Rachmaninoff, and Tchaikovsky. As the grand finale, Bock busted out with "Boogie Woogie Bugle Call." The panel admitted him.

Harnick, too, showed early signs of what would make him such a successful and sensitive lyricist. Growing up in Chicago, where he was born in 1924, Harnick shared the family penchant for writing verses to commemorate special occasions. (His first published effort, a Thanksgiving poem, appeared in his grammar school newspaper when he was in the fifth grade: "The turkey has my sympathy. / Why must we be so mean? / What has the turkey done /That he deserves the guillotine?") More substantively, he was studying violin seriously and by the time he was a teenager he would sometimes play in the orchestras for Gilbert and Sullivan shows put on by amateur groups. He was "bowled over" by the technical feats of Gilbert's lyrics and began to play with puns and with internal and multisyllabic rhymes in the songs and sketch comedy he was writing with a high school buddy. In the army—Harnick was drafted into the Signal Corps in 1943 and worked as a mobile blind-landing-systems installer—he gravitated to a volunteer unit that threw together a weekly show for fellow servicemen at the Robins Field airbase in Georgia. Harnick joined other cast members in improvisations based on comic scenarios that their director, Sol Lerner, a former theatrical agent from New York, remembered from shows he'd seen back home; Harnick also played the violin and wrote and performed satirical songs about life in his unit. Before Harnick received his honorable discharge in early 1946, Lerner tendered a version of "If you ever come and try your luck in New York, look me up, kid." First, though, Harnick went back to Chicago and enrolled at Northwestern on the GI Bill. There, he studied violin and wrote for the storied student revue, the *Waa-Mu Show*. His classmate Charlotte Rae, costumed in overalls as a wartime munitions worker, sang his freshman contribution, "I've got those gotta-go-home-alone tonight blues." She also gave him a copy of the original cast album of *Finian's Rainbow*, and Yip Harburg's lyrics lit a spark. "I thought it was extraordinary that a man could have such fun with words and yet be saying something important," Harnick explained, and he wanted to do the same. He continued to pursue a violin career after graduating, even landing a seat in a prominent dance orchestra with a standing five-night-a-week gig at the Edgewater Hotel. But when tension in his arms (caused by his clenching with nervousness when microphones descended nightly to broadcast the music on radio) along with layoffs in the orchestra left him jobless, he moved to New York. If he was going to be penniless, he figured he might as well do it where he could try to break into showbiz.

Harnick did call upon Lerner soon after he arrived in the summer of 1950 and Lerner helped by hooking him up with some television variety shows that needed songs. Bock had arrived some eighteen months earlier, a semester short of finishing at Wisconsin. He, too, had been writing for shows in college—a full-length musical for which he served as composer won first prize in a student contest sponsored by BMI—and with Larry Holofcener, a talented college pal, as lyricist, the two quickly snagged a job with television's *Admiral Broadway Revue*, which starred Sid Caesar and Imogene Coca and eventually morphed into *Your Show of Shows*.

Musical variety shows still had a few years of life on Broadway in the early 1950s—and for a bit longer Off-Broadway, on TV, and at summer resorts in the Catskills, Adirondacks, and Poconos—and they provided invaluable on-the-job training for theatrical songsmiths. Often turning out a new show every week, the writers honed their skills for all kinds of swiftness. They had to write fast and what they wrote had to establish a lot of information quickly: in a variety format, each number presented a new character (or at least a character type), a new story (or at least a joke), and its own tone. The satirical recounting of a dud of a date, from attraction to disappointment in a seething but censorious town, for example, comes off in six short stanzas—less than two hundred words—in Harnick's first hit, "Boston Beguine" (from *New Faces of 1952*). "How could we hope to enjoy all the pleasures ahead," the frustrated singer concludes, "when the books we should have read were all suppressed in Boston?" These shows were also crash courses in what worked in front of an audience and what died. Many a writer of book musicals shaped up for the complex dramatic demands of that genre—and for coming up with good new songs in a day or two during on-the-road tryouts—by cranking out tunes for the second-class form.

Encouraged by a meeting with Yip Harburg, Harnick considered working with a partner while he concentrated on lyrics, but he never stopped writing music and his sense of composition can be felt in the supple phrasing of his words. As for Bock, he put aside his lingering literary ambitions and focused on music, becoming even more adept at producing tunes for any dramatic situation, from clomping cowboy syncopations to calypso beats to sliding Gypsy flourishes, as fanciful revue settings—or costumes— demanded. By the time they met in 1956 (introduced by their mutual friend, the performer Jack Cassidy), both had written for book shows— Harnick for a comedy called *Horatio* that was a huge hit in Dallas but flopped at an Adirondack resort and never came to New York and Bock for *Mr. Wonderful*, a Sammy Davis Jr. vehicle that ran nearly a year on Broadway (and brought Bock recognition as well as royalties for its frequently covered songs "Mr. Wonderful" and "Too Close for Comfort"). Harnick and Bock had begun to make lives—and even a living—in the theater.

As partners, they gave each other new occasions to rise to in song after song: Bock's contrapuntal flourishes invited Harnick to build character conflict into his lyrics; Harnick's haiku-like turns offered Bock chances to mark subtle emotional shifts in the music. Without having to discuss it, they concurred on a core principle: that songs served the show and shouldn't be written as stand-alone commodities. That's why, though they typically wrote three songs for every one used, they seldom had any recyclable trunk songs.

Fiorello! showed off their adroit and witty use of songs to convey heaps of dramatic information, draw audiences into the characters, and comment on a situation—often all at once. "The Name's La Guardia," for instance, shows the hero's idealism tempered by political savvy while also poking fun at the exploitable ethnic voting blocs of the urban electorate: as multilingual La Guardia campaigns for Congress in the first act, he sings in English, then Italian, then Yiddish as he meets different groups of constituents, and Bock keeps up, shifting from Sousa-like march to tarantella to the festive dance tunes known as *freylekhs*.

Bock and Harnick had been hired separately for *Fiorello!* and the astounding success of the show—it even won that year's Pulitzer Prize for drama—cemented their partnership. The show's coproducer, Hal Prince, signed them up as a team (along with Abbott and Weidman) for a new project while *Fiorello!* was still in rehearsals. (The new show was *Tenderloin*, a tale of whores, church reformers, and corrupt cops in 1890s New York. With an appealing score but lumpy libretto, it opened to mixed reviews in October 1960 and closed six months later, while *Fiorello!* was still running strong.) But Bock and Harnick were beginning to talk about developing a project through their own initiative. And they were talking about it with the librettist Joseph Stein, who had coauthored the book for their first musical together, *The Body Beautiful*, a clunky effort about an aspiring boxer. It opened in late January 1958 and lasted about seven weeks. Nonetheless, the three men liked working together and in 1960 an idea for a musical began to hatch.

Stein, born in 1912, was also smitten by theater in high school and he loved to write. At City College he continued to work on plays and to contribute to the school newspaper and magazine, but without dreaming of pursuing writing as a profession. After completing a master's degree in social work at Columbia University, he found a job as a psychiatric case worker—but he kept writing in his time off. In 1942, over lunch with a mutual friend, he met a comic who needed some new material for radio monologues. Stein made some off-the-cuff suggestions and the performer said, "Why don't you write that up?" The fifteen dollars he paid Stein for the material marked the beginning of Stein's professional career as a writer—and it was not the last time Stein would write for Zero Mostel.

Stein's comic sensibility was warm, even kindly—like the man himself. His radio sketches found humor more in the absurdity of situations and in the sure-fire Jewish outsider stance that dominated much comedy of the period than in ridicule or caustic jokes. They were funny enough to open doors to Broadway revues and TV; through the early 1950s, Stein, too, wrote for *Your Show of Shows*. And he crossed paths with Jerry Bock again when he and a writing partner, Will Glickman, were hired to write the book for *Mr. Wonderful*. But two other musicals he wrote before 1960 set him more directly down the path to the new project with Bock and Harnick.

The first was *Plain and Fancy* (1955), a commission bankrolled by a Philadelphia department store owner who wanted a show about the Amish to do for Pennsylvania what Rodgers and Hammerstein had done for Oklahoma—or so Stein remembered it. (Accounts from the period explain that a woman from Pennsylvania had tried to sell the producer on her script about the Amish a couple of years earlier.) Stein and Glickman (again, writing partners) researched Amish customs, dress, and speech; the producer brought a Mr. Zeek from Pennsylvania to school the company in the ways of his tribe, and he also planted a tape recorder mic among the celery in a Lancaster County market stall to try to capture the local lilt for the cast. Preshow press coverage emphasized the exoticism of the simple-living Mennonites, but the script took pains to portray the community in a positive, even wistful light. It relied on a well-worn plot device: two city-mouse New Yorkers, Dan and Ruth, alight in Bird-in-Hand, Pennsylvania, where Dan is selling a farm he inherited to a local man. In the process of helping to right a romance, the outsiders come to appreciate the meaningful way of life they witness, and the community reaffirms and tightens its ties to tradition (displayed most wondrously in a second-act opening number, in which a barn is raised onstage). Utterly conventional in form and quaint in spirit, the show offered a frisson of the foreign in a pleasant, familiar package. It ran for more than a year despite lukewarm reviews.

Stein turned to themes of family conflict within a tight, rigid community once more when, in 1959, he adapted Sean O'Casey's *Juno and the Paycock*. Working on his own as librettist this time, Stein stayed faithful to O'Casey's close study of the crumbling Boyle family in the period of Ireland's War of Independence—stalwart mother, drunkard dad, stool pigeon son, besotted then spurned (and pregnant) daughter—while also coloring in the social background. The show featured several big ensemble scenes that brought 1920s Dublin to life, with women commiserating comically on front stoops, men cavorting in a pub, neighbors viciously turning on the Boyles when the family's ballyhooed inheritance fails to materialize. The show offers a surprising critique of masculinity in times of war—the son's death at the hands of IRA avengers comes across as part of a violent culture that's out of control, the dad's drinking renders him entirely ineffectual, and the women leave to make a better life, daughter following mother "to my sister's place, to the farm, where you can take a full breath without the smell of sadness in it." Despite a rich score by Marc Blitzstein and stirring, Irish-inflected choreography by Agnes de Mille, *Juno* closed after sixteen performances, criticized for failing to find a convincing middle ground between bubbly musical numbers and O'Casey's bitter tone.

Stein didn't have either musical consciously in mind when he suggested that he, Bock, and Harnick take a look at Sholem-Aleichem's short stories as possible source material for their new venture. He was simply reminded of the stories after Harnick proposed they adapt Sholem-Aleichem's *Wandering Stars*. A friend had given Harnick a copy of the novel and he saw great potential in the rollicking, epic, and tumultuous love story that traces the parallel paths of a cantor's daughter, Reizel, and a wealthy man's son, Leibel Rafalovich, who are separated as youngsters as they try to run off from their shtetl together to join the theater. Each traipses across Europe and, eventually, comes to America as a star—Rosa an admired singer in the Gentile opera houses, and Leo Rafalesco a celebrated leading man of the Yiddish stage. Literary critics have long pointed to the book's choppy plotting, melodramatic emotion, and expositional cop-outs (epistolary chapters that fill in skipped-over events, for example) as key evidence of Sholem-Aleichem's failure as a novelist. But theater people have frequently found it irresistible, both for its vivid portrayals of the mendacious managers, conniving costars, and imperious divas who nonetheless consistently manage to put magic on the stage and for its direct (critics would say overly blatant) theme of the theater's irresolvable inner conflict as a commercial art—one that must please a paying audience even as its creators aspire, like

Rafalesco, to greatness. Harnick loved it. So did Bock. The Broadway musical seems like the story's natural habitat—the form, after all, was invented and sustained by scrappy Jewish artists who learned to balance seriousness and shmaltz, assimilation and ethnic assertion. *Wandering Stars* looked perfect as Harnick, Bock, and Stein's next project.

Except that it was too sprawling for even a three-hour stage adaptation. Or so Stein contended. Traversing a dozen locales and as many years, populated by hordes of colorful characters and twining around two central plot lines, the novel couldn't be contained in the taut structure of a book musical. (If the *New York Times* reviewer is to be believed, Maurice Schwartz's 1930 dramatization with songs by Avrum Goldfadn bore out Stein's judgment: it played as "a succession of insufficiently fused fragments." How the Moscow Yiddish Art Theater's version fared is hard to say; the June 1941 debut was overwhelmed by other events.)

But the short stories—those, Stein told his collaborators, might be more suitable for the stage. He remembered that his father, an immigrant from Poland who was now living with him, had read them in Yiddish when he was young. That pious, affable milkman with his tangled Talmudic quotes and rebellious daughters. Those tragicomic tales of ruin and survival. Couldn't those make a good musical? Even Rodgers and Hammerstein had thought so, though Stein didn't know it at the time.

But where to find the stories in English in 1960? Frances Butwin's *Tevye's Daughters* had been out of print for nearly a decade and even though some Sholem-Aleichem was still available in translation, Stein wasn't having any luck locating it. Neil Klugman and the other caustic characters in *Goodbye, Columbus* seemed to be shouting from every bookshop window, asserting themselves, controversially, as the irreverent new voice of Jewish America. Stein called all over the city and finally, at O'Malley's secondhand bookstore on Park Avenue South, he put his hands on a volume with a fading gray green cloth cover, the title *Tevye's Daughters* looping across it in a gilded cursive font. Inside, he rediscovered the sympathetic, stalwart hero who made him laugh so hard he cried. In March 1961, Bock, Harnick, and Stein met formally for the first time to discuss staging the stories.

Harnick was surprised by how much the stories appealed to him. He remembered reading some Sholem-Aleichem when he was in high school on the recommendation of someone who'd heard how much he enjoyed American humorists like Robert Benchley and James Thurber. But stories by "the Jewish Mark Twain" left him cold. Harnick "wrote them off, just dismissed them" at the time. But twenty years later they came across as "wonderfully human and moving and funny." For what reason—emotional maturity? more refined literary sensibility? inchoate postwar fondness for the old Jewish world? simply the availability of a better translation?— Harnick couldn't say. They simply resonated. Bock and Stein had the same reaction: the stories were "so warm and human and emotional that they cried out for music." Only later would Harnick acknowledge a buried basis for the appeal. "Over and above the beauty of the stories themselves, there was another reason why we were all drawn to this material, which can per- haps be best illustrated by a title which Mr. Stein suggested: 'Where Poppa Came From.'" But in 1960–61, the men did not recognize that motivation. "It never entered our minds that it was Jewish," Harnick recalled. "We all felt the same way about the stories, that they were just very beautiful and we couldn't wait to work on them." Or, as Stein liked to put it, "These were stories about characters who just happened to be Jewish."

Like a lot of other American Jews, that's pretty much how Bock, Harnick, and Stein felt about themselves. Stein, the oldest of the three, was the only one raised by Orthodox immigrant parents in a Yiddish- speaking household. But he "was never very involved in religion" and after his bar mitzvah found whatever spiritual calling he may have felt in the collaborative world of the theater. Bock and Harnick came from less observant families—Harnick in a mostly Gentile neighborhood, where a brief adolescent interest in becoming a rabbi was quickly supplanted by music and writing, and Bock in a secular family where it was his grand- mother's singing of Russian and Yiddish folk songs that infused him with what he referred to as his ethnic "juices." All three—like ever-growing numbers of other Jewish Americans—felt comfortable in this era of grow- ing acceptance and integration. Being Jewish was not the governing fact of their lives, but neither was it an issue. They would never deny that they were Jews, they just responded to the identity with the quintessential Jewish gesture: a shrug.

From the beginning, Bock, Harnick, and Stein ran into discouraging, even derisive, reactions to their effort. The first came from Stein's own agent, who let him know she thought he was wasting his time on a ridicu- lous project. "I'll go through the motions of making a routine contract," she told him with some irritation when he asked her to draw up a standard agreement among the three partners; she expected that it would not amount to anything. The writers had plenty of their own doubts. "Who would be interested in producing a show about a shtetl?" Stein wondered. But they kept at it, simply out of love of the material and the desire to work together. "It was pure speculation and pure affection," Stein said.

Of Sholem-Aleichem's eight Tevye stories in the Butwin volume, they initially chose to work from five: "Modern Children" (the story that focuses on Tzeitel's marriage to Motel the tailor), "Hodel" (the daughter who chooses Perchik, the revolutionary, and follows him to Siberia), "Chava" (the one who marries a non-Jew), "Shprintze" (who drowns herself after her wealthy beau's uncle calls off their betrothal), and "Get Thee Out" (in which Tevye and his family are evicted).

Stein's first order of business was figuring out how to weave the distinct and separate stories—written over the stretch of two decades—into a single drama. He had adapted works before, but not from fiction, and Sholem-Aleichem presented difficulties that went far beyond the need to spin full scenes and dialogue out of narration, some of it quite minimal. (All that is said in "Modern Children," for instance, about Tzeitel and Motel's nuptials is a near throwaway line—"the next day they were engaged, and not long after were married"—yet it inspired what eventually became *Fiddler*'s lengthy and elaborate act 1 finale. In the movie, the scene lasts a whopping twenty-one minutes.)

The stage's demand for incident was the least of Stein's challenges. The bigger problem lay in the clash between the musical's essential means—full frontal delivery—and Sholem-Aleichem's thickly layered indirectness. In the original series of prose monologues, the action emerges more from Tevye's way of recounting events than in the events themselves—in the twists of his language, the ironic drama of his dawning self-consciousness, the sheer relentlessness of his verbiage (in contrast to his tragic failure to speak up during the events he now relates), his vital need to narrate himself through every situation. Stein would have to determine how—and where—to use monologue in a way that didn't reduce Tevye's complexity. For starters, without Sholem-Aleichem as his listener—the frame the original author created—to whom would Tevye be speaking?

Then, there was Tevye himself. He is far more complex than *Juno*'s blustery Captain Boyle or *Plain and Fancy*'s conservative Papa Yoder. If Tevye occasionally shares a few of their characteristics—some self-inflated

PHOTOFEST

Jerry Bock (at piano) and Sheldon Harnick: songs should serve the show.

authority, some delay in recognizing what's transpiring around him—they are neither what make him funny nor what make him affecting. Comic and tragic incongruities combine in Tevye, this man of unshakable faith who constantly questions God. Enduring one catastrophe after another, the man with no power confronts the Highest Authority. He even quotes Scripture in the process: Tevye throws the Book at Him. But that's the easy part for Tevye. "I wasn't worried about God so much. I could come to terms with Him, one way or another," he says in the Shprintze story as he heads home from hearing her suitor's uncle break the engagement. "What bothered me was people."

This is a mirthless humor that would prove difficult to translate to the commercial theater, even half a dozen years after Samuel Beckett's comic bleakness had been introduced to the Broadway stage (where it found less than mass enthusiasm). Stein labored to keep Tevye lovable and funny without sacrificing—or sensationalizing—his pathos. He understood that when the audience laughs at Tevye, it must not be with condescension or there would be no emotional truth in their show. But understanding a critical point is one thing, applying it credibly in the theater another.

Stein pored over the Butwin volume, numbering sections with a light pencil to create a workable sequence of connected events. He encouraged himself with the certitude that any adaptation is a new thing in itself, not a literal translation: "I'm not a stenographer." Even so, he wanted to capture what had touched and stirred him and his collaborators in Sholem-Aleichem's work in the first place. Otherwise, what was the point? He was determined "to be very true to the original in terms of mood and feeling."

Keeping faith with those qualities tested the three men as they met periodically over the spring and early summer of 1961 to exchange ideas and as they weighed a couple of outline variants that July. One question thrummed beneath their labors even if it was never explicitly named, a version of which (unbeknown to them) had vexed even Sholem-Aleichem himself when he tried to adapt the material for a popular theatrical audience: to what extent could they maintain the tragic tone of the Tevye stories when writing for the chipper expectations of Broadway? How they'd treat the Chava story provided one key answer. Like Sholem-Aleichem before them, they changed its ending. Their first outline has Chava returning to the family fold at the play's close: "With pogrom threatening, her place is here. Her husband knows where she is, she feels he will come. Tevye accepts her." And though Stein would rewrite the scene many times before settling on a final version, that essential action stuck.

Even so, the collaborators worried that the second act piled one sad event upon another: apart from Chava's marriage to Fyedka, there was Hodel's departure for Siberia, the town's eviction and exodus, and, in an early variant outline, even Shprintze's suicide.

Couldn't they use some comic relief? They thought of removing Chava's story line entirely and replacing it with a vastly modified version of "Shprintze," Sholem-Aleichem's most painful story of all. They imagined that with "light and humorous treatment" they could exploit the story for its "valuable social elements" addressing the class divisions among Jews. What if, they wondered, instead of Shprintze's drowning herself when her suitor's wealthy family tears him away from her, Tevye tries to calm his heartbroken daughter? The scene could have "high humor and tenderness without any Second Avenue quality." And more: "We will also be able to make another kind of comment because we will see the wealthy family being evicted together with the other Jews."

Like any number of bad ideas entertained in a creative process, the suggestion was quickly abandoned. Wringing humor from "Shprintze" would have required too great a distortion for a weak payoff, especially when compared to the affecting Chava story (one that they would come to use to escalate the challenges that Tevye faces, just as Sholem-Aleichem did). They dropped "Shprintze" altogether. They wouldn't have time for five stories and, in any event, it was too dark for the show that was beginning to take shape.

Besides, Stein had settled on a means of bringing the material home to contemporary audiences: he was sending Tevye's family to America at the end of the play. Though in the first outline Tevye himself was to remain behind—"he is too old, he is afraid of new things, this is his home; he will survive; survival, he assures them, is his strongest trait"—a letter from an uncle who has already emigrated persuades him that his children should do the same. To Stein it just "felt right" that they should come to the United States. It was historically true that the wave of Jewish immigration surged in the period after the failed 1905 revolution and the subsequent pogroms. Sholem-Aleichem and his wife and son were among more than 150,000 who came in 1905–06 alone. Stein's own parents arrived only a few years later. Stein entertained giving the daughters less "exotic" names like Rachel and Sarah.

Where Tevye and his family were coming from proved just as significant an adjustment. At first, the script didn't specify. "Does Tevye live in Boiberik?" the authors asked in some early notes, naming the summer resort town to which Tevye delivers his milk and cheese. In the original stories, Tevye lives between Boiberik (which Sholem-Aleichem based on the real-life Boyarka) and Yehupitz (based on Kiev) and sometimes bemoans his remoteness from a Jewish community. Kasrilevke (Golde's hometown) and Anatevka (where the butcher Lazar Wolf and the tailor Motel Kamzoyl live) lie some versts away. But like the earlier radio adaptations of the stories, Stein moved Tevye to the center of Anatevka, collecting all the characters in a single setting. Dramaturgical expediency ended up serving the postwar Jewish immigration narrative, flagging the trajectory's end points: shtetl to America.

With an outline all three men approved, Stein started to flesh out the scenes. He built upon what little dialogue he found in the stories and kept much of the book's language in Tevye's monologues. He pulled in some bits and pieces of background from other stories in the volume that aren't part of the Tevye series. He invented—as he had to—many of the interactions. In mid-October 1961, he completed a draft of act 1.

"Move! March, you foolish animal!" ran the first line—the voice of Tevye heard from the wings, urging his tottering horse to get a move on. Then a stage direction: "Tevye enters, sits on a rock, sighs wearily." He spills his heart out to the audience, complaining cheerfully about his "stubborn animal." He ponders aloud: "Well, even a horse is one of God's living creatures and he has the same rights as other living creatures—the right to feel tired, the right to be hungry, and the right to work like a horse!" He explains that he sells milk and cheese for a meager living, that he has a wife and five daughters—"One more beautiful, smarter, livelier than the next. . . . And I have only one question about my daughters. How do I get them off my hands?" He all but announces an ambivalent fatalism: "The good Lord made many, many poor people. And if He wants it that way, that's the way it should be. You see, if it should have been different, it would have been. (*Pause.*) And yet, what would have been wrong to have it different?"

Soon Tevye meets Perchik, the young revolutionary, and invites him home for the Sabbath. The scene shifts to Tevye's home, where the girls are peeling potatoes, sewing, and doing laundry and their mother, Golde, is cracking wise. When Tzeitel wants to know where to put the potatoes, Golde answers, "Put it on my head! By the stove, foolish girl." When a younger daughter complains that she can't abide kasha, Golde carps: "Did I ask you what you hate? Eat it. . . . If you want to hate, hate a crazy dog, hate a drunken peasant who beats up people, why should you hate kasha? Kasha's not to hate, kasha's to eat!" The letter arrives from the uncle in America (a good occasion for a song, Stein notes) and the daughters' romances are introduced in parallel scenes even as Tevye promises the first to the butcher, Lazar Wolf.

Bock and Harnick pulled no punches in expressing their disappointment in the draft. They objected to the opening monologue as "pure, unadulterated exposition" holding up the launch of the story. They didn't like the way the daughters "have one-liners here and there that don't begin to reveal them as people." The scene when Tevye goes to meet Lazar Wolf wasn't working. Stein had wanted to avoid a hackneyed routine, so he changed the story's comic mix-up of the two men talking at cross-purposes, Tevye thinking they are discussing the sale of a cow while the butcher thinks they are talking about his interest in marrying Tzeitel. Stein had Tevye come right out with his understanding of why Lazar wanted to see him—"You are interested in my cow"—and that, his collaborators told him, made the scene seem "neither fish nor fowl."

Most of the comments addressed dramaturgical points—how simultaneously to build and streamline the action, how to fill out the characters—that would be ordinary in a critique of any script's first pass. But some responses show the writers grappling with enormous questions they may not have uttered aloud but that would determine the show's prospects as much as any technical shaping and pruning they would do: What was its attitude toward the Jews of Anatevka and the world around them? And, as a corollary, what did it have to say about their own times?

They wondered whether the constable who warns Tevye of the coming pogrom that he will oversee should be "a subtle anti-Semite, a some-of-my-best-friends-are type guy rather than a Nazi?" They favored the former characterization. "This man seems to be both friend and fiend," they reasoned. "And this leads to a feeling that if we could extend the symbol of Government and Gentile or peasant hostility [toward] the Jews beyond this one man we would have less of a black and white villain and more of a truthful examination of the problem." At the same time, Bock argued for some ethnographic color: "I think a big Sabbath meal could be fascinating for its ceremony, warmth and uniqueness on stage as well as providing a background that's part of the fabric of our show."

Two days after Bock delivered Harnick's and his comments, Stein's father died. Whether propelled by a redoubled desire to honor his father's legacy or stirred to action by his collaborators' ideas or both, Stein was back at work on the script within a week. He met with Bock and Harnick on November 6 to discuss a new outline. Two months later, he delivered a funnier, more tender new draft that featured preparations for a big Sabbath meal.

In the meantime, Bock and Harnick got cracking on the score. With their first collaboration, on *The Body Beautiful*, they had established a simpatico way of working together: first they'd discuss the show's subject and source material, then they'd go off and work independently. Bock would sketch some tunes—"musical guesses," he called them—and give them to Harnick on a tape. Meanwhile Harnick read more deeply, came up with song placements, and began to hatch some notions for lyrics. He'd work with the tapes from Bock. When he had lyrics that didn't seem to fit any of the recorded tunes, he'd send them along and Bock would compose in response. Back and forth they would go, each stimulated by the other.

"Sheldon, here's a little gay folk thing that I think has some interest for us," Bock told his partner on the first recording he sent him in the fall of 1961. Bock plays oompahing chords on a piano in need of tuning as he sings his skipping melody with nonsense syllables: "bup-bup-bup-bup-bup-yaaaa, bup-bup-yá, bup-bup-yá." Figuring that the dream scene in which Tevye tricks Golde into agreeing to let Tzeitel marry Motel would stay in the book no matter what direction Stein took it, Harnick had been picturing the nightmare's coming to life: deceased Grandma Tzeitel appears to bless her namesake; then Lazar Wolf's first wife, Fruma Sarah, comes to threaten revenge if, as the Butwin translation has it, Tevye should "let your daughter take my place, live in my house, carry my keys, wear my clothes." When the tape arrived in the mail, Harnick quickly affixed the words "A blessing on your head, mazel tov, mazel tov. To see a daughter wed, mazel tov, mazel tov" to the first set of "bup-bup-yá's," and the rest of the lyrics to "The Tailor Motel Kamzoil" seemed to flow by themselves, guided by the language in Sholem-Aleichem's original short story and the contours of Bock's accelerating tune.

Through the fall and early winter, the pair sent music and lyrics back and forth between Harnick's Manhattan apartment and Bock's home in the Westchester suburb of New Rochelle. Now and then, they'd come together in their publisher's office on West Fifty-seventh Street and sit for hours at an upright piano singing through their creations, smoothing out bumps in the transition from page to sound, and musically doodling. In the neighborhood where popular American song was born, bred, and brazenly peddled, the ghosts of Tin Pan Alley were harmonizing with strains from the Pale: Bock fused his jaunty pop proficiency with a deeply absorbed feel for the thick harmonies and sweet-and-sour falling fourths of Russian folk music, the melancholy modes of Yiddish song, the spiraling frenzy of Jewish wedding dances. Bock didn't need to do any research to compose this score. He "felt it was inside me" and found that the "opportunity to now express myself with that kind of music just opened up a flood of possibilities."

He had also soaked up the styles from late 1950s LPs, such as the Moiseyev Dance Ensemble's compilations of Russian folk tunes and Theodore Bikel's recordings of Yiddish songs. (Bikel maintains that more than soaking up styles, Bock siphoned some tunes.) When on one of the tapes he sent his partner Bock sings a melody for Harnick with "a certain Yiddish-Russian quality" that he says is "overly sad, which might be a point of humor," his rich voice breaks, beautifully, with cantorial *krekhts*—half-tone hiccups that distinguish the technique. Maybe that's why Harnick heard something devotional in it. The lyricist pulled directly from Jewish liturgy—"May God bless you and protect you"—to shape (with some variation and invention) the song Tevye's family would sing around the table on Friday evening, "Sabbath Prayer," a yearning song that saw barely any revision over the next two and a half years as the show slowly made its way to Broadway.

But it was another plaintive tune, a waltz, that most stirred Harnick when he played the tape Bock had sent him and heard his partner croon through it with place holding la-da-dee-dee-da-da syllables. Bock thought the melody might express a "flirty idea" for the daughters, but Harnick heard something different. He took to heart Bock's suggestion that the tune was "unashamedly sentimental." Words just came—they "crystallized" on the music: "Is this the little girl I carried? Is this the little boy at play? I don't remember growing older. When did they? . . . Sunrise, sunset . . ." He couldn't wait to share the words with Bock. He took the train up to New Rochelle and sang it at the piano in the composer's basement studio. When they called Bock's wife down for a listen, she started to cry and Harnick realized they'd struck deep. Years later, he could count this moment as an early inkling that the show they were making out of sheer love might come to be loved by others.

* * *

It was way too soon, however, to let in such grandiose thoughts. The creative team didn't even have rights to the material yet, and without them the project was going nowhere. Almost as soon as Bock, Harnick, and Stein had started talking seriously about the Tevye stories, their representatives had initiated what they all thought would be a routine licensing process. Negotiations with Crown Publishers began in August 1961 and quickly resulted in a letter of agreement. Bock's lawyer expected a contract within the first few days of November. By the new year of 1962, Stein had completed a second draft and Bock and Harnick had written at least a dozen songs, but they still lacked a signed deal. The unexpected snag had a name vaguely familiar to the authors: Arnold Perl.

When Perl licensed the stories for his production of *Tevya and His Daughters* in 1956 (after Rodgers and Hammerstein had let their option go), he secured exclusive rights from Crown Publishers and the promise of access to any Sholem-Aleichem material he might want from the writer's son-in-law B. Z. Goldberg, who took a liking to Perl. Four years later, the former Communist was driving a shrewd capitalist bargain. The new Tevye team was buying access to the stories published by Crown, not to Perl's play. (Though Perl's family would maintain that *Fiddler* is based on it, Stein claimed never to have seen *Tevya and His Daughters* and, apart from their significant structural differences, there are no overlapping lines that don't come either from the Butwin translation or from Maurice Samuel's *The World of Sholom Aleichem*.) Perl held out for an 8.2 percent royalty (larger than the 4.8 percent Sholem-Aleichem's family was granted) and, most important, a line of acknowledgment on all title pages and ads forever: "by special arrangement with Arnold Perl." The deal was done in July 1962.

At last they were ready for a producer. Finding one made the haggling with Perl seem easy.

As the authors started to raise the subject with various contacts, they heard variations on the same dismissal: no producer could make money on a show that would appeal only to a small coterie audience. "What will we do when we've run out of Hadassah groups?" asked one of several who turned them down. He was only the most blunt about fears others shared: the show was "too Jewish."

Were they kidding? Wasn't worrying about Jews on Broadway just a wee step away from worrying about Jews in synagogue? The director Tyrone Guthrie once quipped that if all the Jews were to leave the American theater, it would "collapse about next Thursday." What was so threatening about *Tevye* (as the show was now being called)? After all, whether or not one accepts the academic argument that a coded Jewish

sensibility underlies almost every show since the invention of the musical, by the time *Tevye* was seeking a producer, the Great White Way was
not a restricted neighborhood.

The very same week Stein was finishing his tentative first draft, in October 1961, *Milk and Honey*, the cheery Zionist musical by Don Appell (book)
and Jerry Herman (music and lyrics), opened; it enjoyed a sixteen-month
run. Soon after, Shelley Berman starred as the comic father in *A Family
Affair*, a farce about plans for a big Jewish wedding by James and William
Goldman (book and lyrics) and John Kander (music) that, savaged by the
critics, lasted only a couple of months; somewhat more successfully, *I Can
Get It for You Wholesale*, a bitter tale of greed in the garment industry with
a loathsome hero, opened in March 1962, introducing the world to an
explosive nineteen-year-old sensation, Barbra Streisand. Streisand went
right from that show into her first blockbuster, the bio-musical about the
comedian Fanny Brice, *Funny Girl*, which ran for three and a half years.

But potential producers sensed something different about *Tevye* even
if they couldn't quite put their finger on it. These other shows—even *Milk
and Honey*—were about Americans. Their Jewishness was not hidden,
but it was not thematically important, except insofar as characters moved
away from it: the protagonists visiting Israel in the Jerry Herman show fall
in love with each other, not with their putative homeland, and return to the
United States at the end; *Wholesale*'s Harry Bogen (Elliott Gould) tromps
on anyone in his path as he tries to get to the top; and Streisand's Fanny
Brice turns away from her background as she rises to stardom. At least as
Harnick understood them, "those shows weren't Jewish." And producers
who, after all, were investing in Broadway to make money hadn't seen
any Yiddish-related material make a killing in a good long while. If ever.

The *Tevye* team hoped that the young sensation of a producer who
had enlisted Bock and Harnick for *Fiorello!* would take a chance on them
again: they asked Hal Prince to direct their show. He read the script in
the summer of 1962 and simply couldn't connect. There was "something
overall that bothers me," he fumbled as he broke the bad news to Bock.
He found the text "so languid" and full of "let-downs." Could the material even accommodate a more dramatic shape? "Or is it all charm and
warm humor?" he wondered. "It's just so gentle," he concluded, before
suggesting that Bock spare Stein's feelings and not share his remarks.
Later, he allowed that the problem may have boiled down to a cultural

difference. As the descendant of German Jewish forebears, Prince felt no attachment to the Yiddish world of Eastern Europe. He felt "as foreign to the shtetl as I am to Buckingham Palace."

Prince did offer one piece of advice, though, attached to a promise: he recommended that they ask Jerry Robbins to direct and said he'd consider producing if Robbins came on board. Prince had watched Robbins reinvent the musical with *West Side Story* and had recently called him down to Washington, D.C., for a pre-Broadway repair of *A Funny Thing Happened on the Way to the Forum*, the frisky Plautine musical comedy by Burt Shevelove (book) and Stephen Sondheim (music and lyrics) best remembered for the outsize buffoonery of its star, Zero Mostel. Robbins had turned that flabby mess of funny material into a trim comic machine. Robbins's fluency in the language of theatrical metaphor was what *Tevye* would need to move it beyond "being simply an ethnic folk tale" toward its promise of "larger things." The more Prince thought about it, the more he was sure that Bock, Harnick, and Stein simply shouldn't proceed without Robbins. And he so advised them.

But the writers didn't wait. Arnold Saint Subber, who had produced (and, as legend has it, conceived of) *Kiss Me, Kate* fifteen years earlier, was interested. It turned out that he had been raised with Yiddish, having been taken in by a Jewish grandmother after his father was killed in an accident. "He knew Sholem-Aleichem better than we did," Harnick marveled. Despite Saint Subber's personal tie to the material, though, the authors perceived that he was having a rough time raising money after a couple of flops and they didn't think they could count on him. On July 25, they played the score for Fred Coe, the rumpled southerner who produced work on stage, film, and TV. Bock cited the film director and producer Arthur Penn as having expressed interest, too. "Negotiating," wrote Bock in his diary a short time after meeting with each of them, with no further comment.

On August 20, 1962, more than a year after the men had started to work on the project, an item in the *New York Times* made it official: "Aleichem Stories Inspire Musical," the page 18 headline announced, noting that the production was being "considered" by Coe and would probably be presented in the fall of 1963.

Then nothing happened. Or not much apart from a presentation for friends two months later in Stein's New Rochelle home, where Stein narrated events while Bock and Harnick sat at a piano and sang through the score. If any of the guests took out their checkbooks, their pledges didn't amount to much. Coe, who had indeed signed on, needed to go out and raise money. *Tevye* simply had to wait.

The artists did not. Stein went off and wrote a new play of his own, an adaptation of Carl Reiner's comic bildungsroman *Enter Laughing.* The "side-splitting," "uproarious," "marvelously funny" play—as the *New York Times* declared it—opened in March 1963 and played for a solid year. Meanwhile, Bock and Harnick responded to an invitation to adapt the film *The Shop around the Corner* (based on a play by Miklós László) for Hal Prince, and over the autumn and winter of 1962–63 they wrote and rehearsed their little gem of a musical, *She Loves Me*, which premiered in April 1963. Though appreciated, the small-scale charmer that tells the tale of a surprise romance couldn't compete with splashier spectacles and it closed after eight months. At the same time, the song duo wrote what the *New York Times* called (in an otherwise negative review) "three snappy numbers" for a tame space adventure for children featuring puppets by Bil and Cora Baird, called *Man in the Moon.*

As for the possibility of Robbins, his schedule was packed all through the season. Coe had duly called him in December 1962, but there's no indication that Robbins even accepted a copy of the script at that point. He was up to his ears with a trying production of Brecht's *Mother Courage* (for which he adamantly refused Brecht's instruction to use a turntable onstage). Soon after it opened in late March 1963—right between *Enter Laughing* and *She Loves Me*—Robbins was preparing a new Broadway opening. If the financial loss, mixed reviews, and miserable experience of *Mother Courage* disturbed him, he didn't lose stride: he moved right into work on transferring Arthur Kopit's mordant play *Oh Dad, Poor Dad, Mamma's Hung You in the Closet and I'm Feelin' So Sad*, which he'd staged Off-Broadway the previous season. And a project with Richard Rodgers was in the planning stages. But somehow a sliver of mental space opened long enough for Robbins to think about what would challenge him anew after the Kopit play.

In July, he wrote to his friend and erstwhile collaborator Leonard Bernstein to ask whether the composer had any further ideas about a ballet version of the mystical Yiddish play *The Dybbuk*, which they'd once talked about. Robbins thought they might pull it together in time for the next year's Spoleto festival in Italy. (They finally got around to it in 1974.) Robbins floated a new idea: "Also, have you read *Another Country* by James Baldwin?" he asked. "There's a marvelous new and strange kind of musical theater to be evolved from the book [which] touches me enormously."

Coe reached Robbins at this auspicious moment when thoughts of new forms, Yiddish material, and issues of racial tolerance were mingling in his mind. On August 15, Bock and Harnick came to his Upper East Side home office to play him the score. He didn't have to be coaxed. On the twentieth, his lawyer called to tell him they'd come to terms with Coe—including the agreement that Robbins would be cut in as an uncredited author—but warned Robbins not to make any decisions about the Richard Rodgers collaboration on his docket until they had the *Tevye* deal in writing. Robbins wasted no time. Within a week, he wrote to Rodgers to withdraw from their plans, explaining that the Tevye material "is something I feel deeply related to. maybe it's my heritage. I'm aware of the fact that a lot of people have considered this material and gave it up as impossible. but i want to try and have decided to. Both of you are creative enough to understand what is moving me, and believe me the background of my parents and their parents plays a big role." The next day he heard back from Rodgers. Expressing "deep disappointment" and the "equally deep hope that we'll work together some time soon," Rodgers allowed how "this sort of decision has to be made on a personal and emotional basis."

When Robbins cabled his favorite stage manager, Ruth Mitchell, on August 23, to entice her to join the project, he gushed, "I'm going to do a musical of Sholem Aleichem stories with Harnick and Bock. I'm in love with it. It's our people." A few days later, Robbins wrote to his longtime close friend Nancy Keith: "I'm going to do a musical which should really star my father," he happily announced. "It's all about the background he comes from." And then he added, with the sort of winking self-criticism only an intimate could appreciate, "So I have to start getting into my usual black mood for work."

The *Tevye* team had heard of Robbins's notorious "black mood" and, as delighted as they were to have won the musical stage's greatest living director, they stashed away some caution. When they were about to offer the helm to Robbins, Harnick checked in with Robbins's friend Sondra

Lee. She told him they couldn't do better than Robbins for the project but should give him a wide berth as the opening approached. "He becomes obsessed by his demons," she told Harnick. "He is so worried about failure." And since Robbins's father had imbued him with the fear that if you're Jewish everything you've accomplished will be taken away from you, she thought he might feel especially vulnerable on this show, perfect as she felt they were for each other. If he starts brooding under a cloud, she cautioned, you can expect terrible thunder. If you hear it rumbling and you can't reach him with humor, she said ominously, "stay out of his way."

In the summer of 1963, when Robbins stormed into the project, he blew in like a gale force, bringing fresh perspective and exhilaration— and a slew of precise, rigorous demands.

* * *

Robbins immediately threw himself into preparing for *Tevye*, despite rehearsals for reopening *Oh Dad*. Robbins always conducted extensive background research where a project warranted it, but never before with as much fervor. He started amassing books, articles, photographs, records, and films about Jewish history, culture, and practice. Early on, he rented Maurice Schwartz's movie *Tevye der milkhiker*. Perhaps Schwartz's knack for shifting nimbly between humor and poignancy, his ability to be at once grand and pitiable, helped shape the image of the Tevye that Robbins would want center stage, but his working notes don't discuss the heartrending movie or Schwartz more generally. It's a telling omission: Robbins had made his own acting debut under Schwartz's direction at the Yiddish Art Theater in 1937.

Robbins's first serious dance teacher, Gluck Sandor, had been hired by Schwartz as a choreographer and he brought Robbins (as well as his sister, Sonia) along with him. The show was I. J. Singer's *Di brider ashkenazi* (*The Brothers Ashkenazi*), an epic novel adapted for the stage the moment it came off the press. Sprawling and full of twists, rises, and falls, the plot traces the fate of Poland's Jews—and of the industrializing city of Łódź—from the late nineteenth century to the First World War by telling the story of enterprising brothers who become rivals in business and romance. Robbins danced in two numbers, served as supernumerary in the many lavish crowd scenes, and, just shy of his nineteenth birthday and appearing much younger, played a boy in a two-word walk-on. "Yoh, tata," he had to say—"Yes, Dad."

Playing eight or nine times a week for six months (to packed houses) could have provided Robbins with a solid sense of at least one big slice of Eastern European Jewish life (albeit in melodramatic form), despite his not knowing Yiddish. The novel had been published in English, but even if Robbins hadn't read it he could have followed the stage action, with all its pomp and pious protocol, easily enough. But that was the last thing that interested him at the time—the first instance in which young Rabinowitz was listed in a program under the name Jerome Robbins. He focused, instead, on Schwartz's technique and showmanship. He found the maestro to be "stern, serious, not smiling except when the play called for it," and "autocratic" but also a tremendously skillful and compelling actor. Robbins particularly liked to watch the climactic scene in which Schwartz, playing the assimilating brother, cuts off his *payess*—his ritual side curls—"in an act of defiance, . . . puts on a tie & with a deep determined breath & chin lifted, he strides out to meet the world. (End of act 1.)"

Apart from projecting into his admiration of the scene his own teenage desire to separate from his Jewish heritage, Robbins likely picked up some early lessons in pacing and the power of a portentous first-act curtain. As Robbins would be, Schwartz was a stickler for realism and ensemble playing, and he knew how to build, and milk, big flashy scenes. He gave plenty of stage time and meticulous attention to dramatized religious rituals. *The Brothers Ashkenazi* featured a solemn, extravagant wedding—one Robbins nowhere mentions in his notes even as he is called on to create one himself.

Perhaps Robbins was so resistant to *Yiddishkayt* in his youth that the substance of *The Brothers Ashkenazi* bounced off him and genuinely made no lasting impression; perhaps he needed to engage the artistic project of cultural recovery as a parallel process of personal retrieval, with no interference from another domineering theatrical imagination. Whatever the reason, he approached *Tevye* research as if he'd had no exposure to the century-long history of Polish Jews recounted in the Singer work—or to the culture of the scrappy company at the Yiddish Art Theater. It was *Tevye* that provided him a chance to fill in a wide and aching gap in his under-standing, to make up for his father's teaching him "nought about the reli-gion, Torah, traditions, language or most of all the WHY of it . . . fasting, davening [praying], payess, tzitzis [fringes] or any pride or history of our tribe." Among the books Robbins bought: *A Treasury of Jewish Folklore*, *Nine Gates to the Hasidic Mysteries*, *The Jewish Woman and Her Home*, *Great Ages and Ideas of the Jewish People*, *The Lifetime of a Jew: Throughout the Ages of Jewish History*, *The Jewish Festivals*, *Everyman's Talmud*, Mau-rice Samuel's *Little Did I Know.*

But the first item Robbins looked for was a photograph. He wanted a portrait of Sholem-Aleichem. By the time the *New York Times* reported on August 29 "Robbins to Direct 'Tevye,' a Musical" (a full year after the paper's last mention of the project), Robbins had already put in some calls to experts at New York's Jewish Museum and the Jewish Educa-tional Committee. With a long-standing, serious interest in photogra-phy, Robbins may have expected to glean some insights by gazing into the wide, bewhiskered face of his onetime namesake. Or perhaps he simply wanted to see what the debonair voice of the people looked like. Or to keep the author's smiling eyes nearby as a sort of charm as he worked on the show. In any event, a picture of Sholem-Aleichem would have served as a strong visual rejoinder to a photograph that character-ized Robbins's feelings about Jewishness heretofore.

Hebrew Lesson, a haunting image by Cornell Capa, had been hanging in Robbins's home office for at least a few years, depicting a teacher with pointy beard and spiraling side curls leaning like an ominous shadow over boys reading in a *kheyder*. The photo, made in 1955, may have struck sentimental chords for some viewers, but Robbins's own brief experience with a bar mitzvah tutor had been traumatic and the appeal of this pic-ture, though beautiful, was complicated, to say the least. The hovering figure in the photo evokes the "old wizened, decrepit white bearded, unshaven man [who came] to the house every afternoon to train me to read the Torah, that part of the Torah I had to learn." But the scarring lesson Robbins took from him was "Jewish submissiveness." Neighbor-hood boys taunted Robbins through the window while he had his lesson. The teacher did nothing. "If he'd taught me to fight—if he'd stood up and yelled at them back, but no, he accepted the fact that we were curs and

Henri Cartier-Bresson, 1960, Magnum Photos

Jerome Robbins at home with Cornell Capa's "Hebrew Lesson"
looming behind him.

we got off the sidewalk when we were commanded to." Yet here on his
wall Robbins had prominently displayed a reminder of "the horror, the
embarrassment and the shame" of Jewish wimpiness.

Even if Robbins never obtained or never hung up a portrait of Sholem-
Aleichem, his work on *Tevye* would mitigate the fear and frustrated
desire evoked by the Capa image. With this show, at last, he would stand
up for Jews; he would stand up as a Jew. "The play must celebrate and
elevate the life of the shtetl and its people," Robbins scrawled on a yellow

legal pad in early September, as he jotted down his preliminary reaction to the material. And he quickly added a corollary: "We must keep away from the sentimental." This imperative guided Robbins's work on the play as much as any of the research he was soaking up.

This principle was at odds with much of the background material he was consulting, which included the mawkish paeans to the hermetic, homogenous, poor-but-pious shtetl invented in the 1940s and 1950s: Samuel's *The World of Sholom Aleichem*, Herzog and Zborowski's *Life Is with People* (Robbins called it "our guide and our Bible"), and Roman Vishniac's *Vanished World*. (He purchased at least six copies to distribute to his designers once he had assembled them.) For all the heat Robbins and the *Fiddler* team would take later for "discard[ing] the richness of texture that is Sholem Aleichem's greatest achievement" (as Irving Howe put it in a famously cranky *Commentary* essay) and for "falsifying the world of Sholem Aleichem, not to mention the character of the East European Jew" (as the theater critic Robert Brustein chided), in truth, Robbins labored mightily to burn away the shmaltz that for two decades had encased the world of the shtetl like amber.

From his first reading of the script, Robbins warned against the show's "being in love with the material." Jumbled as his hasty handwritten notes were, his feelings were clear, visceral: the work was "not a 'musical'" in any conventional sense and "must not be thought of as 'Bway.'" It must avoid "making all the Jews & all the people understanding, philosophic & hearts of gold, wry of expression & compassionate to the point of nausea." The creators would need to let an honest reckoning with the material dictate the appropriate theatrical form, one that would "keep the guts, flavor, humor, color, smell, sound, gesture & cadence of the life," but in a way that would transcend "the realistic & the expected." In a likely swipe at the Arnold Perl plays, Robbins wrote an instruction, "Only by striving & tenaciously struggling to find [the right style] will we be able to make this show rise above what has already been seen & played."

Right away, a visual image struck Robbins that came closest to what he had in mind: the paintings of Chagall. Robbins had long admired their poetic quality and, as a young dancer on tour with the Ballet Theater in 1942, he had met Chagall in Mexico, where the artist was supervising his set design for a Léonide Massine piece in the repertoire. A decade later, as a star choreographer discussing a possible production of Stravinsky's *Les*

Noces, Robbins rejected the idea of Chagall as its designer. As "wonderful" as he thought Chagall's "fantasy and knowledge of Russian village life would be," Robbins worried that such scenery would upstage his dancers. But now, another decade later, he could see how such imagery would enhance the spirit he wanted *Tevye* to convey.

Perhaps the idea occurred to Robbins when he opened one of the volumes of Sholem-Aleichem's writings he had acquired for his research, *The Great Fair*, the childhood autobiography published by Noonday Press in 1955 (in a translation by Sholem-Aleichem's granddaughter, Tamara Kahana). The book featured a Chagall drawing as its frontispiece, a charming sketch of the young artist at an easel, painting the bespectacled, goateed author sitting for the portrait. It was as if Sholem-Aleichem's playful prose self-portrait of his youth inspired Chagall's own visual one. Chagall had talked about how he loved Sholem-Aleichem as a boy and climbed a fence to catch a glimpse of him when the author came through Vitebsk on a reading tour. Now he was paying homage. Robbins recognized the same complementarities the publishers at Noonday must have seen between the two artists when they commissioned the book's frontispiece—what Robbins called the painter's "fantasy & poetry" and the writer's "wry irony, earthiness & criticism, detached observation." He set out to unite them onstage.

Chagall, too, had been squeezed too tightly in sentimentalizing American embraces but Robbins appreciated a wider, more worldly aspect of the work: "In his fantasy atmosphere, particulars; in his free & nonrealistic choice of colors & form, in his child's fantasy evocations & artist's sophistication & elegance, his evocations of the time life & richness of shtetl life becomes so very riveting, exciting, & stimulating. He has translated & elevated the material above the limited appeal of those who recognize its sources, & revealed & endeared it to all peoples everywhere. This is also our job."

Just as Hal Prince had anticipated, Robbins was looking for a way to make *Tevye* both particular and universal and one key was visual: combining earthly detail with spiritual fantasy. On September 4, Robbins cabled Chagall: "We would be very honored if you would consider designing the décor and costumes for a musical play based on the Sholem Aleichem stories that I will choreograph and direct this winter." Within days, he had the reply: "MERCI VOTRE ATTENTION REGRETTE

TROP OCCUPE POUR ACCEPTER FAIRE DECORS." The painter was not simply making an excuse—he told friends how much he would have liked to work with Robbins had he not been so busy—but even without his direct involvement (and much to his annoyance), Chagall hovered over the production like one of his floating figures. One recurring image in Chagall's work gave Robbins an early defining idea. The fiddler sawing out a sound track for the shtetl from his precarious rooftop post would guide the show like a magician: coming down to the stage and weaving into the action unseen by the characters, he would foreshadow their fate in movement and melody.

Chagall or no Chagall, Prince kept his word. By mid-October he had joined Fred Coe as a producer.

Meanwhile, the scenic designer Boris Aronson was waiting for a call from Robbins. A successful and confident artist, Aronson wasn't the sort to sit by the phone, but he had contacted Robbins the very day the *New York Times* announced Robbins as the director of *Tevye*. Aronson had created the set and costumes for Robbins's 1952 New York City Ballet piece, *Ballade*, a melancholy take on commedia dell'arte characters, set to music by Debussy, and had been eager to work with the mature Robbins on a full production. More important, he felt quite simply that *Tevye* was his show to do. And he was right. No other designer in New York knew as much about Sholem-Aleichem and Chagall as he did. No other designer anywhere. The call came—even before Robbins had received Chagall's "regrette."

Aronson was born in 1900 (or so he said; some accounts correct the date to 1898) in Kiev, where his father was the grand rabbi. From early boyhood through his celebrated fifty-three-year career in New York theater, Aronson chafed against orthodoxy of all kinds: as a child, he boldly told his father he had no interest in religion; he resisted the Kiev art school's rigid devotion to French realism; he fled the sharp turn toward what he called "rampant cultism" that Soviet art took after a thrilling period of postrevolutionary experimentation; and in New York he upended, sometimes literally, the predictable furniture of prevailing efforts to put a replica of "real life" on the stage. He believed that designers "must be reborn with each show," creating the style that suits each project.

If his style was never fixed, Aronson's principles were set in the heady years right after the Russian Revolution and the First World War, when directors like Vsevolod Meyerhold were inventing radical new approaches to theater production. Aronson had been unconsciously waiting for such dynamism and abstraction since his adolescence. "By the time I was fourteen," he always maintained, "I was past crying over *The Cherry Orchard* and no longer cared whether the three sisters arrived safely in Moscow." In Kiev—which had become a center of the Jewish avant-garde only a dozen years after Sholem-Aleichem had cowered in a hotel there, hiding from pogroms—Aronson emerged as a key figure, helping to organize a show of Jewish artists and exhibiting his own work. He studied for at least two years in the Kiev workshop of Alexandra Exter, an acclaimed modernist painter who served as the chief set designer for the experimental director Alexander Tairov at his Moscow chamber theater, the Kamerny. Aronson assisted her on a 1920 production of *Romeo and Juliet*, long remembered for its multiple angular playing areas and its use of mirrors. Under her tutelage—and absorbing the new visual and movement vocabularies in Moscow, where he moved in 1921, calling it "the mecca of the theater world"—Aronson learned to think of set designing as a means of giving dynamic space to the actor, highlighting mood, fostering action, and creating a thing of beauty.

He left Russia for America in 1923, anticipating the taming of the avant-garde into "home-sweet-home calendar art" and the coming political clampdown on creativity. On his way, he spent some eighteen months in Berlin, where he presented work in the first Western exhibit of Soviet art and wrote two books. The first, on "contemporary Jewish graphic art," essentially argued that there really was no such thing because Jews, living all over the world, created in response to the conventions and tendencies of the cultures in which they resided. The other was a monograph about Chagall.

Aronson became friendly with Chagall in Moscow and admired his wily Constructivist scenery and costumes for the Sholem-Aleichem plays and his panoramic murals that impishly depicted the people associated with the theater and their surroundings. Aronson especially appreciated the "tonal juiciness" and "coloric strength" that, much more than formal technique, gave Chagall's work what Aronson called its "weighty lightness." (When he became a father in 1950, Aronson named his son Marc, after the artist.)

When Aronson arrived in New York in November 1923—"with awkward baggage, crowded emotions, little money, and less English"—it wasn't only the verbal language that led him to seek work in the Yiddish theater. Much to Aronson's surprise, the Yiddish stage was the realm where Constructivism and other new approaches were most welcome: the mainstream American stage seemed stuck in static realism. Beginning with the avant-garde *Unzer* ("Our") Theater in the Bronx, where he designed the fantastical subway car in which advertisements come to life in Osip Dymov's comic critique of consumerism, *Bronx Express*, Aronson moved down to Second Avenue and then into the English-language theater. In addition to a long association with Harold Clurman and the Group Theater, there were many Broadway projects, including two that catapulted him into the limelight: *The Crucible* (1953) and *The Diary of Anne Frank* (1955).

Robbins was impressed by the materials on Aronson's past projects that he'd asked his assistants to gather for him. When he met the big, solemn man with the Russian accent on October 1, he was ready to offer him the post. But Hal Prince was unsure, and the writers, though they had no objection, were rooting for a designer they knew. Aronson had designed some recent flops, and while it was Garson Kanin's noisy book for *Do Re Mi* that sank that show about a small-time wheeler-dealer in the music business, Aronson's set—an enormous jukebox—was considered overwrought by as many critics as found it witty. Prince wanted to know that Aronson would not overdesign their delicate show.

It so happened that the Storm King Art Center, not far from Robbins's second home in the woods north of the city, was exhibiting a retrospective of Aronson's paintings, collages, and scenic designs that fall. Robbins took the team up to see it. There, they were struck by the versatility and imagination in Aronson's models and color renderings of diverse settings. For *J.B.* by Archibald MacLeish, who described the locale for his version of the Job legend as "a traveling circus which had been on the road of the world for a long time," Aronson suspended a huge circus tent. For the Marxist parable at the ARTEF (Arbeter Teatr Farband), *Jim Kooperkop*, in which a nasty hypercapitalist sends a mechanized golem to quell the masses, Aronson built a clamorous, expressionistic metropolis.

But it was his design for Maurice Schwartz's 1929 production of Sholem-Aleichem's *Stempenyu*—the play that first flopped with Boris Thomashefsky in 1907—that did most to win over the *Tevye* team. The main set piece was the exterior of a house that swiveled around to frame an indoor domestic space. Everyone loved the effect and wanted to use it (though

Robbins regretted that it depended on a turntable). Maurice Schwartz had helped launch the careers of both Robbins and Aronson. Now, the Yiddish actor who was best remembered for his poignant portrayal in *Tevye der milkhiker* had indirectly sealed the deal between them for a new *Tevye*.

Robbins filled out his design team with two artists with whom he'd done substantial work already. He was one of the lucky few who could count on Jean Rosenthal's clearing space for him in her crowded calendar. The small, soft-spoken woman with a mop of short brown hair and big, round blue eyes that gave her a perpetual expression of wonder dominated the emerging field of lighting design from the late 1950s through her early death from cancer in 1969. She worked on nearly every concert Martha Graham ever presented as well as on myriad ballet and Broadway productions. For Robbins, she had provided the diffuse whites against a three-walled cyclorama for his *Afternoon of a Faun* and the sharp urban shafts cutting through the city of *West Side Story*, among many other projects. She was a perfect match for him. Perhaps it was her temperament, perhaps her education at Manumit, an experimental socialist boarding school upstate whose aim was to help children "to become men and women who can think for themselves, stand on their own two feet and fight injustice and oppression." Rosenthal quipped that the most important thing she learned there "was how to walk into a chicken house without disturbing the chickens": excellent preparation for a life in the theater. She was unflappable.

Studying at the Neighborhood Playhouse School of Theater and then in the design program at the Yale Drama School, Rosenthal entered the profession just as the Depression began. At age twenty-one, she became the technician in charge of the Federal Theater Project's wagon theaters playing in the city's parks. As she worked her way through Orson Welles's Mercury Theater and onto Broadway, she was self-conscious about the closed male world she was entering. She "used courtesy" and "cultivated a careful impersonality," but mainly "my only real weapon . . . in the battle for acceptance was knowledge. I did know my stuff, and I knew that the technicians knew theirs." More than that, she had an artistic vision. "Dancers live in light as fish live in water," she'd say by way of explaining the role of the designer in creating their "aquarium." And with dramas, "the play—the playwright's play—comes first."

The industry's burly stage electricians, who towered over her, famously adored Rosenthal—and without any condescension. They respected her great technical skill. Aronson, who resented her at first, ended up refusing to do a show without her if he could help it. He saw in her a unique and inspiring combination of "technician and dreamer."

"Bring six to half, darling," she'd quietly command, requesting that a particular light dimmer be set at a certain intensity. "Thank you, honey." When others would start storming and stomping with frustration during the long technical rehearsals that are the lighting designer's special hell, she'd stay calm and cheerful. And while she loved the give and take with directors or choreographers over the look they wanted to achieve, she held her ground when she was asked to make a change that she considered wrong. She fought to serve the work, not to butt egos, so she had no trouble standing up to Robbins. And he was as besotted with her as the tech guys were. He lined her up on September 12.

For costumes, he tapped Patricia Zipprodt, who had been designing for Broadway since the late 1950s. Born in Evanston, Illinois, in 1925, Zipprodt came to New York after graduating from Wellesley, filled with Beat Generation dreams of a bohemian career as a painter. Waitressing and ushering to cover the rent on her fifth-floor walkup and the fees for some art classes and wearing "all black and my hair in a bun," she was "doing the 50s bit" to a T. Even the "floundering around and wondering what to do with myself" seemed to fit the ambition. Then she had a conversion experience. On the spot, at a performance of the New York City Ballet, she determined she'd devote herself to the stage: Karinska's bejeweled costumes for Balanchine's *La Valse* overwhelmed her with their sculptural use of tulle, the light glinting off beads, the shimmer of the overlapping hues. "I saw them as pure painting with fabric," she said later. "It wasn't like I was seeing yellow and green and red. It was very layered, color upon color, air and light filtering through it." The effect "swept me away." She talked her way into a scholarship at the Fashion Institute of Technology (which wasn't inclined even to admit a student who already had a BA—Zipprodt's was in sociology), and there she learned sewing and draping. She took a job making samples in the garment district.

Then one day she stopped in her tracks on Fifth Avenue to gape at the "architecture" of camel-hair coats by the couturier Charles James on display in the windows of Lord & Taylor. She all but hounded James into letting her work for him, barraging him with letters and phone calls until he let her start at the bottom, picking up pins. Watching James for a year, she learned "how to create the structure for anything."

Zipprodt wanted to study design formally but couldn't afford the programs she looked into at Yale and Carnegie Mellon. Borrowing just enough money to take time off from working to spend a year in the public library, she gave herself an intensive tutorial in the history of costume, from ancient Egyptian tunics to Balenciaga's tunic dresses, so that she could pass the exam for the United Scenic Union, the requisite ticket into the profession. With a union card in hand, Zipprodt took jobs as an assistant for various Broadway designers and passed up her first offer of a show of her own to assist the legendary Irene Sharaff (*The King and I, West Side Story*) on *Happy Hunting* (1956), a vacuous marriage comedy and comeback vehicle for Ethel Merman.

Like Jean Rosenthal, Zipprodt had heeded a theatrical calling and methodically set out to learn her craft, without taking any shortcuts or expecting special favors. Such absolute resolve and such a scrupulous work ethic not only enabled both designers to fulfill their talents at a time when women had to prove their excellence simply to be considered acceptable, even in the relatively open realm of the theater, but also made both of them fitting collaborators for the exhaustive taskmaster Jerry Robbins. It didn't take much to push them to give their all, and then some more—but he couldn't push them around.

Zipprodt was beginning to come into her own as a designer when Robbins saw her mix of urban duds, stark white masks, and flashy, power-flaunting court attire in *The Blacks*, Genet's "clown show" of racial construction and illusion, which opened Off-Broadway in 1961 (and ran for more than three years). He hired her to design *Oh Dad, Poor Dad* and her costumes hit just the right skew between reality and absurdity, featuring such elements as arm-length black gloves for a mother in a peculiar state of mourning and a white safari suit for her lover. Just as important, Zipprodt was not cowed by Robbins. Not too much, anyway. For *Oh Dad*, she had made a big black evening dress for Jo Van Fleet to wear, with red flowers sewed onto its partition—very expensive inset roses for which she and Robbins had "gone over eight thousand reds to figure out one that would be right." When Van Fleet put it on for dress rehearsal and suggested "it should have a little more blue in it," Robbins, to Zipprodt's astonishment, instantly acquiesced. Zipprodt confronted him on the way out of rehearsal and "shook him until his hat fell off. 'How could you do this! We picked this! We spent hours!'" Robbins sent her a big box of tulips the next day by way of apology. She knew exactly what she was getting into when she agreed to join *Tevye* that fall.

* * *

Except when it came to subject matter. The Pale was entirely foreign to the tall Episcopalian from the Midwest and, like a college thesis adviser, Robbins quickly sent her into a deep review of the literature. She was to read the Sholem-Aleichem stories, look at production shots of his works by the ARTEF, spend time in the archives at YIVO, and contact some experts who could show her historical photos—for starters. Robbins also expected her to watch films with him.

Aronson, too, was summoned to Robbins's home for screenings of rented 16mm movies. Despite Aronson's expertise on Chagall and Jewish modernism, the Kiev native knew as much about the shtetl as a New Yorker knows about Appalachia. (Rosenthal, too, knew close to nothing about Eastern European Jewish life at the turn of the twentieth century— her parents, Jews who had come from Romania in the 1880s, were both secular doctors. She, however, was excused from the research assignments, since lighting would not in itself represent the world of the play. And she was too busy with other productions.)

Along with Robbins and his assistant, Tommy Abbott, Aronson and Zipprodt gathered at Robbins's home on East Seventy-fourth Street to watch obscure films meant to give them historical and, more important, visual information about the Pale in 1905. One, *Ghetto Pillow*, features a camera panning across Impressionist watercolors of the shtetl Balagoris, "deep in the woodlands and marshes of White Russia," painted by Samuel Rothbort—scenes of townsfolk traipsing through deep mud in the rainy season, women bringing gifts of sugar to a new mother, men receiving back massages in the bathhouse, boys playing cards, women feather dusting before the Sabbath. The film takes its title from an image toward its end: women ticking and stuffing goose-feather pillows to hand down to daughters embarking on married life, as if Rothbort's paintings were a new way of passing along an heirloom. ("Ghetto" was a peculiar but common translation of "shtetl" in English-language discourse; usage slowly shifted toward "shtetl" in the post–World War II years. The film itself is a telling example: made in 1961, it was reissued in 1989 under a changed title, *Memories of the Shtetl*.)

Rothbort had traveled through the shtetls and cities of White Russia as a boy soprano with touring cantors in the 1890s and later as a yeshiva student. (He arrived in the United States in 1904.) In his "memory paintings," created in the 1930s and 1940s and exhibited beginning in the early 1960s, Rothbort depicts a diverse, if isolated, modernizing community: men both with long beards and with clean-shaven chins, families arranging marriage dowries and young men proposing, scenes of Yom Kippur lashes meted out in synagogue and scenes of American émigrés returning for visits. With dabs of brown, black, and bright color, masterfully highlighted with thick brushstrokes of white, the paintings showed the *Tevye* designers one wistful way of seeing a world in transition.

Ghetto Pillow's score of symphonic music, cantorial prayers, and a Yiddish lullaby, along with narration in the detached, bemused voice of an ethnographic filmstrip, also go a long way toward lodging the movie within the post-Holocaust project of fond remembrance advanced by so many of the books on Robbins's research syllabus. That's why Robbins especially wanted the designers to see the other reel he rented, *Skvoz Slezy* (*Through Tears*—or, as it's often called in English, *Laughter through Tears*), a pre-Holocaust feature film that might push them in a harsher direction. As a Soviet production made by the official All-Ukrainian Photo-Cinema Administration in 1928, the film joined a handful of works in Yiddish whose primary purpose was to depict the backwardness and impoverishment of Jewish life before the revolution gusted through, bringing, as the film needed only to imply, the light and abundance of emancipation in its wake. Based loosely on pieces of Sholem-Aleichem's "Motl, Peysi the Cantor's Son" and "The Enchanted Tailor" (the story that was tamed and folklorized in Arnold Perl's *World of Sholom Aleichem*), it served Robbins's agenda, too. "Don't romanticize the characters," he told Zipprodt. "We are not to see them through the misty nostalgia of a time past, but thru the every day hard struggle to keep alive and keep their beliefs."

The Soviet film was certainly less generous toward those beliefs—in one scene a toddler makes a doll out of a prayer shawl and phylacteries, in another the local rabbi is depicted as out of touch with reality and dismissive of the local folk. One of the several main characters, the tailor of the original short story, falls sick from the innkeeper's prank of changing a billy goat for his nanny goat because he remains fixed in a benighted religious mind-set and imagines that some demonic force must be at work. Little surprise that the film blames the innkeeper's petit bourgeois contempt for the poor tailor and his ilk and emphasizes class conflict more generally, contrasting czarist officers' lush life of tea service and gramophones with the shoeless, starving Jews they enjoy harassing.

Where Soviets depicted hapless, destitute folk stifled by czarist antisemitism, lack of access to land and livelihood, and their own superstitions, Robbins saw "the guts and toughness of the people" treading onward despite their hostile environment. The film helped him show the designers how the world of *Tevye* should be "a rural unsophisticated area . . . it is poverty stricken. Everyone just about ekes out an existence. The honey mists of time do not make life beautiful for them."

The opening shot reveals a line of crooked houses with crumbling wooden shingles on their sloping, sagging roofs—a look that Aronson would capture with a fanciful overlay on his painted backdrop of a ring of shtetl homes. He knew his set would have to "combine elements of fantasy and reality"—elements, that is, drawn from both Chagall and *Through Tears*; the Soviet film was deliberately shot to look like a documentary. Robbins hired a professional photographer to take high-quality stills from the film for the designers to scrutinize. Aronson took dozens of them to his studio. He adapted their details—cubbylike shelves built into homes for storing clay pots, lopsided wooden fences, rough-hewn plank benches, zigzagging laundry lines—to ground Anatevka in the gritty reality Robbins demanded, while a swirling moon or somersaulting houses painted along the proscenium lofted it toward the mythic.

The movie offered models for costumes, too: the women's printed blouses and mismatched skirts, the innkeeper's rolled-up shirtsleeves under a woven vest, the tailor's simpler vest buttoned up tight over his tallis *katan* with its stripes and fringes dangling from his waist and the tape measure draped over his shoulder. Archival research was not enough, however. Robbins also wanted his designers to see—and was eager to see himself—the way such clothing was worn and how customs were lived in the flesh. Lining up fieldwork in Orthodox and Hasidic communities was one of the first efforts he put in motion when he agreed to work on the show.

Since the early 1950s, Hasidic sects had been rebuilding their bases in Brooklyn after their centers had been decimated, and groups from Poland, Hungary, Ukraine, Belarus, and Russia were scattered throughout the borough. Non-Hasidic Orthodox communities had been in the area, of course, since the migrations of Sholem-Aleichem's day. While together they made up less than 10 percent of American Jewry, which was filling the ranks of the Reform denomination as it was suburbanizing, they were consciously claiming themselves as America's most "authentic" Jews. At its inception in the eighteenth century, Hasidism represented a radical challenge to rabbinic Judaism; now it asserted itself as the most conservative element in Jewish life, the keeper of the flame—whose imagistic torch *Fiddler* would help to carry. Over the following months, a woman named Dvora Lapson became the *Tevye* company's guide into this closed world otherwise beyond their reach.

On Robbins's instruction, Lapson took Zipprodt to observe people in Hasidic and Orthodox dress. They visited yeshivas, factories, and synagogues in Hasidic neighborhoods of Brooklyn and paid calls to residences of the elderly in Manhattan. Lapson showed the designer her collection of photographs and Eastern European Jewish art. The two watched throngs of Hasidim see off their rebbe as he departed for Israel on the *Queen Elizabeth* that November.

But most important, Lapson brokered Robbins's entrée into community celebrations so he could observe their dancing. A pioneer in Jewish dance, Lapson had studied at the Isadora Duncan School and with Doris Humphrey and Michel Fokine (whose work Robbins performed in his early years at the Ballet Theater) and had begun a career on the stage in 1929. Early on, she decided to dedicate herself to Jewish dance and set about studying, presenting, and teaching both religious and nascent Israeli folk forms. Before the war, she traveled to Poland, where she presented popular recitals and gained permission to study the dancing of the Bluzhever Rebbe and his followers (and she maintained a friendship with him when he emigrated to the United States after the war). In Israel in 1949, she forged connections with the Inbal Yemenite Dance Theater (which Robbins had championed after seeing their work on a trip to Israel in 1952) and with developers of national folk dance and became one of their greatest ambassadors in North America. Like Aronson and Robbins, she passed through the Yiddish Art Theater, with stints staging dances for Maurice Schwartz. Robbins caught up with her in the fall of 1963 through the Jewish Education Committee, where she was promoting the innovative idea of integrating dance into children's school curriculums. Then in her midfifties and still carrying herself with the long-necked elegance of a woman trained in ballet, Lapson enthusiastically took on the job as "dance research consultant" to the world-renowned choreographer. She promptly supplied copies of her booklets and articles— "Folk Dances for the Jewish Festival," "Dances of the Jewish People," and "Jewish Dances of the Year Round"—inscribed to him "with best wishes and with devotion."

Robbins's timing in locating her couldn't have been better. The autumn festival of Simkhes Toyre—commemorating the completion of the annual cycle of reading the Torah—was coming up in early October and Lapson knew a *shtiebl*, or small community prayer house, where this typically ecstatic holiday would be celebrated with special abandon. When the night arrived, Robbins headed across town to pick up his guide at her home on West Seventy-third Street. His assistant reminded him to bring yarmulkes. Bock, Harnick, and Stein joined them, and they set out for the wild wards of Hasidic Brooklyn—specifically to the blocks where a Hungarian sect resided in Borough Park. Dozens of men were crammed into the tiny *shtiebl*, singing, clapping, knocking back schnapps after schnapps after schnapps. Their dancing came as a revelation: the secular showmen expected gentle folk forms of all hold hands and mosey one way round a circle and then the other; instead, they felt the room shake from floor stomping, body twisting, athletic flinging, and writhing. This was a holiday less for noshing than for moshing. The next day, Robbins sent Lapson a big bouquet of flowers.

Weddings, as private affairs, would be harder to crash, but Lapson knew the way in: contact the kosher caterer. A little more than a week after Simkhes Toyre, she met with a Mr. Tennenbaum of Broadway Central Hotel Caterers and explained her interest in attending upcoming events under his supervision. What exactly she told him is lost to history, but she doesn't seem to have mentioned anything about a Broadway musical. When she followed up with a note, she emphasized her own dance scholarship and knowledge of Hebrew and made sure to drop some venerable names: "I am a friend of the Rabbinical families Halberstam, Unger and Spiro and have attended their family simchas [celebrations] in the past." Finally, she assured Mr. Tennenbaum that she was familiar with the rules of dress for these occasions and would, "of course, be escorted by a male member of my family because of the lateness of these events." That escort would be none other than Jerry Robbins.

They scored an invitation for the very next night for a wedding at the Riverside Plaza Hotel, at the time a venue with opulent ballrooms on Manhattan's Upper West Side. Once again, the dancing enthralled Robbins with its "virile ferocity," as he came to describe it. As the weeks and then the months of research and preproduction meetings wore on, Lapson also drew on her rabbinical connections and began calling Robbins regularly to tell him when weddings would be open to him and which ones would feature a lot of dancing, which would allow men and women to dance together, which would be particularly huge, involving the marriage of children of prominent families, which would have balconies from which people could observe, and when holidays would prevent weddings for a while.

When Robbins planned to attend, as he often did through the fall of 1963, she'd call with reminders: it will begin promptly at 9:00, so pick her up at 8:15; you can bring two people this time; don't forget change for the beggars. For a fee of $500—plus reimbursement of $37.50 that covered cab fare, tips at weddings, and two dozen yarmulkes—Lapson became Robbins's regular date for the devout. Time and again, they saw the bride and groom lifted up in chairs by the cavorting guests and, often, a flimsy cord hastily stretched between stanchions instantly acquire the force of a high concrete barrier, separating women from men.

But every time, it was the men's dancing that amazed Robbins. "My great wonder, watching the dancers, was how people weren't hurt & bruised as bodies were flung centrifugally from out-of-control circles," Robbins later marveled in handwritten notes for a letter. "Hats flew off, chairs overturned—but the rough dominant force that was released by all this kinetic energy was overpowering—for in spite of each man improvising as he felt—in spite of primitive variations of the basic rhythm—two things held them together. Their constant hand grip— when if broken by the external momentum of the dance, or by another body flinging itself into the dancer, was always regained, reunited. And secondly, the deep & powerful assertion—a strength I never knew—a dedication to a rite, claiming survival & joy, procreation & celebration. An explosive foot thrust to the floor that shook the room that said Yes I am here, & I celebrate the continuity of my existence."

It was as if the shame Robbins had long felt about "weak" Jewish (and gay) masculinity was pulverized by the whirling frenzy of these homosocial dances, then kicked up and blown away like old, dry dust. This dancing provided the proof positive, and further inspiration, for his demand that the show express Jewish robustness and resilience—the strength that not only he "never knew" but that had been obscured in popular representations for decades.

He was intrigued, too, by a man with a rusty beard who seemed to be a regular at these weddings, entertaining the guests by weaving among them with a particular trick. Lapson had seen such antics during her research in Europe and mentioned them in an article for the *International Folk Music Journal*: he was performing a *flashen-tantz*, a caper in which "the man balances a bottle on his head as he dances, perhaps to prove himself sober." Robbins referred to him as "Mr. Redbeard," but it didn't take long for Lapson to identify him and track him down. And more: this Rabbi Ackerman from Borough Park would be glad to meet with Robbins.

Yet Robbins said little about how he would use dance in the show. All fall, he was meeting daily with, or at least taking calls from, the writers or designers or producer, or all of the above, to discuss the script, the music, the costumes and set, the budget. The only clue that he expected dance to play a significant role in the show was his insistence, when he agreed to take the job, on an atypically long rehearsal period of eight weeks before hitting the road for tryouts—four for his work as choreographer, four for the staging of the book.

But rehearsals were still more than half a year away, and in those months when his "intense research on the Sholem Aleichem musical" was "taking most of my time," as he told a friend (by way of apologizing for not getting to the scripts she'd sent him), he was putting the authors through their paces. He tasked them, too, with conducting deeper, more personal research. Stein felt his own family background exempted him from such homework, but he did the reading. (An exchange Stein adapted for Perchik and Tevye—"Money is the world's curse." "May God smite me with it!"—comes not out of the Butwin translation of the stories but from Maurice Samuel.)

Beyond the booklist, Harnick dove in. He started questioning his own relatives about a background he had never heard about before. "You want some Jewish customs for your new play?" Harnick's mother wrote in reply. "Here goes." His aunt Choni also sent letters detailing what she recalled from her childhood. Between them, they told how their mother (Harnick's grandmother) spent two hours chopping gefilte fish in a wooden bowl for Shabbos, how she covered her head and circled her hands to light the Friday night candles, how a "Shabbos goy"—a Gentile neighbor—came each Saturday morning to light a fire in the kitchen and parlor stoves so the family would be spared breaking the religious commandment to refrain from all work. The earthenware pot with a philodendron climbing out of it on Harnick's mother's patio in 1963 had once been used by his grandmother every week for making the long-simmering Sabbath stew called cholent, which cooked overnight in an oven at the corner bakery; the children fetched it home at lunchtime on Saturdays, when their grandfather returned from shul. Through these revelations and the show's development, Harnick began to "feel more Jewish." As the work went on, "as a writer and as a person, my life came together," he said. "I knew who I was and who Sholem-Aleichem's people were, and where our lives touched."

For his part, Robbins interviewed his father, learning for the first time about the ruse and bribe that enabled Harry to steal out of Rozhanka at age fifteen on an "underground railway," as Robbins likened it. Harry traveled by foot with a deserting Russian soldier, all the way to Amsterdam. Robbins was moved by the rare opportunity to "feel my father's feelings so strongly." He asked Harry, too, to explain how and why he had discarded Orthodox practice. Answer: his recognizing how his relatives and other Jews engaged in "juggling and bending" the religious laws to accommodate the demands of American business and culture. Robbins also pondered his maternal grandmother, who had come to live with his family when Robbins was an adolescent, "a wonderful tiny, amazingly wrinkled little woman" who "never lit a stove or turned on electricity after sundown on Sabbath eve; kept separate dishes for dairy & meat foods; attended shul religiously & was always reading the Talmud." He could still picture how beautiful she looked on Sabbath evenings in her dark velvet dress with a tiny handmade lace collar, lighting the candles and reciting the blessing. As a child, he was "both awed and scornful of her ritual gestures." He "'despised' her Jewish backward ways," which he could not ask her about, even if he'd wanted to: she spoke only Yiddish. Some thirty years later, he was finally allowing himself to make sense of this heritage that had been "laid open for me and more gently than i ever realized, i absorbed it, drank it in and let it sink to a place deep within me, quietly building up a rich & glorious storehouse of cherished sacred and touching knowledge—all stored away—deep & away." Now he was not only opening the vault but spelunking into its many caverns, hauling up one treasure after another to enliven the world of the play, in order to make it specific. And true. The more he delved, the more he pressed the writers to toughen and tighten the script.

* * *

The version Robbins first read had come a long way since the initial draft, with its stagnating action and some sections sticky as damp sugar. In response to Bock's and Harnick's notes, Stein had restored the ironic confusion in the meeting between Tevye and Lazar with a light, humorous hand and, in place of a series of escalating insults between them that had ended the scene before, the men now concluded with a happy toast "To life!"—and broke into song. In this draft, Perchik was charmingly introducing the subject of marriage to Hodel as a "political question," and in general humor was emerging more out of character than from set-up jokes. A scene in which Tevye goes to the local priest to demand his daughter Chava be returned to the family ends with him reeling away, rebuffed. Following Sholem-Aleichem, Tevye wonders in a troubled monologue, here set to music, why God bothered to make different kinds of people: "Forgive me for asking / But why did you choose / to make of your children / both Gentiles and Jews? / These questions, almighty God / I hope you'll excuse / But I had a daughter / Too precious to lose." The action finds a spot of uplift when Motel acquires a sewing machine at last and sings it a love song, but then the constable delivers a new, irrevocable blow: eviction. In acquiescing to the decree, Tevye stands up to its minion (and plays to the house): "We are not strong, we have no power in the government. But we have a special talent to survive. We are a peaceful people, we do not win great wars, but we survive—we flourish and survive!" Then Chava joins the family, pledging to emigrate with them no matter what her husband decides. (He shows up and, after a tense silence, Tevye tells him to help with the packing.)

In addition to "Sabbath Prayer," "Sunrise, Sunset," and "Tevye's Dream," Bock and Harnick had already written a touching musical plea from Tzeitel begging not to have to marry the butcher, "Poppa Help Me," and a "Letter to America" in which the community, led by Tevye, responds to mail from relatives overseas by singing of their love of Anatevka, asking, "Who needs America? / Who needs a new community / changing our ways to I don't know what? / Maybe there's opportunity / Maybe I'd like America, but . . ."

All of these developments gave the show more dramatic tension and shape. Stein was fattening the characters and the songs were advancing action or thickening context.

Robbins had complaints from start to finish. To begin with, something about the opening number, "We've Never Missed a Sabbath Yet," rankled him. Famously inarticulate about what he thought was needed when it came to text or acting, Robbins could only repeat that it wasn't working. He couldn't explain why; he just didn't like this song that uses the rush of Gilbert and Sullivan–style patter (but in a minor scale) to convey the family hurrying to complete all their preparations before sundown. The whole day leading up to the Sabbath was "a race with time," *Life is with People* informed, and the song begins at a gallop. First Shprintze, then Bielke, begs Golde to let them go play. They've rubbed, they've scrubbed, they say, but their repeated pleas of "Momma, Momma" are rebuffed by Golde's insistence that they stay inside and do their pre-Sabbath chores.

Now the older daughters join in, following Golde's instructions to set the table, even as they urge her to calm down. But there's no calming their mother: "So who can relax while there's so much to be done, keeping one eye on the soup and the other on the sun?" The daughters try to

Jerome Robbins and Joseph Stein: book changes.

reassure her—there's plenty of time, no need to be nervous—and keep reminding her in the refrain, to little avail, "We've never missed a Sabbath yet."

On they sing, Golde frantic as she lists all that remains to be done: preparing noodles, plucking chickens, chopping liver, making challah, washing woodwork and dishes, peeling potatoes, dressing the smaller children—many of the tasks itemized in *Life is with People* that govern a woman's life each Friday as she "darts from broom to oven and back again peering, stirring, prodding, dusting, giving commands to her daughters. . . ." The song captures the frenzy—and the reward.

Everything slows down and in a simple, almost liturgical passage that leans longingly on an augmented fifth, Golde and the girls reflect on the peace that enters their home and their hearts as the sun comes down: "For Sabbath, Queen Sabbath / Sabbath Queen and Bride / All work and all worry / Must be set aside."

That beautiful respite is broken and the staccato enumeration of chores takes off again, as the family returns to the sweeping and plucking and scouring and cooking. What was Robbins's problem? "We've Never Missed a Sabbath Yet" condenses event into song and presents the weekly ritual that binds and sustains the community. It appears to accomplish what a standard opening number needs to do: it tells the audience where they are, who lives there, what matters to them. Still, Robbins wanted the writers to change it. He didn't explain that the song merely establishes a situation without setting an action in motion. He just said the show needed to start someplace else. But he couldn't say where.

Instead, in meeting after meeting at his home, Robbins kept asking the authors a question that struck them as unnecessary for having such an obvious answer: "What is this show about?" He'd lean back in his chair and await their answer, but the authors were dumbfounded. Robbins knew full well that the show traced the trials of Tevye, a simple Jew trying to scratch out a living in the Russian Pale of Settlement at the turn of the century. They had nothing new to tell him. Still, Robbins kept hammering the question like a district attorney and, every time, one of the creators gave the same answer: "The show is about a dairyman and his marriageable daughters."

One late autumn day, Robbins snapped, "No, no, no, that's no good." He let out a gust of exasperation. "That's not it. That's not enough. That's 'The Previous Adventures of the Goldbergs.'"

Nobody said anything, but the team understood what Robbins meant about "the Goldbergs." And they agreed with him. None of them wanted to create a show like the long-running sitcom that had carried a warm if meddlesome Jewish mother into American hearts for nearly three decades. From 1929 to 1950 on radio and then for another half-dozen years in various forms on TV, *The Goldbergs* presented a lovable Jewish family of Yiddish-lilting immigrant parents and slang-slinging American-born children. Gertrude Berg wrote each episode and also starred as Molly Goldberg, the dizzy dame but ultimately can-do matriarch who found the way out of—and a comforting lesson in—any predicament. *Life* magazine likened the program to "a pair of comfortable old shoes which never seem to wear out."

Bock, Harnick, and Stein had no interest in cobbling their show on the same last. A prequel to *The Goldbergs* meant not only something too soft but something pleading too hard for acceptance. They were past all that, they knew. *The Goldbergs* had been off the air for more than five years.

No one remembers who uttered the words that finally provided the answer to Robbins's persistent question, but they seemed to rearrange the molecules in the room. "It's about the dissolution of a way of life." Robbins leaned forward. "That's it! That's it," he said. He wasn't the sort to cry out or slap the table—more a "quiet, growling presence," as Hal Prince describes him—but his enthusiasm was unmistakable. "It's tradition," he asserted. "Yes, that's it. We have to establish the traditions at the beginning and then the audience will see how they're breaking down. That's the show."

Instantly, Robbins saw how this theme could give him a pliant and powerful dramatic tension around which to stage the action. The forces breaking down the traditions would press from both the inside and the outside. In the first instance—modern children challenging their parents' staid ways—the generational conflict would make the story universal. At the same time the violent antisemitism of czarist Russia would exert pressure externally. The persecution endured by Tevye and the people of Anatevka was on account of their Jewishness, expressed by the very traditions that were in danger of unraveling. That would make the show simultaneously universal and a very particular story. Through his own personal pursuit for a reconnection to his heritage, Robbins intuited that the story could also be embraced by Jewish audiences in search of a usable past, as their own ties to tradition attenuated.

Right away, an image took shape in his mind. Robbins saw exactly how to open and close the show. "I'll begin it with one of the oldest folk forms: the circle," he told the authors. "I'll bring the cast out and make a folk circle. And at the end, we'll bring the cast out and the circle will disintegrate." (Aronson's use of two turntables, one set within another, would share this idea.) Robbins sent Bock, Harnick, and Stein away with instructions to make every scene relate to the theme of traditions breaking down. Then he turned more attention to the question of who, exactly, would be in that circle. "Shtetl means my community, more than my location," he wrote in his research notes, echoing *Life Is with People*. "The people made the shtetl, not the place." In casting, he had to follow that principle: the actors, working as an ensemble, would have to make a community. Together, they would have to manifest a tenable oxymoron: a gritty, gutsy Broadway shtetl.

CHAPTER 4

IT TAKES A SHTETL

IN SEPTEMBER 1963, ROBBINS HAD BEGUN ONE OF BROADWAY'S longest, most arduous casting processes ever—not a surprise, given that he'd taken an unprecedented six months to put together the company for *West Side Story*. Back then, in 1957, his effort to cast previously unknown, young, credibly hoodlum performers came as an innovation: he was creating a couple of gangs, not an assembly of chorus boys. More unusual, he expected each of them to sing, dance, and act—and to do all three well with a score and set of movements that were far from easy. Until then, typically only the stars of a musical had to deliver song and character brilliantly and at least passably make it through some choreography; a chorus carried the big songs while a troupe of hoofers took care of the dancing. Robbins overthrew that formula forever.

Besides, he was notoriously indecisive. For major roles, he'd call actors again and again, settle on one, then change his mind, then change it once more. He was looking not only for the qualities actors could bring to a role but also for how they worked in relation to others with whom they might play scenes. For *Oh Dad, Poor Dad*, Austin Pendleton auditioned seven times for Robbins, as did Barbara Harris. Neither was offered the job until the day they read together.

Pendleton was the only actor Robbins knew from the start that he wanted for *Tevye*. He had enjoyed working with him on the Kopit play and thought the young midwesterner's winning earnestness would work well for the new project. Pendleton was the first actor he invited to audition. Twenty-three, and just a couple of years out of Yale, Pendleton read for the role of the revolutionary, Perchik. He loved the part and didn't complain that, over a period of several weeks beginning in September, Robbins asked him to come in a second, third, fourth, and even fifth time to read the same scenes. Every hungry young actor in New York, it seemed to him, would do whatever it took to land a part in a musical directed by Robbins. He floated away from every audition, no matter how arduous it had been, flattered and thrilled that Robbins believed in his acting enough to consider him for a part so different from the shy, stuttering boy he had played in *Oh Dad*. One day, Robbins handed Pendleton some unfamiliar pages. "Since you're here, would you mind reading this other part?" Robbins asked. The character was called Motel and, as Pendleton recalls, he wasn't yet well defined or as interesting as Perchik: "He was a sincere young guy who wants to marry the oldest daughter and who's poor and honest and all that, but there was nothing really vivid about it." Robbins dismissed Pendleton with a standard issue "very nice, thank you," and Pendleton went on his way, preoccupied with how he'd bring Perchik's fervor to life onstage.

His heart could hardly sink, though, when he learned through the grapevine in October that Robbins would offer him the role of Motel. "I was going to be in a Jerry Robbins musical," he told himself. "What was there to be disappointed about?" Some days later, when he ran into Robbins in the street, the director grabbed him by the shoulders and exclaimed, "Since we cast you, we're reconceiving the role of Motel. He's this utter loser, but just absolutely tenacious—it's you!" Once rehearsals were under way, months later, Pendleton would wither under Robbins's even sharper stabs at his vulnerabilities. In the meantime, though, he eagerly awaited the work's start.

On and off, from October to January, Robbins saw hundreds of actors for the other forty-five roles, often spending six-hour days with hopefuls scheduled at ten-minute intervals. They poured in on the recommendation of casting agents and in response to ads posted in trade papers that offered standard brief character descriptions most notable for signaling to actors that some roles would require them to "look"—or maybe even "act"—Jewish. Among them:

Golde: wife of Tevye, middle-aged, stern, sarcastic but with wit. A devoted mother with good humor and sentiment that embarrasses her. Sings.

Lazar: Jewish, middle-aged butcher, rather crude and loud but with a likable streak. Sings.

Yente: Jewish, middle-aged matchmaker, talks steadily, a real "yente."

Fyedka: not Jewish, young, sensitive but determined. Sings.

Bock, Harnick, Stein, and Prince frequently joined Robbins behind the table, a thick stack of résumés, 8 × 10 glossies, and schedules spread out before them. On some days as many as twenty-five auditions were crammed into two hours, and dozens of actors returned several times over the months. Exacting as Robbins was, he encouraged and supported the performers who interested him: he might attend a voice lesson with someone whose singing was unsure (as he did with Joanna Merlin, who was called back seven times and was eventually cast as the oldest daughter, Tzeitel) or send someone for special movement classes (as he did with Robert Berdeen, originally cast as Fyedka, so that he could learn Russian character dance) or dispatch his assistant, Tommy Abbott, to coach a promising actor privately (as he did for a Perchik contender, Stuart Damon). In part, the outside help was Robbins's way of overcoming objections of his collaborators: "Excellent actress," Harnick had scrawled on the audition schedule next to Merlin's name at her first tryout. "Can't sing." But Robbins sent her to work with Bock and Harnick, too, and they got to know her range and ability to sell a song; they knew she could combine Tzeitel's fortitude with real warmth and soon agreed that the seasoned actor (who had played all of the girls in a scaled-down touring company of Perl's *Tevya and His Daughters* a few years earlier) was the strongest contender for the role.

Robbins was planning a ballet for the second act that would express Chava's pull toward Fyedka and the stretching, then breaking, of her tie to her family. So he made dancing skill the highest priority for that part. He chose Tanya Everett, a seventeen-year-old redhead from North Carolina with no significant professional experience and less knowledge about Jews—she was a Baptist who had gone to a Catholic boarding school. She did have solid dancing and plenty of charm. But compared with her, Merlin sang like Callas. The team knew they needed a sturdy singer for the third sister to help carry the other two. Besides, settling for anything less than a great soprano for Hodel, the fiery second daughter who would go off to join her arrested paramour in Siberia, was impossible. She would sing "Far from the Home I Love" in a tightly focused emotional moment in act 2. Robbins liked Anne Fielding, who had performed in the chorus in Stein's *Juno* and taken over for a lead role in *Once Upon a Mattress*. (She had also played Chava in Perl's *Tevya* at the Carnegie.) She possessed a robust voice and intense stage presence. "Marvelous. Sings well," Harnick noted on her audition sheet.

Robbins put all three women onstage together at a 12:30 audition on Friday, November 22, and was pleased enough with the combination to present the trio to Bock, Harnick, Stein, and Prince early that afternoon. The creative team watched as the women learned a short dance routine and the men appreciated the easy rapport among the actors: not only was each a capable, appealing performer, the connection among them meant that they could pass as sisters. The group parted happily for the scheduled lunch break, planning to return at 3:00 to look at some potential Yentes and Perchiks, beginning with Bea Arthur. On the way out, they saw actors huddled around a radio, crying: President Kennedy had been shot. Auditions were called off for the rest of the day and Broadway went dark that night—the first time it had ever done so for any reason other than a strike.

In ways that couldn't yet be assessed, Kennedy's presidency had been emotionally in synch with the *Tevye* project. His administration has long been associated with the 1960 Lerner and Loewe musical, *Camelot*; a week after the assassination, Jackie Kennedy, with some embarrassment, told *Life*'s Theodore H. White that she couldn't get a passage from that show's title song out of her head, a track her late husband had loved to listen to:

> *Don't let it be forgot*
> *That once there was a spot,*
> *For one brief, shining moment*
> *That was known as Camelot.*

The sentimental appeal can't be denied. Camelot's king, who seeks a peaceful reign and yearns to know "what the simple folk do" (as one song wonders) and has a beautiful wife (who needs to be "handled," as he frets in another song), provided a facile pop culture overlay for taking stock of the end of the slain president's presumed era of "happily ever-aftering, here in Camelot." But *Fiddler* ended up having more affinity for the values and domestic policy ideals of the Kennedy White House than the 1960 romantic fable could. Anatevka may not have been as "shining" or as "brief" as Camelot, as the title song describes it, but if "shtetl" had rhymed with "spot," an adjusted lyric might serve as the true background song for Kennedy's convictions about his country. "This was the secret of America: a nation of people with the fresh memory of old traditions who dared to explore new frontiers, people eager to build lives for themselves in a spacious society that did not restrict their freedom of choice and action," Kennedy wrote in his 1958 essay "A Nation of Immigrants."

Only a few months before the assassination, he made the first nostalgic trip of an American president to his ancestral homeland. During his four-day state visit to Ireland, Kennedy told the people of Limerick, "This is not the land of my birth, but it is the land for which I hold the greatest affection." Kennedy's trip had been calculated to reopen American hearts—and its doors. And the show in auditions the autumn of his assassination would pull with gentle persuasion on those same heartstrings. Both nudged along the shift in the locus of America's origin story, as the scholar Matthew Frye Jacobson has put it, from Plymouth Rock to Ellis Island. Kennedy pressed for reform of American immigration law, which from the mid-1920s had cut off the further entry of Eastern European Jews, among others: for four decades, no more tempest-tossed Tevyes had been welcome on these teeming shores. (In 1965, the Johnson administration would abolish the country's national origin quota system.) As a defender of immigrants, Kennedy was a friend to the Jews. In March 1963, the Anti-Defamation League gave its annual America's Democratic Legacy Award to the president to honor his "enrichment of our democratic heritage." Instinctively, *Fiddler* paid homage to Kennedy's principles. The show—created by the sons and grandsons of immigrants, now fully assimilated and prospering—at once celebrates the world left behind and the leaving of it for freedom and opportunity in America; it would give audiences an emotional correlative for their murdered president's vision.

But at the time of the assassination, that theatrical solace—and the public's readiness for it—lay nearly a year away. When *Tevye* auditions resumed on November 26, the national mood remained glum: postwar optimism seemed to have crashed in an instant. Simmering tensions—over civil rights, the war in Vietnam, the emerging counterculture—would rise through the rubble, and also be reflected in *Fiddler*'s plot. The show—every show—would go on. (Jackie Kennedy came to see *Fiddler* one year after the assassination and enjoyed it immensely.)

Robbins kept searching for a special "ordinary" quality for his cast—he didn't want actors who looked too polished or flashy to be convincing as poor Jews. Yet he and his collaborators also didn't want actors who, in their view, overplayed some put-on idea of Jewishness. They rejected stereotypical portrayals that showed vestiges of the American vaudeville "stage Jew" with Old Country accents, flailing hands, or singsong intonations; they quickly eliminated anyone who seemed to have arrived at the audition hall directly from Yiddish Second Avenue or the borscht belt (though they did make an arrangement with the Hebrew Actors' Union—the sixty-five-year-old association of Yiddish performers—to audition some of their members). Robbins's notes on the show repeatedly sound his contempt for representations of Jews as "lovable schnooks," and his collaborators shared his concerns. Joe Stein asserted that, especially for Yente, since "the part is written very Jewish . . . I think we ought to cast away from the obvious Jewish." While the team's jottings on audition sheets next to names taken out of consideration reveal the usual negative comments that can grow increasingly snide as long days of casting calls drag on—"DULL, DULL, DULL," "rotten actor," "his sullen charm wears thin," "sang like a parody of a Methodist spinster choir lady"—more notably, they dismiss those who have "too much of an accent," "Reform rabbi delivery," "the Jewish quality I find unappealing." The Jewishness they sought had to well up from character, not sit upon an actor like external trappings—they looked for acting from the inside out, as common theatrical parlance had it, not from the outside in.

Though less common to the presentational form of the musical than to realistic dramas, this approach reigned in general in the American theater of the period. It was no mere coincidence that "The Method" in its local incarnations had been developed and taught by children of Jewish immigrants (born in the States or brought as youngsters); it rejected "exteriority" and coached actors to dig for psychological reality. Robbins joined its orbit, working backstage in his youth at the Group Theater, studying at the Actors Studio, and taking scene analysis classes with Stella Adler, the youngest daughter of Yiddish theater royalty, Jacob P.

Adler and Sara Adler (and sister of the actor Luther Adler, who later played Tevye in *Fiddler*). Stella Adler had broken with the other pioneer, her Group Theater colleague Lee Strasberg, by emphasizing research and ingenuity over "sense memory" of personal emotional experiences in building character. "Don't use your conscious past," she counseled actors. "Use your creative imagination to create a past that belongs to your character." Robbins's undated notes from the Adler sessions he attended emphasize her teachings along these lines, especially on the difference between "organic action" and "stated action." He was looking for actors who did not "play Jewish" but who played their characters. His cast members didn't have to be Jewish—and, it turned out, most of the principals Robbins hired were not—they had to be Lazar or Perchik or Golde or Rivka the Villager, who were Jews. This was a pillar of faith for Robbins, as an artist and as a man. He knew that if he cast well he would not have to waste time in rehearsals explaining the distinction.

Easier said than done. Though Robbins settled quickly on Pendleton as Motel, selecting the suitors for the other two sisters proved more difficult than if he'd actually been arranging the actors' marriages. Apart from possessing a strong baritone, the Perchik had to combine the blustery certitude of a militant with the endearing timidity of a romantic neophyte. And, of course, fit well into the growing ensemble and, especially, spark off some chemistry with the Hodel. Over several months, the team saw scores of eager young men, among them Joseph Chaikin (on the verge of founding the influential Off-Off-Broadway company the Open Theater), Elliott Gould, Ron Liebman, Tommy Rall (a Broadway regular who'd played a featured romantic in *Milk and Honey* and a leading dance role in *Juno*), Ron Rifkin, George Segal, Sam Waterston, Gene Wilder: every top-grade white actor then in his twenties, it seemed, and plenty more who weren't so top-grade. None satisfied Robbins. The new year dawned with Perchik still not chosen—and, worse, with the search for Hodel reopened: Anne Fielding had decided two months on the road was too long to be away from her husband and she bowed out before signing a contract. And while the team liked Joanna Merlin, they continued to audition other potential Tzeitels.

At least Robbins had nailed down his Tevye before the end of 1963. The choice had been obvious, even inevitable. But that didn't make the process simple.

Accounts differ on when, exactly, Zero Mostel was offered the role. And they differ more when it comes to why he took his time accepting it, requiring the team to keep auditioning other actors just in case. Brilliant, riveting, deeply familiar with *Yiddishkayt*, Mostel was the first candidate anyone thought of, as Stein remembered the deliberations, but because Robbins "insisted on examining every possibility before making up his mind, we auditioned some awfully good actors who would have been fine."

Robbins was decisive about one thing from the start, however: "fine" would not suffice. Whoever played Tevye first would have to combine the realness Robbins insisted on in general with the magnetism and virtuosity— the ineffable "it"—that make a Broadway star. The actor would have to live in two places simultaneously onstage: inside the world of the play as a convincing Pale of Settlement patriarch and on the outside of the dramatic action as a crowd-pleasing performer of magnificent feats. And he would have to be equally and constantly lovable in both realms: intimate with the audience and beyond their ken, winning their empathy and their awe. The conventions of the musical require a measure of duality from all the cast members, who shift in and out of representational acting and presentational song, but star power is charged by an extraordinary alternating current that allows a lead actor to run both modes at full wattage at all times. In the late 1950s and early 1960s, especially, the most popular musicals pointed with glitzy self-consciousness at this very quality, featuring flashy numbers that named and framed the star ("Hello, Dolly," "Mame") or that gave her (usually her in these years) a big blowout song ("Rose's Turn" in *Gypsy*, "Don't Rain on My Parade" in *Funny Girl*). Within the context of a musical drama with an ensemble cast, and without the help of histrionic extravagances (whether campy or not)—a fanfare entrance; finery, feathers, and a bright follow spot; a thunderous eleven o'clock number—*Tevye*'s star would have to exude theatrical ebullience without breaking the illusion that he was a poor, simple dairyman. There would have to be some madness in his Method. And he would have to balance gracefully.

Bock and Harnick championed Howard Da Silva, the strapping baritone who had originated the role of Jud Fry in *Oklahoma!* and delighted the songwriting team as the conniving Republican machine boss Ben Marino in *Fiorello!*; Bock and Harnick had also seen him in *The World of Sholom Aleichem* and knew he had an attachment to the material. Harnick was drawn by Da Silva's "natural voice, sense of nobility, and charisma" but couldn't persuade Robbins. According to oft-told lore, Robbins said he required an actor "larger than life," a quality he thought Da Silva lacked. In any event, the actor never auditioned for Robbins; perhaps the longtime activist harbored his own doubts about inhabiting the same rehearsal room as a friendly witness to HUAC. And if Robbins, meanwhile, did not want his show to be thought of as in any way derived from Perl's work, that would have disqualified Da Silva from the start.

Da Silva was just one in a first-class lineup of seasoned actors considered for Tevye that fall; others included Danny Kaye, Joseph Schildkraut, Rod Steiger, Eli Wallach. The roster may simply have been a function of the run-around Zero Mostel was giving the creators. Accounts of the initial approach to Mostel vary—not least because the antic actor infamously told interviewers different stories about his life, sometimes simply embellishing the facts, sometimes clearly enjoying how far he could take journalists on a ride. The actor's family recounts that the first overture came in late 1962, when Stein visited Mostel backstage at *A Funny Thing Happened on the Way to the Forum*, bearing an early draft of *Tevye*, and that the star fumed at home about what "*shund*" the script was, vowing that he would never deign to appear in such a sentimental bastardization of the great Sholem-Aleichem's stories, which, Mostel said, his parents read to him in Yiddish when he was a boy, making him "roar with laughter." Stein maintained that he made no such trip to Mostel's dressing room.

In any event, in September 1963, Fred Coe reached out to Mostel, after Robbins was hired. But Mostel put off answering for weeks on end, meanwhile pursuing a TV pilot for a sitcom involving his own family (it never panned out), and the team at least needed some backups. They kept auditioning esteemed actors and spoke with several more, as they waited in vain through September for a response from Mostel. Robbins was growing frustrated. "Would somebody tell Zero that this show will be good for him?" Robbins huffed.

During the first week of October, Robbins and the authors played the score for Mostel at his apartment on West Eighty-sixth Street. Bock and Harnick sat at the piano and sang through a number of songs. Bock, for one, left in high spirits: Mostel loved their tunes. The actor promised that they'd hear from him by the sixteenth. When no word had come by 4:30 on that date, Stein called Robbins to ask: "What's happening with Zero?"

Mostel had made money on *Forum* and wasn't desperate for work the

way he'd been less than a decade earlier, while the blacklist still suffo-
cated him. He could afford to devote himself to his painting—he called
acting the side work that supported the art that mattered more to him—
but Tevye tugged at him irresistibly. According to family lore, it was
Mostel's wife, Kate, who insisted he take the role. A retired dancer, she
had a good nose for a theatrical hit, and even in the audition draft of the
script she could smell a winner (and thus she could see the mink coat she
coveted, as one of their sons recalls, adding that the couple fought bitterly for weeks over whether Mostel should accept the part). Friends,
though, remember Mostel's excitement over the opportunity and his
sense of entitlement to the role. He considered Tevye not only "the greatest Yiddish character ever created" but by all rights his. No one else possessed the background, the affinity, the chops he could bring. Hal
Prince—who had pushed for Mostel in *Forum* as producer of that show—
agreed, emphatically enough to offer a then whoppingly generous salary
of $4,000 a week against 10 percent of the weekly box office gross (a
higher base pay than the $100,000 one-year contract Mickey Mantle was
about to sign with the Yankees).

On the twenty-fifth, Robbins wrote Mostel that he so wanted him for
the show that he'd postpone it until the fall of 1964 to accommodate
Mostel's schedule were he not "stuck with" a signed commitment "to go
this spring." He fairly begged in signing off: "Please don't make me do
this without you. Please." Maybe Mostel had been waiting to hear Robbins grovel. In any event, it worked. (And, it turned out later, the schedule was postponed to accommodate Robbins.)

On November 1, Prince started cranking out letters to the likes of Red
Buttons and Tom Bosley (who'd starred as Fiorello): "I'm sorry that it
hasn't worked out with Tevye," Prince wrote, politely reassuring them
that it was "a very difficult decision" or that "[I] hope and expect that one
of these days we'll do a show together."

Mostel and Robbins had worked together briefly before and did not
like each other. So Robbins's eagerness to cast Mostel and Mostel's zeal
for the part spoke to both men's prevailing sense of artistry—they recognized and respected each other's talents. Even more, the draw of the
Sholem-Aleichem material trumped their mutual distrust and distaste.
For both of them, albeit in vastly different ways, this project was personal.

Their first professional encounter (after crossing paths a number of times over the years) had been in 1962. Prince had called Robbins in to help out with *A Funny Thing Happened on the Way to the Forum* when it was in trouble on the road. He reached Robbins in Los Angeles, where he was receiving best picture and codirecting Oscars for the film version of *West Side Story*, and implored him to catch the next possible flight to Washington, where the show was losing half its audience at every intermission. Prince felt that only Robbins could figure out how to rescue it. He also knew that his leading cast members might object to his number one fix-it man. Not only might Zero Mostel resent the "rat fink"; his costar, Jack Gilford, might hold a particular animus: Robbins had named Gilford's wife, Madeline Lee. Gilford flared at the news and threatened to quit, but when he phoned home Lee counseled him to keep his job: "Don't blacklist yourself," she told him. Mostel famously marched up the high road: "We of the left don't blacklist," he told Prince. He agreed to work with Robbins. But he added, "You didn't say I had to have lunch with him."

Mostel and Robbins agreed on one cultural and political point: "Naming names," Mostel had proclaimed, "is not Jewish." And that, at least as Robbins explained the deed to himself, was why he did it.

But it wasn't just the political bad blood that caused Mostel to call Robbins "that sonofabitch" in place of his given name. Two more opposite temperaments are tough to imagine. Mostel was an unstoppable force, Robbins an immovable object. Mostel was confident and free as an actor could be, Robbins a sack of insecurity as a director. Their very bodies exemplified the contrast between them: an uncontainable, jiggling mass on the one hand, an utterly flab-free, erect carriage on the other. If a time machine could put a story about them on the Yiddish stage of earlier decades, charismatic, outsize Thomashefsky would have to play Mostel and haughty, blazing Jacob Adler would embody Robbins.

Like those brilliant rivals of yore, Mostel and Robbins arrived from opposite directions at a consummate sense of artistic showmanship. Both were alternately considered highfalutin for their pronouncements about capital-A Art and scorned for pandering with base entertainments. In other words, they were masters of Broadway, making popular works with serious ambitions. *Fiddler* counted on both.

Mostel would have seemed the perfect choice to Robbins for a deeper reason, too: he represented an image of Jewishness that Robbins had done all he could do to distance himself from but that exerted a pull on him all the same. He described it in one of his journals as a "crude, vulgar, but healthy and satisfied" way of being, a way of saying, "I don't care what they think. Fuck them!!! Ha!" And he recounted a scene he witnessed in a Paris restaurant: a Jew and an Englishman were conferring over a business deal at a nearby table, the first man's boorishness starkly contrasting with the second's tamped-down scorn. "How I wish the Jew had gone further," Robbins wrote. "Slammed the table, dribbled down his chin, ate with his hands and spilled the wine, pushed the table over and danced some demoniacal freilach. He should have farted and laughed, spit." Robbins could well have been describing Mostel at his most deliberately, histrionically coarse. (In one of many displays of outrageousness recounted by a journalist, Mostel once roguishly buttered a roll in a restaurant and, as if carried away by the sheer motion, kept slathering the spread up his arm, then up the sleeve of a stranger at the next table.) Mostel represented all that Robbins had repressed. Perhaps Robbins sensed that *Fiddler* needed the tension between decorum and the threat of vulgarity, between dignity and populism, polite assimilation and that self-assured "Fuck them!" Certainly Robbins knew that alone he could supply only the half of it.

Like Robbins, Mostel fought an inner war over Jewish identity, but the enemy fire came from a different place. Mostel never sought to evade his Jewishness—on the contrary—but he rebelled against, and came deeply to resent, the Orthodox practice his parents maintained and expected their eight children to carry forward. The family lived in the concentrated community of some 230,000 Jews in Brownsville, Brooklyn, in 1915, when Zero was born (his given name was Samuel), and later (after a failed sojourn on a farm in Connecticut) moved to the Lower East Side. Yiddish was spoken at home and in the neighborhood. Despite the second-commandment prohibition against graven images, Mostel's mother supported his attraction to art as a youngster, encouraging him to visit museums, where he copied paintings for hours on end. Quickwitted and apparently in possession of a photographic memory, Mostel would have made an excellent rabbi, his father thought.

Mostel understood that choosing to pursue painting and performance meant leaving his family's world behind. "Could you imagine my father, a Jew in a black hat with a long beard, sitting in a night club?" he once asked a journalist who had wondered whether the performer's parents had ever

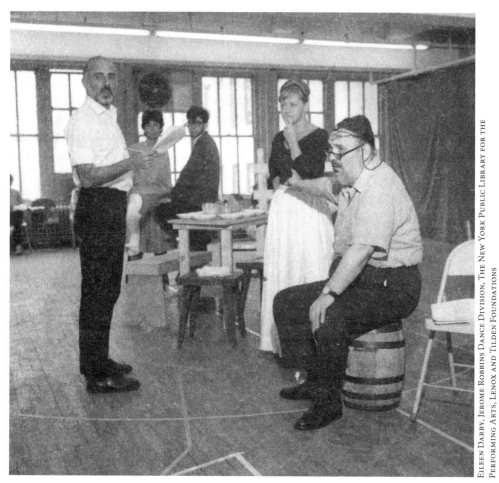

Jerome Robbins directs Zero Mostel and Maria Karnilova as Joanna Merlin and Austin Pendleton await instruction.

seen his routines. As Mostel saw it, the life he chose was fundamentally at odds with the life he abandoned. The problem with religion, the inveterate joker told the audience at a Harvard lecture in 1962, is that it is "devoid of comedy." Mostel put his faith, instead, in the universal will to laughter. "Comedy," he continued, "is rebellion against hypocrisy, against pretense, against falsehood and humbug and bunk and fraud, against false promisers and base deceivers—against all evils masquerading as true and good and worthy of respect. It is therefore the role of comedy to put to the test whatever offers itself as piety, to examine all claims." As a performer—on stage and often off—he devoted his life to that proposition.

If Mostel's calling as a comic conflicted with his upbringing as a strictly observant Jew, he experienced a further shove away from religiosity in 1944 when he married Kate Harkin, who came from an Irish Catholic background. His parents would not accept her, and supposedly they sat shiva for him. The extent of his estrangement from his mother and its impact may have been exaggerated—one Broadway reporter went so far as to invent, and publish, the story that Mostel almost refused to go onstage for the New York opening of *Fiddler* because he couldn't bear to play the scene in which Tevye disowns Chava for marrying the non-Jew Fyedka—but certainly she kept her distance. Mostel's two sons didn't spend time with their grandmother. The older brother, Joshua, remembers his reaction as a boy upon hearing that Zero's mother had just died: "He has a mother?"

On the other hand, Mostel sustained a lifelong grudge against his mother-in-law because she served him creamed beef the first time Kate brought him home to meet her; he considered the ostentatiously nonkosher dish a deliberate anti-Jewish slur. And though Mostel did not raise his children with any religion, he could not altogether abandon the one in which he was raised. Tobias Mostel remembers that throughout his teenage years he'd see his father praying privately at home late at night, hunched and bobbling over a Hebrew text, yarmulke tilting atop his bald spot—as if the daily practice of Mostel's upbringing hung on like vestigial cartilage, lacking utility or significance but too familiar and ancient a part of himself to question, too painful to remove.

Then there was Yiddish. Mostel peppered his outbursts with its pungent insults. He coarsened his jokes with its salty phrases. He muttered in *mamaloshn* when he didn't want others to understand—or, perhaps more to the point, when the content of the utterance was less important than indicating that the emotional size of his response was so great it required his secret language. Yiddish never stopped gurgling within him; often it spilled out. Besides, Mostel was well read and as refined in his aesthetic sensibility as he was obstreperous in his outward behavior. In addition to pre-Columbian objects and fine art books, he collected Judaica—including dozens of dreydls from around the world. He loved to discuss—and show off his knowledge of—Yiddish culture and literature, which, he took as a given, required no special pleading to be considered among the world's great works. When he listed the supreme masters of the comic form in his Harvard lecture on comedy, he included—alongside the likes of Rabelais, Swift, and Dickens—Sholem-Aleichem. Tobias, born in 1949, was told his name derived from Tevye.

Playing Tevye, then, was not just another job or even just another starring role for Mostel. The part offered a kind of vindication, a reconciling of Mostel's past with his present, a means of honoring the background he had to reject in a form that, in itself, expressed, even celebrated, that rejection: playing Tevye on Broadway, he could have his kreplach and eat it too. Robbins, in contrast, had run from an image, from a specter of incivility and weakness that rose from his ignorance and fear and from his desire for acceptance. Mostel knew what he had given up and could represent it with affection as a trace of the past; Robbins was joyously discovering a cultural wealth that he'd been denied and that the show could display as a gleaming treasure—but, crucially, one from long ago and far away. In different fashions, both men were internally making the show's primary contradictory gesture: embracing Jewish practice at arm's length. *Fiddler's* own dialectics—Tevye's constant on-the-one-hand, on-the-other-hand reasoning—expressed this ambivalence and made space for audience members, whether Jewish or not, at any point along several spectrums of observance, knowledge, or parallel experience, to find a place of emotional entry. Robbins was right that the theme of "tradition" solved everything. It gave the show dramatic conflict that could be reiterated with new variations in every scene, but beyond that all-important technical necessity, the theme performed an alchemical feat that would be the key to the show's success: by turning *toyre* (Torah)—Jewish law and religious practice—into "tradition," it handed over a legacy that could be fondly claimed without exacting any demands. Heritage, after all, is not something one does; it is something one has. Through *Fiddler*, Mostel and Robbins—and millions of spectators in the decades to come—could cherish, honor, and admire a legacy in the safely secular, make-believe space of a theater.

* * *

By the end of 1963, with a headlining director and star nailed down, designers studiously at work, and the script and score already in passable shape, the *Tevye* project needed only one thing more: cash. Fred Coe had neglected to raise any in the year and a half since he'd become its producer. Nor had he managed to draw up contracts for the designers and the actors Robbins had selected. The enthusiastic southern gentleman was in over his head—including in drink. And he had a new project on his plate, directing the film version of *A Thousand Clowns* (which he had produced on Broadway the previous year). Prince had come into Tevye sharing duties and future earnings equally with Coe, but Coe's piece of both dwindled. Eventually, he was relieved of all responsibilities, cut back to 12 percent of the producers' interest, and taken out of the credits entirely.

Hal Prince already had a coterie of investors who had raked in profits on some of his earlier ventures, and plenty were willing take a chance on *Tevye*—as the team was still calling it at the beginning of 1964. In January, the producers drafted an initial prospectus to entice investors. It got some key facts wrong, as such documents, written by office staff who haven't spent much time talking to the artists, often can. The errors shine some light on the way the business side of a project thinks about its "property"—and often shapes how the public will think about it. Dated January 21, 1964, and aiming to raise $376,000 in shares worth $7,500 per unit, the "preliminary prospectus" describes "an original musical comedy" that is "based upon the TEVYE folk stories by Sholom Aleichem and a play by Arnold Perl, based on said stories."

Jerry Robbins and the authors would have objected to almost every word in that description: they didn't think of *Tevye* as a musical comedy— "it is more a combination of an opera, play & ballet," Robbins had said in his notes—and they insisted that they were not following Perl's lead. The common but inadequate designation of Sholem-Aleichem's masterful creations as "folk stories" would not have disturbed them, however, and indeed when the final version of the prospectus was completed a few months later, on April 16, that phrase was one of the few that remained intact. The reference to Perl's play was whited out and a clarification added: "It is based upon the TEVYE folk stories by Sholom Aleichem" was now followed by a blank space and then an emphatic new line: "It should be noted that the works comprising 'THE WORLD OF SHOLOM ALEICHEM' written and adapted by Arnold Perl, are not included as basic material for the proposed Musical." It's impossible to know whether the writers of the prospectus were simply making legalistically sure that their document accorded with the agreement Bock, Harnick, and Stein had signed with Perl and Crown Publishers back in 1962, in which they asserted that they were taking over the license to the Tevye stories and not to the material of Perl's earlier play, or if the prospectus writers were confused about the two different Perl productions and their differing source material. Perhaps they knew the difference and were fudging the distinction on purpose. Clearly enough, though, they wanted to emphasize the originality of their venture.

By that point, the producers had attracted nearly 150 investors, whose involvement ranged from partial shares at the minimum amount of $500 to a few gambles of as much as $22,500. If names are a reliable measure, the list of limited partners was not dominated by Jews. Along with some Adlers, Levys, Feldsteins, Grossmans, and Cohns, the contributors included Dempseys, Buckleys, McVeys, Kelloggs, Farrells, Peccis, Wilsons, Catagnolis, and Vanderbilts, among others: in other words, those with disposable income in their bank accounts and a show tune in their hearts who typically backed Broadway productions in those days. Prince's track record—and that of Bock, Harnick, Stein, and Robbins—would have counted more than the content of the project. The producers made no special effort to reach out to Jewish investors who might have supported the play as a matter of ethnic pride or interest; if anything, they downplayed the tribal appeal. Neither the word "Jew" nor "Jewish" appears in the prospectus's description of the play; nor does "Yiddish" or "shtetl."

The April version—completed after most of the investors had signed on—adds some plot summary, describing the travails of a milkman in Eastern Europe and the fortunes of his three marriageable daughters; the theme, it announces, is "the conflict between the new generation with its modern ideas and the older generation with its traditional ideas." Then, in a surprisingly insightful bit of dramatic criticism, the prospectus makes a point that the Yiddish literary scholar Seth Wolitz would discern years later in analyzing the show's tremendous success: "The resolution is the decision of the family to break with the old and move on to the new world—the United States. It is the major step in their acceptance of the changing times and their attempt to change with it."

Capitalizing at $376,000, the show was not expensive for its time. Nearly a decade before, *My Fair Lady* had cost as much, and only a few years earlier *Camelot* ran up more than $600,000 in start-up expenses. Prince had little trouble raising the funds. And Robbins had none spending it. Early in 1964, with the beginning of rehearsals still six months off, he was already showing signs of dithering his way over the budget.

* * *

Design meetings had been continuing regularly since the fall. In those days long before designers could e-mail digital photos and scanned sketches around, Robbins met Aronson and Zipprodt frequently—often several times a week—and separately. Robbins preferred to serve as the controlling relay point between the two designers, the filter for their communications. He would decide which costume sketches Aronson could see when, which set renderings were appropriate for Zipprodt's discerning eye. The feisty costumer quickly caught on and balked. She called Aronson to say that they couldn't possibly do their work in isolation from each other and the two started meeting clandestinely at his home, away from Robbins's dominion. Though twenty-five years apart in age and artistically bred in disparate worlds, the two were, in the words of Aronson's design partner (and wife), Lisa Jalowetz Aronson, "intuitively related in style." Both worked from impulses about color, Zipprodt amassing and layering swatches of complementary hues and textures

Patricia Zipprodt's costume sketch for Hodel
as she sets out for Siberia.

next to one another, Aronson rendering his myriad ideas in watercolors or gouache sketches. They continued their research together—they added a Russian film about Gorky's childhood and Maurice Schwartz's Tevye movie to their syllabus—and they compared palettes based in browns and blues with splashes of red and yellow. Zipprodt always thought about color dynamically—its changing over the course of a play parallel to dramatic developments and, especially, through the relationships between characters. "Colors bump into one another," she once put it. When characters encounter one another, their clothes interact. With Aronson, she expanded her sense of how the costumes combine meaningfully with scenery, too: Golde's muted claret dress against the red overtones in her home's wooden furniture, the greens and ochers in Chava's layers echoing the pastoral backdrops of wheat sheaves and trees. The two formed a strong bond, and though they were wary of Rosenthal at first—Aronson, especially, feared her gelled lights would throw off the delicate color balances that meant so much to the sets and costumes—she won them over when they saw how beautifully she brought out their intentions. Still, Rosenthal worked mostly on her own. And she had little time, and maybe less cause or inclination, to join their kvetch sessions about Robbins. He was driving Aronson mad.

Every day or three, Robbins called Aronson on the phone or summoned him to a meeting to rave about a new idea he wanted the designer to try. Robbins went constantly to art exhibits and performances—from the flashiest commercial productions to the funkiest avant-garde experiments—and he sopped up what he saw with enthusiasm. If he liked a forest represented with shimmering materials, he excitedly told Aronson to make a shimmering forest. Aronson would hurry back to the studio to sketch some possibilities. When he brought them to Robbins, the director would already have another new notion that thrilled him. Before even looking at how Aronson had responded to the earlier suggestion, Robbins would send him away to try the next one. As the design concepts had to start taking more concrete shape, Lisa Jalowetz Aronson and others in the shop put together models of set pieces and painstakingly began the building drawings that would enable the ideas to be transformed into real, life-sized scenery. Time and again, they would have to start over from scratch as Robbins issued new instructions without considering what Aronson and his assistants had already made.

Boris Aronson's rendering of Tevye's house: combining elements of fantasy and reality.

Aronson threw out a lot of work that hadn't even been given the chance to be rejected. The materials and labor, meanwhile, were mounting up on Prince's account sheets.

When Robbins finally did settle on a specific design element, he changed his mind about its details as finically as he might change his mind about what color shirt to wear. For the wedding scene at the end of act 1, Robbins and Aronson agreed on a painted backdrop of swirling night-sky blues with a whorled bright moon shining against it, stage right. The brushwork gave the drop a Chagall-like sense of motion and dynamic color—the evocation of the master's painterly style, which was what Aronson preferred to the more literal allusions to Chagall's imagery that Robbins insisted upon elsewhere in the design. Both men loved that pretty moon, which worked within the realistic frame of the story while also casting a glow of mysticism over it. But Robbins couldn't decide where, exactly, the wispy white circle should be positioned. One day he wanted it a few inches higher, the next day lower; one day farther to the right, the next more to the left—and day after day, new permutations:

higher to the right, lower to the left, higher to the left, and so on. Aronson and his assistants had to repaint the drop repeatedly to accommodate Robbins's minute adjustments. After countless iterations, Robbins finally nodded his satisfaction. He offered no thanks, no eureka, no acknowledgment of the extraordinary paces he'd put the painters through. But at least it was done. The moon looked gorgeous.

And so Robbins found another detail to fuss over. "The height of the house isn't right," he told Aronson. Changing it threw off the relationship of the rooftop to the moon behind it. Aronson's crew had to paint the drop again.

Still, Robbins had obsessiveness to spare. Casting continued at an accelerated pace in the new year. So did research—more weddings, more reading, more poring over pictures. Robbins purchased another five copies of Roman Vishniac's book of photographs to share with collaborators; he rented *Laughter through Tears* again. He was on the phone or in a meeting with Joe Stein every couple of days, and almost as often with Bock and Harnick. He was hounding the designers, coaching hopeful actors, and, apparently, dodging phone calls from Hal Prince, who was leaving messages every day or two. When Robbins retreated for a weekend to his secluded house at heavily forested Snedens Landing, about a thirty minutes' drive north of his city apartment, he brought along background reading and notes to "mess around with" and sometimes he brought Stein himself for an intensive session on the script. When Robbins dashed to London for five days the last week of January, his return flight was due in New York at 1:55 p.m.; he scheduled auditions for 4:00 that afternoon. He would have had to go straight from the airport to the theater.

The show was taking firmer shape in his mind's eye. Though his activity speeded up, his ideas seemed to coalesce. "The drama of the play," he scribbled down on the first day of the new year, "is to watch a man carefully treading his way between his accepting of his sustaining *belief* (that way of life that is centuries old, practiced as if it were still in the middle ages, which protects & defends him & makes his life tolerable)—& his wry questioning of it within the confinements of the belief. He always asks *why*. He ducks & weaves with the events around him still managing to straddle both sides—his traditions & the questioning of it." The tests of Tevye's ability to stay astride the widening gulf become more difficult and finally, when Chava chooses Fyedka, "he *is forced* either to move forward into being a new Jew or embrace the strict traditions of his life." Robbins was clearly siding with the "new Jew" option, an interpretation of Tevye befitting midcentury America. From a liberal standpoint that holds tolerance and equality as supreme values, Tevye's crisis over Chava's non-Jewish spouse comes across as old-fashioned indeed. Sholem-Aleichem's Tevye is most undone by Chava's apostasy, but that simply does not register on Robbins's radar as such, so the high-minded director has to conclude, "The conditions that [Tevye] has lived under have made him become as prejudice[d] as his attackers."

Robbins seems to have been rereading Sholem-Aleichem's stories that winter. Little wonder, given the story's agonizing sadness, that "Chava" was stirring him deeply. As he describes Tevye's torment, Robbins seems to merge emotionally with the character. He slips into Yinglish syntax in his notes: "Underlying all his actions is the frightening question 'Why?'—Why? Why Chava? Why on me is this visiting?" And he could well have been describing his own decades-long anguish when he continues in Tevye's voice: "Why Jew & Gentile," as the dairyman allows himself to wonder in Sholem-Aleichem's story and, in turn, in Stein's script. "It is a fearsome question, with terrifying ramifications—& it is this which so deeply flings him into a panic." Robbins began to picture a surreal scene in which Tevye would "careen and come apart" as he tried to win his daughter back and would be shown confronting "an event too large & catastrophic for his capabilities." Book musicals in the 1960s still sometimes featured "dream ballets"—dance sequences in which a character expresses in movement a fantasy that can't be put into words, or even into song. Robbins imagined giving Tevye a nightmare ballet.

The schedule barely let up even as Robbins answered the call for a rescue mission on another show. *Funny Girl*—which he was originally to have directed—was foundering in Philadelphia and in late February and early March Robbins spent extended periods there cleaning up the mess. (Robbins loved working with Streisand. "Her performances astound, arouse, fulfill," he noted later. "When she sings she is as honest and frighteningly direct with her feelings as if one time she was, is, or will be in bed with you. The satisfactions she gives also leaves one with terrible and pleasurable hunger.")

Robbins arrived for a March 18 read-through of *Tevye* at the Hellinger Theater with *Funny Girl*'s unwieldiness and five postponed opening dates curdling in his mind. The main problem with Isobel Lennart's book, he thought, was that "it was not written within the time and tempo schedule of a musical, and when it was ripped to pieces to bring it down to size, only a soap opera paste job could be done to make anything recognizable and tell the story." He listened to Bock and Harnick's new numbers, Stein's new scenes, and, especially, the overall movement of the play, with sharpened attention.

About twenty actors were on hand to help, many of them already cast—Pendleton, Merlin, Everett among them—and others willing to pitch in for the fifteen-dollar fee required by Equity for their unrehearsed labors. (That wasn't enough to conjure Mostel, apparently. Jack Gilford read Tevye.) Now the script began with the milkman's direct announcement of the theme Robbins had pulled out of the script conferences: "Good evening. My name is Tevye. I may be a stranger to you, but I am very well known to those who know me well. We live in the little town of Anatevka and I'd like to tell you about our life there. . . . The main thing is that we live as our fathers before us and their fathers before them. (*Sings*) Tradition, tradition!" Bock and Harnick had taken a stab at a song addressing their central theme.

At the end of a couple of hours, the writers felt pleased. Robbins said little as he dashed away for a three o'clock meeting with Aronson. That night, he grumbled his reactions into a Dictaphone, noting that he felt he had "the treasure of the season" and then launching into lengthy explanations of cuts, tucks, and rearrangements the script required. Before those remarks could be typed up by Robbins's secretary and then shaped into what he wanted to present to the authors, Bock and Harnick had left the country. *She Loves Me*—produced by Hal Prince—was opening on London's West End at the end of April. They were going to attend rehearsals and also make some adjustments to the score.

Robbins came down with a nasty case of bronchitis. But a raging fever didn't stop him from working. He used the time he was laid up to go over the script even more minutely and to build on those recorded remarks to prepare a document of several pages outlining "book changes to be completed by author in April." He sent it to Stein on April 3. The next day, he dispatched an even longer set of "notes on the score" to London.

His experience on *Funny Girl*—now selling out nightly at the Winter Garden—made Robbins push Stein all the harder to produce a performance-ready script before rehearsals started. "Having been through terrible fire and insolvable problems with *Funny Girl*," he told Stein, "I absolutely refuse to repeat the same experience and have anyone else suffer from it." Forty pages had to come out of *Tevye* right away, Robbins commanded. "If this means reconstructing of scenes and events it has to be faced now." Changes affecting scenery especially had to be made immediately. If there's anything that would have "ramifications for Boris," Robbins ordered, "let's solve it now and save screaming later."

His specific demands were mechanical—in the way that building a Swiss watch is mechanical: refining all the delicate parts and fitting them together efficiently and gracefully. But making material tick according to Broadway clockwork always means interpreting it in a particular way. That he wanted Stein to let audiences get to know the daughters better— who Tzeitel is, "what she is, what she wants and what she is like," Hodel changing "from a traditional girl with a mind to one who weds the revolutionary idea," Chava as an individual rather than someone "colorless until her meeting with Fyedka"—mattered not only because stick figures bore audiences. Just as important was what they represented: coming social upheaval, a resonant matter at a time when Betty Friedan's *Feminine Mystique* had just spent six weeks on the best-seller list and Congress was about to outlaw discrimination on the basis of sex. In the context of 1905, the daughters' rebellion remained in the still restricted realm of marriage (Hodel, after all, does not run off on her own to join the revolution) but they and their suitors were the means by which modernizing forces assailed Tevye from outside and within. "This should be the most vital part of our show," Robbins correctly argued. Instead it remained "ordinary, conventional and colorless."

Tevye's relationship to the daughters had to be richer and more focused, his reaction to Perchik and Hodel played not in the current script's "passive humorous nebbish terms" but more substantively. Stein had made an "essential error" in the Chava sequence: "its climax is now the cliché lamenting and agonizing scene by a Jew whose daughter married a Christian. Let's throw all that out and put there instead *the trial* of his ability to swing with the times, and the climax of that trial is his denial of Chava. Get out after that immediately."

The director saw the potential wide appeal of the *Tevye* musical in its "vital and universal" story about "the changing with the times we all have to make, and the conflicts and tensions made by these changes." And he understood that the universalism would emerge most potently from Tevye's anguish. Unless the play traced his "attempts to keep his tradition and still follow his heart," Robbins enjoined, "we are back with a better 'Rise of the Goldbergs.'" Plus, he added in an especially telling complaint, the script was "still terribly anti-Gentile and Jewish self-loving."

Robbins had been pounding these points for months with Stein and the notes betray his impatience. He calls sections of the script "muddy," "boring," "bland," "killing with monotony." As if to soften the blow, his cover note offers some stroking lines about how "diligent" Stein has been and assures him that "all we need is this final two months' energy to get set and go." Perhaps he meant to make Stein feel better by revealing that he worried even more about Bock and Harnick's work: Robbins was "pleased" with "the shape of the book at the reading and not so much with the score."

In his letter to the songwriters, Robbins began, "Dear Boys," his typical form of collective address that at once expressed affection and reminded them who was boss. In a single paragraph he carped, chided, nagged, even threatened. He found it "incredible and unforgivable" that they were overseas writing new songs for *She Loves Me* and had also taken time to churn out several songs for *To Broadway with Love*, an extravaganza at the World's Fair. He warned that the project would require "another, and this time, much more lengthy postponement" if the writers didn't hop to. A handwritten postscript made a wan effort to dull his bite: "The tone of this letter is nasty I know—I'm sorry for it. But the points I believe in firmly all around."

"Though most of the songs are charming even the charm wears thin," Robbins slammed with faint praise. Instead, the show had to convey the "toughness, tenaciousness, robustness, virility and hard core resilience of the people." In his most emphatic assertion of the image he wanted to produce—and, most of all, the image he wanted to avoid—Robbins explained: "We err in begging for love for our 'kindness,' 'sweetness,' 'gentleness,' 'understanding,' 'patience,' 'pixie humor' and boy scout virtues. What we should be asking for is admiration for our tenacity, effort, frailties, vigor and not holier than thou qualities." What that could possibly mean in musical terms, Robbins didn't say. But one thing was certain: "If every song is sweet, sentimental sad, touching and nostalgic, all will come off as Second Avenue."

Bock and Harnick tried not to bristle. "Please, Reb Robbins, don't holler or we'll come home by horse," they answered, affecting some banter on thin blue airmail stationery. Though Bock was keeping an eye on the London show, he had plenty of time to work on the *Tevye* score, he explained—he even had a piano in his flat—and Harnick was working on it all day. In fact, the situation was "ideal for writing" and they wanted Robbins to feel "it's both *credible* and *forgivable!*" But either way, they could get more done without his microscopic meddling. Their letter was blunt: "any more talk and conferences at this time" would be counterproductive.

Still, they trusted Robbins. They knew he was motivated by artistic considerations, not by ego. Or at least not by ego alone. After they returned—Harnick on April 29 and Bock on May 5—they cut an amusing song for Lazar about "a butcher's soul" because it stole focus away from what the scene was supposed to be about—Tevye's difficulty in deciding whether to give Lazar Tzeitel's hand ("What gave you the idea / That a man who makes his living / Handling liver, lungs and kidneys / Has no heart?"). They dropped a rousing number called "Make the Circle Bigger" because it was "agitprop." They ditched a short tune called "Baby Birds" for reiterating the ideas of "Sunrise, Sunset." A minor but beautiful script change had gone in. In the early scene when the men gather to hear the newspaper read by Avram the Bookseller, he tells them about a shtetl whose residents have been evicted. In the earliest drafts, the town was called Graznia; now it was Rozhanka.

By then, Robbins's overall point had been vindicated. *Cafe Crown*, Hy Kraft's adaptation of his own 1942 play, had opened at the Martin Beck Theater on April 17, proving true what its composer, Albert Hague, had boasted to Joe Stein: that their Jewish musical would make it to Broadway before Stein's. The show offered an affectionate, humorous peek inside a bygone Second Avenue eatery where the royalty of the 1930s Yiddish theater assembled to brag, bicker, and vie for glory. It was packed like a pickle barrel with waiters' slow-burn wisecracks and impresarios' bumptious speechifying (the protagonist, based on Jacob Adler, is preparing an adaptation of Shakespeare's *Lear* called *The King of Riverside Drive*). The characters are rehearsing a musical within the musical, *Au Revoir, Poland—Hello, New*

York, which offers some ample opportunities for wry and wacky songs. And in a heartwarming, only half-mocking act 1 denouement, the inge-nue's beau, so troublingly named Logan, turns out to be the son of a rabbi.

This thickly layered shmaltz fest played thirty preview performances on Broadway. Holding tryouts in town, the producers figured, not only saved travel expenses but kept the show close to its target audience—more than 42 percent of America's Jews still lived in the New York metropolitan area at the time. Even so, the show attracted Jews at about the rate of Eas-ter Mass at St. Patrick's Cathedral. The deterrent wasn't just musty writ-ing or actors fumbling their lines or Theodore Bikel (in the role modeled on Adler) failing to keep his wig on straight. Jews who came of age in the postwar period—now the adults making up much of the Broadway audience—were, for the most part, fleeing from neighborhoods like the Lower East Side and their nostalgic representations. If they were going to splurge on a night on Broadway that month, they were more likely to choose ethnically neutral (i.e., Anglo-Saxon) entertainments like *Hello, Dolly!* or a new, lightweight musical called *High Spirits* based on a Noel Coward play. *Funny Girl* was also an option, its irony and assimilationist plot enough to keep it on the far side of the sentimentally "Jewish"—a category that Streisand was brashly blasting open in any case.

Some nonmusical, more high-brow offerings invited theatergoers to explore current liberal concerns: the modern-dress *Hamlet* directed by John Gielgud and starring Richard Burton (opening less than a month after he'd married Elizabeth Taylor amid a media frenzy); James Bald-win's *Blues for Mister Charlie*, the time-fluid crime drama about the murder of a black man by a white man in the South; and Rolf Hochhuth's *The Deputy*, the theatrical *J'accuse* of Pope Pius XII for having failed to speak out against the Nazi genocide of the Jews. Its telling subtitle was *A Christian Tragedy*. The play stirred enormous controversy in New York (as it had done in earlier productions in Europe)—and no small measure of anxiety among mainstream Jewish institutions, which feared it could tear a rift in hard-won "harmonious interfaith relations," as an Ameri-can Jewish Committee representative put it. Opening night was picketed by a joint group of 150 Catholic, Protestant, and Jewish protesters object-ing to alleged bigotry against Catholics—and they were joined by a dozen American Nazis in storm trooper uniforms. *Hamlet*, in contrast, drew throngs into the streets night after night that spring, well beyond the premiere, but in this case the thousands who turned up each evening from April through August were trying to catch a glimpse of glamour and express their adoration of Burton and Taylor, who met her new husband at the theater after the performance most nights; the crowds more than compensated for an Ohio congressman's earlier effort to have Burton's visa revoked on the grounds of his "moral turpitude."

All three plays dealt with the question of an individual's responsibility to the claims of history—whether the ghost of his father calling Hamlet to action, racist violence illuminating the moral crisis of white America in *Mister Charlie*, or the pope choosing silence in the face of cataclysm—and did so with a crescendoing demand for civil rights and sexual liberation gathering outside the walls of the theaters. This was the tide Robbins wanted to catch, at least to the extent possible in a musical form. As for *Cafe Crown*, before its official opening on April 17 the producers posted a closing notice; its curtain came down for the last time on the nineteenth. Robbins could not have invented a clearer object lesson.

* * *

Robbins was slowly assembling the rest of his cast. To the amazement of his colleagues—and even surprising himself—he offered the role of Golde, Tevye's down-to-earth wife, to his dance colleague and Ballets: USA member Maria Karnilova. Slender and sturdy, with high cheekbones and smiling eyes, she projected the motherly groundedness the character needed. She had never carried a major Broadway role before, but under Robbins's direction she had bumped to great acclaim in *Gypsy* as the stripper Tessie Tura, advising, "If you wanna grind it, wait till you've refined it," in the song "You Gotta Get a Gimmick." She was a friend, a known quantity to Robbins. He knew that physically she could do anything and that she was a reliable, low-maintenance company member. And, no small thing, perhaps an ally in what was sure to be an endless battle with Mostel.

Bea Arthur, a more experienced Broadway actor, had auditioned well for that part—Harnick thought she was "great" and Stein knew her from the days she had understudied the ingenue in *Plain and Fancy*—but she killed her chances to play Golde when she read the nosy, nattering role of Yente the matchmaker. She was the first to make the authors laugh and they lobbied hard for casting her, though Robbins had his doubts: he found her too American, he said, without elaborating. Perhaps he was commenting more on the character herself. Stein had created Yente, transforming the male matchmaker Efrayim, who makes a brief appearance in Sholem-Aleichem's "Tevye Leaves for the Land of Israel," into a larger, familiar type: the garrulous busybody, obliviously revealing her peccadilloes through comic business (stuffing extra cakes into her purse when she visits Golde) and ironically contradictory remarks ("Other women enjoy complaining, but not Yente," she crows, after complaining about her late husband). Such jokey devices are as old as Aristophanes, but when combined with her rapid-fire speech rhythms, her singsong cadences, her tendency to ask and answer her own questions and, more generally, to speak for her supposed interlocutors, Yente's humor seemed to be thickly cut with borscht. It was an American Jewish sensibility that poured forth from Yente when she was played as written, and it made Robbins nervous. (By calling her Yente, Stein made one of his book's few concessions to the Yiddish language, which the authors had vowed to avoid; it was too associated with cheap plays for laughs, they believed. A common enough name, Yente had come to mean meddlesome gossip-monger, and that was one old-biddy yuk Stein was willing to exploit.) All the same, no one else who'd auditioned for the role made Yente come alive at all, and, recognizing Bea Arthur's skill as a character actor and comedian, Robbins gave her the part.

The rest of the supporting characters posed less daunting problems—other than Robbins's indecisiveness. But eventually he pieced the company together with performers both long known and totally new to him. He tapped his first dancing teacher, Gluck Sandor—the one who had snagged a spot for him in the Maurice Schwartz production of *Di brider ashkenazi* back in 1937—for the part of the rabbi. He took a chance on young Leonard Frey (whom he'd seen in a play in Spoleto), as the rabbi's son, Mendel. It wasn't until the end of April, though, that he found a Perchik and a Hodel to replace Anne Fielding: two fine singers, Bert Convy (even though Robbins didn't want Perchik to be "too handsome") and Julia Migenes (who came to auditions while still playing Maria in a short-term revival of *West Side Story*).

Ads in trade magazines announced open calls for singers and dancers—the villagers of Anatevka—and they arrived by the score through the last week of May, up to a few days before the first rehearsal.

Trying to stand out from the crowd, some came dressed in what they imagined the people of the play would wear. (Roberta Senn, for one, attending her first-ever professional audition, donned a yellow skirt and red leather boots and plaited her dark hair into two thick braids.) Men had a chance to express themselves in improvisations that concluded long days of quickly learning and presenting movement sequences. "The Russians are coming and they're strong and they're armed and they're going to kick you out," Robbins told one group, setting up a scenario. "You try to placate them, but it doesn't work. Show me." Robbins saw some of these chorus candidates, too, as many as ten or twelve times. He was searching for performers who could dance and sing well enough to look like they weren't doing it too well: these were poor Jewish folk in the Russian Pale, he kept telling them. They shouldn't sell it onstage. They should come across as regular, untutored dancers when they whirled around at a wedding. Needing townsfolk of all ages, he ended up hiring a number of novices as well as old hands, all with strong training in ballet or modern dance. Hal Prince took a look at the women who made it through the final cuts in their ankle-length skirts and babushkas and was momentarily stunned. "You've never seen such a motley crew of chorus girls in your life," he thought, and then shook off the apprehension, reminding himself that he hadn't gone into showbiz to be Florenz Ziegfeld. Robbins knew what he was doing and Prince didn't doubt him for a moment.

But Robbins doubted himself. With the cast finally set and rehearsals slated to begin on June 1, he sent Prince word through his representative that they'd have to delay the production again because he needed more time to prepare. Prince fired off a telegram: "Don't ever ask me to talk to your lawyer," it concluded, "unless you never want to work with me again. Love, Hal." Robbins retorted by cable: "Then don't give me rehearsal dates via my assistant. Love, Jerry." Prince coolly replied that Robbins could do as he wished as long as he reimbursed him for the $55,000 he'd already laid out for the production. He warned that he'd sue for it if necessary. When the men finally spoke to each other, Robbins cried. He wasn't ready, he protested. How could Prince betray him so? Prince didn't try to relieve Robbins's panic with strokes of reassurance; he just held to his threat. That was the way to push Robbins over the edge. One good shove was all he needed. Within a few days, things between them were back to normal: Prince was calling Robbins again with the reminders to take care of one thing or another. Most urgent since their contretemps was approving the final plans for Aronson's turntable. Prince urged Robbins to go see the designer right away so his crew could have the go-ahead to start building it. Otherwise, Prince warned, they'd go into overtime. With the threat of being docked $55,000 less than a week old, Robbins hurried to see the drawings.

One more issue needed resolving before rehearsals started: what was the show going to be called? The authors and Prince had batted around ideas for months and they all agreed only that "Tevye" was too bland and too vague. "A Village Story," "To Life," "Listen to the Fiddle," "Make a Circle," "Once There Was a Town": their list kept growing, but nothing zinged. "To Light a Candle," "My Village," "Three Brides and a Man," "A Village Tune," "Homemade Wine," "Not So Long Ago," dozens more. The authors liked "Where Poppa Came From," but Prince preferred a name that suggested that the show was a musical. In late March, he called the question. "Anything on the list will do," Stein told him. "I don't care anymore." Prince scanned the list and made the choice. "But it doesn't mean anything," Stein said. Prince shrugged and replied, "Well, that's the title." *Fiddler on the Roof* went into rehearsal on June 1.

CHAPTER 5

RAISING THE ROOF

ON THE EVE OF *FIDDLER*'S REHEARSALS, AN ARTICLE CAME OUT in *Look*, the biweekly general interest magazine—then enjoying a circulation of 7.5 million—that carried a clue to the show's coming triumph. Titled "The Vanishing American Jew," the story described how the Jewish community's very success in America could be spelling its doom. It quoted alarmed rabbis, communal leaders, and sociologists responding to a rise in mixed-faith marriages among Jews and a parallel decline in birthrates and synagogue attendance. The president of the New York Board of Rabbis warned that "the vitality and the entire future of the Jewish people would be jeopardized" if young people continued to marry out of the faith. Despite the splash made by the book *Beyond the Melting Pot*, published only nine months earlier and arguing for the enduring power of ethnic identity among immigrant groups over generations, the sources in *Look*'s story apocalyptically argued that the increasing acceptance of Jews by others, and the thorough Jewish sense of belonging in America, could eventually lead to the disappearance of the people: annihilation by love, not hate.

Anxiety about the Jewish future had been brewing in communal circles for months before percolating up into a mass publication like *Look*. In October, the 1963 edition of the annual compendium *The American Jewish Year Book* came out, reporting in its lead article that third-generation Jews were twelve times more likely than the first generation to marry non-Jews. The article cited two major studies, including one that found that the "children of at least 70 percent of mixed families are lost to the Jewish group." Equally perturbing to its authors, the *Year Book* noted that Jews who went to college were more than twice as likely to choose non-Jewish spouses as those who did not. Could the long-revered values of equality and education really be turning out to be bad for Jews?

Well, yes, in a way, some prominent observers were so bold as to argue—at least if those values were pursued without providing Jewish youngsters with the balancing forces of religious knowledge, communal commitment, and reason for sustained affiliation. In many respects this was an old story: the tension between the simultaneous goals of blending into America and maintaining distinctiveness, between seeking full social acceptance and reproducing Jewish families through endogamy, had weighed on the collective Jewish conscience for as long as there had been Jews in the United States; the theme had been valorized in popular culture for decades. But now, a romantic couple like David Quixano and Vera Revenal at the center of Israel Zangwill's *Melting Pot* in 1908 or Abe Levy and Rosemary Murphy in the long-running 1922 hit *Abie's Irish Rose* were not an abstract symbol of a contentious ideal. Chava's betrothal to Fyedka in *Fiddler*, though set in 1905, represented a growing American phenomenon that was rattling the mainstream Jewish community in 1964. It wasn't just the gradual lowering of social boundaries or Jewish dispersal from urban enclaves into more mixed, decentralized communities; the rising civil rights and sexual liberation movements also pressed the young generation toward one end of the long-standing debate. They faced a "crisis of freedom," Rabbi Alan Miller, leader of New York's Society for the Advancement of Judaism, told *Look*. And if they chose universalism over what sounded to them like Jewish chauvinism, the blame, suggested the research director of the American Jewish Committee, Marshall Sklare, belonged to one nefarious force: Jewish liberalism. So Sklare had argued in *Commentary* in April, in an article responding to the *Year Book* statistics: "The liberalism of the Jewish parent—his commitment to the idea of equality and his belief in the transitory character of the differences which distinguish people from one another—subverts his sense of moral rectitude in opposing intermarriage. For if he is at all in the habit of personal candor, he must ask himself if the Gentile is any less worthy of the Jew than the Jew is of the Gentile." The intermarriage crisis, he predicted, would force the Jewish community to put self-affirmation ahead of such pieties—or else produce "ominous" consequences.

The appeal of *Fiddler* for so many American Jews was not simply that it staged this timely conundrum but that it presented an alternative to Sklare's stark either/or prognosis. The show offered itself as a means of self-affirmation—one that didn't require abandoning, and in fact celebrated, those pro-equality "pieties." Attending the play, purchasing the original cast album, and singing its songs became a form of ethnic assertion.

Fiddler's creators sensed what was at stake in the Chava story. Tevye's reaction to his daughter's elopement and her eventual effort to reaffirm her solidarity with the family would prove to be the most challenging elements of the production, undergoing more rewrites and more restagings than any other sections as the company rehearsed the show and then took it on the road.

Jerome Robbins clipped the *Look* article when it came out and kept it in his *Fiddler* file, but the intermarriage question did not top his issue agenda as he began working with the actors. He was thinking exactly like the sort of Jewish liberal that Sklare distrusted, as his comment on Tevye's "prejudice" betrayed. More telling, the contemporary parallels Robbins found in the plight endured by the folks of Anatevka were related not to any threats faced by Jews of his own day but to those being suffered by African Americans. The script drew no explicit analogies, but Robbins himself drew them, blunt as a protest placard, at his first rehearsals.

For the first two weeks of June, Robbins called only the three daughters and their suitors to the rehearsal hall, a cramped fifth-floor studio at City Center on West Fifty-fifth Street. He started the work by asking them to improvise: "What would it be like if you were in the South and you were a black person and you were buying a book in a bookstore where blacks were not allowed?" he asked Robert Berdeen and Tanya Everett, who were playing the illicit lovers, Fyedka and Chava. Hal Prince had dropped in to see how things were going and was appalled when he heard the actors ad-libbing: "But what do you mean you won't sell to me? Just because my skin color is different?" Prince couldn't decide which was worse, the banality or the irrelevance of the drill. Robbins also had the actors enact an impromptu concentration camp scenario. He seated

Berdeen at a writing table and told him he was a German soldier serving as a bureaucrat who had to process Everett, a Jewish woman. The actors gamely played a scene full of clichés, wondering all the while, "What the hell does all this have to do with czarist Russia?" But they didn't dare complain. "Nobody ever complained to Jerry," Prince affirmed. They were terrified of him.

Within a couple of days, Robbins abandoned the improvs, but not the effort to instill the actors with a sense of the oppression of the Pale. He wanted them to grasp, emotionally, what it meant to be the victim of discrimination, how it felt suddenly to lose everything on some authority's whim and to have no recourse. Most of all, he said, he needed to "make a shtetl out of them." Attempting to give them a visceral glimpse of traditional religious mores, Robbins adapted a famous scheme from his *West Side Story* rehearsals: as he had separated the actors playing Jets from those playing Sharks, even during lunch hours and rehearsal breaks, he now tried to impose gender segregation on those playing the Jews of Anatevka. The actors put up with the contrivance for less than a day. Even Robbins soon saw it was silly.

But even after abandoning the hokey improvs, Robbins did not immediately turn to Stein's script. He didn't want the actors on their feet until they had fully absorbed the pictures, paintings, and prose depictions of shtetl life that he piled onto a table in the rehearsal room: Chagall reproductions, the stills from *Through Tears*, mimeographed excerpts from *Life Is with People*—and for Pendleton, at least, the whole book. Robbins's seriousness about the material—and his eyes always burning "like one of those figures you see on the cover of paperback editions of Dostoyevsky," in Pendleton's view—charged the rehearsal room with an electrifying sense of mission. This was different from the typical energy that juices the early, anything-is-possible stages of any Broadway show as actors begin to learn their parts, banter into relationships, and dream of long-running glory. Robbins didn't seem to be chasing after a hit—not a hit for its own sake, in any case. He was on a quest and he was calling the cast aboard. If his demands were unusual, they were not unwelcome. "You didn't do that kind of research for *Guys and Dolls*," Merlin recognized. "This was exciting."

Of the six actors playing the lovers, Merlin was the only one who was Jewish, and though she was familiar with Sholem-Aleichem, she knew next to nothing about Orthodox practice. She watched with eyes as wide as her colleagues' when Robbins dispatched her and the others to wedding parties through Dvora Lapson. Everett and Migenes tried to blend in among the women at a grand affair at the Ansonia Hotel one hot night, conversing with vague "mm hmms" and silent nods for fear of being revealed as interlopers. Merlin and Pendleton played participant-observers at weddings in Williamsburg in their respective gendered tribes, allowing themselves to get lost in the crowds of hundreds. As a self-described "goy from Ohio," Pendleton was amazed by everything: the groom stomping on a glass, the couple raised up in chairs, the hours of raucous dancing—and astonished more by the transference of the joyous ritual into a staged scene that he would eventually play night after night with genuine, brimming emotion.

Educating the cast mattered enormously to Robbins, but the improvisations and table talk served another function, too: as delaying tactics. Robbins was both the most prepared director anyone had ever worked with and also the most insecure, especially when it came to scene work. He simply didn't know how to talk to actors. He'd blurt out Actors Studio words like "motivation" and "justification" and urge his cast to find their "inner reality," but he couldn't articulate any thoughts about the specific emotional lives of the characters. So he concentrated on the behavior. Obsessively.

But Robbins knew, as a week of rehearsal was flying by, that no matter how much he dreaded the process, he had to get the actors up. He started by staging the early scene where the daughters set the table for the Sabbath and Tzeitel and Motel end up having a private conversation in which she urges him to speak to her father about their desire to marry each other, while he helps her lay down a tablecloth and then add dishes and candlesticks. The action is in the dialogue, the pretext in the business. But Robbins could deal only with the business—and he spent several precious hours on it one afternoon. By Pendleton's count, Robbins restaged the table setting twenty-five different ways: Put a plate down on this line. No, try it after that line. Maybe it would be better on the next line. Never mind, put the candlestick down instead. Not there, over two inches to the left. No. To the right. Switch places and try it again. Go faster. Try it slower. Let's go back to the first way. And so on, well into the night. Merlin and Pendleton grasped that Robbins wanted them to arrive at behavior that seemed effortless, just part of the reality of their characters' lives, but the wavering unnerved them. They had only just gotten started. Were they in for seven more weeks like this?

For the chorus, who joined the rehearsals in the third week, work ran more smoothly (at least at first). Robbins was at ease placing dancers on the stage and showing them their moves. And dancers, in turn, did not expect or need the coaxing and questioning that drew the best work from actors. They did as they were told, even when what Robbins told them deviated from any task they'd been given before. They weren't there to sing and dance, he explained; they were there as vital members of a community. He required all the ensemble members to conjure up characters and write their biographies. Food vendors, hatmakers, cobblers, street cleaners, embroiderers, water carriers: the research materials described many communal roles they could choose from. He mandated that they describe their ages, professions, temperaments, and relationships to everyone else in the town. One night Robbins assembled the entire company to show them *Ghetto Pillow* and *Through Tears*. And a large group of the chorus, too, made a field trip to a Brooklyn wedding.

When Zero Mostel blasted into rehearsals after the second week he started ridiculing Robbins right away. "A couple of weddings in Williamsburg and that putz thinks he understands Orthodox Jews!" he'd snort with a roll of the eyes that seemed to trace the full circumference of the globe. Mostel vied for power with everything he had—comic charm, deep personal knowledge of *Yiddishkayt*, colossal talent, sheer volume and size—but always indirectly. Like an overgrown class clown, he shared his jibes in naughty asides to other actors. He never confronted Robbins directly, but he baited him. One day, every time Robbins turned his back, Mostel shook his ample behind at him. The next day he carried out the same routine, only this time he gave Robbins the finger. On another occasion, when Robbins insisted Mostel stop chomping on chewing gum during rehearsals, the actor stuck the gum behind his ear and popped it back into his mouth and began gnawing lustily when Robbins looked away. Once he tromped across the back of the stage with a bucket on his foot while Robbins was talking to other actors. Day after day he found a way to entertain his fellow cast members at the director's expense. And most of the company—especially the younger actors—cheered him on with their laughter. The more one feared Robbins, it seemed, the more one appreciated Mostel's pokes at his authority—and the prospect that Robbins feared Mostel.

Robbins silently endured Mostel's shenanigans. How hard he had to work to keep from blowing his stack, no one knew, but he never exploded—not at Mostel, anyway. He could be curt with Stein, barely looking up when the writer passed him the new pages he demanded. He could be cutting with actors—he called Everett "fatso," carped incessantly at a couple of chorus members (his "scapegoats," as they were known), and drove Bea Arthur off the stage in tears with an insult. But with Mostel, Robbins stayed businesslike. And if his own acting was involved, Mostel responded in kind. When both were concentrating on a scene, their working relationship simmered, in Stein's description, at "two degrees below hostile." Robbins put as genial a spin on their antagonism as he could when questioned by a journalist shortly after the show opened. "Mostel likes to test you when you work together," he said, removing some of the sting by generalizing with the second person. "There was a certain amount of squaring off at each other, but I think we both felt some good healthy respect beneath it all."

Robbins said little to Mostel by way of direction and that was plenty since Mostel, endlessly inventive, needed little prodding. When they argued at all, it was over substance, and often over Jewish substance. "What are you doing?" Robbins demanded at one rehearsal as Mostel touched the doorpost of Tevye's house and then brushed his fingers over his lips. Mostel offered the obvious answer: "I'm kissing the mezuzah." Robbins responded bluntly, "Don't do it again." But Mostel insisted that Tevye, like the Orthodox Jews with whom the actor had grown up, would never neglect to make the customary gesture of devotion that acknowledges the case of sacred parchment affixed to doorways of Jewish homes. Robbins bristled. Mostel held firm and kissed the mezuzah again. Without raising his voice—in fact, the more emphatic he became, the more firmly and calmly he spoke—Robbins demanded that Mostel stop. The actor relented. And then, when he walked through Tevye's doorway once more, he crossed himself. He'd made—and won—his point. The mezuzah kissing stayed in.

Less contentiously, Mostel deepened the Jewish texture of other elements of the show. When Bock and Harnick wrote "If I Were a Rich Man," they had been inspired by a mother-daughter duo they'd heard singing a Hasidic song at a benefit for the Hebrew Actors' Union. Bock went home with the song's harmonies of thirds and sixths in his ears and wrote the music for "Rich Man" that very night. For lyrics, Harnick began with the hero's fantasy in the first Tevye story in the Butwin volume, "The Bubble Bursts" (not otherwise dramatized in *Fiddler*), in which Tevye invests his entire savings with his speculating relative, who ends up squandering every cent. After handing over his "little hoard" in the story, Tevye has visions of "a large house with a tin roof right in the middle of the town," with a yard "full of chickens and ducks and geese." He sees his wife, Golde, as "a rich man's wife, with a double chin," who "strutted around like a peacock, giving herself airs and yelling at the servant girls." Earlier in the story, he imagines being wealthy enough to purchase a seat by the synagogue's eastern wall, build the synagogue a new roof, and take up other magnanimous works. Harnick shaped these fantasies to Bock's melody (including a verse, eventually cut, about dispensing charity) and elaborated them into a more complex version of a Broadway musical standard, the so-called I Want song. Typically, such a number comes early in the show and lets the protagonist tell the audience what she or he desires—for instance, Eliza's "Wouldn't It Be Loverly?" in *My Fair Lady* or Rose's assertive "Some People" in *Gypsy*. "Rich Man" does the same, but only up to a point.

Where characters usually reveal the goal that motivates them—the driving force of the action to follow—Tevye expresses a flight of fancy, poignant for two differing reasons. First, both he and the audience know that he won't become wealthy and, anyway, that material riches don't truly motivate his actions. And second, audience members (of any ethnicity "beyond the melting pot") can tacitly recognize that they, the descendants of struggling ancestors, have fulfilled Tevye's idle dream. "Rich Man" instantly took the place of an earlier song the team had written for Tevye, a charming but less telling number about his recalcitrant horse. ("Matchmaker" is also a complicating variation on an I Want song: through singing it, the girls come to understand what they don't want. It replaced "To Marry for Love"—which pointed out how "love doesn't put a turnip on the table"—as Bock and Harnick reshaped the score around the capacities of the cast. The melodically simpler waltz, "Matchmaker," was easier for Everett and Merlin.)

Mostel could convey the ironic texture of "Rich Man" by heaving a heavy yet wistful sigh during the pauses built into the tune. No other actor could find as many layers and shades in an audible exhalation. Harnick gave him a chance to indulge in his hallmark faces and animal noises, too, by adding in lines about crossed eyes and the squawks made by those chicks and turkeys and geese.

But it was Mostel's religious background that enabled him to give the number its fullest dimension. Bock and Harnick had been especially impressed by the sound of particular passages in the Hebrew Actors' Union performance and wanted to capture it in their song: the duo had burbled beautiful nonsense syllables. Harnick found it impossible to render such phonemes in prose, so he wrote down, "digguh-digguh-deedle-daidle-dum." When Bock and Harnick played the song for Mostel, he understood instantly what Harnick had been after and offered to "try something." "If I were a rich man," he began, and then, in place of the "digguh-digguh" phrase, he quietly emitted a soulful half-hummed, half-articulated incantation derived from the murmur of daily davening—a "dream-tasting spiral of Yiddish scat-syllables," as the critic Richard Gilman later described this tender, primal sound of yearning itself.

Meanwhile, Harnick worried that the song took too serious a turn. He proposed cutting the verse in which Tevye dreams of the synagogue seat by the eastern wall and imagines how he'd "discuss the holy books with the learned men seven hours every day. / That would be the sweetest thing of all." Mostel protested. "If you change that," he boomed, "you don't understand this man." Harnick yielded, and said later, "He saved me from myself."

For all his goofing around at rehearsals, Mostel could switch instantly into a state of intense focus on the work. Other actors watched him in awe, spellbound by his freedom and self-confidence as a performer. He would try anything and never doubted himself. "He can do the same thing four ways," Stein remarked, "and they all seem right."

He became so totally absorbed in his character that, like a guru walking on hot coals, he shut down the distress signals being sent to his brain. In 1960, Mostel had exited a Manhattan bus on a January night and slipped on the icy pavement. The bus ran him over, crushing and mangling his left leg. After five months in the hospital and four complicated operations, he was spared the amputation that had originally been recommended, but he lived in a state of severe, perpetual pain and walked with a cane—except onstage. The moment he came off, the agony rushed in. Tanya Everett or his dresser, Howard Rodney, would bring him swaths of cloth that had been drenched in water and put in a freezer, to apply to his leg after a performance.

Mostel's injury made his unlikely gracefulness all the more astounding. At a bulky 230 pounds when he played Tevye, he treaded lightly and could even appear dainty. Robbins compared him to "a bagful of water [that] has gotten up and started to float around." For a man without formal movement training, he had exceptional control. Robbins exploited it in the first big number he staged, "L'Chaim," the celebration at the inn after Tevye assents to Lazar Wolf's proposal to marry Tzeitel. Working on this scene had to be one of the occasions when the friction between Mostel and Robbins was superseded by their brilliance, each man recognizing— and feeding—the creativity of the other.

To Bock and Harnick, "L'Chaim" was simply a song. But Robbins saw much more in it: an opportunity for bringing together Russians and Jews, exploring their long-standing animosity and opening up, then closing, the possibility of rapport—all through dance. He divided the male corps into the two groups, putting, as one of them remembered, "the butchest dancers in the Jewish roles." Despite looking tougher, however, those playing Jews were told to keep their movement small and contained at first, to express a physical submissiveness when Russians are around. "Keep it all inside," Robbins instructed, as he showed them their celebratory steps: they hold up their arms, elbows bent at right angles, and clasp hands with the men on either side, and, thus lined up, snake through the inn. When Russians unexpectedly leap into the revelry, they slap their feet in a set of rhythmic steps, perform jumping splits, vault over the furniture, kick their legs, and generally dash about. They are the masters of the universe, Robbins explained, and their boisterousness, though friendly in this instance, threatens the Jews.

The climax of the scene comes when, in the frenzy, a Russian bumps into Tevye. Everything pauses as the two glare at each other and, without moving, approach the precipice of a physical fight. Then the Russian— played by Lorenzo Bianco—thrusts out a hand, inviting Tevye to dance with him. Here, Mostel's dexterity allowed him to be funny and piteous in a single moment and small gesture: slowly, he moves his pinky into Bianco's hand, expressing with just a finger Tevye's eagerness to trust his neighbor as well as his apprehension. In the instant their hands connect, Bianco flies into a toe-and-heel-tapping caper, and Mostel seems as if he will take flight. At half Mostel's girth, Bianco pulls him through the dance like a weightless kite and the men from both factions join in, their clashing styles meshing in the celebration not only of the engagement but now also of the rare and temporary suspension of hostilities. In a line, the Jews take small sideways steps and the Russians come bursting through between them, scooting along the floor on their knees and swooping in all directions. The number was a triumph for Robbins and for Mostel. The first time Prince saw it in rehearsal, he figured it wouldn't take long before he'd be sending checks to investors.

But as the work continued, Robbins didn't stage any more dancing. Six weeks of rehearsal had gone by and the male dancers hadn't learned anything else; the women hadn't done anything at all. Robbins had wangled the unusually long eight-week rehearsal period by insisting he needed four as director of the actors and four as choreographer. So where were the rest of the dances? "Oh, I'll do them," Robbins said, with a nonchalant wave. Prince fumed quietly.

The members of the cast, too—especially the women—were beginning to wonder. They had learned and practiced the prologue's song, "Tradition," but as they entered their seventh week of rehearsals and the departure date for Detroit neared, Robbins still hadn't staged it. Given how tediously they'd labored over the simplest scenes, actors were getting nervous. At the rate Robbins was going, they figured he'd need at least a few days to put the opening number on its feet. And it wasn't going to be fun.

One day toward the end of the last week in New York, after the lunch break, Robbins clapped his hands and called the full chorus onto the stage (meanwhile, the principals were sent off to the lounge to work on their scenes with assistant director Richard Altman). He put the group in a line—young Roberta Senn at the lead—and told them to hold their arms up at a 90-degree angle and to link pinkies with the person on either side of them. His dance assistant, Tommy Abbott, helped show them what to do: maintaining their line, walk in from the stage-left wing, stepping on the downbeat of a four count, knees pulsing lightly, and circle the stage. Nothing could have been simpler. The variations flowed out of Robbins with an effortlessness that seemed casual: some

"You're proud," Robbins told them. "Tradition!"

performers were to shift their head position from left to right every four beats, some to turn around entirely. When the circle was complete, with all twenty-four performers onstage, the two positioned downstage center were to let go of each other's hands and lead their lines in opposite directions, heading upstage, walking underneath hand bridges formed by pairs of actors and coming to rest in two semicircles.

Robbins gave each group with a verse in the song—the papas, mamas, sons, and daughters—a series of defining movements to perform as they came downstage, in turn, to sing about their lives and obligations. Papas slap their chests with their right hands, point an index finger skyward, turn around with arms raised at 90 degrees, palms toward their faces, snapping their fingers. Mamas fold their hands on their stomachs, wipe their brows with the back of the right hand and thrust the hand toward the floor, walk toward the audience rolling their hands in a paddle-wheel motion. Robbins presented the sons with a little skipping crossover step and incorporated into their sequence a pensive hand to the cheek, a shrug, and the rhythmic swaying—the *shukhel*—of men's prayer. For the daughters, he assembled a couple of curtsies, some swaying motions of the arms, a series of side steps with a foot flexed and heel scuffing the floor: the moves combined an image of deference with a hint of mischief.

In less than two hours, the villagers learned their steps. "You're proud," Robbins told them as they got set to run the whole sequence from the top, this time with music. "You're very proud of your tradition." They straightened their spines. "All right," said Robbins. "Here ya go." Mostel picked up his opening speech toward the end: "And how do we keep our balance? That I can tell you in one word." The rehearsal pianist hit the opening chords, Mostel stomped his foot in time, threw his arms upward, and cried, "Tradition!" Out came the line of villagers, chins up, chests forward, spiraling onto the stage as they sang. From the house, Austin Pendleton (who wasn't in the number) was watching and what he saw forced him to change his own posture: he sat up and leaned forward with attention. Right away he grasped how tremendous the staging was. The steps were not complicated but the patterns were rich and meaningful: the cohesiveness of the circle, the abstracted gestures that distinguished each family member not only functionally but temperamentally, the vertical motions that connected the people to their God and to history. Most of all, Pendleton recognized that the number set forth the show's high stakes. "When the tradition gets repeatedly challenged in the course of the play," he marveled, "you'd know it's something huge. Jerry wanted the audience to feel that instantly. Now they would."

The performers felt it, too. A couple of hours earlier, they had been a cluster of theater gypsies, frayed and fearful, awaiting instruction from a man who could turn tyrant at the drop of a cue. Now, onstage at least, they were a community, elevated by the pride in their way of life. The scene wasn't completely finished that day. The song "accumulated" over time, as Jerry Bock later remarked. "It just kept rolling to a bigger moment." And Joe Stein would continue to weave more strands into the prologue "like a tapestry." He kept writing new lines—"a piece of dialogue here to introduce the rabbi, another to introduce Yente, others to introduce various other characters." Bock was adding layers to the music: toward the end of the song, all four separate groups sing their parts simultaneously in a folkish fugue that produces some surprising dissonant clashes that hint at the familial discord to come.

Even the unfussy staging would see some adjustments. Senn would have to relinquish her lead place in line to the dancer Mitch Thomas, and Peff Modelski would have to walk backward in her spot. Everyone's positioning and timing would have to be recalibrated once the floor contained an orbiting turntable. But the very first time through, on that July afternoon, they knew that Robbins had nailed the curtain raiser. The company now had an inkling that whatever trials were to come over the next eight weeks in Detroit and Washington, they could very well be worth it. The troupe would have to dig deep sometimes to remember that.

* * *

For now, everyone's attention was fixed on preparations for the road. On July 18, actors dressed for the standard costume parade, a one-by-one walk across a stage that would allow Robbins to see what Zipprodt had made of the sketches and the collection of swatches that he'd been responding to for months. Again and again, Robbins had reminded her that the people of Anatevka "are not 'characters' but laborers, workmen, artisans, and the effect of their work on their clothes and bodies must be apparent." That meant more than putting the butcher Lazar Wolf in a bloodstained apron or draping a tape measure over the shoulders of Motel the tailor, Zipprodt knew better than anyone. She labored to make the clothes look aged and worn without seeming fake and, just as important, without losing texture under theatrical lighting. Through trial and error, she invented a technique of dyeing, painting, and rubbing fabrics with tools like vegetable graters, wood rasps, and steel wool to create the look she wanted. Perchik's burnt-orange pants began as a pleasant rust color. Zipprodt dyed them brown, then scraped away at the material, as if laundering the pants against a washboard, abrading the added color so that the rust peeped through irregularly. Many pieces underwent what she called a "bleach and overdye" process: first their original color was faded down in a chlorine bath and then they were dipped in a dye of a compatible hue. Even the *tzitzis*—the fringes religious Jewish men wear under their clothing—were tinted and treated for the sake of authenticity.

From underwear to overcoats, Zipprodt used natural fibers that would have been available in 1905 for the 165 costumes she made: silks and cottons for the shells and pink knee-length bloomers, belted calf-length shifts, and striped camisoles with skirts that the three sisters wear as they change into their Sabbath clothes and sing "Matchmaker"; various grades of wools for the buttoned cloaks, patterned shawls, and heavy jackets the Anatevkans bundle into after the order of expulsion. It may have been July in New York, but when the play ends it's winter in Anatevka. There was no scrimping on the heavy layers.

As the actors walked around in the clothes and saw their Anatevkan neighbors in full attire for the first time, their world started to come to life in a newly thick, visual way. The cast had yet to work with Aronson's set pieces, which were already packed into shipping crates and on their way to Detroit. The costumes would join them that night in the ten trailers heading west at the outrageous cost of $9,000. When Prince signed up the trucking company, he figured they'd need six trailers. "It never occurred to me that we would have one of the biggest monsters ever sent out!"

Robbins knew how much work he'd have to do in Detroit. Days before departure, Robbins told his assistant to ask his doctor for eight weeks' worth of "those very mild pickups with SKF printed on back" (no doubt, Smith Kline French's readily dispensed Dexedrine). It would be the work of clarifying, fine-tuning, trimming, and shaping—the kind that could be harder than a major overhaul.

According to *Fiddler* lore, the show *was* overhauled on the road. But satisfying as the mess-to-megahit narrative may be, that's not what happened. Unlike *Man of La Mancha* or *Funny Girl* or other shows that saw changes like major characters jettisoned and whole plot lines rerouted, *Fiddler* basically remained intact. Although half a dozen songs that were performed on opening night in Detroit were replaced by new ones, when the show returned to New York in September it told the same story it had told in July—but with more emotional depth and more theatrical high points. It didn't change so much as become more fully itself. And like any sincere process of self-realization, getting there was grueling.

The first on-the-road rehearsal was called for noon the day after the company arrived in Detroit. The set crew was installing the scenery on the stage, so Robbins and the actors—having abandoned an alternative space that had no air-conditioning—worked in the Fisher Theater's lush lobby. The building, designed by Albert Kahn and erected in 1928 as a "cathedral to commerce" by the seven Fisher brothers, who had made a fortune by developing a covered body for automobiles, stood as an opulent reminder of the city's industrial heydays—first in the early, pre-Depression years of car manufacturing, then during the war as the "great arsenal of democracy," and finally for a time after the war, when the economic boom raised the demand for cars and America dominated the world market. The twenty-eight-story art deco structure, faced with pink granite at the base and with marble the rest of the way up, housed offices and retail space and, in its first decades, a grand movie palace on its ground floor, fitted out in a local notion of Mayan decor: spewing fountains, live macaws, and banana trees in the lobby, bright red and yellow fixtures in the auditorium, gilded frog ashtrays in the restrooms. When it was renovated as a playhouse in 1961—modern neighborhood cinemas and proliferating televisions having commandeered the clientele of the extravagant old movie palaces—the birds and fruit and decorative waterworks gave way to designs more modest only in relative terms. Audiences in the 1960s still came into the building through a high arched entryway lined with bronze and granite reliefs and passed through part of the vast interior marble arcade, its vaulted ceiling covered in elaborate murals and mosaics and bedecked with gilded chandeliers.

The Fisher's sheer extravagance drew the public as powerfully as did the chance to see road companies playing New York's latest hits—and the tryout shows that could be Broadway's next ones. Even if audiences weren't so keen on spending an evening with a work in progress, the pre-Broadway productions were part of the subscription they had to buy if they wanted to secure seats for the visiting blockbusters. Between those deals and steady sales in group benefits, the Fisher could guarantee decent houses for at least the first couple of weeks of a tryout. That gave Prince some solace. Robbins wanted to go to Boston instead of traipsing to what he called the "milk towns," but Prince couldn't make the switch. Boston theaters were not available and besides, Prince told him when he signed for the midwestern house in February, "The subscription in Detroit is hefty, but only available if we book for a full four weeks. I think we need this protection." By July, the protection felt thin. The Fisher had booked moderate audiences for the first two weeks of the Detroit run; the other two would have to build from good word of mouth. Harnick, for one, found the situation scary: even if the show were in good shape, "we could die in Detroit."

The company set up for rehearsal in the theater's lounge, entering under the watch of naked Muses with flaming orange hair who floated on overhead frescoes with harp or tambourine on a background of hemlock branches and starry skies. One cast member who had taken a small detour came rushing back, squealing, "You should see this ladies' room!" and the troupe, male and female, marched in to admire the thick purple carpets, the velvet princess couches, and the gold-plated faucets. The Fisher's flamboyance made for an amusing foil to the tattered grays of the fictional world of Anatevka the troupe inhabited in a day's work, but it disturbed some company members, too. The city's entrenched segregation was obvious enough to anyone who noted who filled up the 2,100 seats at Fisher performances—and who cleaned underneath them in the morning. To the extent that *Fiddler* evoked nostalgia—as some of its critics would charge—it may have been not only for the benighted life of the shtetl but as much for a guileless, giddy moment in America when, as Michael Harrington had just recently put it, if you didn't make a point of looking for "the other America," then it was "easy to assume that ours, indeed, is an affluent society" that anyone who works hard can enjoy.

For that first rehearsal in the lounge the musical director and vocal arranger, Milton Greene, led the actors and orchestra through all the songs. The musicians' easygoing response to adjustments in accents and phrasing set the tone for the afternoon's labor—intent but unruffled professionals simply getting the work done. When everyone moved into the theater at around 4:30, however, the collective good mood began its monthlong collapse. Initially, the culprit was the usual suspect that always frays nerves: the incorporation of all the show's technical elements. The eight-hour tech rehearsal that Wednesday night—it ran until 1:00 in the morning, with the company getting through just the first act—gave Robbins new reasons to abhor Aronson's turntable. Teaching the actors to step onto the revolving piece of floor without falling down—and then while maintaining a natural gait or a dance step—ate up two days of rehearsal. The snaking line of dancers in "Tradition" had to time their movements to the pace of the turntable, and they spent much of that first day marking out the moves. Sandra Kazan was the first to tumble to the floor and she learned shortly thereafter—through a backstage pay-phone call to a local doctor she'd seen that morning—that she was pregnant. Fear of falling again almost forced her to leave the show, but her doctor back home in New York reassured her that she could keep working and, more important, Aronson slowed down the speed of the rotation. Robbins made the troupe walk through the blocking again and again, and by Friday the cast had finally gotten the hang of it.

Not a moment too soon. The first preview audience was due on Saturday, and Robbins's dread was spreading. On Friday night, he upbraided Greene for the mushiness he alone heard in the music. Dismissing the orchestra for the night, he turned his attention to the actors, all of whom he felt fell short—Motel couldn't sing, Perchik lacked urgency, Fyedka was too meek. Not one cast member, he complained, seemed capable of walking across the stage without bumping into the scenery. And that, of course, had to be Aronson's fault, as Robbins did not hesitate to tell him. In a fit of frustration, he called a halt to rehearsal and sat, silently, in the auditorium with his head hanging low. The actors milled quietly backstage, afraid to move or speak. After five awkward minutes, Robbins beckoned Prince to his side. "What are you going to do about this, Hal?" he asked, loud enough for the company to hear, more plaintive than angry. "In my entire career, I have never put on a show in this condition."

Prince kept his affable cool. "Whatever it is, Jerry, just tell me and I'll take care of it." The two whispered together briefly and then Prince moved away. Robbins sat, quiet and motionless, for five minutes more, then suddenly clapped his hands to call the actors back to work. They instantly assembled onstage and rehearsal went on as if nothing had happened.

The first preview did its job: it began to show the creators where audiences were responding and where their attention flagged, where the play's emotions gathered and where they failed to materialize, where the laughs landed and where they died. Most of all, it showed the whole company that they had something that could hang together. Until that evening, they had never played the entire second act from beginning to end, in costumes and with all the light cues and set changes. Though the performance lasted nearly four hours that first evening and suffered some technical glitches—noisy stagehands in the wings, a drop entangling itself in a set piece, crew members caught in the light—most of the audience stayed to the end and then applauded heartily. A few walked out during the long, loose second act, but Harnick found a silver lining: "They were inching out backwards. That was the one encouraging thing." Stein, too, held his confidence in check, noting that much of the crowd that night was part of a Jewish group benefit. At the intermission he heard some of them talking in the lobby: "Well, *we* like it, but will *they* like it?" The performers weren't even noticing the audience that night. They were just glad to have completed the whole show without a major disaster. The dancer Duane Bodin was not the only one thinking, "Well, we got through that one."

To get through the one the next night better, Robbins began tinkering at rehearsal first thing in the morning. One audience reaction that perplexed him came after a charming song near the top of the second act, Motel's paean to his "Dear, Sweet Sewing Machine" in which he promises, as if taking a matrimonial vow, to love and honor it, to keep it clean and oiled if, in turn, the machine will help him make a living, transforming "satin and silk" into "butter and milk." True, Pendleton's singing scraped by on spirit (and Merlin's didn't compensate when she chimed in with some counterpoint), but he was a terrific actor and his weedy voice fit Motel's nebbishy character. The song had always been a favorite at backers' auditions.

Robbins had staged it so that at the end the townspeople came running in to see the tailor's amazing new contraption. During the first preview, they took up their places in the wings as the song began, and as Pendleton finished they did what every pro knew to do: they held for applause. They would rush on as directed once the clapping had peaked. But there was barely any clapping that night. Almost none. Mostly an awkward silence until the Anatevkans realized they should go ahead and make their entrance. Robbins discussed the problem with Harnick and Bock afterward—there were production meetings late each night after every performance—and at the rehearsal, they told Milton Greene what to do: the orchestra should play slower and more softly. "I'm afraid they're not getting the lyrics," Harnick explained to Greene. Pendleton and the musicians practiced it at the new pace and the new version seemed delightful.

But not to the second-night audience. Once again, they greeted the song with indifference. Otherwise, the second preview ran more smoothly—except for when Tevye's house, moving into place on the turntable, collided with a backdrop and the show had to be stopped. Prince came out to apologize while the technicians rescued the scenery.

The audience didn't mind. Even Pendleton "could feel their warmth" throughout the show despite their coolness toward his love song to his mechanical apparatus. Stein also felt the receptiveness from the house, and this time *they* were there: a non-Jewish benefit audience from an insurance company. The playwright started to allow himself "a feeling that we might have something very special."

The official opening the next night put a damper on that feeling. Not so much because the audience wasn't appreciative—though they still did not take to "Dear, Sweet Sewing Machine," despite the orchestra's now playing new underscoring at the end instead of stopping and leaving a hole that should have been filled with applause. The problem was the critics. There weren't any—or hardly any. The Detroit newspapers were on strike, and word was out that the fate of the show could rest in the hands of a single reviewer, the local stringer for *Variety*. Writing under the byline Tew, he was rumored among the cast to be moonlighting for the showbiz daily from his day job as a Chrysler vice president. In fact, he had studied theater at Northwestern—Harnick remembered him as a classmate. But the car-company quip seemed to fit, as if Chrysler in the 1960s conditioned him to appreciate designs with imposing front ends and squared-off rears; he had few favorable words for *Fiddler*, with its tidy first act and its still baggy second. His dismissive assessment plunged the actors into the doldrums, even though they had to know that Tew was wrong from his first line: "Everything is ordinary about *Fiddler on the Roof* except Zero Mostel." True, Mostel was sui generis, but a show about Jews living in the Pale of Settlement that begins without an overture, brings down the first-act curtain with a pogrom, and ends with a mass eviction—that was not ordinary, either. Tew declared the songs unmemorable, the sets, costumes, and lighting merely "serviceable," the direction "workmanlike," and the choreography "pedestrian."

But despite Tew's legendary pan, long remembered as the only Detroit review, other critics did, in fact, attend that night and they recognized—as the striking *Detroit News* writer Jay Carr said on local radio and TV (instead of in print)—that *Fiddler* was shaping up to be "an uncommonly fine musical." In an upbeat letter to investors on July 28, Prince quoted liberally from Carr and from enthusiastic reviews from Toledo and across the river in Windsor, Ontario. (There would soon be one in Chicago, as well.) The newspaper strike forced Prince to buy more expensive and less effective advertising on TV and radio, but the show was getting favorable coverage by critics. The producer was not worried about the "bum review" in *Variety*.

But back in New York, *Variety*'s was the only notice easily available, and apart from the investors on Prince's mailing list, few interested parties had seen any balancing accounts—until the *Times* reported a week later that *Fiddler* was "receiving good response in its run" in Detroit. In the meantime, doomsday rumors flew. Pendleton's agent called him from Manhattan the day Tew's review appeared saying she'd heard Robbins was going to be fired and replaced by George Abbott. Though Abbott had directed Bock and Harnick's *Fiorello!* and *Tenderloin*—only two of the dozens of shows "Mr. Broadway" had written, directed, or produced by then—Robbins had recently rescued *A Funny Thing Happened on the Way to the Forum* for his early theatrical mentor. What's more, Abbott—a buttoned-up WASP who had spent much of his boyhood on a Wyoming ranch—had not a stitch of affinity for *Fiddler*'s material. Besides, rail as Prince did about rising costs, he never lost confidence in Robbins as the only director who could make *Fiddler* robust. That the actors lent any credence at all to the false gossip was a measure of how done in they felt—and of their half wish that Robbins would just go away and leave them alone. He didn't.

The night after opening, with the *Variety* review and the New York sniping clouding their moods, the members of the company repaired to the bar across from the theater after the show and congregated around several tables. Pendleton noticed Robbins sitting off by himself at the bar and, after knocking back a Jack Daniel's, summoned the temerity to approach him. "So, Jerry. What are you going to do?" Pendleton asked. Robbins answered calmly: "Ten things a day."

One of the first was dropping "Dear, Sweet Sewing Machine." Not because Tew, in his only accurate judgment, had recommended excising the "forgettable" number but because Robbins, already realizing why it was failing, was planning to take it out as soon as Stein and the rest of the team could sew up the incision. "It's forward motion," he explained to Harnick. Tzeitel and Motel's romance has already been resolved by the time that song comes along and the audience is interested in what will happen with the other daughters and their suitors. "You can keep the first couple alive, but you can't give them a major number," Robbins said.

"The audience doesn't want to hear it. They want to go on." He broke the news to Pendleton, offering the same explanation along with his commiseration. Pendleton let him pretend to be sorry, though at heart the actor was relieved: "It's no fun being in a number that doesn't work." And anyway, he still had a song in the first act, "Now I Have Everything," his exuberant response to Tevye's accepting him as Tzeitel's intended: "Did you see what I did / When he laughed in my face? / I stood there and stiffened my spine. / The nerve of a tailor to ask for a queen / Without having goods or a sewing machine. / A nothing turned into a Samson, no less, / And lo and behold! You are mine!"

Accelerating the forward motion—in act 2, *finding* it—consumed Robbins as the work continued in what Kazan described as "agonizingly long" rehearsals that were "hell to go to." A sagging second act is a common enough problem in musical theater making to be a cliché—the exposition is over, the denouement is obvious, and getting to it just takes too long. *Fiddler* heaped on a few more troubles: there was still a lot of plot to go, and most of it was depressing.

And how could it be that, though they'd been talking about it since New York, Tevye had no second-act song and Golde had none at all? Although Harnick had imagined Tevye responding to his daughters' romances by suddenly wondering whether his own arranged wife loved him, he couldn't figure out how to make it work. He took long walks around Detroit trying to raise some ideas. Finally, he sent some words to Bock, apologizing that they sounded more like dialogue than lyrics. Bock came back with a setting that didn't change a word. It took Robbins no more than fifteen minutes to stage "Do You Love Me?" Its sweetness charmed audiences, as did its assurance that the hidebound elders learned from their modern children.

If scrapping the sewing machine song and giving the parents an unlikely love duet allowed focus to sharpen on the two other couples, that focus only made their shortcomings more obvious. Between Chava and Fyedka, Robbins didn't feel the spark—and how could their romance set off Tevye's sense that his world is collapsing around him if it wasn't convincing? Simply telling the actors to find some chemistry did no good. Reblocking them with approach-and-retreat patterns, to emphasize the physical attraction that they had to resist, didn't help, either. Robbins concluded that the problem was visual. Robert Berdeen was not much taller than Tanya Everett and looked young and innocent, even pretty. To convey that theirs was not mere puppy love, Robbins decided that Fyedka had to look more mature, like someone who could take care of her. He would have to replace the actor. Prince remembered a tall actor with a likable stage presence from some earlier shows he'd produced and found him on summer vacation in a cabin in New Jersey. Joe Ponazecki caught the first flight to Detroit that he could make; he needed a job and this one was offering $175 a week. (Berdeen—a fine dancer—was shifted to the chorus.)

Perchik and Hodel, in contrast, would take more work. Robbins had been complaining for a while that Bert Convy and Julia Migenes had to be pulled away from "that 'golly–oh gee shucks' business they've been indulging in." They were playing shiny, smiley Broadway lovers instead of fervent idealists of 1905, Robbins chided, saying they reminded him of the cloying Nelson Eddy–Jeanette MacDonald movies that aired on late-night television. He worked with them day after day on the scene when Perchik proposes marriage and, in the same breath, announces that he is going away. Frustrated and searching for a way to make Convy understand Perchik's revolutionary zeal, he told him—only a month after the murders of James Chaney, Andrew Goodman, and Michael Schwerner—to imagine that he was a student on his way to Mississippi to assist with voter registration. "You are not going to Coney Island for a ride on the Ferris wheel," Robbins prodded. "You are going on a dangerous mission. That's the urgency I want to feel in this scene."

Bock and Harnick struggled with Perchik, too. Trying to write a number for him that would express his fire as well as his charm and also push the action became what they called their "bête noire number 1." They wrote about a dozen different songs—some of them duets with Hodel—but couldn't hit the mark. Perchik ended up sounding too propagandistic ("You'll hear a rumble and the earth will shake / And Romanovs will crumble and the chains will break") or too cornball ("A dairy farmer's daughter / And a cigarette maker's son / Met in a tiny village / And there became as one"). Or too propagandistic *and* too cornball ("When we're free to be free / What a world that will be"). Finally, they came up with a satisfying argument song in which Perchik schools Hodel in how he'd behave "if I were a woman" ("I'd want to know why / I had to take orders / from men not a quarter as smart as I").

Detroit audiences always rewarded the tune with some laughs and a nice hand. So Bock and Harnick were stunned when, at a postshow meeting one night, Robbins said he was cutting it. "Are you out of your mind?" Harnick said. "It works!" Robbins answered with the impassivity of a mechanic explaining some minor engine trouble: "I know it works. But it's a four-and-a-half-minute number and the show is very long. I think I can accomplish the same thing in thirty seconds of dance and it may even be stronger. Let me try it." Bock and Harnick had heard that polite plea many times and understood what it really meant: "I will try it or you guys are fired." But Robbins also promised that if his plan didn't improve the show they would go back to the song. Sure enough, when Perchik pulled Hodel into a social dance he says he learned in Kiev, the action showed, in Harnick's words, "a transformation of tradition being broken, of men and women dancing. You saw the two of them falling in love, you saw her embarrassment. You saw him changing—a warmth you hadn't seen before. It was wonderful."

Still, Bock and Harnick were not going to waste the two best voices in the company. They had also produced a humorous love song for the top of the second act called "As Much as That," to come after the couple tell Tevye they plan to wed: "As much as I love the people, the workers, the peasants / As much as I love the work we plan to do / As much as that / And maybe more. Yes! More! / Do I love you." It, too, fell to Robbins's time-slashing crusade at the Fisher. The marchlike tune didn't tell the audience anything they didn't already know, he reasoned. Besides, Prince never liked it. The producer thought it crowed about "what a lot of fun it is to be a member of the Communist party."

In its place, the team gave Perchik a short reprise of Motel's act 1 song, "Now I Have Everything," with new lyrics Harnick dashed off in his hotel room. Convy brought out the lushness of the song, which, like all the other lovers' numbers in the show, musically marked the gap between the children's and the parents' generation, between the individual and the community—and, by extension, the New World and the Old. But Convy couldn't raise more than a tepid response from the house, despite his beautiful high baritone. Reprises didn't belong to the style *Fiddler* was forming for itself and the audience seemed confused by recognizing a tune they'd already heard.

But Robbins let it be for a bit while he focused on the more crucial, emotional pivot point of the second act: Tevye's anguish in response to Chava's elopement. Robbins had created the "nightmare ballet" he had planned—a complex, wrenching sequence that ran some ten minutes long, as Tevye reeled from place to place, searching out his beloved daughter. Robbins scored the movement precisely following an outline Stein drew with only a little variation from Sholem-Aleichem: Tevye goes to the priest's house—which Robbins instructed Aronson to place on one side of the stage—thinking he has been summoned over an issue with a cheese order, only to find that Chava has run off to marry Fyedka. At that moment, Robbins noted, "his world begins to tilt, careen, and come apart. Realistic time and place changes: events are condensed . . . his world becomes flooded with associative fantasies." He totters home (on the other side of the stage), where he slaps a child, screams at Golde, and knocks over a stack of his milk cans, kicking and beating them, and collapses. The family disappears and he gets up and rushes back out, searching for Chava. Robbins planned that, next, "through the village he charges in pain and the shtetl comes apart, fragmentizes and flies around him. . . . What pieces of scenery appear is treated normally at first, but as the sequence progresses, the bits and pieces of props etc. representing village etc. become transparent, unrealistic—swimming—detached and loose—a Chagall swirling past in pieces. The performers move these pieces themselves and in this way we arrive at the end in the shifting woods."

To realize this vision, Robbins placed villagers onstage going about their business in an abstracted sort of pantomime and then had them freeze as Tevye staggers among them. Others execute more complex steps while holding the whirling scenic pieces. (At last there was some choreography for the women in the corps.) Chava appears—then a second Chava. Tevye freezes, then lurches impulsively toward them, then abruptly stops himself and changes direction, running from Chava's entreaties. As he rushes through the woods, the trees—the chorus in a forest ballet—tilt and tumble as the stage is bathed in gradually intensifying washes of red light. The result was a wrenching expressionistic spectacle, an external rendering of Tevye's inner torment.

By all accounts, Mostel melted down before the audience's eyes in a disintegration as complete and convincing as his famous transformation into a rhinoceros. He didn't tear his hair or beat his chest in ever-larger histrionic gestures; instead, it looked like the air was slowly leaking out of him. He became weaker with confusion and despair, wordlessly questioning why God created both Gentile and Jew.

Harnick loved the sequence—"it was sensational"—but reluctantly had to agree with Stein that after it "the show died." The audience barely applauded at the end, and if Robbins wanted to think that they were too emotionally devastated to clap, he couldn't help noticing that they never fully reengaged the show from then on.

At rehearsal each day he reduced the sequence further, trying to distill the action and emotion to their most concentrated essence. The smaller it became, the larger the audience response. "If he takes it out altogether," Bock joked, "it will be a showstopper." Bock was basically right. Over a couple of weeks of condensing, Robbins converted the elaborate episode into an elegant, heartbreaking event, just a minute or two long: the daughters, upstage—as if seen in Tevye's mind—are courted in dance, accept their suitors, and go off, as Tevye mourns the flight of his "little bird." He can't make sense of what's happening: "Everything is all a blur. / All I can see is a happy child. / The sweet little bird you were / Chaveleh, Chaveleh." In one of the show's most effective shifts from the particular to the universal, Tevye's despair over Chava's apostasy boils down to a father's grief over the loss of a daughter.

If Robbins felt any chagrin over tossing out weeks of work, he didn't show it. He held nothing—and no one—too precious if it didn't serve the show. Having cut the character of the priest, he dismissed the actor Charles Durning. Robbins realized, he told the authors, that the expressionist mode was totally out of character with the rest of the show and yanked the audience away from the fictive reality the artists had worked so hard to establish. In contrast, the Fruma Sarah dream sequence in the first act unfolded within the reality of the story: Tevye was, in fact, recounting a dream (albeit one he had invented to persuade Golde to let Tzeitel marry Motel instead of Lazar Wolf). And that comic aspect helped them get away with a big expressionistic production number. But the Chava nightmare didn't belong. "It was a mistake," Robbins said, placidly dismissing the result of the company's long, exhausting labor. "I should have known that."

For all the diminishment of the Chava episode, Mostel did not let up on playing Tevye's rage and bewilderment over Chava's challenge to his core beliefs. And in this instance, he agreed with Robbins: the simpler framework made Tevye's distress more legible and specific. In the early part of the scene—which preceded the deleted choreography—Tevye refuses Chava's plea for acceptance. When he commands, "You are never to speak to him again, never to mention his name again, never!" Mostel yelled the word "never" as though he wanted to be heard in Chicago. Night after night, Everett felt like she'd been socked with a sandbag, even though she knew the shout was coming. The force of his voice was tremendous and terrifying every time. And he looked at her "like he wanted to kill me." Even the audience started, as if physically stunned by his volume and emotion. Mostel was channeling the severity of what his mother had done to him, his son Tobias Mostel reckoned: "That's why it cut the audience in half every night." This scene was the play's emotional climax as far as Mostel was concerned. Future actors would save the highest feeling for the eviction at the end, but for Mostel, Tevye's tragedy was his separation from Chava.

Mostel was playing lighter scenes with just as much comic intensity and, as early as Detroit, was beginning to test the limits of the script with his infamous embellishments. In "Rich Man," Robbins gave him a bit of business at a moment where the song calls for him to sigh: he should raise his hands to God with the sigh, then drop them—only to catch one in a milk barrel. His sleeve would come out wet and Mostel was to shoot a look heavenward as if to say, "Even this?" and then wring out the sleeve and go on with the song. Within two days, endlessly inventive Mostel was performing five minutes' worth of lazzo. He dabbed milk behind his ears like perfume, used it to grease the wheels of his cart. On the third night, he sighed, lowered his arm, and took it out—dry. Robbins had instructed the crew to leave the barrel empty. He won that round. But the battle had barely begun.

Once the schedule of performances started, Mostel was excused from most rehearsals to rest up his leg. His understudy, Paul Lipson, stood in, and Robbins's assistant relayed any changes to Mostel a couple of hours before curtain. That's all Mostel needed. To the other actors' amazement, he could learn new lines in a glance and absorb physical and interpretive adjustments without rehearsal. If his absence from the daytime labors left the cast without their comic relief, it also spared them the endless hostility between him and Robbins. The director was giving off enough rancorous vapors without Mostel in the room, and who knew how much more toxic the air would have become if Mostel had been goading Robbins as he smoldered. As each day wore on, the company felt more certain that the show was a disaster. After all, Robbins was not satisfied with anything—he found fault even with the scenes that seemed to be playing well. At one point he suddenly decided that Fruma Sarah should make her entrance in a coffin, and Aronson and his crew had to snap to and produce one, despite Prince's hollering about the budget. The coffin went in—and came right out the next day, when Robbins decided he didn't like or need it.

Zipprodt, too, could hardly keep up. She remade Everett's skirt fifteen times because Robbins wanted it to flow a particular way when she moved. Meanwhile, he was demanding rewrites from Stein every day and, at least once, threw new pages at him, denouncing the writing as amateurish and embarrassing. Stein just kept bringing the pages. Robbins's sniping at Bea Arthur escalated as the size of her role dwindled and her own temper flared. Karnilova, ever Robbins's champion, tried to boost the others' spirits. "The man is a genius," she reassured them. "He'll pull it together." But she didn't persuade the troupe. If nothing else, the cast was simply too fatigued from what seemed like arbitrary changes and colossal disregard for their toil to recognize how much better the show was actually becoming.

The proof was in the local word of mouth. Even after the subscription audience ran out, houses kept filling up. By the third week, *Fiddler* pulled its first hint of profit—$1,600—on a deal with the Fisher that gave the show 70 percent of the box office up to the first $20,000 in sales and 75 percent of any amount over that sum. The show cost about $50,000 a week in operating expenses so when, in the fourth week, the profit reached $8,300, Prince silently congratulated himself. The Detroit run closed on August 22 with total losses to date of $5,335.65—a better outcome than most.

Pendleton likened Robbins's refinements large and small to the work of an art restorer removing smudges from a canvas: "Suddenly all the composition and color scheme of the painting are revealed. It was just like that." With several outstanding additions still to come that would send the show over the top, *Fiddler* left the Midwest in good shape.

* * *

The cast, on the other hand, was in a shambles—actors sick, dancers injured, everyone in a state of advanced exhaustion. But from their point of view, Robbins was faring even worse: he was "having a hard time," in Kazan's generous phrase; Pendleton deemed him "in a torment"; Bodin thought he was "unraveling." Harnick cracked a joke in a discussion about a song revision, and when Robbins glared at him and snapped, "I want that lyric as soon as you can get it," Harnick remembered Sondra Lee's advice: "With the tone of his voice and the look in his eye, I thought: 'Okay. This is the time. Stay out of his way.'"

That wasn't really an option, though. Rehearsals resumed in a hotel ballroom within hours of the troupe's arrival in Washington, while the scenery was being put in at the National Theater, and production meetings continued every night. In the absence of the Chava sequence, Robbins was still struggling to find a big production number for the second act—he thought the audience wanted one. When he renewed the notion of a company song about Anatevka, Bock and Harnick came face-to-face with their "bête noire number 2." In the first, light and humorous version, spurred by the arrival of a letter from New York, the villagers asked, "Is it really such a paradise, America? / Nothing but unhappy people go there / People who hunger for letters from where? / Anatevka, Anatevka." For bringing the action to a halt, this song was abandoned after a few performances at the Fisher.

But Robbins clung to his desire for an act 2 wallop. Though *Fiddler* was successfully defying many of the conventions of a midcentury book musical—no overture, no flirty chorus girls, no reprises, no simple plot line, no happy denouement—Robbins wasn't letting go of a presumed need for a big number to start off the second half with a surge of energy and to win the sort of ovation that "Tradition," "Tevye's Dream," and "L'Chaim" were drawing in act 1. At the nightly meetings, he pushed for an occasion to put in something splashy. He liked Stein's suggestion that a refugee from another town passes through Anatevka and, on his way out, disparages the town as a "mudhole," prompting the locals to defend their home in a tuneful boast charming for its modesty. Bock and Harnick responded with a zesty song called "A Little Bit of This," which began with Golde intoning, "What does he mean, a mudhole?" and soon had Tevye chiming in: "Let him go to Minsk or Moscow or Pinsk / Let him go to America. / What does he think he'll find? / Everything is here! /

Maybe not a lot / But every little thing a man could need or want we've got." They wrote two more introductory options, all three of them leading to a chorus in which the people catalog their worldly possessions: "A little bit of meat / A little bit of fish / A pot and a pan and a glass and a dish / A little bit of wood / A little bit of twine / A slice of bread and a drop of wine / All very small, small indeed / But in Anatevka, all we need." The song expressed a romantic ideal of the shtetl that Maurice Samuel and Abraham Joshua Heschel had made popular more than a decade before: that what the people lacked in material wealth they made up for in spiritual riches and communal cohesion. Though the number went through several transmutations before being fixed as the mournful hymn preceding the expelled Jews' exit, this sentiment remained at its core: both a compliment to contemporary audiences for how far they had climbed from their humble origins and a reminder of all they may have sacrificed for their achievement.

Through the three weeks in Washington, Robbins feverishly built and rehearsed the number, bringing nearly the entire company onstage for the sort of high-energy spectacle audiences would have expected from the choreographer of *West Side Story*. A villager singing about a pot begins to bang on it with a ladle, another thumps a spoon against a pan, a third plinks a cup with a fork. One by one, then in twos and threes, the villagers join in the merry rhythm making with various household utensils. Some hit a table, others stomp the floor in the syncopated beat that builds and builds, until the orchestra comes in with a jaunty melody and the whole town gets caught up in this celebration of simple means. Meanwhile, the individual townspeople—the performers making use of the biographies Robbins had required them to write—present themselves in dance. The fishmonger and hatmaker hawk their wares; the street sweeper twirls in off-center turns with his broom (a bit of choreography made possible by the skills of the man in the role, the dancer Sammy Bayes). The women in the corps, having had their opportunity to dance taken away when the Chava ballet was cut, now weave through the action in a pretty, simple-looking sequence built of complicated steps. Robbins insisted that the troupe retain their bearing as villagers. "Give me klutzy!" he admonished the men. The dancing accelerated into exuberant patterns—and performers, giving him plenty of klutzy, barreled into one another during rehearsals. One of them, John C. Attle, was knocked out in a collision one day. That hardly deterred Robbins. He worked the scene every day for a week.

Meanwhile, Robbins was having his own head-on crashes with various company members. Rehearsing the new number, he snapped at Duane Bodin for moving too gracefully. Bodin took off his hat, flung it across the stage, and stormed off into the wings, where he filled out the quitting notice Equity rules require. Bock, Harnick, and the stage manager, Ruth Mitchell, found him sitting by the electric boards and calmed him down, reminding him they'd soon be in New York, where the show would be a smash. Bodin couldn't believe that prediction in the moment, but the authors had a clearer external view. And they had seen the lines at the box office when they arrived in Washington. With government offices still closed for August vacation, the city couldn't have been deader. The National had not signed on to any Theater Guild subscriptions for the summer. So the queues meant only one thing: word had gotten out from people who had seen the show in Detroit.

As a stagestruck adolescent growing up in the capital whose summer-camp buddy was Joe Stein's son Harry, the future theater critic Frank Rich was hanging out in the National with Harry during *Fiddler*'s tryout and saw the rapture with which the show was received from its first night there. Even for the town's "unsophisticated audience and such a Gentile audience," *Fiddler* was "electrifying."

The local critics thought so, too. They were invited for the third performance in Washington, and when reviews appeared on August 28—with the *Post* declaring, "Joy, there is such joy in *Fiddler on the Roof*," and lauding it as neither a conventional musical nor a folk opera but as a new form "put together with freshness to make you feel and to make you laugh"—some of the creators' anxiety began to lift. The following week a new, bolder thought entered their heads: the show might even succeed without the star.

No one doubted how much Mostel had added to the development of Tevye's character or the magnitude of his unique brilliance—Frank Rich, who went on to see hundreds of first-rate productions, calls Mostel's Tevye "the greatest performance I have ever seen in the musical theater. . . . It was like Scofield in *Lear*." But Mostel raised the unthinkable and unspeakable notion when he fell ill during a performance. After completing "If I Were a Rich Man" during a Wednesday matinee, he apologized to the audience and called out, "Ring down the curtain!" and then crumpled onto the stage. His understudy, Paul Lipson (who played the role of Avram, the bookseller), was hurriedly dressed in Tevye's faded blue vest. A plaid kerchief was tied around his neck and a brown cap plonked on his head, while Prince walked out in front of the curtain to announce that Lipson would be continuing shortly. Though Lipson had substituted for Mostel in many blocking rehearsals, he had never actually rehearsed or acted the role. He didn't know the lines and only vaguely recalled the songs, but Prince deemed canceling the performance out of the question. Lipson went out, with a surprising calm, and did what he could. The rest of the cast pulled him through, while the stage manager fed him lines from the wings when his approximations went too far off course.

Mostel tried to go back into the show that evening, but one of his symptoms was laryngitis, so even if he could have mustered the energy for the three-hour performance—in which Tevye not only remains onstage most of the night but wrings himself out emotionally—he had no voice. He stayed out for several days. To the creators' amazement, audiences did not complain. Not more than a few returned their tickets on hearing that the star was indisposed, and the rest rewarded Lipson with enormous ovations. The playwright Lonne Elder (observing the show's development through a program for young theater artists) incredulously overheard people in the lobby saying they couldn't imagine anyone better. True, Mostel's ruthless talent likely could not be imagined by anyone who hadn't seen it. Still, Lipson, with his lighter, sweeter Tevye, didn't so much carry the show as demonstrate that the show could carry him—that is, the creators could entertain the thought that while *Fiddler* was transcendent with Mostel, it no longer required him. (Lipson eventually led touring productions of *Fiddler* and, later, revivals; when he died in 1996, he had played the role more than two thousand times.)

Lipson's success was not enough to satisfy Robbins. He was certainly not persuaded by Harry MacArthur's concluding remark in the *Star* that "you may just not be able to find anything wrong with *Fiddler on the Roof*." Robbins found plenty. He assembled the cast in the first couple of rows of the theater the morning after the reviews came out and sat on the lip of the stage enumerating the many faults of their show—while Mostel stalked upstage, wagging his behind and giving Robbins the finger.

One day, the thing most wrong in Robbins's estimation was Austin Pendleton. Robbins thought he had fallen into a rut as Motel and—worse than anyone else in the fatigued cast, which had started to coast once the favorable notices had appeared—was simply not working hard enough anymore. More than anything, Robbins hated complacency, and he was not going to allow anyone to slack off. "Last night during the wedding scene I had to leave the theater," he told Pendleton right before a matinee performance. "I couldn't bear the thought of that wonderful young woman being married to you." And that, according to Pendleton, was "one of the milder things he said." The actor refused to speak to Robbins for a week, and as the days went by, he felt his performances getting weaker as his confidence evaporated, until he became convinced that he would be fired—even as Bock and Harnick were working on a new song for him.

Motel (Austin Pendleton) stands up to Tevye (Zero Mostel) and wins the hand of Tzeitel (Joanna Merlin).

Convy had lobbied for "Now I Have Everything" to be taken away from Pendleton and given to him. The song's sentiment fit Perchik better, he argued, and he didn't have to point out who was the superior singer. Bock and Harnick had already begun working in Detroit on a replacement number for Motel. Harnick credits two inspirations: a note Robbins gave him and Bock in a meeting telling them that in response to winning Tzeitel, Motel needed, musically, an outburst of exuberant happiness, and a line Stein had written for Motel in that moment: "It's a miracle!" Harnick fished in the nightstand of his hotel room for a Gideon Bible so he could brush up on some godly interventions and churned out lyrics for "Miracle of Miracles" fitting a pious young man with their references to David and Goliath, the wall in Jericho, and manna in the wilderness. Bock set Harnick's words to buoyant music made to order for Pendleton: the melody and chordal harmonies were simpler than those of "Now I Have Everything" and the range was tighter. The songwriters rehearsed with Pendleton on the sly, and during the second week in Washington they presented the number to Robbins. "Okay, show me," the director said—the first words he'd spoken to Pendleton in days. "Let me see what your instincts are. Do whatever you want to do." The dance music arranger, Betty Walberg, played the accompaniment on the piano and Pendleton sang and strode around a bit. "Play the music again," Robbins told Walberg, and he improvised some simple movement: arms tracing a circle on their way to clapping hands, little skipping steps, a joyous sink to the knees. "Okay, now do those," he told Pendleton, whose excitement swelled even though he was learning the gestures "through a cloud of rage."

Acquiring the number didn't pull Pendleton out of his fury, though, and when Prince caught him backstage one Tuesday night, between his final exit and the curtain call, to invite him for a postshow drink, Pendleton thought he was about to be fired. At a table in the back of the bar at the Willard Hotel, where most of the cast was staying, Prince played what turned out to be one of the most important roles in *Fiddler*: the offstage good cop to Robbins's tyrant. Prince put a double Jack Daniel's in front of Pendleton, sat down, and leaned in. "What's the problem, Austin? Is it Jerry? He's being mean to you?" Prince asked, as Pendleton recalls. Then he added, sounding as conspiratorial as he could, "If I was directing and a producer ever did this to me, I would kill him, but I'm doing it. Don't listen to Jerry. Fuck him. You have two shows tomorrow.

Just go out and do them. Over this past week, we gave you 'Miracle of Miracles,' and you're still out there depressed all the time. It's stupid. It's nothing. What do you want? You have one of the best songs in the show. Just don't listen to him."

In the two shows the next day, Pendleton felt his vitality begin to come back, and then Robbins called the first rehearsal of "Wonder of Wonders" with the orchestra. With the whole cast sitting out in the house, Pendleton and Merlin took up their positions onstage and cued the lines leading up to the song. "It was a miracle!" Pendleton said, and the strings came in with their introductory arpeggios. Pendleton bounded through the song, with the skips and handclaps and a breathless gush in his singing. When the horns blared in for the big finish, Robbins vaulted onto the stage. "Fabulous!" he cried. "You're great!" It was as if the week-long skirmish had never happened. With only a few performances to go before the company moved on to New York, the song went in that night.

Meanwhile, Mostel's favorite song had been taken out. It came near the end of the show, after the eviction edict is delivered to Anatevka. "We've been waiting for the Messiah all our lives. Wouldn't this be a good time for him to come?" Mendel asks. Tevye answers, singing about how the Messiah, when he does show up, will apologize for having taken so long. But the Jews weren't easy to find, "over here a few and over there a few." Still, he'd make everything work out. The song had to go, the authors understood, because at a moment of pathos the audience could not accept a wry comic number. Mostel hollered about how stupid Robbins had to be to reject it, but Mostel was not in the audience, Harnick noted. "From the stage he couldn't see that in the context the song didn't work." True enough: Broadway musicals of the mid-1960s were not yet hospitable to tonally jarring juxtapositions that would become postmodern commonplaces later (in works by Kander and Ebb, for example).

But "When Messiah Comes" didn't fit for deeper reasons that make its ejection more than an amusing footnote to the creation of *Fiddler*. First, the lyrics refer obliquely to the Holocaust—"Would that be fair / If Messiah came, and there was no one there?"—and *Fiddler* was recalling the Old Country as the place left behind for the promise of America, not as the graveyard it became. The Messiah's tuneful apologies clashed with *Fiddler*'s forward-looking way of looking back. More important, the song hammered home the central doctrinal difference between Christians and

Jews—that hardly minor matter of whether or not the Messiah had actually shown up just yet. With its universalizing impulse—and the desire among midcentury Jewish spectators to blend in as a distinct but well-fitting member of the American mosaic—*Fiddler* couldn't afford to draw excessive attention to this contrast. This was the one place the show threatened, indeed, to be "too Jewish," and that, more than the out-of-place comic tone, is likely what caused the audience to feel, in Harnick's estimation, "a little uncomfortable." Robbins pulled the song.

* * *

Even as he kept working on the second-act Anatevka extravaganza, Robbins was quietly preparing what no one dreamed the show needed: another first-act dance number. The wedding celebration featured some embellished horas and then Perchik's city dance. And the inn scene's "L'Chaim," with its athletic feats and comic contrast of Jewish and Russian styles, more than sufficed as a crowd pleaser. Why couldn't Robbins leave well enough alone?

Simple. He could not forget "Mr. Redbeard," the man performing a *flashen-tantz* at the weddings he had visited as part of his fieldwork, and the men's revelry in the homosocial Orthodox world, where, "without any constructing elements except a rudimentary rhythm and an avid impulse to express their communal joy—the men stomped, kicked, hit the floor and . . . tossed their arms about, flung their bodies around." Back in March, when Robbins had written to the authors with the long list of changes he expected them to make to the script and score, he offered only one unqualified declaration of enthusiasm: "The wedding scene is going to be wonderful, I think." Robbins knew an occasion for an elaborate production number when he saw one; less than two weeks from the Broadway debut, he had not yet finished turning the original story's lean mention of the wedding into a showstopper.

As a teenager performing in Maurice Schwartz's production of *Di brider ashkenazi*, Robbins had seen up close how a staged wedding could combine ceremonial dignity and theatrical fireworks. Eight or nine times a week, for nearly six months, Robbins took part as a supernumerary in the Yiddish play's marriage scene. Robbins doesn't mention the solemn, lavishly staged nuptials (or anything else about the production) in his notes and letters on *Fiddler*, but Schwartz's savvy showmanship could not have failed to make an impression. Beyond the spectacle, *Fiddler*'s wedding scene carried forward an impulse that had made Jewish weddings a staple on the Yiddish American stage: they permitted immigrant audiences to maintain, through a secular form, pleasurable ties to ritual practices they may have left behind. At a further remove—over the distance of time and historical catastrophe, as well as geography—the Jews in *Fiddler*'s audiences could lay claim to such a tie, even as the vigor of the dancing refuted the shame that may have been associated with it: the choreography debunked the common stereotype of weak, effeminate male Jews, so recently accused of having gone like sheep to the slaughter.

Coming right in the middle of *Fiddler*, the wedding scene would be central in more ways than one. In thoroughly theatrical terms it makes the show's essential gesture in a brilliant confluence of form and theme. It provides a fond and historically authentic representation of a traditional wedding ceremony—the chuppah, bride's veil, ring placed on the index finger, stomped-on glass, and so on—and swathes it, musically, in an American sensibility. Visually, the scene goes (to borrow key words from the Jewish ceremony) according to the laws of Moses; aurally, it goes according to the heartstring tugs of Tin Pan Alley. Fittingly a waltz, the song Tevye and Golde sing over the action—the tune that had made Bock's wife cry in their Westchester basement when he and Harnick first played it early in their work on the show—lilts with the thoroughly universal wistfulness of parents wondering, "When did she get to be a beauty, when did he grow to be so tall? Wasn't it yesterday when they were small?" Robbins was tempted to cut the song. He couldn't see how to stage it. What are Tevye and Golde *doing*? he needed to know. Bock and Harnick took turns stating the obvious: "Just have them sing it." For once—and crucially—they prevailed.

No one in the company knew about the late-night work sessions Robbins had conducted with Tommy Abbott and Betty Walberg during the weeks in Detroit, trying out choreographic ideas that Abbott kept track of. And though sometimes Sandra Kazan arrived early to rehearsal and caught Robbins onstage, clad in khakis and a white T-shirt, silently sketching out moves with his body, she had no idea what they were for. So the male dancers could not fathom why they were suddenly called for a 10:00 a.m. rehearsal in the theater lobby in Washington a week into their run there. Many who did not have demanding parts in the "L'Chaim" dance had long figured that nothing taxing was being asked of them and had stopped keeping up a daily workout routine.

Robbins didn't say much by way of explanation when the dozen men assembled in the carpeted lobby: "This is the dance at the wedding to entertain the bride and groom. Here we go." He showed the troupe some steps—walking in a circle with some bounce in the knees, to begin—and then passed out glass bottles and told the dancers to put on yarmulkes and do the steps again with the bottles on their heads. One by one, the bottles thudded onto the carpet. Robbins instructed the men to try again. And again. Sammy Bayes finally made his way through the sequence, but the movement looked so tentative and stiff as he used all his energy to concentrate on not dropping the bottle that Robbins finally allowed the men to put on hats. But he permitted no tricks—no holes cut into the crowns, no Velcro. He wanted the audience to feel the tension—for the sheer theatrical thrill as well as for the emotional echo of the precarious eponymous fiddler trying to scratch out a tune without breaking his neck. The dancers definitely felt it. Bodin wasn't the only one "scared shitless": all the men knew they would be dancing on a wooden stage and that the choreography called for some of them to slide across the floor on their knees. Glass splinters were not an option.

But the more they practiced, the more undemanding the bottle balancing seemed—standard for those who had stayed in shape and were used to "pulling up" into the dancer's efficient posture of tucked-in pelvis and lifted rib cage. Robbins selected for the role four men who found the trick easy enough to be able to make it *appear* arduous. Then he showed the group the next section, which most of the rest of the corps would join, featuring far more difficult moves—"whips and hooks," Robbins called them, body flings that required quick twists and jumps and changes of direction. "You're working yourself into a state of joy," he told the men. Within a couple of hours—like magic, to Prince, who watched part of the rehearsal—the men absorbed the choreography. That afternoon, Robbins called a "put-in" rehearsal. The entire cast played through the wedding scene and they burst into applause—and some into tears—when they saw the new number for the first time. That night it went into the show.

It's impossible to know exactly what moves Robbins took from Mr. Redbeard's frolics or from the communal cavorting among the men at

Orthodox weddings, but certainly Robbins embellished on what he observed. Years earlier, when choreographing "The Small House of Uncle Thomas"—the second-act ballet in *The King and I*—Robbins hit a dead end trying to create authentic Siamese dance, despite his extensive research into the genre. Only when Richard Rodgers urged him to take some license with the movement vocabulary was he able to break through his inhibition and devise an exciting fourteen-minute dance drama that conveyed Thainess with its cocked legs, flexed feet and wrists, and wide-stance demi-pliés but that actually borrowed from the Balinese legong dance, Peking opera, Japanese Bunraku and Kabuki, and Cambodian dance—as well as from Martha Graham and, most important, from Robbins's own imagination. In the "Bottle Dance," Robbins similarly captured the spirit of the original by maintaining some essential elements—balanced bottle, arms pumping heavenward, the group in a frenzy—and then built on them with sheer choreographic ingenuity and showbiz panache.

Having seen one man pretending to totter drunkenly, flexing his knees and flicking his wrists, Robbins begins by doubling the spectacle: two men gently pulse their legs, twirl their hands, turn a full circle, and, maintaining their ramrod posture, sink to the floor, then spring back to full height. Facing each other and clasping right hands, they repeat the moves, punctuating them with some formalized handclaps and slow leg swings. Next, Robbins doubles the stakes again, arraying four men balancing bottles in a lateral line, holding hands at head height. To the stately beat of the score's most klezmer-inflected music, featuring a trilling clarinet and a jingling *tsimbl* (or cimbalom, the hammered dulcimer of Eastern Europe), the men slide stage left, then stage right in a series of syncopated grapevine steps: on tiptoe, tracing a semicircle along the floor with a foot, tapping the ground with the heel, or completing a phrase with an emphatic full-foot stomp. The music crescendoes and climbs up the scale like a fanfare signaling that something magnificent is about to happen—and it does. The men back up, still maintaining their line, and lower themselves to their knees. The orchestra's horns kick in, cymbals crash, and the men thrust out the right leg at a 45-degree angle, and then pull themselves forward along that vector, gliding upon the left knee and bringing it in line with the right for a slight showy pause in a kneeling position. Then the same routine to the left, then again to the right and to the left. Finally they rise up and let their bottles drop into their hands. As the music quickens, more dancers join in, and they all break into a wild ecstasy of motion: leaning back and, as if sending a signal to the heavens, clapping hands with a circular sweep of the arms that propels them into a spin. Some swing a partner round, hands on each other's biceps, and they seem to take wing by virtue of centrifugal force. No circle dance ever looked as vehement as the brief, brawny turn they make together before lining up side by side and linking hands with crossed arms. Thus joined, they advance downstage as a mass of throbbing rhythm for the finale: they jump and whirl and land on bended knee, arms outstretched—both a gesture of devout supplication and the quintessential footlight finish, made iconic as far back as 1927 by Al Jolson in *The Jazz Singer* (playing another Rabinowitz/Robbins pulled away from Judaism by show business).

That first night the dance was performed—and forever after—the audience exploded at the end. Here was Robbins's choreographic genius radiantly on display: two and a half riveting minutes of innovative movement that revealed situation and character, fed the action, and, in its very form, encapsulated the show's ideals of Jewish revivification and cultural adaptation. Legendarily, Boris Aronson watched from the back of the house that night and at the close of the dance turned to Richard Altman and said, "Any man who can do that, I forgive everything."

Mostel was back onstage by that point and the show, having been played before audiences some forty times, had found its groove—that place where the performers have absorbed into a kind of muscle memory all their cues and technical tasks and can devote their energies to being wholly present in their fictive reality.

But Robbins was still fretting over the big chorus number at the beginning of the second act he had yet to put into the show. After a week or so of rehearsing it, he had begun to wonder whether he could really justify the scene with the refugee coming through town, given that it so baldly functioned as a setup for the song and dance. And even the song felt like a drag on the action at a point when so much more of the story had yet to unfold. Even so, the pot-and-pan-clanging dance could be the act 2 element that would bring down the house as surely as the "Bottle Dance" was doing in act 1. Robbins hesitated to let that opportunity go.

But he did adjust the play's ending. The moment Mostel returned, Robbins quickly reworked the exodus of the villagers, thanks to some quick revisions from Bock and Harnick. They took out a bitter song called "Get Thee Out" and fused the "little bit of this, a little bit of that" music and lyrics to an earlier, slowed-down version of the Anatevka song to create a rueful farewell that expressed the ambivalence of exile. On the one hand, the townsfolk try to convince themselves that they would be better off somewhere else. "Well, Anatevka hasn't exactly been the Garden of Eden," says one villager over a vamping accordion, as a lead-in to the community's inventory of "a pot, a pan, a broom, a hat . . ." "Someone should have set a match to this place long ago," Tevye concurs. On the other hand, they sing of abiding attachment to home: "Where else could Sabbath be so sweet . . . where I know everyone I meet." They quote the original subtitle of *Life Is with People* in the closing lines of this leave-taking from the "dear little village, little town of mine."

Repositioning the song so that it follows the eviction order gave it a dramatic function—a reason for being that it lacked when placed earlier in the act. Robbins thickened its meaning with the change, too. At the end of the play, the song operates through classic dramatic irony: the audience knows something the characters don't know—that the Anatevkans, or at least their children, will be better off elsewhere. And not just any elsewhere. Tevye, Golde, and the two youngest daughters are heading to New York (and Tzeitel and Motel are expected to follow before long). American spectators can supply the happy ending that the play itself does not explicitly propose. Such warm satisfaction tempers a conflicting emotion that comes from a different kind of privileged knowledge: the future fate of Anatevka, functioning at its most synecdochic in this number that begins to bring events to a close.

The scenes leading up to and out of the song point forward in both affective directions, too: toward the Holocaust and toward American redemption. First comes the edict, delivered by the constable, who professes in act 1 to like Tevye "even though you are a Jew." He brings the decree to Tevye as villagers are gathered outside his home, in front of one of Aronson's most expressive backdrops: the same two trees that were in green bloom earlier now stand bare on an ocher background of a bleak winter. (Zipprodt has dressed the company in heavy coats, mufflers, and hats: the seasons have cycled through over the course of the play.) When Tevye, stunned, asks how the constable, who has known them his entire life, could do such a thing, the officer all but says he is "just following orders." Though the exchange runs only three lines, it marks a rare moment in which *Fiddler* not only evokes the Holocaust but also places the expulsion from Anatevka within a historical continuum in which, as the Passover Haggadah maintains, "from generation to generation our enemies rise up to destroy us." The constable is thus rendered as one more enemy in an eternal stream of Jew haters and the play enters a cosmic Jewish time zone. Now Tevye becomes anachronistic, too. "Get off my land," he commands in response to the constable's excuse. "This is my house." Tevye practically chases him offstage and, for good measure, Mostel spits noisily into the wings after him. Never mind that from Alexander III's notorious May laws of 1882 onward, almost all Jews of the Pale were forbidden to lease or purchase land. Tevye's claim to property grants him some authority and a means of fighting back, if only temporarily. It's one of the feel-good moments the ending depends on.

The other is Tevye's muttered "God be with you," spoken indirectly to Chava and Fyedka, who have come to say good-bye and explain that they "cannot live among people who would do this." This, finally, was Stein's century-bridging solution to a matter Sholem-Aleichem leaves unresolved. The original story cycle ends without its hero having made up his mind whether to embrace his returning daughter or to reject her. Stein sustains a bit of the tension by having Tevye speak under his breath with a nod toward Tzeitel, who repeats his blessing to her sister and brother-in-law. The bigger change is Fyedka's presence—Chava has left him in the original story—and his indignant and self-congratulatory comparison of himself to exiled Jews: "Some are driven away by edicts, others by silence." Tevye's recognition of their marriage, reluctant as it is, catapults him across time, the patriarch of the Pale putting at least one foot into the contemporary parental category excoriated by Marshall Sklare in *Commentary*.

In the penultimate line of the play, Golde tells the two youngest girls to "behave yourselves. We're not in America yet." But figuratively, they have already made the journey, bearing the values of American tolerance and adaptability that need only find the proper setting in which to flourish. In short, as Seth Wolitz aptly dubs them, they are a new generation of Pilgrims running from religious persecution for the freedoms of the New World, and thus (to borrow from an earlier musical) they belong to the land—*this* land.

Audiences embraced them as quintessential Americans, rising to applaud their departure for these shores night after night in Washington. Robbins had staged the exodus to such winning double effect, drawing acclaim in one gushing ovation both for the fact of Jewish immigration and acculturation (and for American tolerance and democracy that enabled them) and for the virtuosity of the show. With his last line— "Come, children. Let's go"—Tevye picks up the handles of his cart and begins to drag it along a counterclockwise arc, with the two girls following behind and Golde alongside; the turntable rotates underneath them, the house rolls off into the wings, and the rest of the company joins in circling the bare stage. As a snare drum rolls, everyone raises an arm toward the sky, recalling the gesture from the opening "Tradition" number, thereby saluting the past they are leaving behind—and then they drop their hands and walk off. The circle of the community established in that first song dissipates before the audience's eyes, "swirling away like in a Chagall," as it felt to Tanya Everett. Left alone with his family, again, Tevye tugs his cart forward and reveals the fiddler, bent over his violin behind it. He plays the four-bar theme, Tevye turns a full 360 degrees to take in his little world for the last time, and then, with a thrust of the chin, beckons the fiddler to join the family. The orchestra takes up the theme, crescendoing into a momentous final chord as Tevye, Golde, the two girls, and the fiddler curve along to exit and the curtain falls.

Robbins maintained the image in the curtain call, keeping the turntable revolving as the company assembled, seeming to be continuing their journey. As they took their bows, the actors began to let "some real excitement" seep in with the ovations. Among themselves—never in Robbins's earshot—they buzzed about the likelihood that they were in for a healthy run. "We all had the feeling that it was going to be enormous," Everett said, though "we were kind of amazed at how enormous."

The more smoothly the show was running, the more Robbins began skipping out to the lobby during act 1. Typically, he lost interest when he ran out of problems to solve, or perhaps he couldn't stand seeing the tiny imperfections that he would never be able to fix. A couple of days before the end of the Washington run, he left town altogether.

The company caught up with him in New York on September 14—after a luxurious rare day off—for a rehearsal at the vacant Barrymore Theater while the Imperial was being readied. First on the agenda, they ran through the act 2 extravaganza, showing it to Prince and the rest of the creative team. The troupe had worked on the number for nearly three weeks and, exhausted as they were, they were flying on the excitement of the upcoming opening and the knowledge that they had made a good show. They presented the number with precision and full hearts. The pots banged, the pans clanged. The women dancers twirled and leapt. When they finished, Robbins offered a simple "thank you" and quietly conferred with Prince while the company just stood around, sweaty and anxious. After a few minutes, Robbins turned to the troupe and, feeling his gaze, they straightened their spines, like recruits coming to attention when the sergeant walks in. "You know what?" he said. "We're not going to put it in." No one groaned. No one sighed audibly. But disappointment swept through the company. "You know why?" Robbins added, almost consolingly. "Because in Washington, the second act we already have came together and this number would violate everything we accomplished in creating a new kind of second act." Besides, in the creators' confab, Prince, who in any event could not bear the possibility that the show might add even two more seconds to its length, condemned the number. "It's not our show," he said. "It's villagers gamboling on the green. Let's be brave." Robbins assured the company that they were standing by a beautiful, quiet second act that was an innovation for a musical and the proper culmination of their story. And with that decision, the making of *Fiddler* was complete.

* * *

But of course Robbins called rehearsals. There was always fine-tuning to do and the actors needed to get comfortable on the stage of the Imperial, a Schubert theater built in the 1920s especially for musicals, with a wide, as opposed to deep, house that allowed the 1,400 spectators to feel close to the action. The backstage area was shallow, too, and performers had to make offstage crossovers beneath the stage, past the male chorus members' basement dressing rooms. Mostel had finally recovered thoroughly from his illness and was tapping replenished reservoirs of energy. He was jovial as a schoolboy on the verge of summer vacation, and even as he continued his jibes against Robbins, they were rounded by the pervasive mood of happy anticipation. Mostel, too, sensed the coming triumph— and he took the credit for it.

The company breezed through three preview performances for a rapturous audience and approached their official opening with a sense of confidence they could not have imagined only a month before. Harnick noticed the long lines at the box office and thought, "For the only time in my life, I don't have to worry about the critics."

The last rehearsal, on the day of the opening, was almost pointless in terms of making adjustments to the production. Robbins gave some notes simply for the sake of giving some notes. But the real point was for the company to feel, collectively, what Lonne Elder observed as a "serene quietness and resolve" about all they had endured and all they had achieved. "We came to love our village," chorus member Peff Modelski said. "We needed the performance to be wonderful."

As usual in theater culture's opening-night bonhomie, on September 22, break-a-leg telegrams poured in for the creators from colleagues in the field. Many hinted—even before the curtain went up that evening—how powerfully Jews, especially, would find connection in the show. In advance of the public, Jews in the Broadway community—that is to say, a high percentage of notable artists—cracked Jewish jokes or invoked religious phrases to wish their friends well, taking obvious pleasure in the opportunity to assert an identity that was seldom declared. "Good luck, but we demand equal time," Robbins's friend Stephen Sondheim wrote to him, signing, as if in a Groucho Marx role, as "Council of Roman Churches Monsignor Fulton J. Sonzheim Dealer." Barbra Streisand, still running in *Funny Girl*, cabled, "Come to our show tonight. Relax. Have a piece of fruit." Madeline Lee and Jack Gilford sent a wire to Bock, Harnick, and Stein promising that "the Talmud says tonight the world is a wedding. Good luck." (And a postperformance congratulatory letter to Harnick from Harold Arlen came half in Yiddish—albeit transliterated into the Roman alphabet.)

The creators expressed a deepening Jewish identification through the gifts they exchanged. Opening-night presents typically reflect a show's themes. Robbins gave beautiful art books—Chagall or Ben Shahn—to all the company members. (To Boris Aronson, who, after all, had written a book on Chagall, he gave a plant and a note of apology. And for the technical crew, he bought bottles of Scotch.) But for one another, the creators purchased ritual objects. Joe Stein, for instance, gave Harnick a mezuzah, the first the lyricist had ever owned. Harnick gave Robbins a shofar, the ram's horn sounded on the High Holy Days. In addition to the sentimental meaning any token of a special event bears, such gifts came imbued with significance that reached far beyond the show's own history and community. These weren't just ethnic tchotchkes but items with sacred functions, bearing power to assert belonging as indelibly (if more privately) as tribal markings, should they ever be used as religiously intended. The troupe gave Robbins a white yarmulke emblazoned around its rim with the words "Fiddler on the Roof, September 22, 1964." Each company member autographed it in ink. Mostel signed his last name only, and in Yiddish—*mem-alef-samekh-tet-lamed*—lording his superior knowledge over Robbins to the very end.

Assembled in the wings at 6:55 p.m., the company awaited the show's first cue. Lights would come up on the fiddler, Gino Conforti. Strains of the violin would play and the orchestra would take up his tune. Tevye would walk out and address the audience. "How do we keep our balance?" he'd ask. "That I can tell you in one word." Four oompah beats would blare from the string and rhythm sections in the pit, and the chorus would link those pinkies, take a collective breath, and strut out onto the stage as Tevye pronounced the key word: "Tradition!"

As the company waited, jitters kicked in. Just before the curtain went up, Mostel turned to the chorus and, eyes sparkling, opened his mouth in a twisted grin to reveal a red Life Saver stuck to his teeth. The gag broke the tension and, when the time came, the villagers strode out confidently for their song. By the end of the number, the company knew they would have gainful employment for a long time to come. They felt it across their backs, Modelski said, "like somebody tiptoeing with a little ice cube between your shoulder blades."

Prince sat calmly in the house, watching the audience as much as the show. They laughed, they cried, of course. But beyond that Broadway cliché, Prince discerned an admixture of delight and emotional engagement that he didn't know what to call. Spectators cooed as they clapped after "Tradition"; they "ahhed" during "Sabbath Prayer" as lights faded up behind the scrim to reveal Jewish families all over Anatevka—all over the world—lighting candles along with Golde and Tevye. He sensed their rapt, if silent, disquiet as Hodel went off to Siberia to join her revolutionary fiancé and as Chava eloped with Fyedka. He recognized the tingle of satisfaction that had become familiar from his successful openings of *Damn Yankees, West Side Story,* and *A Funny Thing Happened on the Way to the Forum.* But something was different this time. Thanks to

Tevye (Zero Mostel) evicted, but heading to America.

Robbins, he thought, *Fiddler* was entering some other realm. If the ovation that night lacked the foot stomping and shouting that had erupted
in Washington and in the New York previews, Prince didn't worry. He
had never been so certain that a show would succeed.

Expecting much to celebrate, Prince had reserved the swank Rainbow Room some sixty floors above his office at Rockefeller Center for the
opening-night party. Actors couldn't wait to take off their heavy, tattered
layers of woolen rags and put on smart suits and velvet dresses for the
festivities. For the first time in almost four months, the company would
not be assembling as Anatevkans. They would walk down the several
rounded steps into the ballroom, to guests' applause, simply and happily
as their shiny selves. Robbins was startled by their transformation. He
had forgotten that they had lives and realities beyond their onstage shtetl.

It was almost midnight by the time the party really got rolling because
throngs congratulating Mostel at his dressing room delayed the star's

arrival. Tony Cabot's Music Masters played to an empty dance floor for nearly an hour, but once Mostel made his entrance, the hully-gullying began, topped by what one observer called "a picturesque twist session that was not to be believed." Kate Mostel high-kicked her way through a jitterbug with John C. Attle. Not to be outdone, her husband whirled around the floor with New York senator Jacob Javits in a raucous hora to a quick medley of the show's music that Cabot inserted into the playlist of American standards.

Then word of the first review started seeping into the room like a noxious odor. In the *Herald Tribune*, Walter Kerr accused the creators of the one crime they felt exempt from: pandering. "I think it might be an altogether charming musical," he chided, "if only the people of Anatevka did not pause every now and again to give their regards to Broadway and their remembrances to Herald Square." Prince took the mic and told the crowd, "This is the biggest hit any of us will ever have gotten near, so party on." But he was too late. Bock and Harnick had left and much of the cast was filing out, too. Pendleton, for one, "didn't want to see Jerry after he read the reviews" and figured his colleagues shared the thought. "We felt maybe we'd let him down." Other reviews turned out far more favorable—in the *New York Times* Howard Taubman declared the show "an integrated achievement of uncommon quality"—but Prince would not have been surprised by the next day's box office lines around the block even without these notices. Harnick's hunch had proved right. Decades before the massive marketing campaigns calculated to render new shows "critic-proof," the reviews hardly mattered. Roberta Senn wrote to her parents in Chicago with a report on the opening (the twenty-two-year-old found the party "too glamorous to be fun") and urged them to let her know right away when they wanted to come in to see it: "We are sold out until December."

Harnick marveled: "There was something in this show that people wanted to see."

* * *

By February, Prince was sending distributions to investors. In June, no one was surprised that *Fiddler* swept the Tony Awards, winning as Best Musical as well as for book, score, direction, choreography, costumes, production, and performances by Mostel and Karnilova. (Mostel famously accepted his statue noting that, since no one else from the show who had been on the podium that night had bothered to thank him, he would thank himself; then he carried on a bit in Yiddish. He left the production in August, month after month of eight shows a week too much for his injured leg—and his contract renewal demands too much for Prince.)

But the "something" Harnick recognized was more than an affecting story, spectacular choreography, good songs, thorough and beautiful designs, and one of the most brilliant performances ever. In fact, *Fiddler* did not represent the greatest work of its creative team. *She Loves Me* boasts a superior score, *West Side Story*, more electrifying dances. The greater sum that *Fiddler*'s parts added up to went beyond the soul-stirring, radiant enchantments of even the best Broadway musicals.

Fiddler gave Gentile post-McCarthy America—and the world—the Jews it could, and wanted to, love. It gave Jews nothing less than a publicly touted touchstone for authenticity. And it did both while capturing the sensibility—the anxiety—of a tumultuous American moment and making reassuring sense of it.

Fiddler did so formally as well as thematically. In this period of transformation in the American theater—and of America in general—one key to *Fiddler*'s success was its status as a transitional work. The era of Rodgers and Hammerstein had ended with *The Sound of Music* in 1959; Stephen Sondheim's groundbreaking concept musical, *Company*, would debut in 1970. As deftly as its title character teetering on the roof, *Fiddler* balanced right on the pivot point between them. Without bidding adieu to the spectacular, sentimental, and storybook satisfactions that the old form provided (romances, explosive dance numbers) but gesturing toward the melancholy and irresolution that were to come (the pogrom and expulsion), *Fiddler* was formally familiar enough not to frighten or disorient audiences, and adventurous enough to excite them. It was a work of cultural adaptation and transformation as well as a work about such change.

In prompting audiences to identify with Tevye's struggle with change—on personal and communal levels—as upheaval bringing loss as well as gain, the show spoke to anyone who had experienced the conflict of leaving behind something profoundly prized, or at least deeply familiar.

Within a decade, *Fiddler* had played in two dozen countries—among them, Australia, France, Germany, Holland, Japan, Mexico, Yugoslavia, and even South Africa. (After a protracted battle against a company that would have performed for segregated audiences without the authors' permission, the authors agreed to an alternative production whose proceeds—as its program prominently declared—would benefit an organization of black artists.) Joe Stein loved to tell that at rehearsals in Tokyo that he attended, a local producer asked him how the show could have been a hit in America when it was "so Japanese." By 1971—just before the film version was released, spreading *Fiddler*'s reach far wider—there had been fifteen productions in Finland alone.

At home, Gentiles were gushing over its ethnic familiarity. In just one of many such congratulatory notes to the creators from friends and colleagues, the music arranger Bobby Dolan praised Robbins for expressing universality through particularity, for "as you must know, these Jewish people are equally Irish."

The response that came from the Jewish community was breathtaking. Today, after *Seinfeld* and Sarah Silverman—and, more apt, decades after the launch of the annual Chabad telethon, with its Hasidim frolicking and fund-raising on commercial TV—it's hard to imagine just how thrilled audiences could have been to see men wearing *tzitzis* and women lighting Sabbath candles on a Broadway stage, and not as a joke. Even the Yiddish press rejoiced. The conservative *Der Tog Morgen Zhurnal* couldn't help finding virtues in the "Broadwayized" Tevye; *The Forverts* declared *Fiddler* "Jewish America's most beautiful monument to Sholem-Aleichem." For those who harbored shame in the Old World ways of their parents or grandparents, as well as the guilt that comes barking after such patricidal feelings, the affectionate portrait of Anatevka seemed to wash humiliation away. Robbins had staged his own passage from Jewish repudiation to conciliatory embrace and perhaps spoke most directly to those who had heeded the same self-abnegating call. From that heritage that had been "laid open" for him, that he had "stored away—deep and away,"

> from all of that I closed my self off—dismissed, rejected & tore out of me. Blacked it out—forgot it & threw out (i was sure). Wash yourself clean of it—bathe & scrub; change your clothes, cut your hair, alter your walk, your talk, your handwriting, recast your future, remold your life, your friends, your taste; convert convert! No, don't adopt the Christian religion—do not go that far; but leave behind forever the Jew part. I became Jerry Robbins.

Making *Fiddler*, Robbins reclaimed that discarded part of himself and, in so doing, returned it, in a glittering package, to those audience members who also had left it behind. "*Fiddler* was a glory for my father," he wrote in the same set of notes toward an autobiography, "a celebration of & for him." At the end of the opening-night performance, Harry came backstage and found the director in the dimly lit wings. "How did you know all that?" he asked. He threw his arms around his son and wept.

* * *

Not that Jewish spectators had to be as hugely conflicted as Jerry Robbins to share in the outsize emotional response to the play. In letters of gratitude they extolled Hal Prince and the authors for showing the world the beauty of their Jewish heritage in a place they never expected to find it. Rabbis sent copies of the sermons they were giving based on the play. (That they were giving sermons at all was a matter of the cultural adaptation that *Fiddler* both embodies and celebrates: Jewish worship had been "Protestantized" in the postwar period and preaching became increasingly important to a congregational rabbi's role.)

One Jack Spiro attended the show on the first night of Passover and wrote to tell Hal Prince, "This is the first seder I've missed in many a year, but I felt more uplifted being in the audience of *Fiddler* than I would have had I passed that time in Temple." With a surprising twist, he added, "I want to thank you for restoring my faith in musical theater"—as pure a testament as there could be to the idea that popular culture answered the spiritual displacement of many midcentury American Jews.

Untold others tapped into this exhilarating public esteem, even if they didn't send notes to say so. One of thousands of such families was the Fiersteins from Bensonhurst, Brooklyn—Irving and Jacqueline and their two boys. From Irving's earnings at a handkerchief factory, they budgeted funds for regular family trips into the city for art exhibits, concerts, and plays. Jacqueline sent in for theater tickets as soon as new shows were announced and, as usual, garnered front-row balcony seats for *Fiddler* early in the run. The younger brother, age eleven at the time, was dumbstruck by the spectacle of men with beards and women with babushkas. In all their theatergoing, the family had never seen a stageful of Jews. The boy found it shocking. Most of all because those Jews were proud. Adults in his neighborhood gossiped about how Streisand ought to fix her nose and Jews needed to change their names to make it in showbiz, but here they were, a few blocks from an unaltered star faring so well in *Funny Girl* and, more astonishing, watching life unfold in a shtetl. Young Harvey Fierstein couldn't get over it: Jews had come out of the closet, exuding self-respect and treasuring their ways. Songs from the show would be played at his bar mitzvah two years later and the sensibility would stay with him a few more years after that, as he became a pioneering gay playwright and actor (and, decades later, played Tevye in a twenty-first-century Broadway revival).

Some audience members wrote in to affirm the show's veracity or, gently, to offer a suggestion or correction. "The play was the life of my grandparents, may their souls rest in peace," began one of many such responses, this one from a woman not yet sixty years old who had been born in Zembrow, Poland, which "was very much like Anatevka." Her grandfather wore a cap and a beard just like Tevye's, she wanted the creators to know, and the show reminded her of a family story about a teenaged cousin shocking the town by dancing with a boy at a local wedding: "My grandparents hid for shame."

A Mrs. Schwartz from East Orange, New Jersey, remembered having left "just such a little town in Russia" at age four and only wished that Tevye's family, like her own, had packed a brass samovar along with the candlesticks. "I'm sure you can pick up a samovar on 3rd Ave," she encouraged. "And believe me it will complete a beautiful scene."

The producer received kind instructions on how the "Anatevka" sign in the train station where Hodel departs from her father should be written in the Cyrillic alphabet, how an actor should properly pronounce "Kiev," how the ring in the wedding scene should be presented to the bride *after* the drinking of the first cup of wine, how Tevye should recite the Kaddish when he disowns Chava, and many more. Such letters suggest how powerfully *Fiddler* hailed members of the public who saw themselves reflected in it.

As *Fiddler*'s run extended over a year, then two, three, and more, the tone of the mail began to change. *Fiddler* was becoming an icon, which burdened it with extratheatrical responsibilities. The show reached its 900th New York performance in November 1966, without having had one empty seat or even an empty standing-room spot. In that short time, Prince had returned a profit of 352 percent to investors (not including the contemplated film sale, well in the works). And national companies were lighting down in cities large and small all over the country.

But one didn't need to be near a theater hosting a production to know and partake of the *Fiddler* phenomenon. In his Tevye costume, arms posed as if playing an invisible violin, Mostel graced the October 19 cover of *Newsweek* in 1964 (paid circulation 1.6 million). The original cast album, released that same month, topped $1 million in sales within a year. Right away, wedding bands all over the country were expected to be able to strike up its tunes on demand. Long before the movie played in cinemas in every small town, Cannonball Adderley recorded a jazz version of the score, Joe Quijano a Latin one. Eydie Gormé sang "Matchmaker" on the *Ed Sullivan Show* only a few months after *Fiddler* opened; the Supremes and the Temptations teamed up for a medley as part of a special broadcast on NBC. (Later, even the Osmond Brothers harmonized and boogalooed through the *Fiddler* songs in pastel three-piece suits.) *Fiddler* belonged to everyone.

The more *Fiddler*'s image of the mythic Jewish past proliferated, the more anxiety some Jews expressed over its duty to hold up a dignified, religiously correct ethnic self-portrait. For such spectators, *Fiddler* wasn't only speaking about Jews; it was speaking for them. And thus they had a personal stake in making sure the show got them right.

Complaints started to trickle in about Gluck Sandor's portrayal of the rabbi. Robbins initially enjoyed the "funny kind of tenderness" his old teacher brought to the role, playing him as a little frail and absentminded but approachable and admired by the community. As time went on, Sandor doddered across the line of dignity and spectators didn't hesitate to make their disappointment known. Beginning with high praise for the show in general, their letters objected to a "stupid ridiculous," "idiotic," "half-witted," "buffoonish" characterization that did "a disservice to the play and the Jewish people." No less than Maurice Samuel issued a public protest in a lecture in St. Louis, deriding the show's authors for presenting the rabbi as "a confused nebbish, a jester," and sniping that "only a Broadway musical comedy could cast the rabbi as a comic." Prince gamely answered the mail, explaining, "The real intention was that we not treat the rabbi pompously, over-reverentially. He's a villager and warm and fallible." Anatevka wasn't Vilna, after all; its rabbi was a provincial, not a world-class scholar. Still, Prince sometimes admitted, "the gentleman who plays the rabbi often gets carried away," and he knew that the authors

Hisaya Morishige as Tevye in Tokyo: within a decade,
Fiddler had played in two dozen countries.

agreed. Joe Stein held little faith that Sandor could go back to playing the "simple, gentle man" Stein had written, and pleaded with Robbins, "for the sake of the show and for my own peace of mind, I'd like to urge that we make a change." Robbins duly wrote Sandor "another letter about you know what—that rabbi problem again" and tenderly threatened his job. But Robbins couldn't bring himself to fire his early mentor; Sandor stayed in the show until 1970—with no impact on the box office.

Nevertheless, the mild outcry in the mail revealed the rising stakes in some quarters of the Jewish community. And soon it wasn't enough for the show to represent honorable Jews; it had to behave like them, too. To be a Jewish ambassador, *Fiddler* had to be a Jewish exemplar.

Never was this expectation more blatant than in a brouhaha over the dismissal of a cast member in the fall of 1966. The actor in question was Ann Marisse, a seasoned though young performer who had replaced Joanna Merlin as Tzeitel in the late spring of 1965. (Merlin left the show when her pregnancy reached the point—four and a half months—where the costume shop couldn't take out her wedding dress any further.) Prince found Marisse "strong and appealing" in her first performances. Taller than Tanya Everett and Julia Migenes, she commanded the space as the oldest sister and she sang well. She had taken over the part of Consuela in *West Side Story* and had racked up several other Broadway credits (including a role in the megaflop *Cafe Crown*). In *Fiddler*, she played for a year and a half without a glitch.

Then, in September 1966, she missed a performance on Rosh Hashanah without advance notice—or so management said. The producers typically allowed actors to take a day off for the High Holidays if they made a request in advance. Marisse called in sick the afternoon of the holiday instead but claimed she had already alerted her understudy. When the stage manager balked at the flouting of procedure, she cried discrimination. That incensed Prince. "It makes me especially angry in that she didn't even ask to miss those couple of performances," he told Robbins. "I called Joanna Merlin, and she seems anxious to return to the company for a number of months. Goodbye, Ann Marisse."

She did not go quietly. "It is true that I am an actress and that you are the producer. I am in your employ and you pay my salary. Does this also imply that you have leased my dignity and my spirit?" she wrote to Prince, reminding him that her father was an Orthodox rabbi and that her husband was ordained, too. (Her husband threw in the tallis, though, for a career in Hollywood; some years later, he directed the slasher flick *Graduation Day*.) Marisse complained to Actors' Equity, which affirmed that management acted within its prerogative, and threatened to go to the state's Human Rights Commission, which has no record of having granted the complaint a hearing. When she took her story to the press, however, journalists couldn't resist the apparent irony. As the *New York Post* put it, she was fired "of all things for not coming to work on the Jewish High Holy Days."

The issue of *Fiddler*'s observance of the High Holidays had come up the year before. It's a ready-made controversy: the contest between shul and showbiz for the soul of an American Jew on Yom Kippur is a sturdy emblematic one, driving the plots of works going as far back as *The Jazz Singer* and the melodramas of the Yiddish theater. The *New York Post* walked right into the trope in 1965, when Leonard Lyons ran a brief item in his column noting that the show would go on Yom Kippur eve, despite some misgivings from Luther Adler, who had replaced Mostel as Tevye. Letters to Prince's office protested that playing on the holiday was "a disgrace," "an insult to all Jews everywhere," and made "such a mockery of the traditions the show celebrates." An executive vice president of the New York Board of Rabbis sent a series of telegrams with such assertions as: "Sholem Aleichem would turn in his grave were he to know that his beloved Tevya who was so close to God would be violating the holiest day of the year publicly."

Prince took care to reply, explaining that canceling the performance wouldn't be fair to people who had purchased tickets more than six months in advance, particularly to those from out of town. "Next Tuesday evening 1500 people will leave the theatre with a warm and edifying impression of Jewish life," he wrote to the cable-happy rabbi. Or, as he put it more pointedly in his letter to Lyons, "The Imperial is not a Temple; it's a theatre, and *Fiddler* makes more friends for the Jews than Yom Kippur does." *Fiddler*'s curtain went up on the evening of October 5, 1965, just as it did at every other Broadway show then on the boards, and at every show on the boards in the past, including those with Jews in their plots.

A few days after the Lyons column that gave Prince "a potful of trouble," the *New York Times* sports pages carried a wire story of scarcely a hundred words. Its headline: "Koufax Out Wednesday." The superstar southpaw's refusal to pitch the World Series opener for the Dodgers on Yom Kippur galvanized American Jews across the denominational spectrum. To the pitcher's own surprise, he was suddenly elevated to a valorous Jewish status he had never intended when he reflexively put into his player's contract some years earlier that he would never take the mound on the holiest day in the Jewish calendar ("comparable to Good Friday for Christians," the *Times* helpfully pointed out).

That Koufax wasn't religiously observant—and probably didn't even attend services on Yom Kippur—made the gesture all the more important in affirming the identities multitudes of midcentury American Jews had been forging. With dispersal from urban centers in the postwar period, affiliation with synagogues skyrocketed, increasing from 30 percent in 1930 to nearly 60 percent in 1960 and rising, even as religious practice declined. By the mid-1960s, a majority of American Jews were living in suburbs, where affiliating with a modern synagogue was the most concrete (and least onerous) way of asserting Jewishness: belonging to and supporting the multipurpose institution—often, as the saying at the time had it, "shuls with pools"—mattered more than ritual observance. Sanctuaries filled up on Rosh Hashanah and Yom Kippur but drew a mere smattering of congregation members on the Sabbath and other holidays. Community leaders derided the growing legions of "twice-a-year Jews" and wrung their hands over the constant crisis of Jewish continuity: yes, all those suburban synagogues operated Hebrew schools where children learned the rudiments of the faith and prepared for bar and bat mitzvah, but without reinforcement in the home, without any lived experience of Judaism's rites and rhythms, the rabbis and Jewish educators worried, what would being Jewish mean for them?

Mass culture was providing some of the answer, though likely not the answer those community leaders were looking for. A real-life Jewish hero broadcast into living rooms across the country, Sandy Koufax proclaimed his Jewishness in a once-a-year observance that not only sufficed for much of the Jewish public but ratified them. Koufax's photo went up on bulletin boards in those Hebrew schools all over America; his name was invoked in High Holiday pulpits. His refusal to play on Yom Kippur was the proudest moment in popular Jewish American culture since, well, the opening of *Fiddler on the Roof.*

So a year later, when Ann Marisse's cry of foul hit the papers and local TV news broadcasts, standing up for the couple of days still held sacred even in the most unobservant precincts was well enshrined as the sine qua non of the *pintele yid.* Still, the letters that swamped Prince's office were shocking in how far they surpassed, in volume and vituperativeness, any previous gripes. If some writers couldn't help betraying their love of the show amid their denunciation—a cantor from a Conservative synagogue in Minnesota threatened that "unless this matter is cleared, we will recommend to this congregation, consisting of 4,500 people, not to patronize your production of this marvelous presentation"—most went for the

Jewish jugular. "Is this what tradition means to you?" one demanded. "I believe you have enough money now from *Fiddler on the Roof* TO BE ABLE TO 'CONVERT,'" another inscribed, no doubt with caustic intent, on a Rosh Hashanah card. A man from the Bronx chastised: "Your 'show must go on' regardless. . . . Six million of our people also had a 'show' of their own when they marched into gas chambers."

These letters weren't merely lodging complaints; they read like writs of excommunication, declaring Hal Prince and, by extension, the show desecrators of everything the community held sacred.

And yet, much of the community—perhaps some of the complainers among them—also had come to hold *Fiddler* sacred. No boycotts materialized when the show, indeed, went on. There was no dent in ticket sales or enthusiasm. Ken Le Roy, who took over as the fiddler six weeks after the show opened and stayed in the role for seven years, said *Fiddler* was the only show he'd ever been in that prompted standing ovations eight times a week—and he'd been in the original productions of *The Pajama Game*, *Brigadoon*, *Carousel*, *Oklahoma!*, and *West Side Story*. By the time *Fiddler* broke the record for the longest-running Broadway show with its 3,225th performance on June 17, 1972, no pounding by the kosher police could diminish its power or the fullness with which Jews took possession of it. And no claims on it made by Jews could reduce its availability to Gentiles.

Not everyone liked it—especially not Yiddishists, somehow fearful that, having "debased" the original Tevye stories, the show might supplant them. (If anything, *Fiddler* has expanded the audience for Sholem-Aleichem; a spate of his works were published in the mid- and late 1960s, capitalizing on the musical's popularity.) Scholars also resented its depiction of "the cutest shtetl we never had," as Irving Howe complained. Musicals always unfold in fake places—the stage itself, of course, but also settings that are mythic by nature. No one looks for documentary realism in the New York City of *Guys and Dolls* or *West Side Story*. But in the absence of a real-life reference point, *Fiddler*'s Anatevka took on a glossy veneer of historical veracity.

This has been one of the burdens—and one of the gifts—that *Fiddler* has carried into the world and that has kept it in a state of constant contention. The show remains a platform on which Jews engage, work out, and argue over the significance and substance of their identity. It persists as a mode in which Gentiles and Jews alike encounter an image of

Eastern European Jewish life. It endures as a story of generational conflict and cultural attenuation that fits just about everywhere.

Fiddler on the Roof is an excellent show, and as it continues to be produced on professional, amateur, and school stages all around the world, that is often the perfectly good reason people choose to present it. But from its opening in 1964 until today, sometimes by design and often by accident, *Fiddler* takes on an inordinate cultural utility that no other musical sustains.

When plans for foreign productions began, the creators worried all over again—needlessly, it turned out each time—whether audiences without warm ties to Jewish culture would connect with it. They authorized the first overseas version for the one place they figured would welcome it without complication. "I am enormously gratified that the first production of *Fiddler on the Roof* outside the United States is to take place in Israel," Joe Stein wrote for the production's program booklet, adding that it was "most logical that a musical based on the stories of Sholem Aleichem be first presented in Israel." The logic was more complicated than he knew.

PART III

─────

TEVYE'S TRAVELS

CHAPTER 6

THE OLD COUNTRY
IN THE OLD-NEW LAND

DAN ALMAGOR HAD JUST COMPLETED HIS FIRST YEAR AS A Ph.D. student at the University of California in Los Angeles in the summer of 1964 when he received an urgent call from back home in Tel Aviv. Giora Godik, Israel's "Mr. Broadway," was on the line. The flamboyant impresario was shaking up the Israeli theater and needed Almagor's help. Despite being only sixteen years old, the state had a solid theater tradition that had begun with the earliest Zionist settlement, when Hebrew plays served as a tool for advancing the language, and it had quickly evolved into a professional artistic culture. By the 1960s, the country supported several full-scale repertory companies and a growing fringe movement. But not until Godik came along had it seen the outsize glamour and glitz of a high-budget musical. His first, *My Fair Lady*, had opened in early 1964 and had sent a charge through the country's cultural scene, as Israel seemed to prove overnight that it was as capable as mighty New York of presenting top-notch, up-to-date shows with lavish production values. The country seemed to take as big and quick a leap in finesse and fashionableness as Eliza Doolittle herself. With *My Fair Lady* still running strong, Godik went looking for more. And he wanted Almagor to find it.

At twenty-eight, Almagor was already an accomplished writer of songs, sketches, and plays—skills he'd refined in an entertainment troupe during his years of obligatory military service—and he had superb command of English. Godik had hired him and a colleague to translate *My Fair Lady* into Hebrew. In a language that was still so new in its modern form that it did not yet have a ripe slang and in a country too small for regional accents, they figured out how to create the quirks in Eliza's speech that signal her status and drive the plot. (Following the recommendation of a linguistics scholar Almagor consulted, they relied on the grammatical errors and playful inventions of children.) Now that he was in the United States, Godik had a new job for him. "Go to New York and look for another show," the producer told Almagor on the overseas call, promising to finance the trip. Almagor caught a flight as soon as he could and landed in a city with no hotel rooms: the 1964 World's Fair was drawing tourists from all over the United States as well as from abroad.

But apart from forcing him to sleep in a dingy men's rooming house, the World's Fair hardly registered on Almagor's radar. Had he followed the tourists to the fairgrounds in Queens, he'd have been able to catch an extravaganza that would have astonished even Godik: the spectacle *To Broadway with Love* in the Texas Pavilion, featuring a cast of seventy-five in a panoramic history of America's commercial stage—and with the songs by Bock and Harnick that had so incensed Jerry Robbins. And he might have caught wind of the months-long dispute about his country's representation that had been raging in the press and in the courts. A mural and poem depicting the plight of a Palestinian refugee adorned a wall in the Jordanian Pavilion. Backers of the American-Israel Pavilion (Jewish philanthropies and communal organizations in the United States) sought to have it removed.

The mural would not have shocked Almagor. He was a leftist with some sympathy for Palestinians—and also (not considered a contradiction, not yet anyway) the writer of some of Israel's most popular patriotic songs. But none of that concerned him when he arrived in New York that August: his attention was trained on midtown. With Godik footing the bill, he went to a show every night and in the afternoons, too, on the days with matinees. Nothing seemed right for Israel. Entertaining as they were, *How to Succeed in Business* and *Funny Girl* exuded such American sensibilities that Almagor couldn't recommend them. *Oliver!* was worse: it had a perceived (if not actual) Fagin problem (as the venerable Habima Theater learned when, in an effort to compete with Godik, they presented it in 1966, drawing more controversy than customers). Almagor decided to try *A Funny Thing Happened on the Way to the Forum*. He had heard about a "funny fat guy" in a major role whom everyone was calling a genius, so he bought a Wednesday matinee ticket. Even if he couldn't deliver it to Godik as a great discovery, at least he'd have a good laugh. What luck, he thought, to score a seat in the third row.

But when he took that seat at the Majestic Theater, Almagor saw that he could have bought the entire row. Where was everybody? An usher explained that *Forum* had been running more than two years and had been barely hanging on since Zero Mostel had left the cast several months earlier. And word was out that the producers had posted a closing notice. The Israeli slumped and waited, regretting that the afternoon would yield neither a prize for Godik nor the thrill of seeing a comic master at work. As he leafed through his program, a flyer advertising a show trying out in Washington and due in New York in a few weeks fell to the floor. "That's where your fat man is now," the usher told him, leaning over to pick it up. It was not the star's name, though, but a line of smaller type that made Almagor do a double take: "Based on the stories of Sholom Aleichem." The moment *Forum*'s curtain came down, Almagor made his way to Penn Station and boarded the next train for Washington. He went right to the National Theater and bought a ticket for the next performance of *Fiddler on the Roof*.

The impulse—and the excitement that fired it—didn't make any sense to Almagor. By his own admission, he was part of the generation that "grew up to despise the sound of Yiddish and anything associated with it." During the early years of nation building, the Old-New Land (as Herzl had dubbed the project of his Zionist dream) had little use for the Old Country, other than as a foil. In place of passivity, the rhetoric went, the new "muscle Jews" would take action. Instead of poring, crooked and bent, over ancient holy books in airless rooms, men—and women, too— would till the earth, standing tall and squinting into the sunlight. The imagery contrasting anemic Europe with Zionism's virile ideal was as selective and spurious as the deployment of Vishniac photos had been in America. In Israel, rather than arouse sympathy, the Old World tropes triggered rejection. Diaspora—*galut*, in Hebrew's emphatic iamb—was weak, docile, defenseless. "We shall not be like them," Almagor remembers learning as a boy. "We will raise our heads and be tough and strong."

Even Holocaust survivors speaking Yiddish in public were aggressively shushed. "Speak Hebrew!" their new countrymen shouted, disgusted by the language they associated with Jewish victimhood. Like many in his generation, Almagor changed his name at age twenty-one to proclaim that he belonged to a new breed. Born Elblinger to parents who had immigrated in the 1920s from Lublin and Warsaw, he chose a moniker that may have followed the original patronymic's cadence but that signified its opposite: in Hebrew, *almagor* means "fearless." (He also dropped his "shameful" middle name, Shmuel.)

Yet Almagor nearly jumped out of his chair at the National Theater. Not only because "my fat man was excellent." The happy shock of seeing a shtetl onstage made him "excited like I had never been excited in the theater. Me, the anti-*galuti*, the sabra, was so thrilled by the show." Somehow, he just knew other Jewish Israelis would feel the same way: the time was right for his generation to find a warm way into the European piece of their legacy. When the performance ended, he summoned the chutzpah to go backstage to inquire about the rights. He poked through a door and found the creative team sitting around "just like in the movies," with "empty glasses and full ashtrays," analyzing the night's performance. He blurted out an introduction, quickly reciting his credentials, and was welcomed in. Some of the *Fiddler* team had read about the Israeli *My Fair Lady* in *Variety*. (The Hebrew rendering of "the rain in Spain falls mainly on the plain" had become famous worldwide: *barad yarad bidrom sfarad ha'erev*—hail fell in southern Spain this evening.) Almagor was even drawn into the performance postmortem.

In the morning, he phoned Godik. "Giora! I found it," he cried. "Sholem-Aleichem!" The Polish-born impresario nearly slammed down the receiver. "No, it's not *galuti*," Almagor pressed. "It's different. It's marvelous."

"No, I don't think so," Godik said. "I want to do *How to Succeed in Business*."

"I saw it, Giora. It's not for Israel."

Godik produced the Frank Loesser show. It flopped.

Almagor headed back to Los Angeles to devote himself to his dissertation on Micah Berdichevsky, an important figure in early Hebrew letters who developed a modernist, symbolic literary style and argued from the Pale in the early twentieth century for a secular Jewish nationalism.

But before turning his focus back to Berdichevsky's complicated narrative techniques, Almagor quickly wrote an article for the Israeli paper *Ma'ariv*—a four-page spread under the headline "The Fiddler Who Went on the Roof." It was one of the first major publications about the show and certainly the first to frame *Fiddler* for Hebrew-speaking audiences. Accompanied by several production photos, the article teeters with ambivalence, as if Almagor was embarrassed to admit to Israeli compatriots what he had gushed to Godik: that he loved the show. Every accolade— *Fiddler* is "intelligent," "agreeable and moving"—is sapped by sarcasm or complaint. He objects to the "tasteless" genre of the American musical, "Broadway's questionable contribution to the world of theater," and, wise-cracking, wonders if there will be "a new Louis Armstrong hit, 'Hello, Shprintze.'" In the end, though, Almagor owns up to his guilty pleasure: "Shmaltz? Maybe. But so beautiful! Kitsch? Terrible. But what a treat!" Having proclaimed his proper wariness, he is able to confess, "Most of the time I enjoyed myself, laughed and was moved to tears."

Could other sabras do the same? Godik had not entirely dismissed the possibility—especially not after the sensation *Fiddler* became in New York only a few weeks after Almagor's call. Godik sent another scout, a young actor visiting the States who had recently made a career break-through in the title role of a hit satirical film about an "Oriental" Jewish family emigrating to Israel, *Sallah Shabati*. His name was Chaim Topol.

Topol and Almagor were friends. Though they hadn't served in the same army unit, they were in the same age cohort, moving from performance troupes in the military to the civilian revue circuit when they were discharged in 1957. Topol directed and performed in pieces Almagor wrote. His most successful role, however, remained Sallah, a character carried over from his ensemble in the army, the one attached to Nahal, the unit for youth committed to kibbutz life, as Topol was as a teenager. The Nahal troupe performed their affectionately satirical sketch comedy and songs in bases and civilian communities all over the country, not only boosting morale but contributing to the construction of a common culture for immigrants from Europe, North Africa, and the Middle East at a time when Israel still lacked national television. Sallah's author was the humorist Ephraim Kishon, recruited by the troupe because of his funny weekly column in an Israeli paper. He and Topol developed the comic character in an ongoing series of skits in which the newcomer from an unspecified Arab country, a ne'er-do-well father of too many children, bumbled his way to moral victory over pesky big shots, bosses, and bureaucrats. When the Nahal troupe morphed into a highly successful civilian touring company, Spring Onion, Sallah's popularity grew even greater. The jokes typically turned on the clash between the patriarch's benighted old ways and the sometimes dubious demands of modern Israel. (The sketches thereby reinforced stereotypes about the "backwardness" of Israel's non-European Jews even as they poked fun at Ashkenazi power.) *Sallah Shabati* opened early in 1964, and while Israeli critics panned it, audiences broke Israel's box office records; the film remained the leading feature in cinemas around the country for some six months. People came, in Topol's view, "as if greeting an old friend." It was nominated for a Best Foreign Language Oscar in 1965 and it won the Golden Globe in the same category. Topol was bestowed with the Golden Globe for "Star of Tomorrow." *Sallah* rose to classic status in Israeli cinema, a passenger entertainment option on El Al flights from New York to Tel Aviv well into the twenty-first century.

But despite some surface similarities between the two patriarchs dragged into modernity by their daughters' marriages, Topol did not recognize a kindred spirit in Zero Mostel's Tevye. Indeed, when he checked out *Fiddler* for Godik, he "fled from the theater with my hands to my ears." He had seen one of the performances in which, he claimed, Mostel infamously ad-libbed borscht belt jokes—"You're yawning, Mrs. Finkelstein, what's the matter? Your husband keep you awake last night, or am I putting you to sleep?" Topol was "absolutely convinced" that *Fiddler* "would be loathed in Israel for precisely the reasons that it was loved in New York": sentimental memories of the old *galut* as imagined from the comfort of the new.

But Topol saw it again one evening, this time with Mostel offering a "clean" performance. Now when Mostel came onstage, "one felt the whole of the Russian Jewish experience, its light and shade compressed in his person. He was not an actor. He was a reincarnation." The awed Israeli recognized a beautiful, emotional truth in the show when it wasn't shrouded in shtick. Of course *Fiddler* could work in Tel Aviv, Topol could now see. It could work anywhere. Godik made a trip to New York and saw for himself. By mid-November—some six weeks after the Broadway opening—the deal was done. *Fiddler* would make its foreign debut in Israel under Godik's command. Out in Los Angeles, Berdichevsky would have to wait: Almagor now had a new translation commission.

* * *

Sholem-Aleichem entered the theatrical repertoire in Eretz Yisrael—the Land of Israel, the biblical name commonly used for the prestate Jewish settlement in Palestine—as one of the most popular playwrights for amateur and budding professional groups alike, playing in translation as early as 1909. His comic plays became a staple at the most illustrious early theater, Habima, which was established in mandate Palestine in 1928, having migrated from Moscow, where the troupe had developed under Stanislavsky's wing, beginning in 1917. From the start, Habima intended to manifest a break with shtetl culture, and performing in Hebrew was one strong sign of that doctrine. Its legendary production of Ansky's *The Dybbuk*, premiering in 1922, was another, featuring scenery and costumes by the avant-garde Soviet artist Natan Altman, whose sketches, by his own account, depicted people who were "tragically distorted and twisted, like trees that grow on dry and barren soil." The company's acting, at first based on Stanislavsky's realism, caught up with Altman's designs: the director, Yevgeny Vakhtangov, gave the performers jerky, stylized movements and frozen poses; in the scenes with beggars, actors wore cubistic masks inspired by animals. Overall, the production achieved a new sort of mythic beauty, but one stemming from the grotesque, glaring otherworldliness of its personae. If Habima did not, after all, entirely relinquish the shtetl as subject and setting, it emphasized its difference from the old culture with its avant-garde distance.

Between 1928 and 1938, Habima presented six Sholem-Aleichem plays amid a repertoire that also included modern European dramas; in the same period, two went up at the Ohel Theater (founded in 1925, initially as a workers' theater under the auspices of the Histadrut, the national union). According to the Israeli theater scholar Freddie Rokem, these "mostly melodramatic adaptations from his stories depicting the life of the Jews in the Diaspora . . . were often given a Zionistic interpretation . . . emphasizing the squalor and small-mindedness of the Galut-Jew." Or, as a newspaper reviewer covering Habima's production of *The Treasure* jeered, the director "drew Kasrilevke not with ink but with poison. A German presenting the same would have been deemed an antisemite. And in Tel Aviv people loved it: Why wouldn't these nobodies say adieu to their ridiculous town and move to the land in the Galilee or the valley?"

To the extent that Sholem-Aleichem was regarded more warmly in Hebrew, it was as a writer for children. Early translations were simplified to aid youngsters in mastering Hebrew, the literary scholar Dan Miron points out. A 1910 translation of "Motl, Peysi the Cantor's Son," for instance, was "diluted, abridged, fragmentary, and, in essence, disrespectful," Miron fumes, adding that it represented a "dumbing down" of the Yiddish master.

That is exactly how Almagor encountered him. Growing up in the 1940s in Ramat Gan, an early agricultural colony that grew into a small city east of Tel Aviv (and that was infamous for the Hebrew-language extremists who blew up a local Yiddish press in 1943), Almagor remembers learning "some of the sweet stories" by Sholem-Aleichem at school, but none of his serious work: "Sholem-Aleichem for us was funny stories for little boys." On the other side of the city, at his school in the Florentine neighborhood of Tel Aviv (named after a Greek Zionist who had purchased the real estate in the 1920s), Topol, too, learned the humorous tales as a child. Clowning around at school, Topol would recite Sholem-Aleichem stories in class; already a captivating performer at age seven, he was never punished for diverting students' attention but was called on to entertain other children with his Sholem-Aleichem material when teachers were absent. He especially loved enacting a story called "Topele Tuturitu" and, given the coincidence of his family name, quickly became known in the schoolyard as "Topele."

Around the time Topol was amusing his classmates, Tevye entered the Hebrew theater. Habima premiered Y. D. Berkowitz's translation in 1943, some fourteen years before Tevye spoke English on the American stage. In contrast to the easygoing portrait of a man overcoming some unexpected twists and turns that Arnold Perl would present, Berkowitz offered a hero besieged from all sides. Following the plot lines of his father-in-law's original dramatization and focusing almost entirely on the Khave story, Berkowitz exaggerated the treachery of Tevye's non-Jewish neighbors. As he had done in the Yiddish version with Maurice Schwartz in 1919, he made the local priest a major character: a violent and ruthless antisemite who tries to pressure Tevye into renouncing his faith. By play's end, when Tevye is expelled along with Tsaytl and her children (Golde and Motl have died), Khave returns, repentant, and joins her father and sister in their eviction. Here it's the hostility of *galut* more than the backwardness of Jews that drives home the Zionist point.

Habima revived *Tevye* (*Tuvia ha-kholev*, in Hebrew) in 1959. By then, Berkowitz's language sounded archaic and the show, as far as Almagor and Topol's generation was concerned, served as just one more example of how moribund the state's classical theater had become. At that point, even the younger, alternative institution, Tel Aviv's Cameri Theater, was fifteen years old, delivering a more realistic and robust style of acting in a more colloquial language—one spoken without accents. Increasingly, Habima, as Almagor put it, seemed like "the theater for the grandparents."

Then Giora Godik swept into the theater world, producing commercial theater in the American mode. With no state subsidy, the self-fashioned impresario, whose father had been a star in the Polish theater, copied the American style as precisely as he could. For *My Fair Lady*, he brought to Israel the original director, set designer, and choreographer to re-create the show exactly as it had been done in the United States— identical in every way, except for the Hebrew. It so happened that the Habima troupe was playing at an overseas festival in the winter of 1964, so Godik leased their theater for his February opening. Though the rental was largely a practical matter, the symbolism was not lost on the public. "A sacrilege!" theater people joked, to see a flashy commercial musical colonizing the venerable stage. *My Fair Lady*'s premiere was a gala affair, with Prime Minister Levi Eshkol and other government officials in attendance; Godik threw an opulent opening-night party and guests drank and danced as they awaited the reviews. Even without the ecstatic press, audiences probably would have swarmed the box office. The scale and skill of the production roused pride in a nation coming of age: it could present the quintessential American entertainment every bit as well as Broadway.

With Habima returning after two months and ticket sales strong enough to keep the show going far longer, Godik searched for a space in which to extend *My Fair Lady*'s run. He found it in Jaffa, the Palestinian town on the Mediterranean coast at the southern end of Tel Aviv that had been left mostly deserted and derelict since the 1947–48 war had driven out most of its residents. Godik was not shy about risks. Besides, a small cabaret that had moved into an old hammam had already proven that audiences would make the geographically short but socially distant trip. Godik took over the Alhambra, a stately Bauhaus building that had been a posh movie palace and performance venue in its heyday in the 1920s to 1940s. Damaged during a devastating three-day mortar bombardment of Jaffa in 1947, the Alhambra stood empty and hobbled now, a startled symbol of Jaffa's decimated glory as a capital of Arab culture. Godik quickly renovated the place, tearing out the back wall, refurbishing the auditorium, and adding his lit-up initials to the signage out front—all in time for *My Fair Lady* to move in that April. After packing the house at the Habima for more than five hundred performances, the show sold out at the Alhambra night after night for months.

Godik's formula fit well with Jerry Robbins's need for fastidious foreign productions that would live up to his standards: the Israeli producer wanted *Fiddler*'s original creative team to come over and reproduce the New York production in every painstaking detail. Robbins sent his directing and dancing assistants, Dick Altman and Tommy Abbott, who kept him apprised in blow-by-blow letters of their progress. The stage manager, Ruth Mitchell, went for a few weeks, as did Boris Aronson and the original builder of the turntable, Fred Feller; later, Stein arrived for the last rehearsals and the opening. (Robbins had been expected to fly in for a final polish—and the taskmaster's imminent arrival was a repeated threat whenever actors slacked off at rehearsals—but in the end he simply sent some encouraging telegrams.)

As soon as the six-week rehearsal period got under way on April 22, Altman and Abbott's enthusiasm collapsed—in part, because they arrived with a false set of expectations about the connection between Israelis and the world of Sholem-Aleichem. Altman naively expected a "cast full of rabbis" and was annoyed and even a little offended by how "forgetful of Jewish ritual" the performers were; he not only had to keep reminding characters passing in and out of Tevye's house to kiss the mezuzah but repeatedly had to insist that they carry out the gesture in the religiously correct way. The Americans' lack of background in Sholem-Aleichem's writing also led them to misjudge Almagor's translation. They didn't understand that when he rendered "If I Were a Rich Man" as "If I Were Rothschild," he was not merely making the line scan in Hebrew; he was using the title of a Sholem-Aleichem story (not one involving Tevye) in which a Kasrilevkite, so poor he can't give his wife any money for preparing a Sabbath meal, daydreams about how philanthropic he could be if he commanded the means of the famous financier.

More important, because audiences laughed in unfamiliar places, the New York team thought Almagor had added extraneous jokes in translation; in fact, he had taken advantage of the audience's grounding in Scripture—a mandatory subject in Israel's Jewish public schools—to restore some of the specific humor of Tevye's quotations, by all accounts the most difficult aspect of Sholem-Aleichem's layered Yiddish to convey in another language. In English, Arnold Perl had sidestepped the issue by opting for generic proverbs; Stein made more of an effort, at least referring to what "the Good Book says." For his first effort in Israel, Berkowitz admitted to changing Tevye's puns and distortions, claiming to have had his father-in-law's blessing in doing so, since Hebrew itself offered no one-to-one correspondences for Tevye's intricate intertextual humor. Almagor believed that the point was to make people laugh, not to send them "to look in the Aramaic dictionary," so he tried for analogues drawn from commonly known sources. For instance, Almagor's Tevye changes the standard blessing over bread, "*hamotzi lekhem min ha'aretz*," into an insult, by saying "*hamotzi lekhem am ha'aretz*": the shift from "*min*" to "*am*" transforms "from the earth" (whence bread is brought forth) into a colloquial term for an idiot. Though Almagor's renditions did not pass muster with the Yiddishists, they did succeed with audiences. Stein couldn't understand why the rhythm of the scenes seemed off and told Godik to get someone to cut the interpolated jokes. He remembered Israel as the "only country where they played around with the script."

But cultural misreadings hardly compared with the frustrations Altman and his colleagues faced in the basic mechanics of getting the show up. Rehearsals were cut short on Friday afternoons as the country shut down for the Sabbath; actors expected days off for religious holidays that none of them actually observed; they balked at the very idea of eight-hour workdays; many of the men refused to grow beards until threatened with being fired. The backstage crew was worse. "It's been constant arguments," Altman wrote to Robbins. "Even the new prop men are slow as molasses, and several items are still missing. (Item: They still haven't given us enough bagels for the Bagel Man—they can't find bagels in Israel?)" A week later, Altman's patience was running out. "The inefficiency here is stupendous and it seems to take people here days what would be done in 10 minutes in the States," he reported. "More than a few times Tommy and Boris and I have been ready to pack up and leave."

The actors, at least, began to give him reason to feel heartened. "They all are responding to our directions beautifully," Abbott told Robbins, "with the exception of the usual one or two nuts who have their own little world, all to themselves." Thankfully, the man selected to play Tevye—Bomba Zur—was not one of those nuts, but word quickly made it all the way to New York that he was irredeemably miscast. Altman shrugged off the dire warnings as so much fractious squabbling, which, he was learning, was a popular national pastime. As he told Robbins, "Everyone—but

Godik's poster: Bomba Zur in *Fiddler* at the Alhambra.

everyone—here has a different (and very positive) opinion about who should be Tevye."

Zur, thirty-six, was a pudgy comedian with a round, innocent face known for his clowning, and he had been well received as Mr. Doolittle in *My Fair Lady*. But apart from some girth and some zaniness, he shared little in common with Zero Mostel: he had scarce experience not playing for laughs and even less confidence. When he auditioned for Tevye, "he read the more serious scenes very well—with a great warmth and simplicity that seemed to surprise Godik's people," Altman noted. "He's scared to death—which is fine with me. He's a sweet man, & I expect him to be quite good." As rehearsals wore on, Zur's panic got the better of him. He'd make strides when working alone with Altman and the pianist but fall apart, losing focus and energy, among the rest of the company. In an early run-through, "'Rich Man' and the monologues were especial bores," Altman complained. When Stein arrived, he wrote to reassure Robbins that Zur "has the equipment to make a good Tevye. . . . He's a little frightened of the part, very insecure, and Dick is bringing him along slowly, and I think quite successfully." By previews— except for one for which Altman chided him for being "shockingly lazy"—Zur was "getting there." And, Altman hastened to add, "the audiences absolutely love him."

By all accounts he projected a sweetness and likability onstage. In his own view, Zur succeeded because he made the role Israeli. "My Tevye doesn't groan, weep, wail, and sigh like a miserable Jew in the Diaspora," he proclaimed. "I dropped all the 'oy vey ist mir's from Joseph Stein's script." The script doesn't actually contain any, but this was a good wisecrack, signaling the actor's proper sabra scorn for the *galut*. With a similar sneer, reporters greeted the American librettist. Stein was startled by how hostile the press interviews seemed, as if the journalists were angry at him. "What makes you think we would be interested in shtetl Jews?" he remembered them demanding. "We're not interested in that culture anymore." Stein shrugged in his good-natured way and answered, "Wait till you see the show."

When Israelis did see the show, they were ecstatic—the public, anyway. The critics and intellectuals, on the other hand, sounded like the Yiddish guardians who had railed against *shund* in America half a century earlier, writing as if trying to outdo one another with the barbed cleverness of their takedowns: they dismissed the show as "cheap, empty, and hollow"; "saccharine water with rose petals made of cellophane"; "*Yiddishkayt* drowning in shmaltz"; "not even fresh shmaltz, [but] putrid shmaltz."

As for Zur, those who knew the original stories recognized what he was doing and despised it, even if they hadn't read the interview in which Zur defined Tevye as "a warmhearted human being who loves his daughters and his home more than his religion." Little surprise that the newspaper of the National Religious Party would resent this portrayal by a sabra who "never knew what an exilic Jew is and can't play one. . . . There is nothing Jewish about this Tevye. He talks to the Almighty as if he were an army major." But more mainstream papers also protested that "he was the least Jewish of all the Jews onstage, with nothing of Tevye in him," that he was "more goy than Sholem-Aleichem-like," and that he was "miscast as Tevye, a character he does not understand." And yet they conceded that "he does his part with grace and charm" and that "Bomba cannot be on the stage and not entertain."

For their part, audiences could not have cared less about Zur's failure to be religiously correct or, more generally, about *Fiddler*'s alleged lack of authenticity. The show was doing cultural work that didn't require such fealty. On the contrary, it likely succeeded because of its distance from the burden of historical accuracy.

Beyond the spectacular dancing, great songs, touching story—the obvious reasons audiences responded to the show—something more profound and complicated was at play that unexpectedly let the show get under the cactuslike skin of anti-*galuti* sabras. *Fiddler* arrived at a time when Almagor and Topol's generation was being shaken loose from its smug repudiation of the European past. "Negation of the Diaspora"—the central Zionist principle that Jewish emancipation requires national ingathering—had hardly gone away as a patriotic precept, but the scorn for those who had perished in the Holocaust, and for the dynamic culture they'd created, was lifting. The catalyst had been another highly theatrical event some four years earlier: the Jerusalem trial of Adolf Eichmann.

A watershed episode in Israeli history, the four-month trial unfolded in the spring and summer of 1961, heavily covered in the newspapers and often broadcast live on the radio. In his eight-hour opening address, Israel's attorney general, Gideon Hausner, vowed to pronounce the indictment in the name of the "six million accusers" who "cannot rise to their feet to point an accusing finger toward the glass booth and cry out at the man sitting there, 'I accuse.' For their ashes are piled up on the hills of Auschwitz and the fields of Treblinka, washed by the rivers of Poland, and their graves are scattered the length and breadth of Europe." He eulogized the history of European Jewry—"the heart of the nation, the source of its vitality"—ticking off the instrumental Zionist thinkers and cultural heroes who had arisen from there. Marc Chagall and Sholem-Aleichem were among those prominently mentioned.

Hausner had fashioned himself—in the Israeli historian Tom Segev's phrase—as the "impresario of a national-historic production." In calling witnesses, Hausner gave stage to more than a hundred survivors who, having been silenced for nearly two decades, testified in detail about the horrors they experienced. Hausner was playing especially to the young generation, aiming to turn their repugnance for the past into respect and understanding. In Segev's view, he largely succeeded. The trial, Segev writes, "marked the beginning of a dramatic shift in the way Israelis related to the Holocaust. The terrifying stories that broke forth from the depths of silence brought about a process of identification with the suffering of the victims and survivors." Almagor, for one, remembers the shame and regret his father repeatedly expressed during the trial over the way his generation had educated their children. Many of those children—then in their late twenties—became motivated to fill in the gaps.

A splashy Broadway musical, of all things, was one medium through which they could do so, in not too taxing emotional terms. Artificial and cheery by virtue of its genre, *Fiddler* brought audiences close to the Old World without collapsing the distance that national self-definition still required. As one local critic covering the show wryly remarked, "The Diaspora is returning to us [after] it was condemned to oblivion, via Broadway."

Which may have been the most expedient way it could have returned. The nine Tony Awards bestowed on the Broadway production even as the Israeli version was opening proved how much America adored Tevye. The most ardent cultural self-loather had to wonder, then: how contemptible could *Yiddishkayt* be?

Even the denunciations of *Fiddler* in the Hebrew press served as a means of elevating Yiddish culture. Those reprimanding the show for its shmaltzification of Sholem-Aleichem were asserting, in essence, that Yiddish literature was better than the commercial entertainment American showbiz had made of it. Whether extolling or reviling the musical, the Israeli critics couldn't help proclaiming the preciousness of Yiddish heritage.

Fiddler played in Israel for some fifteen months; Hal Prince's office bragged that more than one-quarter of Israel's population of about 2.5 million people saw it. (And if El Al's special promotion worked, scores of American tourists saw it, too, booking tickets for the "5,760-mile Off-Broadway production" at the airline office in New York. After all, the campaign pointed out, "It may be forever before you can get tickets for Broadway's 'Fiddler.'")

About six months into the run, Godik replaced Zur—whether because Zur demanded an outsize raise or because Godik could finally get the actor he originally wanted remains a matter of conjecture and dispute. In any event, Godik worked a deal with Habima to pry Shmuel Rodensky away from his repertory contract for two months. Rodensky, born in the Russian Empire in 1904, was a sensitive bear of an actor (who had played the spiteful priest in Habima's 1959 production of *Tuvia ha-kholev*) and he gave the critics a Tevye they could love (while still getting their digs in at the show): "He filled that character with human warmth that is otherwise lacking in that sterile musical. He replaced some of the melodramatic foam with tragic power." The show sold out for almost another year (with Rodensky suspended by Habima for failing to return after his contracted leave) and it took brief tours to Haifa and Jerusalem. Then, in a grand gesture, Godik took advantage of Rodensky's background and produced *Fiddler* in Yiddish. Though the Yiddish production closed within a couple of weeks, it was declared an event of national importance. "It shows how rooted and mature Hebrew is that it can dispense its energy on a production in another language and, even more so, Yiddish, our national language of the past," wrote a critic for the daily *Ma'ariv*. "When the cast—most sabras, and even some Yemenite—does so well in Yiddish, we feel a coming together of people and generations and we are proud that could have taken place in our generation." It was a pride that could not have been felt or named only a few years earlier.

Godik floated the possibility of a European and South American tour of the Hebrew company (playing in some cities in Yiddish), and Hal Prince approved as long as it didn't touch down in cities where an English-language production was planned—and especially not in or near London, "because I think it would give the show a particularly Jewish reputation." The tour never materialized, likely because Godik was already beginning to suffer cash flow trouble that would eventually land him in so much debt that he'd flee Israel. His attempt to mount the French production in Paris also fell through because he couldn't secure a theater before his license to the rights ran out.

But through his casting of Rodensky, Godik had enormous international impact on the future fate of *Fiddler*, if only indirectly. And not only because Rodensky eventually played the part in Germany (pulled past his reluctance by the Israeli ambassador in Bonn, who warned him that if he didn't do it a German actor would embody the Jewish patriarch, no doubt as an antisemitic stereotype). More significantly, because Rodensky couldn't keep up with Israel's brutal schedule of nine or ten shows per week, he handed over the matinees and some other performances to his understudy, Chaim Topol. The younger actor scrutinized the master—"the greatest Tevye ever," in his estimation—watching him from the wings night after night and learning from him the importance of striking the right balance between comedy and gravitas, of not overplaying the humor in the first act so as to avoid undermining the drama of the second. Topol admired how Rodensky "tore my heart" every show and he determined he would "go Rodensky's way" in his approach to the role, too. Rodensky led the cast in the Hebrew-language film of *Tevye and His Seven Daughters* by Menachem Golan (who had produced *Sallah*)—a version based directly on the Sholem-Aleichem play (complete with Shprintze's suicide and Khave's return to the family) in Berkowitz's high Hebrew and with the Zionist tinge of verdant back-to-the-land farming scenes and the remnant of the family heading for Palestine at the end. It was released in 1968. By then, Topol was on his way to starring as Tevye in a movie, too.

* * *

While Topol was going on for Rodensky several times a week in Israel, the Broadway production, nearly two years into its run, was still selling out nightly, a national company was packing houses across America, and negotiations for the motion picture rights were under way. Foreign productions were in the works for the Netherlands, Finland, Australia, Norway, Sweden, and Denmark; the British producer Richard Pilbrow was preparing the London production. The conditions were excellent: not only would the show be staged at Her Majesty's Theater—one of the few decent houses for musicals in London—the space would be available for rehearsals. And the London *Fiddler*, slated to open in February 1967, would be the only big musical coming to town that winter. "There will be virtually no competition," Pilbrow told Prince at the end of September. "London is starting to await *Fiddler* and February is the best possible time!" As soon as the show was announced, orders for charity benefits started "flooding in." The producers were sure they'd clean up. Everything was in place. Except one thing: Tevye.

At first the British producers hoped to cast the stout and likable Shakespearean Leo McKern—they were "wild" about him, saying there was "no other Englishman about whom we feel any enthusiasm at this time"—so when he turned them down in late August, they turned to Hal Prince for help. Granting that Prince would think they were out of their minds, Pilbrow told him that "the one hope, whether any of us like it or not, of the entire theatre knowledgeable public in the U.K. is that the star of *Fiddler on the Roof* should be Zero Mostel." Prince's office opened the negotiations. "If he should turn us down," Prince admitted to Bock, Harnick, Robbins, and Stein, "we are in real trouble." They had "already sounded out Scofield and Redgrave and a list as long as your arm of less likely candidates."

Mostel demanded 10 percent of the show's gross and a four-month commitment, including the rehearsal period. London would go no higher than 7.5 percent and no lower than a six-month contract. And now it was late September.

Prince thought that, barring Mostel, the show should feature an Englishman, but the London producers complained they'd run out of options quickly and wanted Prince to provide a well-known American. He didn't have much time to spare or to consult with the *Fiddler* team, he told them, "when the authors are off in Boston troubling over a new show [Bock and Harnick's *Apple Tree*], when I'm on my way out of town with a new one [*Cabaret*]."

Back and forth went their increasingly testy—and then mollifying—letters and telegrams as the actors under consideration either said "no thanks" or were vetoed by a producer on one side or the other of the

Atlantic (among them, Theodore Bikel, Kirk Douglas, Danny Kaye, David Kossoff, Alfred Marks, Anthony Quayle, Peter Ustinov, even Laurence Olivier). "You must deliver [Herschel] Bernardi or suitable substitute for opening on February 16," one of Pilbrow's partners cabled Prince as the weeks raced by. But Prince saw no reason to imperil the thriving Broadway production, where Bernardi had successfully taken over the central role. What's more, he reminded his British colleagues, since Bernardi was an unknown in London he would not instantly mean box office there. Besides, he sniped, "as the play is being produced in fourteen languages this coming season, obviously there are actors in other countries capable of undertaking Tevye. After all, he's not an American folk hero, he's a Russian."

In the midst of all the to-and-fro, Prince's secretary sent Pilbrow a query: "Hal would like to know if the Israeli movie *Sallah* has been in London and if so, have you seen the fellow who plays the father?" And on October 4, Pilbrow wired Prince with an all-caps list of eight men newly in contention. One name was so unfamiliar to the London producers that they got it wrong: "CHYAM POPAL." Pilbrow elaborated in a follow-up letter: "Somebody totally unknown, if brilliant, with such a gorgeously strange name, could seem like a masterpiece of casting (you will note I can talk myself into almost any point of view)!"

It took more than a week for the producers to get their hands on a copy of *Sallah*, and meanwhile a colleague in Israel raised doubts about Topol's command of English. But when the film finally arrived, the producers fell in love and they summoned Topol to audition in late October. They had no clue that the cable reached him while he was playing Tevye several times a week in Jaffa. They simply didn't know that he had any connection to Godik's production, nor that he had appeared on national TV in the United States six months earlier on "The Danny Kaye Show" singing *Fiddler*'s "To Life" with the host in Hebrew. As for Topol, at first he thought the invitation was a joke.

Joe Stein and Jerry Bock flew over from New York to see the audition along with Pilbrow and his team. When Topol arrived, they wondered if they had contacted the right man. In *Sallah*, they'd seen a charmingly rumpled, sixty-something patriarch, a little bent but not bowed. Into the Drury Lane, where the tryout was held, strode a tanned and slender thirty-one-year-old sabra. But when he sang "Rich Man" and presented some of Tevye's monologues, he thoroughly won them over. The audition,

Pilbrow gushed, was "far more exciting than we ever dared to hope." Amid a marvelous week, he continued, "the most marvelous thing is that Topal [*sic*] is, without a doubt, some sort of special genius. I suppose one should beware of getting too excited, but quite literally, his presence on the stage is like a whirlwind, and a very warm, funny, touching whirlwind at that. I hope I am not exaggerating, but I think he could take the town by storm and make us quite pleased we never had Ustinov, Mostel, McKern or whatever."

That is, of course, what Topol did. But it took plenty of work, including daily tutorials with an English teacher. ("I have five dah-tohs," he'd tell Perchik as he introduced his family, providing grist for comic imitators forever after.) Directly from staging the show in Amsterdam, Dick Altman and Tommy Abbott arrived to do the same in London. Altman worried that Topol's raw vitality would open a wide gulf across from the gentility of the British actors in the rest of the cast (apart from the man playing Perchik, an immigrant from Hungary). And though Prince admitted that he didn't like many of the actors, the Anatevkans eventually cohered as a plausible community. When Jerry Robbins arrived to see the first preview and polish the show—the only time he stepped in to adjust a new production—he found a company that was "doing everything correct." By his standards, though, that wasn't enough. For "Tradition," he told the cast exactly what he'd told the New York actors two and a half years earlier: "Think of long necks. I want pride—you're all proud of your tradition." And in Topol's estimation, at least, the number instantly changed from a nice opener to a galvanizing one.

The production premiered on February 16, 1967, to critical acclaim—apart from the now standard grumble or two from local protectors of Sholem-Aleichem's "authenticity." Houses stayed full; by March the show was fully booked until the following Christmas. Topol moved out of his hotel, rented an apartment, and brought his family from Tel Aviv. He figured he would be staying a good while. In May, Prince's office released figures reporting that *Fiddler* worldwide had so far turned a nearly 600 percent profit.

Then came an unlooked-for boost some four months into London's run: Israel's victory in the Six-Day War. During the tense "waiting period" of late May 1967—after Egypt's president, Gamal Abdel Nasser, responding to false reports that Israel was mobilizing for war on its border with

Syria, massed thousands of troops in the Sinai Peninsula, blockaded Israel's port to the Red Sea, and signed a defense pact with Jordan—Topol spent all but the three hours he was onstage every night in the same state of anxious preoccupation as his compatriots back home. For more than two weeks, Israeli citizens anticipated national annihilation. Though their generals knew this was not a real danger, civilians hastily prepared shelters and rabbis busily sanctified public parks as cemeteries in case of mass casualties, while the Israeli news media, frequently comparing Nasser to Hitler, broadcast his braggart threats to wipe out their nation. In London, Topol raced from the stage to his dressing room whenever he could, to catch the latest updates on the radio.

When fighting began on June 5—with Israel's crushing assault on Egypt's air force—Topol hurried to catch the first available flight home and reported for reserve duty. While his understudy went on at Her Majesty's, Topol traveled up and down Israel, entertaining the troops as he'd done back in his Nahal days, but this time as a solo act. On June 10, it was all over. Israel had not only defeated Syria, Jordan, and Egypt but conquered swaths of their territory, tripling Israel's geographical size and putting some one million Arabs under its rule. As Tom Segev observes, the threat of extermination had never been real, but the fear of it was. And the collective, conclusive relief of victory took the form of a communal euphoria that enveloped world Jewry. (Over the following decades, as Israel's occupation of some of the captured lands persisted, the euphoria gave way to bitter division within Israel and among Jews outside; by the time a generation had come of age in an Israel that had become a regional superpower, a young director would look to *Fiddler* as a means of evoking sympathy for Palestinians. But in 1967—more than forty years before Moshe Kepten would become the first Israeli to direct the show—such an interpretation, like the unending occupation itself, was unimaginable.)

By June 14, Topol was back at Her Majesty's. He had left London as a star; he returned as a hero. *Fiddler* became a site for celebration, drawing Jews as well as Gentiles to the theater—some for repeat viewings—to bask in Jewish perseverance and to pay homage to Jewish survival. The show didn't change, but the atmosphere around it did. As Tevye, Topol the robust sabra embodied the persecuted Jewish past and the triumphant present moment. His recording of "If I Were a Rich Man" hit number five on the British pop charts.

Before long, Topol also became something of a diva. In the fall, he wrote a lengthy letter to Jerry Robbins complaining about too many weak understudies coming on for absent actors and throwing him off his rhythm and about sloppiness among the tech crew. He suggested that Robbins "should come over for a few days and try to save the show." Pilbrow quickly followed up with a note assuring Robbins that the show was in "extremely good shape"; Prince told the director not to take Topol at face value "since the rest of his behavior recently has been so screwy, i.e., his willingness to stay with the company an additional year if we close the production when he leaves (he and it being so closely identified)." A couple of weeks later, Bock and Harnick looked in on the production while they were in London working on a project with the playwright John Arden. While overall things looked "damned good," they reported, "actually the worst offender was Topol, who added about 50 shtick-ad libs, in addition to [playing] heavy handed, almost as if it were about the legend of Topol, not Tevye." The producers did not agree to the star's offer to stay another year if they would close the show when he left. And his proposal left Prince wondering if there was something about the role itself that pushed actors into a state of hubris. After Topol left in February 1968 and Alfie Bass took over, the London production continued to flourish—"history repeats itself," Prince crowed to the show's creators—running for nearly five years. But it was hardly the end of the confident Israeli's identification with Tevye.

Shortly before Topol's last performance, the film director Norman Jewison flew over to catch the show at the urging of his producer, Walter Mirisch. In 1967, the Mirisch Company had tapped Jewison for *Fiddler* and though shooting was not slated to start until the spring of 1970, the search for the star was already on. When Mirisch saw a notice in the paper saying that Topol would soon be leaving the show, he and Jewison took off for London.

Jewison made up his mind the night he saw the show. He wanted Topol. Of course Jewison had thought about Zero Mostel, whose performance he'd seen early in the run a couple of years earlier when he happened to be in New York. Jewison hadn't liked him. Watching from a cushion in an aisle of the balcony—he wangled the perch from Prince in the sold-out house at the last minute—Jewison felt Mostel lacked reality. He was too big, too American, and he was pulling the viewer out of the

Chaim Topol as the bumbling patriarch Sallah Shabati.

play. On film, that hypertheatricality would turn out even worse. At least for the kind of film Jewison wanted to make. From the start, his vision required absolute realism (within the conventions of a musical film, that is). He didn't want any dancing that wasn't part of the plot—in the wedding scene or the "L'Chaim" celebration at the inn—so no gamboling down the lane and singing "Tradition." He didn't want to shoot in the Kansas or Saskatchewan locations the producers were pushing; he wanted to be as near to Sholem-Aleichem territory as he could get in 1971. (That turned out to be Yugoslavia.) "Everything must be rooted in truth and total cinematic believability," he insisted. So, he said, his Tevye had to feel like a Russian Jew and he wanted an actor who was no more than a generation away from that experience.

Mostel, in fact, was closer to Eastern European *Yiddishkayt* than Topol: the American actor grew up religiously observant, speaking Yiddish, while Topol was a robust, Hebrew-speaking sabra. But that was precisely the quality that stirred Jewison. His idea of what a Russian Jew feels like was filtered through—even distorted by—the assertion of Israel as the destiny of the Diaspora, and he would read the coming sabra brashness backward into Tevye's tenacity. "I identified very strongly with

Israel and that's really the reason I hired him," Jewison later acknowledged.

Topol very well could have nailed the offer in the scene toward the show's end when the constable issues the eviction and Tevye tells him to "get off my land." In that moment, Jewison admired how "you could see him stiffen up and stand up as tall as he could." Sure, Topol was a fine actor. But Jewison responded to something more: "It was the Israeli in him. It was the pride, the pride of being Jewish." Even as the Jews were forced out of Russia, you could tell, Jewison marveled, that they were a strong people who "would somehow build a country of their own." Topol connected the same dots: "My grandfather was a sort of Tevye, and my father was a son of Tevye," he told a journalist. "My grandfather was a Russian Jew and my father was born in Russia, south of Kiev. So I knew of the big disappointment with the Revolution, and the Dreyfus trial in France, and the man with the little mustache on his upper lip, the creation of the State of Israel and 'Masada will never fall again.' It's the grandchildren now who say that. It's all one line—it comes from Masada 2,000 years ago, and this Teyve of mine already carries in him the chromosomes of those grandchildren."

In a London theater, in the heady wake of the Six-Day War, Jewison saw Hollywood's future Tevye: one with whom Ari Ben Canaan had merged.

* * *

The Six-Day War galvanized American Jews, too, stirring fears and feelings of attachment that exceeded the surges of support the American community had expressed during Israel's fight for statehood in 1948 and, again, during the Suez crisis of 1956. Zionism had been growing central to Jewish American life for more than a generation—through synagogue sisterhood projects, children's summer camps, youth groups, and other programs—but no one could have foreseen the response the 1967 war provoked. Within hours of the outbreak of hostilities, thousands of American Jews volunteered to fly immediately to Tel Aviv to fill in at work for Israelis called to arms; within a day the community raised $430 million for the cause. Even more powerfully, Israel's victory produced an unprecedented euphoria in Jewish American communities—superseding *Fiddler on the Roof* as a profound, not to mention weightier, source of communal pride—and sealed their identification with the Jewish state for years to come. The historian Howard Sachar characterized the response as nothing less than "the collective incarnation of a new ethnic heroism." This coalescing around Israel saw parallel changes in mainstream Jewish alliances within the United States as the civil rights movement gave way to Black Power. That Black nationalists, New Leftists, and Third Worldists of various sorts (numerous Jews among them) sided with the Palestinians living in the territories Israel had captured and occupied gave mainstream Jewry an extra shove rightward.

But there was more to it than that. Domestic conditions challenged the liberal consensus so recently celebrated in *Fiddler*. While American Jews would not in large number abandon commitments to a range of liberal stances in spheres like civil liberties, workers' access to collective bargaining, and women's rights, their allegiance to Black equality frayed as Blacks themselves challenged the limits of equality as liberalism defined it—which, as they saw it, was not equality at all. By the end of the 1960s, Sachar suggests, Jews not only retreated into parochialism but "wondered if they had not neglected their own interests in championing the cause of other minorities." A prime force behind that suspicion came in 1968. And with it, *Fiddler* became a battleground.

CHAPTER 7

FIDDLER WHILE BROOKLYN BURNS

IN THE SPRING OF 1968, RICHARD PIRO WASN'T PAYING MUCH attention to the winds of controversy gathering around the neighborhood where he worked as a schoolteacher. His hands were full enough as he organized two dozen adolescent performers, as many production technicians, and a student orchestra for a full-scale musical comedy. Piro was about to open *Oliver!* and he was focused on getting the set crew to finish the scenery, the altos to hit their first note in the opening chorus number, and a feisty but talented seventh grader, Teddy Smith, to show up at rehearsal on time and not clown around when he got there. It wasn't that Piro lacked interest in politics—he occasionally participated in demonstrations against racial discrimination and the Vietnam War (and soon would join the nascent gay liberation movement)—but he held his students to high standards and demanded the same dedication of himself. He and his colleague Bruce Birnel, the music teacher and AV coordinator, may have been working in a junior high school, but as far as Piro was concerned, "We were in show business."

With some significant differences. In junior high, lead actors don't always deliver—especially when their voices are cracking. On opening night of *Oliver!* that May, the boy in the title role opened his mouth for his solo in "Food, Glorious Food" and, in place of the sweet countertenor that had landed him the role, out came an uncontrollable caw. He froze, standing silently onstage for what seemed like ages. But in a moment a voice piped up from the chorus and sang the phrases beautifully. It was Teddy Smith, the slight African American boy whose winning smile and innocent-seeming charm often helped him out of mischievous jams. Though academically weak—he couldn't remember multiplication tables or where to put commas—Teddy had absorbed the play's lines as he sat at rehearsals, and when his classmate faltered he stepped in and saved the tune, singing Oliver's lines until the other boy could recover. Piro couldn't get over the discipline and focus Teddy was capable of when he wasn't goofing around. That night the teacher determined that this alert boy would play the lead in the following year's musical.

Piro understood how lucky he was that he could count on there being another musical the next year. His principal, Julius Rubin, sustained an unusual commitment to the arts, all the more rare for his working in one of the poorest districts of the nation's largest school system. Rubin simply saw no reason his pupils should be denied the activities and special courses that were routine in more affluent areas just because they lived in Brownsville, Brooklyn.

By the mid-1960s, Brownsville was the kind of place people meant when they spoke about America's "urban crisis." And like most other such places, it hadn't always been that way. At the turn of the twentieth century, Brownsville had beckoned Eastern European Jews from the squalor of the Lower East Side with promises of fresh air and open space. Real estate ads marketed this section of east-central Brooklyn as a community "where Jews can live as in the Old Country." The bucolic splendor didn't last long. By 1915—the year Zero Mostel was born there—230,000 Jews had settled in Brownsville, making the area one of the country's densest concentrations of Jews, who were crowded into tenements and rapidly deteriorating subdivided houses. It was a radical neighborhood, too, producing strong local advocacy organizations and, as a voting district, consistently sending Socialist and American Labor Party representatives to Albany and city hall.

African Americans began trickling into Brownsville and adjoining Ocean Hill in the late 1920s and the flow accelerated as they were pushed out of the South by shifts in agriculture and then pulled to the North by the wartime boom in manufacturing and shipyard jobs. To accommodate the newcomers, local activists—Jewish leftists and their working-class Black neighbors—pressed for public housing to replace the dilapidated homes that blighted the area; they insisted that it maintain the neighbor-hood's character by rising no higher than three stories and, most impor-tant, that it mix low- and middle-income occupants. But, as the historian Wendell Pritchett has shown, these efforts came to naught as liberal community organizations—churches, the NAACP—refused to join forces with radicals for fear of being tainted as Communists. In any case, they would not have been much of a match for the heedless bulldozing of Robert Moses. Soon, thousands of families displaced by his "urban renewal" programs in Manhattan and elsewhere were relocated to Brownsville's crumbling tenements. And not long after, the city erected hulking sixteen-story housing projects there, restricted to low-income residents.

From the outset, Brownsville had been a stepping-stone neighborhood—the literary critic Alfred Kazin, also born there in 1915, characterized it as "notoriously, a place that measured all success by our skill in getting away from it." Jews moved out as they gained solid economic footing, taking their tax dollars with them. But Blacks had few places to go—they were excluded from many of the "nicer" neighborhoods—and anyway, with many occupations still closed to them and blue-collar jobs drying up in the 1950s, they had little chance to amass the nest egg they'd need to move up. Ocean Hill–Brownsville continued to decline. By the mid-1960s, its jobless rate hit 17 percent—five times the city average—and spiked to 36 percent for young men. Three-quarters of the population was receiving some form of public assistance. The schools, more racially segregated in 1964 than they had been in 1954, the year of *Brown v. Board of Education*, were in a shambles. Experienced teachers invoked the priv-ilege of seniority to transfer out of neighborhoods like Ocean Hill–Brownsville, and when community activists tried to persuade the Board of Education to rotate personnel periodically in order to guarantee their children some strong instructors, the teachers' union balked. Classes were severely overcrowded (even as desks sat open in white neighbor-hoods) and some 73 percent of the local children had fallen below grade level in reading, a whopping 85 percent in math.

Local Black and Puerto Rican parents, recognizing that their chil-dren languished on the losing side of New York's separate and unequal system, joined the citywide movement to desegregate the schools. For a decade they lobbied, picketed, and met with city and state officials, but plan after plan, promise after promise, met massive resistance. An opposing organization called Parents and Taxpayers, which boasted more than a hundred chapters around the New York boroughs by 1963, eventually totaling some 500,000 members, aggressively challenged any hint that white children might be bused from their own pleasant neighborhoods into dysfunctional ghetto schools.

Julius Rubin's school—Harry A. Eiseman Junior High School 275—was designed to offer a fresh solution. Situated on the border of the racially divided communities of Canarsie and Brownsville, the three-story building, occupying a full square block of Rockaway Avenue at Linden Boulevard, was meant to be the anchor for a campus that would next add a high school and eventually perhaps even a community college. The idea was that it would draw students from both sides of Linden—the boundary between the white middle-class and the impoverished Black and Puerto Rican neighborhoods—relieving the overcrowding and enrolling an integrated student body without any busing or unnatural manipulations. The new school was outfitted with a spacious gym, a 600-seat auditorium with a real stage, and three music classrooms that featured not only raked horseshoe seating ideal for choral singing but also acoustic tiles along their walls.

What it didn't have when it opened on September 9, 1963—just two weeks after the historic civil rights March on Washington—was the diversity it was supposed to ensure. Numerous white families in Canarsie and nearby Flatbush had managed to steer their adolescent children into schools south of their border with Brownsville—some even suing the Board of Education on the grounds that the constitutional rights of white kids had been violated because they were denied admission to their old schools on the basis of race. Consequently, far less than the anticipated one-third of the 1,800 kids entering Eiseman that fall were white. The teaching staff of a hundred, meanwhile, reflected the demographics of the citywide system: more than 90 percent were white (and most, Jewish). Throughout the summer of 1963, civil rights leaders across the city had threatened to boycott all the schools if the Board of Education had not come up with a convincing timetable for integration by September 1. At the eleventh hour, the city managed to stave off the boycott by promising results by December. But on the first day at Eiseman, Rubin opened the doors to the incoming classes surrounded by community protesters.

Under Rubin's leadership, Eiseman (named after a deceased progressive Brooklyn educator) put out a school newspaper, published a literary magazine, fielded a band, maintained an organized athletics program, and, most splashily, produced first-rate choral concerts and plays directed by Piro and designed by Birnel. Rubin firmly believed that kids needed spheres where they could "taste excellence" and that those confidence-building experiences, in which hard work paid off, would encourage them to strive in their academic subjects, too. That philosophy sold Piro on Eiseman when he applied to the New York City system as a music and drama teacher. Principals from other districts who interviewed him were flabbergasted by his choice. Piro had a degree in music education from Boston University and a few years' experience at schools in his native Massachusetts and in suburban Westchester, and he performed well on the qualifying exams. "With your scores, you could teach in Queens," they urged him, not needing to spell out the racial and economic implications of their entreaties. But Piro thrived at Eiseman. "We are not martyrs in Brooklyn," he told colleagues who labored in middle-class neighborhoods and in the suburbs.

Students loved his inventive approach to music class, where they could bring in their own records to share at the end of the lessons. The classroom rocked with the rhythms of Aretha Franklin, the Temptations, Stevie Wonder, and the Marvelettes—after the kids learned the assigned material. A chorus of a hundred children prepared Randall Thompson's setting of Thomas Jefferson texts, *The Testament of Freedom*, and performed it not only in Brownsville but in an unprecedented weekend field trip to the placid New England town of Somerset, Massachusetts (where Piro had once taught)—and the white kids from Somerset made a return visit to Brownsville later. One strong student, Beverly Cannon, had loved the music experiences so much that when her family moved to Richmond Hill, Queens, after she completed sixth grade, she stayed enrolled at Eiseman the two more years (using an aunt's address in Brownsville as her residence) and gamely made the hourlong commute to school each day, taking two subway trains and two buses. She did it for one reason: "For Mr. Piro."

Rubin had not managed to staff an entire school with personnel that dedicated and demanding—it was still Brownsville, after all—and many young teachers were just putting in their time before they could move on. Eiseman kids sensed that some of their teachers regarded them as uneducable, incapable, not worth their time, and that made the contrast of Piro all the greater. For a studious girl named Sheila Haskins, Piro's music room was "the only place you could feel free" in the whole school; small Stephan Hirsch, one of the few Jewish or white kids in the drama class, found refuge there from the racial tensions that governed so much else around school. For the wiry class cutup, Duane McCullers, Piro was the rare teacher who could have fun with students until it was "time to get down to business, and then we *got* down to business"; to quiet Maritza Figueroa, who had to scrub floors, do the laundry, cook, and babysit her baby brother while her strict mom folded dresses in a clothing factory, he was "a big brother and father figure all wrapped into one and we wanted him to be proud of us." They all worked hard for Piro—even Teddy Smith, whose gifts were matched only by his recalcitrance. Often, the students surprised themselves with what they achieved.

What would be their challenge in the upcoming 1968–69 academic year, Piro wondered as the *Oliver!* scenery came down and the costumes were stashed away. Piro chewed over some options in the faculty lunch-room. *King and I*, Rubin suggested. Only if the principal could guarantee $3,000 for sets, Piro replied. "I don't do assembly-type shows with crepe paper costumes and butcher paper scenery," he reminded Rubin with a haughtiness that was only half in jest. How about *Sound of Music*? Not enough parts for boys. *Man of La Mancha*? Not enough for girls. Bruce Birnel had just seen the all-Black version of *Hello, Dolly!* on Broadway, starring Pearl Bailey and Cab Calloway—such a triumph that the *New York Times's* Clive Barnes suggested, "Maybe Black Power is what some of the other musicals need"—and whimsically floated *Fiddler on the Roof.* Or what about *Carousel*? Nah, too risky for immature voices. Piro wanted a show that would give Teddy a chance to shine. And one that would be enjoyable and also meaningful for the children after a difficult school year that had begun after a tense summer of inner-city riots around the country and was coming to an end shortly after Martin Luther King Jr. had been assassinated. As summer approached, authorities were bracing for more unrest. (Mayor John Lindsay requested some special performances of Broadway show excerpts in city parks and public housing courtyards to help "calm the city's ghettos" during the summer; Hal Prince responded by offering to provide transportation and some scenes from *Fiddler* and *Cabaret*.)

Tension was growing around Eiseman, too. In the five years since it had opened, the meager white student population had dwindled even further, and while the courts had upheld the city's right to zone school districts with racial diversity in mind, they also reasserted the illegality of denying any student admission to a school on the basis of race, effectively undermining any innovative zoning plans. With the disappointing results at schools like Eiseman as evidence, activists across the city concluded that New York's public schools would never be desegregated. So they tried a new tactic, taking a cue from the Parents and Taxpayers chapter in Jackson Heights, Queens, that had opened its own elementary school as a way of evading a desegregation plan for their area. In 1966, Black and Puerto Rican parents, reversing their longtime call for integration, began to demand community control of their neighborhood schools and set out to show that they could do a better job of educating their children than a neglectful, bureaucratic white establishment. With funding from the Ford Foundation, the city agreed to an experiment in school decentralization in three "demonstration districts" where residents would elect local governing boards to run the neighborhood schools. Ocean Hill–Brownsville was one of them. Though Eiseman fell just outside the trial district, it was singed by the explosive battles soon to erupt two miles away at the experiment's epicenter, Ocean Hill's Junior High 271. The war cry was sounded just as Piro was basking in the success of *Oliver!* and mulling over how to top it with his next musical. That next show would be embroiled in one of the ugliest conflicts New York City has ever known. But the show would go on, sending up a defiant signal of hope through the spreading flames.

* * *

In early May 1968, the new local governing board's district supervisor, Rhody McCoy, wrote to nineteen Ocean Hill–Brownsville teachers and administrators (most of them Jewish) telling them to report to the Board of Education for reassignment for the coming year; they would no longer be working in the experimental district. To the United Federation of Teachers (UFT)—the union—which had made its emphatic opposition to the experiment in community control well known, McCoy's action represented an egregious denial of its members' due process (though McCoy's defenders insisted that such transfers were routine). The union ordered the ousted teachers to report for work despite McCoy's instruction, and they were escorted by police past furious community protesters. To retaliate—or to flex its muscle or maybe simply to try cooling things down—the community board closed some schools for a few days. When they reopened, some 350 UFT teachers—of about 500 in the district—stayed home in solidarity with their dismissed colleagues, and they never came back. Their boycott didn't quite close the schools for the remaining month of the academic year, but two-thirds of the district's 9,000 students did not answer the morning bell: they stayed home, too. These May clashes merely hinted at the protracted struggle over the limits of the community board's power that was to come. And playing by the rules was not all that was at stake as far as the union was concerned. "If community control as we see it in Ocean Hill–Brownsville becomes a fact," UFT president Albert Shanker exhorted his delegate assembly on May 16, "there will be 'Jew Bastard' signs and swastikas in all the schools."

Piro had not attended that meeting—glad as he was to belong to a union, he was not an activist within it—but Shanker's warning filtered down to the rank and file. The rhetoric on both sides of the policy dispute had begun at an overheated pitch and the temperature was only escalating. Proponents of community control had charged the teachers with "coming into the ghetto to cripple our children's lives" and of committing "educational genocide," while Shanker frequently fulminated about the "hoodlum element" and "mob rule" among the people of color in charge of the experimental districts. In lobbying to defeat a comprehensive decentralization bill before the New York State Legislature in those same weeks of May, Shanker distributed union leaflets implying that under the proposed plan school districts would be handed over to Black racists and antisemites.

"Yes, *Fiddler,* that's it," Piro began to think as controversy swirled. He imagined how Teddy just might carry off the role of Tevye, picturing the young teen in a paste-on beard and spectacles. Then one day Piro lost his temper with a student ostentatiously disrupting a class and he swept her books off her desk; she blurted an insult in return, calling him "a white motherfucking Jew bastard." He found the profanity far less shocking than the use of "Jew" as an epithet, especially since the kids well knew that Piro, a trim man with bushy black hair, jaw-skimming sideburns, and a thick mustache, was an Italian American Catholic of Sicilian descent. (He got genial laughs from his students the first day of class when he introduced himself by writing the four letters of his name on the board—P-I-R-O—to show them, emphatically, that it was not SHA-piro.) Piro realized that for his students "Jew" had come to mean any white adult from whom—or toward whom—they felt hostility. He called Rubin right away and told him that next year he would present *Fiddler on the Roof*. He thought that doing the show would give the kids a fuller and more sympathetic understanding of who Jews really were.

"Can't you do *Guys and Dolls*?" Rubin implored. Eiseman had escaped most of the fever-pitched controversy disrupting Ocean Hill–Brownsville schools and he wanted to keep it that way. He couldn't shake the hunch that *Fiddler* would mean trouble. He reminded Piro how "unsettled" things were in the neighborhood and urged him to choose something "less prone to controversy." But Piro—and Birnel, too—kept after him. They had come to learn that if their principal pooh-poohed an idea without issuing an absolute no, he was still open to it. And frightened as Rubin was, he had to admit, at least to himself, that the idea intrigued him. He just didn't want to offend the community at such a "sensitive time." Local parents might resent that their children were having Jewish culture jammed down their throats.

Rubin was looking over the wrong shoulder: it was members of his faculty who leapt to complain. Several Jewish teachers charged that the Black and Puerto Rican kids in the cast would use the show to make fun of them, and that couldn't be allowed. Besides, they didn't trust Piro. They resented what they saw as his hogging of attention and resources and they begrudged his jeans-and-blazer and pop-music ways of being so hip with the kids. Hadn't *Oliver!* been proof enough that he disrespected Jews? Never mind that in the musical version of the story Dickens's Fagin had been softened into a "queer old auntie," as the *Guardian* reviewer of the original production had said. Nor did it matter that Piro had cast a teacher in the role, both for the sake of realism and to ensure a mature actor who could be counted on to avoid stereotypes. A few Jewish teachers had complained about *Oliver!* early on, and now they were determined to shut that provocative Piro down for good.

By virtue of their makeup, schools have always been in the business of what came to be known in the 1980s as "nontraditional casting": they use whom they've got, so in all-female schools girls play both Romeo and Juliet; in predominantly Asian schools Chinese Americans play the ranch hands of *Oklahoma!* And even where there is plenty of diversity among students, the key roles go often to the kids who can best carry them, regardless of race or ethnicity (though gender is seldom discounted except in single-sex schools). Educational drama departments may, in fact, be one of the few places in America where the liberal ideal of race-blind meritocracy is consistently practiced. After all, it's acting, make-believe, the magic of theater. Nobody blinks. Except when the ethnic or racial identity of the characters is a marked part of the theme, a dicier prospect still if that identity belongs to a beleaguered minority: Joe and Queenie in *Showboat* (leaving aside the separate argument over stereo-typical representations) wouldn't make sense played by white actors (unless one were deliberately being provocative). These issues were con-fused and compounded in the conflict over *Fiddler*—and the wider Ocean Hill–Brownsville conflict—in ways that stirred some Jewish anxi-eties. *Did* Jews display marked, visible differences that a little crepe hair and spirit gum couldn't address without being as offensive as blackface? Were Jews, in other words, white? To the local community they were part of the power structure, whether teachers, principals, landlords, social workers, or store owners—as James Baldwin had boldly explained in a *New York Times Magazine* article a year earlier—but Jews often experienced themselves as an oppressed minority, especially when anti-semitic rhetoric was sloshing around.

The students didn't show much more enthusiasm than the aggrieved teachers for Piro's choice. When he told his drama class about the show he'd picked—"It's called *Fiddler on the Roof* and it's a story about Jews"— they reacted with silence, the most polite response they could muster. He played them the record and told the kids they'd be learning some chore-ography for the show. Duane took that as a cue to crack up his class-mates by jumping out of his seat to dance a mismatched jerk to the music. But this was a teacher who could rouse a few dozen inner-city adolescents to prance around in a minuet (even pretending to powder their seventeenth-century wigs and fluff their imaginary ruffles) and to analyze Brahms. It took a couple of days, but by the end of the week he had the group singing "Tradition" with gusto.

Piro could look at the students and see the roles map onto them almost automatically, but he always held auditions, beginning with a basic pitch-pipe test. Then he listened as they sang tunes of their choice and he cast them in parts like any other director—according to capability, constancy, and chemistry with others. Beverly was a natural for Golde (even though she thought she'd have more fun as Yente and the girl playing Yente, a high achiever named Olga, coveted the role of Golde). At thirteen, Bev was a year younger than Teddy, but she towered over him and gave off a vibe of solidity and good sense. She was active in student government, a natural leader, and, as she understood later, in character and out she would help Teddy "keep it together." The others fell into place: lanky, self-assured Linus made a defiant Fyedka; Duane had the compact size and, as an athlete, the ability to play physical comedy as a cowering Motel; confident Reginald was testy enough to be the convincing revolutionary, Perchik; and petite Maritza, one of the few Puerto Rican kids in the company, had a sweet voice and a sad tinge of dislocation about her that would tear up the audience when she sang "Far from the Home I Love," so she was his Hodel. Piro was surprised that quiet Sheila could sing with such charm—he knew she'd help carry "Matchmaker" beautifully and he cast her as Chava—and the seventh grader who belted like Mahalia Jackson would play the grandma who comes from the grave in the dream scene. Some thirty more kids filled in the rest of the roles and the chorus of villagers. When the fall rolled around, Birnel would gather the set and lighting crews—the tech and special effects were his special contribution—and he was already hatching design plans that involved projected film. While the New York City school system as a whole was finishing the year on an ominous note, Piro was filled with excitement—heightened, he could admit later, by the air of controversy.

Over the next couple of months, in his annual summer school drama program, Piro directed Shakespeare's *Comedy of Errors*, grooming a new set of incoming chorus kids and refining the actors who had just finished seventh grade and would be playing lead roles in *Fiddler* as well as in a

DAN O'NEIL IV

Beverly Cannon and Teddy Smith: "Do You Love Me?"

scheduled production of *The Crucible*. While Piro instructed the kids in theater basics—most of all, he never tired of telling them, actors must truly love the characters they play—the dispute between the UFT and the community governing board of Ocean Hill–Brownsville simmered down and returned to full boil several times as various arbitration efforts showed promise and then failed. In general, the country was barely keeping the lid on discord and division that summer, which had seen the assassination of Bobby Kennedy in June, angry demonstrations at the Oakland murder trial of Black Panther Huey P. Newton in July, and 23,000 police and National Guardsmen violently attacking antiwar demonstrators at the Democratic National Convention in August in Chicago. When Connecticut senator Abraham Ribicoff condemned the "Gestapo tactics in the streets of Chicago," during his nominating speech for George McGovern, Mayor Richard Daley erupted in anger: "Fuck you, you Jew son of a bitch!"

But it was a new scourge of "black antisemitism," the UFT's Shanker insisted, that fueled the fracas in Brooklyn. Only a year earlier, the

Anti-Defamation League (ADL) had issued a report concluding that African Americans were far less likely than white Gentiles to harbor negative attitudes toward Jews. That didn't stop Shanker from framing the dispute as, at its core, a Black-Jewish battle. And he did everything he could to make others see it that way. The notion seeped deeply enough into the discourse that *Variety* joked in September that, taking a cue from the all-Black *Hello, Dolly!* Hal Prince was "mulling an all-Negro company of *Fiddler on the Roof.*" The producer was not amused.

A few days before the start of the new school year, Rhody McCoy announced that he had hired 350 new teachers (many of them white and Jewish, recruited from progressive college organizations around the country) to replace the UFT members who had walked out the previous May. And on the first day of the semester, the UFT called a citywide strike, closing all the schools for two days with the demand that the ousted teachers be welcomed back to their duties. When they did go back, once again they had to push through protesting crowds, and when they made it inside they found that they were not assigned to classes. Out went the UFT again, this time for more than two weeks. After another brief return, the union called its third citywide strike in mid-October; it lasted until the third week of November.

Over those autumn months, newly recruited teachers crossed picket lines to hold classes, accosted by striking UFT members, who were themselves confronted by local supporters of community control. It got nasty. Working teachers told reporters that picketers not only yelled "Scab!" at them but also called them "Commie fascists," "Black Nazi lovers," and "nigger lovers"; strikers, in turn, said they were branded "racist pigs."

Shanker raised the panic level, wielding a leaflet filled with Jew-hating invective. It was a composite of two flyers: one, he alleged, had been placed in teachers' mailboxes in two Ocean Hill schools, demanding "absolute" Black control of community schools; the other had been "phoned in to a UFT representative" and decried the "bloodsucking exploiters" and "Middle East murderers of colored people" dominating the public education system. The community governing board swiftly disavowed and denounced the material. The flyer bore the crude letterhead of an organization that did not exist and a phone number that did not operate. Later investigations concluded that the leaflets, in the temperate terms of the ADL, were not the product of any organized effort; in the blunter words of the New York Civil Liberties Union, they were the means by which the UFT had "perpetrated multiple fraud." In the hot moment, they changed the public terms of the debate. Shanker ran off hundreds of thousands of copies and handed them out widely as "proof" that the movement for community control was driven by hatemongers. Media conversation about the school standoffs shifted from issues of teacher accountability and quality education to the specter of black anti-semitism. Mayor Lindsay, a champion of community control, was shocked to find himself jeered at and shouted into silence when he went to speak at a Brooklyn Jewish center in October.

The Black and Puerto Rican adolescents who would be learning almost incidentally about Jewish history and ritual practice as they sang "Sabbath Prayer," put up a chuppah for *Fiddler*'s wedding scene, and contemplated why Tevye and his family were being evicted, for the most part stayed out of the fray. Those with parents involved in community activism may have talked over the issues at home, but unlike kids in the demonstration district whose schools remained open during the strikes, the Eiseman students didn't walk the gantlet of sniping factions to attend classes. Piro's students, in fact, got out of the neighborhood. When Piro had voted with his union to strike, he was thinking about the due process question, not plotting to win extra time with his drama kids. But when the teachers stayed out most of the fall, he was delighted to be able to work on what he deemed "a professional theater schedule": he held daily rehearsals at his Manhattan home.

The principals in the cast—except for Maritza, whose mother would not allow her to go—rode the LL train in to Sixth Avenue and walked the couple of blocks over to Piro's studio apartment at Seventh Avenue and Sixteenth Street. The subway took less than an hour, but for many of the students the seven-mile journey was as momentous as a trip to the moon. Some seldom went to Manhattan, and none had hung out in a white teacher's apartment. The tiny place, stuffed with fabrics and trims Piro had scrounged for costume making and with a rented sewing machine stashed in a corner, made him wonder, drolly, whether "it looked like a drag queen lived there." The dozen kids who crowded into the narrow room didn't make anything of it. And as blustery as they were about their own bombastic hormones, they expressed no curiosity about Piro's private life. He was a teacher, after all. The students couldn't imagine he had one (though a few of the girls admitted to having crushes on him). They arrived midmorning and arrayed themselves on the two daybeds that served as sofas, playfully whacking one another with the covered pillows they shoved aside to make room.

Piro began with discussions about the scenes they'd be rehearsing later. He drilled them on standard actor stuff, which made the kids feel very serious about their labor: Did they grasp each scene's situation? What their characters wanted? Could they understand it better by relating it to something in their own lives? Sheila found quick identification with Chava. Her own strict parents did not permit her to date boys—and her five brothers kept a close eye on her. Chava's desire for forbidden Fyedka made good emotional sense to her. When they worked on the edict scene, Olga thought about kids she knew who faced evictions from their homes. Though her own family was solid, many of her classmates lived in precarious households and recognized the feeling of "leaving because you're thrown out, leaving because you're not wanted." Teddy, quietly coping with a fraught homelife in a shabby apartment that stank of urine, where he had to look after young siblings whenever his mother unexpectedly and unaccountably stayed out—liked to put it simply: "Tevye—he's a poor milkman who lives in a ghetto just like we do." But these weren't political claims or arguments for their right to do the play. The students didn't perceive any irony or incongruity in their efforts—it was cynical grownups who imposed that interpretation—and the Black-Jewish conflict raged mostly beyond their radar. They were drawing actors' parallels. As Olga understood, it was "all about getting into character."

The afternoon work turned technical. To depict the attraction between Chava and Fyedka, Sheila and Reggie had to stand closer together while trying not to. The girls had to sing "Matchmaker" from their bellies and "feel the joy." Olga had to make Yente's speech more spontaneous—less of a prepared shtick—but still get the lines absolutely right. And Teddy, that tough bundle of talent, like all other Tevyes, had to be restrained from hamming. Even at fourteen, he could read an audience's pulse and play for extra laughs or attention. In Piro's apartment, the other kids were his audience and he sometimes displayed his dominion by drawing back lazily or provoking a power struggle. "I'm not going to do it like that," he brashly told Piro from time to time, more for the drama of the altercation than for the sake of any principled interpretive disagreement.

The other kids waited out the storm. It wouldn't take long before Piro yelled. All of the kids had been on the receiving end of his outbursts, though none as often as Teddy, and all of the students understood them as expressions of Piro's passion and perfectionism. The flare-ups never contained any malice or insult. When Piro raised his voice to say "I *told* you twice to do it like this!" or "*What* could you have been thinking?" the students were motivated by how much he cared that they get it right. Sometimes he just stared at them silently, right in the eye, and they knew they had failed to live up to his expectation.

For extra coaching and to work on the songs, the company bounced a few doors up Sixteenth Street to the apartment of Piro's friend, the actor Joe Sicari, whose minuscule ground-floor one-bedroom had an upright piano. Sicari was a stickler for expressing character *through* singing, he repeatedly explained to the kids as they worked through the show's score. It took session after session for Teddy and Bev to find the right dynamic in "Do You Love Me?" For all the maturity of her thirteen years, Bev could not understand why Golde would not admit she loved Tevye unless she really didn't. Or maybe it was just that Bev didn't want to encourage Teddy's blossoming infatuation. Either way, Sicari had to work hard to remove a few layers of Golde's irritation.

Between the morning conversations and the afternoon scene work, Piro served lunch. Serious lunch. Piro was a good cook, and a proud one, and he prepared meals for the *Fiddler* group as if he were planning a sophisticated dinner party. He fussed over chicken *al forno* and fancy pasta salads; he assembled English muffin pizzas. Sicari sometimes pitched in by baking apple pies. The kids helped clean up.

Piro took the students to see *Fiddler* on Broadway—balcony seats were still cheap in those days. He and Birnel shepherded the group to the Majestic Theater (the 1,600-seat house into which the show had moved in February 1967) for a matinee. Harry Goz—the fourth Broadway Tevye—led the cast. A more measured performer than Mostel or even Herschel Bernardi, whom he replaced, Goz let emotion build gradually over the course of the show, and he was the best singer of the bunch. Rae Allen played a wry, pleasant Golde. Piro enjoined the kids both to get involved in the show *and* to keep an analytical eye on the choices the actors made. He invited them to see themselves commanding the same power that could have an audience "living and breathing your words." Most of the children were riveted. Teddy and a couple of the other boys, though, hung out in the men's room smoking past the intermission break; Piro nearly dragged them back to the theater.

Through the trips to Manhattan, the focused labor, the lunches, the goofing around, the dribbled-out sharing of details about home, and the joint struggle to create something, the children bonded—like all other kids in all other school musicals everywhere for all eternity. But seldom are the attachments as tight and indelible as they became for Piro's *Fiddler*, or as meshed with the play's themes. These kids, as they wistfully described it, grew into a family. In trying times, they established their own secure communal circle—the image so central to Jerry Robbins's conception of the show—and soon, like Anatevka itself, it would be assailed by nefarious outside forces.

Shortly before Thanksgiving, the UFT settled with the Board of Education—the ousted teachers would return to their Ocean Hill–Brownsville schools (the plummeting number who still wanted to, that is) and the experimental governing board would be temporarily suspended—and the schools reopened. In the meantime, Richard M. Nixon had been elected president. (Shifting alliances in New York City notwithstanding, national electoral politics were still an arena in which Jews remained closer to Blacks than to whites: Nixon garnered 17 percent of Jewish votes and less than 5 percent of African American—he won 43 percent overall.) But the animosity incited on the picket lines and in the press hardly abated. Jewish hackles stayed raised; Black resentment redoubled. The Eiseman teachers who had objected to *Fiddler* when it was first announced stepped up their campaign to close it down. They called themselves the Maccabees, emboldened, perhaps by the recent emergence of the Jewish Defense League, the far-right organization pledging to protect New York's Jews from the genocidal peril it saw everywhere; the JDL took some rhetorical cues from the Black Panthers ("Every Jew, a .22" became its notorious slogan) and had sprung into being just in time to rally behind the UFT. Though small in number, its members managed to splash plenty of gasoline on the controversy long past the end of the strike.

The Maccabees returned to Eiseman fired by new grievances against the musical. In addition to taking exception to the "defilement" of sacred garb—boys in the cast putting on yarmulkes and prayer shawls—they decried the way the show depicted Jews as weak and docile. Brownsville, they maintained, needed to know that Jews could not be pushed around. One fellow teacher told Piro that if he didn't cancel the show he'd find his personal secrets blazoned in the newspaper—an only slightly indirect threat to "out" him. Another teacher threatened to kill him.

Piro could think of only one answer: the show itself. He offered to present the opening number and first scenes at the school's upcoming Friday assembly. The opposition would see how honorable the students and his intentions were, he was certain. The kids had been taking great leaps in their roles now that they could move around on the school's stage, whose thirty-five-foot-wide proscenium opening and twenty-five-foot depth made it seem like it could contain Piro's and Sicari's apartments several times over. Maritza and the other children who hadn't trekked to Manhattan had been slotted into their parts and were working hard to catch up. Maritza had to stop waving her arms and hyperventilating through her lines like the divas in the telenovelas her mother watched. Piro urged her to feel what Hodel was going through and to forget that she was acting. Piro leveled with the cast, telling them bluntly that the show's future depended on how well they would perform at the assembly.

Two days before their presentation, Rubin called Piro into a meeting. After the turmoil of the fall, the principal had become warier than ever. More than about how the parents would react to Jewish material, he worried about the trust that had been broken between the community and the teachers: the UFT had denied the children almost a whole semester of school. It was necessary to tread lightly, Rubin warned. He was canceling *Fiddler* and wouldn't even consider reinstating it without a written letter of support from the Brownsville Community Council, the elected neighborhood body that had started under the Johnson administration's Model Cities program.

On the day of the assembly, the children gathered quietly backstage. The boys put on the black overcoats Piro had rescued from discard bins and they donned the yarmulkes Stephan and a Jewish boy on crew had scrounged up. The girls draped shawls over their shoulders and head scarves over their hair. There was no teasing or fooling around, not even as the adolescents changed clothes in full view of one another. When showtime came, Piro pressed the play button on the reel-to-reel tape of the "Music Minus One" karaoke-style LP Birnel had recorded, and Teddy walked onto the stage, paste-on beard cascading down his chin, to begin Tevye's monologue. When the chorus came on—two halves from opposite wings—bopping in a line and singing "Tradition," they radiated excitement and joy. True, Teddy didn't sustain good, direct contact with the audience and Olga's Yente went a bit overboard, but in general Piro knew they had nailed it. The audience of their eighth-grade peers hooted and clapped in appreciation. The Maccabees, however, had stayed in the faculty lounge drinking coffee. The cast returned backstage high on how well everything had clicked and by how much fun they'd had making it happen. Bev, for one, was in a state of amazement. For the first time, she had fully entered the play's world, suddenly feeling like "it wasn't make-believe anymore. It was real."

Piro showered the kids with the praise they deserved, and then dropped the bomb of Rubin's ultimatum: "This show has been canceled." Some actors burst into tears; some shrugged with studied nonchalance; Duane cursed "those fucking Jews." None understood why anyone could object to the project they were so earnestly pouring their hearts into. Sheila plunged into sadness over the prospect that she would no longer get to play Chava: "The girl giving me freedom was being taken away." Piro announced that they would pick up *The Crucible* again. Arthur Miller's play about the Salem witch hunts was now acquiring its own unwelcome relevance, he thought.

That night, Olga's mother, Lillian Carter, called Piro at his apartment. His show's Yente had arrived home heartbroken and Carter needed to know why. The teacher's detailed explanation of events hardly satisfied her. Why, she wondered, could the principal accept this project for the two months her child was traveling into Manhattan and then suddenly withdraw his approval? And why had it been all right for Al Jolson to "black up" for minstrelsy or for whites to assume the voices of Amos 'n' Andy on the radio, and for it not to be all right for Black and Puerto Rican children to play Jews, sincerely, in a play? A member of the school board for Eiseman's district, she pledged her support. And she gave Piro the phone number of a mover and shaker on the Brownsville Community Council.

Frances Brown had been waiting for his call. Little happened in Brownsville without the Community Council's knowing about it and Brown, active on the organization's education committee, had been hearing rumors of the strife over *Fiddler*. She couldn't figure it out. "That's a good show," she thought. She knew that the Broadway cast had many non-Jewish actors in it and that productions had played without any Jewish actors in Finland and Japan. No one objected. On the contrary. These were proudly advertised examples of the show's universal appeal. So what was the fuss? Brown could only conclude, she told Piro, that his opponents thought the neighborhood children were not capable enough, or else they had a problem with Blacks and Puerto Ricans participating in the play. Either way, the council could not accept their stance. She promised that the show would go on.

That left the students in a spot just like the fiddler's, Teddy told his fellow cast members when Piro decided to resume rehearsals of the musical: they were merely trying to "scratch out a simple tune" without losing their balance.

Piro kept them teetering as he maneuvered Rubin's absolute permission for the show like an ace Machiavelli. A few mornings after their first conversation, Frances Brown reported that a letter was on its way to Rubin from the Community Council urging Eiseman to present the play. Right away, Piro posted a notice stating that the spring play would be *The Crucible*. Rubin caught him in the hall and thanked him for his cooperation. Piro knew exactly what would happen when Rubin opened his mail the next day. "We urgently request that Junior High School 275 be allowed to put on the *Fiddler on the Roof* play," the council's letter read. "The performing arts know no boundary of race. Therefore this play, as an experience dealing with Jewish culture, can be a great enlightenment to the Black and Puerto Rican youth of Brownsville, especially as staged by Black and Puerto Rican students." Rubin called Piro into his office and all but commanded him to reinstate *Fiddler*. The school could not cross the will of the community.

The Maccabees did not give up so easily. They had one last tactic: ratting. Because *Fiddler* was still running on Broadway, amateur rights were not yet available; it was impossible to license the show and illegal to produce it, even in a junior high auditorium. Schools all over the country flouted such rules frequently, but if they were caught they usually received a cease-and-desist order. Whoever contacted Music Theatre International to expose Piro's pirated *Fiddler* was no doubt counting on that ax to fall. When MTI phoned Rubin to warn of legal action, the principal called a faculty meeting and, with fury and dread, said he would have to write to the Community Council to explain why the show was being canceled after all. It was Birnel who suggested he wait a few days while he tried to work some showbiz connections.

Not that he really had any, but the bluff bought some time—and it worked. Piro reached the lawyer at MTI who had phoned Rubin and won him over with the story of his intent and of his colleagues' betrayal. The lawyer connected him with Hal Prince's representatives, who contacted the authors. It took Bock, Harnick, and Stein less than five minutes to decide to get behind the production. (Robbins was away at the time and his assistant didn't bother him with the kerfuffle.) Harnick found the Jewish objections "embarrassing"; Stein likened them to "saying Hamlet can only be played by a Dane." He thought, in fact, that it was "quite a marvelous thing for these Black children to be involved in this production in view of what is going on in Ocean Hill and what is going on in the city." They authorized the production so long as the program would note their granting of special permission. Piro didn't try hard not to gloat in the faculty lounge.

By that point, the Broadway production had realized a profit of 1,300 percent on the original $375,000 investment. Prince noted that it would pay more to its investors than all his other shows combined. Meanwhile, currents of Black-Jewish hostility continued gusting through the city. They stormed most ferociously in the cultural realm.

First, the issue was a poem. Late in December, Julius Lester, the host of a Black radio program on New York's progressive listener-sponsored station, WBAI, invited onto the air a teacher from Junior High 271, the school at the center of the Ocean Hill–Brownsville experiment, and asked him to share some of the pieces his eighth graders were writing in response to the strife engulfing them. Lester urged the teacher, Leslie Campbell (who later changed his name to Jitu Weusi), to read a particularly belligerent twenty-six-line poem by a girl in his class. The poem was titled "Antisemitism" and dedicated to Albert Shanker. It began, "Hey, Jew boy, with that yarmulke on your head / You pale-faced Jew boy—I wish you were dead," and it concluded, "Guess you know, Jew boy, there's only one reason you made it / You had a clean white face, colorless and faded / I hated you Jew boy, because your hangup was the Torah / And my only hangup was my color."

The media firestorm that ensued was not a literary debate over the merits of the final couplet's use of forced rhyme. Some of the reports got the facts wrong, crediting Campbell as the author of the hateful work. Shanker filed a complaint with the Federal Communications Commission. The JDL organized protests at the radio station. Julius Lester began receiving anonymous threats on his life. The door to Leslie Campbell's home was doused with gasoline and set alight.

At the same time, the most venerable art institution in the city was trying to tamp down a Black-Jewish conflagration of its own. The Metropolitan Museum of Art was just opening a show called *Harlem on My Mind: Cultural Capital of Black America, 1900–1968*, its first exhibition featuring African Americans. Black artists and their supporters protested the Met's uncharacteristic ethnographic approach to its subject: organized by Jewish curators, the exhibit presented a photographic display chronicling the neighborhood over seven decades, but no paintings or prints, as if to declare that no Harlem-based artists had ever produced work worthy of the Met. Picketers outside the museum carried signs asking "Harlem on whose mind?" and claiming that they were, metaphorically, "On the auction block again." Then Random House published the Met's catalog for the show, which included an essay by a recent high school graduate from Harlem proclaiming that "anti-Jewish feeling is a natural result of the Black Northern migration. . . . Behind every hurdle that the Afro-American has yet to jump stands a white Jew who has already cleared it." The essay added that Jewish shopkeepers exploited Blacks and that "our contempt for the Jew makes us feel more completely American in sharing a national prejudice." Mayor Lindsay called the essay racist; the ADL's president pronounced it "akin to the worst hatred ever spewed out by Nazis." The city threatened to revoke the Met's funding if the museum did not cease selling the catalog. The museum complied (though bookstores continued to carry it).

In the roiling controversies, arguments about representation subsumed the issues behind the community control experiment—distribution of power, equal opportunity, self-determination, the needs of minority schoolchildren. Now the front pages were filled with Black-Jewish disputes over images and words, what could be shown and what could be said. In this context, Piro's *Fiddler* made for a great news story. A local CBS correspondent, Jeanne Parr, brought cameras to Eiseman to shoot a seven-minute segment for the six o'clock news in late January, featuring rehearsal clips and interviews with oppositional teachers who smugly insisted they had no objection to the children playing the roles but simply thought such students should be working on a play more culturally "appropriate" to their "Afro-Caribbean" experience. A documentary filmmaker named Howard Enders had caught wind of the production much earlier and had been gathering his own footage for an ABC special. CBS's *60 Minutes* called Piro and eventually produced a segment. Rubin hated the publicity, but the children were electrified by it. Largely oblivious to the allegory the media were making of them, they basked in the cameras like stars.

Enders's hour-long film, *Black Fiddler: Prejudice and the Negro*, framed the Eiseman production as an emblem of Black-Jewish discord, using high-flown language to describe (in the sonorous timbre of Frank Reynolds's narration) "the world's most oppressed peoples alienated from each other." Though it didn't air until August, well after the school year had ended, the process of making the movie churned up the issue that had originally worried Rubin as Enders went around the area interviewing people. He filmed Leslie Campbell. "Kids in that play don't know their own origins," Campbell told Enders. He thought it would be better if they were "secure in their own culture" before being steeped in someone else's "for the sake of integration." Enders didn't include— maybe didn't find out—that Campbell's cultural nationalism had been fostered, in part, by the Jewish left's harnessing of Yiddish culture for group solidarity and activism. In the mid-1950s, Campbell was one of a handful of African American kids who attended left-wing Camp Kinderland in New York's Hudson Valley. At fourteen, he was a counselor in training, participating in the Yiddish singing and folk dancing led by Edith Segal (founder and choreographer of the aptly named Red Dancers of the 1930s). Campbell came to love the stories of Sholem-Aleichem. He appreciated the *folkshrayber* as "the equivalent of an African griot, who has the history of his people, recounts their epic times, and, by recounting them, strengthens the people's resolve and struggle." If Black kids wanted to take a cue from *Fiddler*, he thought, it should be in discovering their own storytellers.

Similar sentiments began to buzz among some Eiseman parents, though Frances Brown's enthusiasm never wavered. She didn't see why kids couldn't have Black history *and* the musical—in fact, the Community Council had been making inroads in the Brownsville curriculum over the last couple of years. Besides, she wondered, how many appropriate Black musicals were there to choose from?

To fortify the parents' support, Piro decided to offer a preview of the first act at the next monthly PTA meeting, an affair that usually drew a couple dozen participants. The program would also include the choir's presentation of *Testament of Freedom*—a means of drawing a greater number of parents to the event. More than five hundred showed up.

By now Birnel had completed the lighting and all the kids had costumes and makeup. The night of the preview, they got something else: laughs and real emotional engagement from an audience. The response lifted them to new discoveries. Beverly and Olga played the encounter between Golde and Yente with well-timed business; Duane found a hilarious way of freezing in fright when Motel can't quite summon the courage to ask Tevye for Tzeitel's hand, and Teddy instantly recognized what Duane was doing and didn't step on his lines. Piro beamed as he watched "ensemble playing in the finest sense." That night he wrote the cast one of his periodic memos. They were masterworks of encouragement, good humor, and specific, constructive criticism. Students looked forward to them as if they were cash in the mail. He addressed this one to "The Beautiful People of Anatevka" from "Your Czar." "Boy, oh boy, oh boy!" it began. "This was some evening." The nearly 1,000-word note singled out some of the highlights of the presentation—Maritza's acting from the inside out instead of all on the outside, the warmth of Sheila's singing, the chorus's precision in "Tradition." And it told kids exactly what else they had to work on: Duane was speaking too fast; the "Matchmaker" girls shouldn't smile out at the audience; Teddy had to stop mugging in "If I Were a Rich Man," which made the number into "a stand-up comedian's bit instead of a real indication of Tevye's way of making up dreams." Piro was quick to add, "I'm not criticizing you in any way. I am proud that you had the guts to try it that way. If all of it doesn't work, we just search for what does and insert it in between all that WAS excellent about the number. This is why we rehearse."

Birnel was galvanizing his tech crew, too. Some of the boys took foraging trips along Pitkin and Belmont Avenues looking for props. They shot 16mm film for the special effects—birch trees to project onto the curtain during the overture, flames to lick the scrim in the pogrom scene. At last, the show was coming together.

But the city's schools were coming ever more unglued. Legitimate student protests over moribund curriculum, overcrowding, and proposed budget cuts for the City University system so many of them planned to enroll in sometimes included violent factions, who smashed windows and ignited gasoline bombs. Police responses more often escalated the violence than quelled it. Frequently, the unrest closed schools for whole afternoons or even for several days in a row. In mid-March, Mayor Lindsay assembled a special committee for the purpose of coordinating systemwide efforts to stanch school violence. But, as the press reported, "demonstrations, rampages in the streets, and the setting of fires continued to plague the city's public schools."

Eiseman's district was hardly immune. Canarsie High—the predominantly white Italian school where Eiseman's graduates became racial minorities when they matriculated into its student body of 4,000—often saw whites ganging up on Black and Puerto Rican students in its schoolyard. In the climate of heightened mayhem, end-of-class bells seemed more like boxing ring signals to resume tribal brawling.

The fighting flowed down to the junior high, where the ethnic imbalance tilted the opposite way. A Jewish eighth grader was beaten unconscious by an adolescent mob while scores of other students stood by silently. (The following fall, Stephan Hirsch, a gung ho Russian in *Fiddler*, was set upon and suffered a broken nose and arm; he suspected that the attack stemmed in part from the admittedly racist remarks he felt Enders had goaded him into making in his documentary.) On days Canarsie High closed, its students from Brownsville hung around Eiseman egging on their younger siblings to organize their own demonstrations. For their safety, white kids had to be barred from the raucous cafeteria at lunchtime and picked up by their parents at the end of the day. The drama students mostly ducked the disorder—if for no other reason than expulsion would mean their having to leave the play— though as a student leader, Beverly tried to organize a calm grievance session with the principal. More militant peers hijacked the effort.

Piro kept after-school rehearsals going in a locked auditorium in what felt like "a battle-zone atmosphere." One day he entered this haven to find the set trashed by vandals: the scenery splattered with paint,

Tevye's cart shoved into the orchestra pit, the piano's hammers ripped out. He and Birnel had only a few weeks to fix everything up.

As the performance date approached, agitation increased. Canarsie High had been closing early again and teenagers let loose were stopping by Eiseman to hurl bricks and stones at the building. The district superintendent determined for the first time that the junior high should close early, too, with all extracurricular activities canceled, lest the kids cowering in classrooms be harmed by shattering glass and missiles. Not to mention the bomb scares. *Fiddler* was now missing out on all-important rehearsal time, especially for the tech crew. The day before opening arrived without their ever having worked a run-through. That day, some two hundred high school kids broke twenty-five of Eiseman's windows.

The next morning, May 1, Piro tried to keep his mind off all that could go wrong by reading the *New York Times* on his way to Brownsville. Bitter conflict at schools of all levels made headlines that day. The paper reported on a number of cases of scholastic unrest. One described parents pulling their children out of an elementary school in Harlem where they didn't approve of some teachers. Another detailed how student activists had seized two buildings at Columbia University. A third recounted how more than 150 Brooklyn College students had broken into and torn up the office of the college president, smashing a lamp, setting his mail on fire, and ripping out telephone wires as part of their protests against tuition for Black and Puerto Rican students. Meanwhile, at Queens College, protesting students had been occupying the thirteen-story administration building for three days; a two-day occupation of a Manhattan Community College midtown campus was just ending after a seven-and-a-half-hour meeting where faculty considered student demands for a program in third-world studies; and the entire campus of City College had closed down in the face of student demonstrations and was likely to stay shut for at least the rest of the week.

A piece on page 49 especially caught Piro's eye, "School Battered by Band of Youths," the story about the damage at Eiseman. "That's some way to attract an audience," he joked to himself. He knew full well that the show was sold out.

Piro grazed past another story in the *Times* that day that had just as much to do with the travails he and his drama kids had endured over the last nine months. Carrying an Albany dateline, it was front-page news:

the state legislature had just passed—and Governor Nelson Rockefeller had signed—a law that restructured public school governance in New York City, decentralizing some aspects of the system but essentially killing the experiment in community control. At the end of a tumultuous school year, the Ocean Hill–Brownsville governing board was finished; the UFT had prevailed.

The process shifted Jewish New York's position as a local political faction. Scholars who have studied this pivotal year—and it is one of the most written-about periods in the city's history—describe it as a defining station on the Jews' long, zigzagging path to whiteness. The journalist Jonathan Kaufman shows in his book, *Broken Alliance*, how 1968–69 betokens the moment Jews begin to vote less with Blacks and more with ethnic white Catholics, emphasizing issues of security and fiscal restraint over civil rights and antipoverty programs. Jonathan Rieder, a sociologist, sees Ocean Hill–Brownsville turning outer-borough Jews from "optimistic universalism" toward "nervous provincialism," aligning them with most of the rest of the city's white population. And that, says Jerald Podair, in his book *The Strike That Changed New York*, marked "the Jewish passage from racial ambivalence to unmistakable white identity." Thus, he argues, Jews helped to reify the "white" and "Black" New Yorks that had gestated over three decades and to cement the shift of New York City's central dramatic agon from worker versus boss to Black versus white.

Eiseman's Maccabees may have seen *Fiddler on the Roof* as a station on the same path, presenting a progress narrative for Jews in the United States as they journeyed toward whiteness. The ethnic particularity celebrated in the show enabled their full entry into American universalism, providing an immigrant origin story that made them, in their own distinct way, just like the Irish, the Italians, the Pilgrims themselves. The play couldn't possibly mean the same thing for Blacks and Puerto Ricans in the ravaged ghettos of the late 1960s: among other myriad reasons, that path was closed to them. But a couple dozen kids at Eiseman made *Fiddler* mean something else to them, something their own.

The children arrived backstage for their opening with more than the usual first-night trepidation. The school had suffered another bombardment that morning: the two hundred teenagers were back, breaking another twenty windows, four fluorescent lights, and four electric clocks.

Rubin closed Eiseman after lunch—but allowed the *Fiddler* company to stay for an afternoon tech rehearsal in the locked auditorium. At 4:15, Piro sent them home for a nap, but Enders waylaid them for interviews and some shots of *Fiddler* dialogue played in streets—the most forsaken local streets, full of abandoned and deteriorating houses, streets where none of the *Fiddler* company actually lived. When the kids returned, exhausted, for their 6:30 call, they passed a row of squad cars lined up in front of the building. Rubin was out there talking to police brass, trying to keep the lid on. While the cast dressed and got into makeup, Rubin was convincing the officers to keep their cars and even their uniformed men out of sight. He didn't want to provoke a confrontation with teenagers who had threatened disruption or to upset the audience with signs of expected unrest. The cars drove away, leaving thirty-five policemen hidden on Eiseman's second floor with radios and four on duty by the exits to project just the right measure of reassurance.

* * *

By 8:00, the house was packed. Jerry Bock, Sheldon Harnick, Hal Prince, and Joe Stein took seats among members of the Brownsville Community Council and eager parents—even Beverly's mother, who never attended school events. The authors' special permission was duly noted in the program; so was their "dedication to the idea and the act of universal brotherhood."

Before assuming his post by the tape recorder in the pit, Piro gave the kids the requisite backstage pep talk: Speak out. Project. You know you can do this. If you mess up, keep going. If all the people out front are making you nervous, imagine them in their underwear. And one more thing: Don't chew gum.

The show ran without a hitch. Amateur, sure, but honest and felt and according to plan. Teddy may have conveyed disinterest months earlier when Piro had taken the troupe to the Broadway production, but he performed "Rich Man" with confidence and directness and gurgling "daidle daidle dum"s that perfectly copied the expressive, chanting prayer he had heard at the Majestic. Beverly visibly melted—and melted the audience—in "Do You Love Me?," revealing Golde's dawning realization that she does, indeed. The song finished with Beverly settling cozily onto Teddy's tiny lap, the two of them harmonizing

DAN O'NEIL IV

Teddy Smith performs "Rich Man" with confidence and directness.

through "it's nice to know" with a charm exceeded only by Teddy's wide grin and slow, sure wink.

The company's emotion gathered as the final number approached. The sadness of the eviction scene contained the sorrow of the parting the students knew they would soon experience as the year—and their own Anatevka—came to an end. As the dirge-like half-note toggle on an accordion introduced the song, Tevye and his family assembled as if posing for a last portrait and were bathed in a sepia light. As the song built, the chorus filed down the steps of the stage into the aisles and quietly invited members of the audiences to join them. "Come on. We have to go," they said, offering a gentle hand. "It's time." Film Birnel had made flashed along the walls of the house: winter landscapes and old black-and-white documentary footage of a pogrom he'd dug up somewhere. Grown-ups cried as they joined the children, walking to the back of the house as the cast sang of their precious hometown. Then silence.

It's hard to imagine any company that had done more to earn the standing ovation that erupted as the "L'Chaim" music played and the kids bounded back onto the stage for their bows. Beverly and Teddy pulled Piro into their curtain call and the cast wept openly as the audience cheered and stomped.

The memo Piro wrote to the group late that night was properly ecstatic. "The one word which keeps knocking at my brain about you," he told them, "is 'respect.'" They had touched the community "not because we delivered a message, but, rather, because we gave them the best show the town has ever seen." Now, he promised, the people of Eiseman and Brownsville shared their views—"no, not on Jews and Blacks—but our deep belief that the boys and girls of our school are FIRST-CLASS CITIZENS OF THE WORLD AND ARE CAPABLE OF CONTRIBUTING FIRST-CLASS CONTRIBUTIONS TO SOCIETY."

He urged them to take in their achievement: "Remember—there are various kinds of poverty and only ONE of them deals with money. The others deal with poverty of the spirit, poverty of ambitions, poverty of good feelings about yourself." The experiences of Jews and Blacks in America were historically too different for the neat parallels that media coverage—and liberal sentimentality—wanted to draw from the Eiseman production of *Fiddler*. But in unwittingly invoking the romantic old trope of the materially poor but spiritually rich shtetl, Piro was not doing something so facile. For this invited no nostalgic harking back to a vanished, varnished place some ancestors may have come from; it encouraged a frank coming to terms with the place they were living in today, some with stable families, some not. But all of them, now, with an Anatevka of their own making that could be looked to as a source of pride and strength. *Fiddler*, the pop culture icon of Jewishness, had become the vehicle, for a handful of children, for the assertion and agency that community control aspired to give the whole city. It's not something *Fiddler* could have done by itself, but it's also not something *Guys and Dolls* could have provided.

Did the Eiseman *Fiddler* change attitudes, as Piro had initially hoped? Looking back after more than four decades, cast members couldn't speak for the wider population, but they recalled the experience with surging emotion, describing the genuine love for their characters and their world and for one another that sustained them through that tempestuous year. "It helped me to embrace all these different people," Maritza summed up. "Including myself."

Piro answered with Tevye-like dialectics. On the one hand, beyond the kids immediately involved in the show, his efforts seemed "all in vain." But, on the other hand, one shouldn't expect too much, especially

DAN O'NEIL IV

Richard Piro directs Sheila Haskins (Chava)
and Linus Sellars (Fyedka).

from a play, whose duty, after all, is to be a play, not an act of social work
or political activism. "It takes a lot of bricks to build a cathedral," he said.

Trouble is, kids in Brownsville were more and more apt to be throwing those bricks. Piro took a semester's leave the fall after *Fiddler*, and
when he returned to Eiseman in February 1970 he found it more chaotic
and unruly than ever. Stairwells were filled with litter, graffiti, and kids
having sex; a critical mass of students had become hostile and disruptive.
Even the drama students lacked drive and discipline. He was finding it
impossible to connect with more than a few of the kids. Rubin had trans-
ferred to a middle-class white school in Queens, and the following fall
Piro followed him there. A year later he left the school system altogether
and moved to California.

* * *

By then, *Fiddler on the Roof* had opened as a widely distributed movie—
one of the last big successful Hollywood musicals. Someone, perhaps
fancying that if representational art could divide Blacks and Jews it

might also bring them closer together, had the idea that young African Americans might see themselves in the pluck and plight of its characters. A special screening was arranged in Washington, D.C., as a fund-raising benefit for Howard University. A university official on hand said the movie "brings better understanding between Blacks and Jews." But the students in the audience begged to differ. "Jews are in some position of affluence now and refuse to see themselves as part of Black oppression," one said. A faculty member, asked if she felt any kinship with the Jews in the film, was blunter: "Jews are white, period."

Plenty of frustrated African Americans could have said as much when Piro and the Eiseman kids put on their play. Divisions did widen as inner cities continued to decay and movements to redress inequities became more militant still. But the experience of creating a show differs vastly from the experience of watching one; watching a play differs from the more passive, atomized experience of watching a film.

And, to the Howard University audience, at least, the film's imagery could seem at odds with progressive analyses of American racism. Tevye and his townsfolk seem to live in a vast, gorgeous countryside—big sky, verdant fields, charming river, all brimming with vitality (despite the film being shot with pieces of stocking stretched over the camera lens to produce the "diffuse" look Jewison wanted). And while they may be poor, Golde has her *shabbos* pearls, Motel gets his sewing machine, Tevye owns his house (and even, anachronistically, his land): no resemblance to inner-city squalor. The Anatevkans suffer unaccountable discrimination, but no apparent structural inequality. More than that, the anti-semitism is over there, in the old country; Tevye and his family are leaving it behind when they declare they are going to "New York, America," where they will find religious freedom and opportunity (and escape the genocide that awaits those who do not emigrate, the film blatantly hints). Like a wedding at the end of a comedy, the departure for the United States implies a happily-ever-aftering (as another musical put it) for these Jews—and, presumably, for anyone else who comes and works hard. It supports a by-the-bootstraps narrative of American success that was fast becoming a standard against which African Americans were being unfairly measured and, predictably, found wanting. It's no wonder savvy Howard students and professors bristled when invited to identify with these soon-to-be model immigrants.

What's worse, a movie presenting a comic yet noble paterfamilias as a new American folk hero, trying to hold family and community together in the face of enormous pressures, could have felt like one more club with which to bash African Americans for their alleged pathology: the infamous Moynihan Report of 1965 ascribed abiding poverty in Black communities to single-mother households and a culture that emasculated its men. The accusation remained an open wound for years, not least for its status as a government rationale for social policy. William Ryan's book, *Blaming the Victim*, had come out just months before Jewison's film and its skewering of Moynihan's argument was still causing a buzz when gruff but lovable Tevye, feminized on stage but downright macho in Topol's cinematic performance, trundled in Panavision into the Howard auditorium.

In any event, it was absurd to imagine that screening Jewison's *Fiddler* would produce warm feelings of identification that would wash away the anger and resentment at injustice. Racial healing was not a function the celluloid *Fiddler*—nor any movie musical—could possibly perform.

CHAPTER 8

————

ANATEVKA IN TECHNICOLOR

IF IT WAS TOO MUCH TO EXPECT *FIDDLER ON THE ROOF* TO improve Black-Jewish relations, Norman Jewison was nonetheless on a mission when he made the movie. He regarded it as "the most important film" that would be released in 1971 "and the most important film that perhaps United Artists has ever released." What, exactly, made it so important Jewison never boiled down to a simple slogan, but a weighty sense of purpose can be felt in every frame of the three-hour epic.

Jewison typically insisted on making pictures that did more than simply entertain—at least, once he was in a position in Hollywood to insist on anything. Having come from Canada to launch a successful career in live American television in the late 1950s—he directed *Your Hit Parade* and *The Andy Williams Show* for CBS, and, among his proudest projects, the first Harry Belafonte special in 1959 (during which twenty CBS affiliates in the South went off the air rather than beam a Black star into local living rooms)—he broke into Hollywood with a Tony Curtis comedy in 1962 and a contract with Universal for seven pictures, including some deft Doris Day fluff. Feeling that "my life was being wasted on these commercial comedies where everyone ended up happy and went to the seashore," Jewison wiggled out of his contract on a technicality and went on to salvage *The Cincinnati Kid*, replacing the fired Sam Pekinpah after shooting had already begun. That was his real launching pad—"the movie that made me feel I had finally become a filmmaker"—and he

signed a two-picture deal with the Mirisch brothers, whose limber independent production company had been feeding hits to United Artists for
half a decade. Jewison "wanted to make films about political problems."
He not only got his wish with *The Russians Are Coming, the Russians Are
Coming* (1966), whose slapstick story of a Soviet submarine running
aground near the New England coast made a lighthearted hash of Cold
War paranoia. He also had a hit, topping the box office that summer and
winning a Golden Globe for best picture and several Oscar nominations.
That emboldened Jewison to press for *In the Heat of the Night*, the tense
crime mystery starring Sidney Poitier and Rod Steiger, reluctantly work-
ing together to solve a murder in a racist Mississippi town. It won five
Oscars for the 1967 season, including for best picture. And it cemented
Jewison's reputation as a strong, multigenre filmmaker with a social conscience.

So he was surprised, at first, when he was summoned to the office of
United Artists chairman Arthur Krim and offered the reins of *Fiddler*.
(Jerry Robbins never got a hearing; the Mirisch Company had also produced the *West Side Story* movie, and they'd fired Robbins from his post
as its codirector.) Jewison had loved the Broadway show, but was "never a
big fan" of movie musicals. He could appreciate the confections from the
1930s and 1940s, but "they were fantasies and we don't make fantasy films
in the very realistic world of today's cinema," he told a journalist while
working on *Fiddler*. "The musical belongs more naturally to the theater
from which it derives." Still, Jewison came to see the Broadway adaptation of Sholem-Aleichem as an excellent candidate for cinematic treatment: "*Fiddler* breaks through in certain areas as there are moments of it
which are sheer fantasy, almost magic, and yet the setting and the characters are all real and the historical background of the piece is real," he
explained.

From the point of view of the studios in the late 1960s, the "almost
magic" of musicals was to be found in what they did for the box office.
The *New York Times* noted Hollywood's banking on the genre in an
October 1968 article, "Studios Again Mining Gold with Lavish Film
Musicals." At that moment, American studios had invested $91 million
in eighteen major musical projects about to be released or in production,
among them *Funny Girl, Finian's Rainbow, Oliver!, Chitty Chitty Bang
Bang, Paint Your Wagon, Sweet Charity,* and *Hello, Dolly!* The trend had

begun with *West Side Story* in 1961, which had raked in profits of $32.5 million by the date of the *Times* article. Other hits soon followed: *Mary Poppins* ($44.6 million), *My Fair Lady* ($55 million), *Thoroughly Modern Millie* ($30 million). But none made studio executives see dollar signs as vividly as *The Sound of Music* (1965), earner of the largest box-office gross in history in its day. Within only three years it boasted international returns of more than $112 million.

Interest in *Fiddler*'s movie rights followed the Broadway opening almost as quickly as the first-night reviews. Walter Mirisch saw the show during its opening week and immediately told Krim he wanted to make the motion picture. Krim dismissed the idea at first, Mirisch recalled, sounding the common refrain that it lacked wide enough appeal, but he changed his mind when the show's sustained popularity proved him wrong. United Artists went after it. They did not get there first. In April 1965—just after he finished *Ship of Fools* and before he got started on *Guess Who's Coming to Dinner*—the producer-director Stanley Kramer put in a bid, offering $750,000 against 10 percent of the gross (with a willingness to go as high as one million if necessary). Additional inquiries came in that spring.

But *Fiddler*'s authors felt no sense of urgency. So as not to compete with the show, any film would have to wait until demand slacked off, and by spring 1965, they giddily understood that day was not coming any time soon. They had plenty of time. And leverage. By December 1965, they had drawn up a "memorandum of terms" to share with prospective buyers. Among its provisions, which served to protect the aesthetic integrity of the show: there would be no interpolation of new dance, and no new music and lyrics if not written by Bock and Harnick. And the film would not be released before 1971. Producers who'd put out feelers early did not hang on into the winter. Earnest discussions began with United Artists alone.

The negotiations moved along in standard fits and starts until, once again, Arnold Perl entered the scene. According to the original contract for the Broadway show, he (and the Rabinowitz estate) were entitled to royalties on any sale of the property, and he stood to receive some $100,000 as his share of the movie deal. He bargained for more, driven by the belief—disputed by the authors—that *Fiddler* was based on his own groundbreaking work. Also, he still owned the rights to his play,

Tevya and His Daughters, and United Artists needed to be sure that no movie based on it would vie with *Fiddler*. "Perl is now in a position to hold up the deal, and will, presumably, want to exact a high price," Jerry Robbins's lawyer told him. Indeed. Perl demanded $250,000 for the movie rights to his play. He got $75,000 for them on top of his $100,000 royalty. He kept his "by special arrangement" credit, too.

After nearly a year of negotiations—and a last-minute, $2.5 million bid from another producer in the fall of 1966—United Artists closed the deal for some $2.75 million. They planned a splashy "roadshow" presentation (one of Hollywood's last, it turned out): opening at first only in select large theaters in major cities, requiring viewers to buy reserved-seat tickets in advance, and trumpeting the grandness of the experience with a curtain, overture, intermission, entr'acte, exit music, and glossy program booklet for sale—a set of lavish formalities that exceeded those of the Broadway show itself.

In the five short years between the start of contract negotiations and the beginning of shooting in 1970, Hollywood, like the rest of America, had been rocked by change. Studio heads had banked on musicals to feed an audience hungry for escapism in tumultuous times; audiences, instead, began to prefer movies that at least acknowledged the tumult. And such movies were becoming available. The censorious Production Code was dissolving in the tide of the sexual revolution; maverick directors were finding inroads into picture-making as the old studio system finally sputtered through its decade-long death throes. Soon after Jewison signed on for *Fiddler*, he saw popular interest shift away from hits like *The Sound of Music* and *Mary Poppins* toward films like *Who's Afraid of Virginia Woolf?*, *The Graduate*, *Bonnie and Clyde*, *Guess Who's Coming to Dinner*, and *2001: A Space Odyssey*. And while *Funny Girl* held its financial own in such company, most of the musicals released at the end of the 1960s with cheery high hopes and even higher investments utterly tanked. *Camelot*, *Star!*, *Chitty Chitty Bang Bang*, and *Hello, Dolly!*— among others—lost millions at the box office, and *Doctor Doolittle*, a $29 million disaster, nearly ruined 20th Century Fox.

The market was mirroring Jewison's own taste for engagement and innovation. His 1968 heist picture, *The Thomas Crown Affair*, hinged on a hot sexual twist and also gave him a chance to experiment with split-screen effects. More significantly, months before *In the Heat of the Night* snagged the Oscar for best movie, he was tapped to make a film intended as a stirring response to the rising demands of Black Power: an adaptation of William Styron's highly acclaimed—and highly controversial—novel about the leader of the bloody slave revolt of 1831, *The Confessions of Nat Turner.* The mere announcement of the project sparked protest from Black activists, who had objected to what they considered negative stereotyping and historical falsification in the book. They organized to demand that, among other things, Jewison and his producer (David Wolper for 20th Century Fox) depict Turner as less brutish, less sexually fixated on white women, and generally more righteous. Though Jewison assertively told the press at the time that he would listen to concerns but make the film as he pleased, the script was altered in response to the outcry.

Jewison had been feeling discouraged for months as the controversy played out. He took the assassination of Robert F. Kennedy in June 1968 as a hard personal blow, sensing in it a "defeat" of "all the causes and ideals that I had believed in." He couldn't get over how violently he'd been attacked by mounted police at an antiwar demonstration in Los Angeles. He saw adapting Styron's book as an opportunity to portray a "revolutionary hero," while some African Americans regarded it as an affront that a white man would have the gall to take up the story, and this also unsettled him. Plus, he later quipped in his autobiography, "Nixon was president. Reagan was governor. I was losing my sense of humor." In February 1969, he officially bowed out of *Nat Turner,* and the Canadian-born director with his wife and their two boys moved to London. In a bitter and futile protest, he returned his family's green cards, asserting that they no longer wished to live in the United States.

In London, Jewison planned to put "all the grief and disappointment of the sixties" behind him and restore the "joy and hope" he knew he needed to film the musical, though he had no intention of making the sort of fluffy Broadway adaptation that was sinking at the box office. *Fiddler* was granted a budget of eight million dollars (which he eventually pushed to nine million). It wasn't an outlandish sum by the day's standards, but it was substantial and United Artists was counting on *Fiddler,* as *Variety* reported, "to bring it into the big money for the first time in a couple of years." Jewison may have left his disappointment behind, but pressure followed him to England.

Some of it weighed upon him like the complaints about white men's fitness to make *Nat Turner*, but now the onus had to do with a Gentile making a Jewish film and it felt less fraught. Indeed, Jewison relished the tale of being offered *Fiddler* and told it often: At the meeting in United Artists' midtown Manhattan office, Krim popped the question. "What would you say if we asked you to direct *Fiddler on the Roof*?" Jewison answered with a question: "What would you say if I told you I'm a goy?" Krim calmly explained—inadvertently betraying some vestigial Hollywood shame in Jewish display—that they were not interested in a Yiddish Second Avenue approach. "He covered so beautifully," Jewison said. "I'm sure he was in shock." (Topol, ever the Zionist, later ascribed the film's success in part to its Gentile director: "He could make a film free of complexes typical to Jews in exile.")

Though the son of an Anglican and a Methodist, Jewison had a long-standing affinity for Jewish culture, even a sense of identification. It began in his childhood in Toronto, where his name had made him the target of some "hey Jewboy" bullying, and he bristled at "Gentiles Only" signs on the shore of the Balmy Beach Canoe Club; he gleefully joined a Jewish friend for synagogue services on a regular basis. Prejudice of any kind rankled and rattled him for as long as he could remember and he recognized the historical persecution of Jews as part of a deadly human virus that had to be eradicated. To that end, "we need to feel how 'the other' feels," he maintained, and he believed his work could make a modest contribution to that daunting project by touching audiences' hearts. "I'm not a cerebral filmmaker," he said. "I make emotional films and I want my audience to become emotionally involved." He expected *Fiddler* to be every bit as socially relevant as *In the Heat of the Night* or even, perhaps, as *Nat Turner* might have been had it ever been made. He took on *Fiddler* with an enormous sense of responsibility.

Like Robbins before him, but with the burden of being an outsider, he plunged into research: He purchased at least 37 books (the usual suspects: Heschel, Maurice Samuel, and, of course, the Sholem-Aleichem stories, along with art books of paintings and photographs of Eastern European Jewish life). He sent copies of *Life Is with People* to those responsible for set decoration, wardrobe, script supervision, makeup, hairdressing, and props, among others. In the fall of 1969, he took a whirlwind five-day trip to Israel, under the guidance of Rabbi Moshe

Davis, the influential Jewish-American educator who had consulted with Arnold Perl years earlier and was now a professor at Hebrew University. The professor set up visits to archives and museums dedicated to Sholem-Aleichem, Russian Zionism, and Jewish music; screenings of historical footage and Yiddish films; visits to observant families in religious neighborhoods. At a kibbutz, Jewison interviewed old immigrants from a Ukrainian shtetl, who described a pogrom they had witnessed as children. (One couple's recollection of feathers flying from slashed pillows made it into Jewison's pogrom scene.)

Jewison also turned to *A Vanished World*, not only by studying the work; he also spent an afternoon with "dear old Roman Vishniac." Jewison considered the photographer particularly influential in developing his own visual vocabulary, especially for "the look of the people." Some listings in his "casting breakdown" notes for Anatevkans—"Sheftel—A tanner—lean, wiry . . . A hard-working generally stoic individual"; "Berl, Blacksmith—a giant, massive, full bearded man . . . a gentle creature"; "Farcel . . . Fishmonger . . . solid, mustached, square-built . . . Adroit in his dealings with the women who buy from him in the Square"—are followed by a page number referring to an image in *A Vanished World*.

Most striking, Jewison made the character of the rabbi resemble the cover of Vishniac's book, projecting, with his full white beard and crinkly eyes, gravitas along with warmth and good humor.

Having assured the preemptive Rabbinical Council of America that the rabbi would be portrayed "in a dignified manner," Jewison cast Zvee Scooler, a longtime actor and Yiddish radio personality who had been born in Ukraine in 1899 and performed for years in Maurice Schwartz's company—including in *Di brider ashkenazi* with Jerry Robbins; he also played the innkeeper in the original production of *Fiddler*, staying with the show for its entire seven-plus years. Jewison thought that in addition to location, actors like Scooler would help him make a "direct connection" with Sholem-Aleichem. Thus he cast Molly Picon, also in her seventies and a peppy star since girlhood of Yiddish stage and screen, as Yente, and she dodders through the movie, head atilt, as Yente's job is rendered obsolete.

Jewison had hoped to add two more Israelis to the company, believing they would provide the same kind of authenticity: for Perchik, Asaf Dayan (son of the famous defense minister, Moshe Dayan), whose English turned out not to be up to the task; and for Golde, Hanna Maron, a leading actor at Israel's Habima and Cameri theaters. On their way to the audition in London, the actors had to change planes in Munich; there, at the airport, members of a pro-Palestinian group moved to hijack their flight, throwing live grenades when a pilot resisted the militants' orders. Maron was among the injured, losing her left leg. The incident "devastated" Jewison and added to his resolve to portray a tough, persevering people.

Like Robbins, Jewison also sought the direct participation of Marc Chagall; he hoped to set a spirited, spiritual tone by using some of Chagall's paintings in the opening title sequence. This time, the refusal was harsher: "MADAME CHAGALL SAYS HER HUSBAND HATES FIDDLER BASED ON FRENCH TELEVISION EXCERPT OF PARIS STAGE VERSION," declared the cable to Jewison from Saul Cooper, a United Artists representative, who looked into the prospect in Paris. But, like Hodel appealing to Tevye, Cooper added, "BELIEVE POSSIBILITY STILL REMAINS FOR OBTAINING CHAGALL'S BLESSING IF NOT HIS PARTICIPATION." Three months later, Cooper updated Jewison: Even after receiving an extensive, French-language synopsis of the film, the artist's answer remained *non*.

Even if Jewison had won the master's cooperation, it's difficult to imagine how Chagall's airy images would have related to the film's earthy specificity. The stage is a land of metaphor, but narrative movies are, by nature, literal—and Chagall hated realism. With movies, "you're taking the story out of the theater and putting it in the real world," Jewison believed, "where there are animals and carts and people." That's why he insisted on shooting in Eastern Europe, and Yugoslavia was as near as he could come. In the Soviet Union he figured he'd be too prone to unpredictable delays. He also had to give up a location he fell in love with in Romania during a six-week scouting trip because no one would provide insurance—for fear of Soviet invasion. "That's when I turned to Tito. He had the largest standing army in Europe and he loved movies," Jewison said. He loved movies "almost as much as he loved hard currency."

Filming in a country run by an autocrat provided many advantages. If Jewison needed to take down telephone poles to keep such anachronisms out of his shots, no problem. If the local farmers had to shut off their tractor engines when he required quiet on the set, all he had to do was sound a horn to alert them to do so. If the fourteen November days of unseasonably warm and sunny weather put him behind schedule as he waited for snow, he could go ahead and cover the ground with marble dust, never mind what it might do to the farmland. The site comprised two rural villages—Lekenik and Mala Gorica, some forty-five minutes' drive from Zagreb (where the cast and crew stayed during the four-month shoot), plus an enclosed square within Zagreb where Jewison filmed a scene he added, supposedly set in Kiev: Perchik arrested after stirring up the masses along with his comrades. "The winds of freedom are beginning to blow all over Russia," Perchik cries as mounted Cossacks close in while John Williams's underscoring swells with thick Russian chords turning ominously dissonant. (The new song Perchik was given in place of "Now I Have Everything"—a rousing march called "Any Day Now"—reiterated his speech and, though recorded, didn't make it into the film.)

As for the villages, their wooden, weathered buildings could be used almost just as they were, with their ramshackle shingles, log fences, and crooked arrangement around a curving road (whose tarmac need only be covered in mud). Jewison was instantly smitten with the setting: "I could almost see a Chagall fiddler standing on a roof," he marveled. "All we had to do was build a synagogue."

* * *

In fact, they had to build a bit more—Tevye's house and barn, a community well, some other structures. But the two-story wooden synagogue was the most significant addition. Overlooked in the reviews, the synagogue defined the film's tone as much as—and in tension with—Topol's toughness. Though the stage *Fiddler* required no synagogue and no scene is set in one, the building plays a crucial role on screen: more than anything else in Jewison's Anatevka, it represents the "tradition" that distinguishes the lusty Jews (as he portrays them) from the local thugs who hate them. If the "people made the shtetl" for Zborowski and Herzog, (and for the stage), the shul did so for celluloid. Decades before wide interest arose in restoring or documenting these structures, Jewison and his production designer, Robert Boyle, constructed a painted shul in painstaking detail, building it from the timber of old barns to give it a sense of age. It is a stunning, syncretic replica of architecture and decor, forgotten for decades as the beautiful old synagogues of Eastern Europe had been destroyed in the war, had decayed in the absence of caretakers, or been appropriated for use as garages and groceries.

Jewison and Boyle visited whatever standing synagogues they could during their East European scouting trip and were inspired by the ornate Baroque elegance of the Dubrovnik synagogue—the second-oldest in Europe, dating from 1652. In Targu Neamt, in northeastern Romania, they saw an abandoned one that served, in part, as a model for the gold filigreed red velvet panels they placed on either side of Anatevka's ark. (The design team even tried to purchase the intact prayer stands, Torah scrolls, ark, and "miscellaneous other appurtenances which would be ideal for the Synagogue in our film." The request was denied.) Following custom, they placed a railed-off *bimah*—the raised platform on which the Torah is read—in the center of the shul and draped the reading table with embroidered red velvet. A heavy curtain of matching fabric covered the holy ark, where the Torah scrolls are kept. Structurally, the building was based on the wooden shuls of eighteenth-century Poland.

But it was by re-creating pastel murals that Boyle performed the film's most beautiful act of recovery. Boyle adorned the Anatevka shul with images of a curly-horned ram against a lavender sky, a pair of scales balanced just so, a brown scorpion crawling on a blue field. These are *mazoles* (from *mazel*—luck), Jewish zodiac motifs that once marked the months of the Hebrew calendar on sanctuary walls, especially in Galicia (today's western Ukraine and southeastern Poland). Beneath them, in panels framed by decorative borders, black Hebrew letters spelled out prayers and psalms, edifying Bible passages—or names of big donors. This enchanting folk art, which mixed images of nature and text, secular hope and sacred prayer, was not widely known among Americans, Jewish or not, in 1971 (though some immigrants had brought the convention to New York's Lower East Side, where *mazoles* can still be found in a few old synagogues). It made the movie's shul lovely and strange: an old-world relic of quiet grandeur.

From the very start, Jewison visually presses the point that the synagogue is the locus of all that will be left and lost. The movie opens quietly, with the camera panning over the rooftops, revealing the fiddler, silhouetted against a brightening sky, and then cutting to Tevye, who, speaking right to the camera, leads viewers into Anatevka. "How do we keep our balance?" he asks as he climbs aboard his milk cart. He slaps the reins against his horse as an alarum for his answer: "Tradition!" The orchestra blares in, and keeping time with the big chords, the camera jolts from image to image in the synagogue: a patch of painted mural, the red

Norman Jewison shows Zvee Scooler how to carry the Torah when he departs his shul forever.

Torah cover with gold star of David, some Hebrew text on the wall. The technique is repeated in the song's brief instrumental passages: jump-cuts that flash the core symbols of a civilization—an open Torah scroll, various segments of the *mazoles*, a golden menorah.

These interludes alternate with the song's verses, in which each part of the community describes its role. No matter that they tell of tradition: their daily lives are not depicted as infused with the sacred. Jewison presents them laboring in rhythm with the music: men stripping animal hides, banging anvils, planing wood; women plucking feathers, punching down dough; girls sewing, churning, pitching hay. Boys, per the song's verse, go to Hebrew school. These are hearty, self-sufficient people, in harmony with the world and each other. (The film drops the play's cacophonous section of the song, where the verses overlap, as if competing for dominance.) Although there's a moment when a shul image illustrates a line of verse, a shot of men wrapped in *tallisim* rocking in prayer, the nine-minute sequence juxtaposes toil and Torah, but doesn't much connect them. The robust folk who know they belong to the land seem visually and sonically separated from those markers of Judaism. They intersect in the film only in the Sabbath scene, lengthy wedding sequence and, at the end, when Tevye removes the mezuzah from the house he is leaving and pockets it for the journey. As in America, in this Anatevka, it is religious worship, represented by and contained in the synagogue, that marks Jewish difference.

Onstage, Robbins wanted to depict and commemorate a "way of life" and for his cast to express pride in that culture. In making the movie, Jewison was compelled by the example of a people carrying on in the face of bigotry, taking pride in brawny fortitude. The issue for him was persecution. "I wanted audiences to feel the racial hatred," he said.

The pogrom that interrupts Tzeitel and Motel's wedding celebration was the obvious opportunity for displaying baseless belligerence. Jewison tightened the tension by bringing the intruders in quietly, brandishing torches. Tevye, in a close-up, is the first to notice and he signals the musicians to stop playing. Quickly the guests stop dancing. Anticipation builds as the two groups stare silently at each other for several seconds, the camera cutting back and forth, first in medium shots that take in the groups, then in tighter ones that linger on faces and on the itchy hands of pogromists clutching their clubs. Silence. A horse neighs, one of the marauders shouts, and what was only hinted at onstage erupts in full fury in the film. Someone snatches the white cloth off a long table; crockery and candlesticks fly. Tables are overturned; bottles crash and splinter. Perchik throws himself at two men who are slashing the goose-down pillows Tevye and Golde just gave to the newlyweds, and he's clobbered. Only when Tevye runs after him does the constable shout, "That's enough." It is perhaps the most chilling moment in the scene, the longtime neighbor standing idly by when he could have prevented the violence. The camera follows the mob outside as they torch shops, break windows, and yank the innards from featherbeds.

The sequence seems symbolically to flash forward to the Nazi destruction, evoking the coming slaughter much more explicitly than the play: Jewison closes in on images of burning books and smashed windows, tropes that had become familiar in the years between the Broadway show and the movie, a period in which "the Holocaust" emerged as a distinct entity. Though not so thoroughly ignored in the postwar years as a recurring assertion long held, the Holocaust did become more widely recognized and represented; it was now the subject of an emerging academic discipline. In pop culture terms, the change is starkly denoted by two major movies that referred to the Holocaust between the stage and screen *Fiddlers*: Sidney Lumet's somber, searing portrait of a traumatized survivor (Rod Steiger) in *The Pawnbroker* (released in 1965) and Mel Brooks's outrageous satire, *The Producers* (1968, starring Zero Mostel), in which Hitler is hilariously mocked. Jewison needed only to make a few clear gestures to invoke the devastation awaiting those who don't leave the continent.

The expulsion, when it comes, an hour after the pogrom, draws this association even more directly. Jewison drags out the departure into twenty gloomy minutes as the community sings "Anatevka," packs up, trudges away, and, in an image inspired by Vishniac, rides huddled on a barge across the river as the sound track reprises the Anatevka dirge.

Within this sequence, the synagogue again plays the central role as the emblem of rupture as Jewison gives the rabbi more than a minute of near-silent action vacating the shul. With no sound other than creaking planks as he ascends the steps to the ark, he takes out a Torah scroll and hands it to his son, who drapes it with the red velvet table cover and exits. Alone, the rabbi picks up the other Torah scroll and cradles it like a baby against his shoulder; with his free hand, he takes a small stack of books by the string that is binding them: This is his luggage. He turns toward the door, pauses. As he looks around for the last time, the camera slowly pans the walls: it inches across the *mazoles*, the Hebrew, the pale painted animals, moving one way, then the other. The camera takes in the whole space in an overhead long-shot, now revealing it as shorn of all decoration, save the wall paintings, those suppliers of beauty and comfort that cannot but stay where they are. As the rabbi shuffles away, muttering a melody to himself, one senses that this could very well be the last time anyone gazes upon them with understanding.

Jewison couldn't stand that idea, no more in real life than in the fictive frame of the movie. Just as he rescued Tevye's horse, Shmuel, from the glue factory after the shoot—he sent monthly payments to a local farmer to care for the animal until it died of natural causes—he wanted to save the beautiful shul. As "the only wooden period replica now existing in Europe," he reasoned, "it seems somehow wrong that it should be destroyed." Before January 1971, while still working on the film, Jewison was already sending inquiries to scholars in Israel who had helped him with research, offering to donate the structure to the country and make a personal contribution to the dismantling and rebuilding costs of some $30,000. His query made it to the ear of the mayor of Jerusalem, Teddy Kollek. "Seriously, I think Jerusalem has enough sites that are original including Synagogues and does not have to import recently made copies here," he huffed. But the minister of religion was reported to be "quite fascinated by the idea." It took a year for the minister to come up with a plan: in March 1972, he suggested placing the structure on the expanding campus of Bar Ilan, the religiously oriented university near Tel Aviv, where he thought it could serve nicely as a study house, a space for learning Talmud and other sacred texts. There was just the matter of raising all the funds for the move. Jewison and Mirisch went to work soliciting donations in the United States while the interested Israelis sought contributions at home.

By the time the funds were assembled in December 1972—and one can imagine Tevye delivering the news—the new old shul had been torn down. What Jewison had come to consider "a symbol of that old shtetl life" was gone.

* * *

When it came time to release the movie, "that old shtetl life" didn't get much of a hearing, either. The marketing and publicity team at United Artists, in their London and American offices, didn't expect to sell seats by highlighting shul, *shabbos*, and prayer shawls. The show's fame presented them with both a boon and a challenge. How could they bank on its status as beloved icon, whose movie version every fan would want to see, while also expanding its reach? Hollywood's marketing machinery—a huge apparatus compared to Broadway's—went into high gear, with an advertising budget of more than $3.3 million (the initial allocation of $1.4 million had grown once Jewison complained). Jewison stayed unusually involved in the rollout plans. "We must not merchandise a Winston Diamond the same as we would a gold filled bracelet from Maceys [*sic*]," he instructed Mirisch.

A special sales director targeted Jewish audiences and, a full four months before the movie's premiere, "logged the largest group sales advance in motion picture history"—$1.25 million—as *Variety* reported in July 1971, with tickets going fastest in New York, Los Angeles, Boston, Chicago, Baltimore, and Detroit. Advance sales were going so well in New York that the advertising director didn't think it was necessary to spend any money on an ad buy there for months. But beyond what Jewison called the movie's "strong initial ethnic pull" lay the question that had troubled *Fiddler*'s authors seven years earlier and that, surprisingly, still worried the movie's marketers: What about *the others*?

The publicity director in London had an answer: "It is essential that we establish the universality of the film," he insisted, "and avoid stressing its Jewishness." To that end, he proposed submitting *Fiddler* as "the 1971 UNICEF film" and "tying in all of its national premieres to charitable events for the worldwide children's organization." Or, he offered, they should develop "a campaign aspect which involves making comparisons between our village and oppressed villages in changing times in other countries. There are Anatevkas everywhere." Neither suggestion was pursued. But the anxiety behind them drove much of the marketing. Press materials sent out to journalists and group sales directors repeated, again and again, Joe Stein's story about the Tokyo producer wondering how Americans could relate to a show that was "so Japanese." Jewison repeated the anecdote in interview after interview.

The promotion team targeted one non-Jewish market that turned out to be especially receptive to the celebration of "tradition" at a time when the rising counterculture was threatening its authority: America's mainstream white churches. The Lutherans published a study guide on *Fiddler* (as they had done through their "Dialogue Thrust in Film" program for movies like *Up the Down Staircase*, *The Heart Is a Lonely Hunter*, *Guess Who's Coming to Dinner*, and Jewison's own *In the Heat of the Night*). The guide appeared in the February 1971 issues of *Lutheran Teacher* and *Resource* magazines, bringing the film to the attention of more than 100,000 educators in the Lutheran Church of America and the American Lutheran Church. In May, the Missouri Synod also printed the guide in its magazine, which meant, Jewison noted, that "90 percent of Lutheranism in the U.S. will have some direct contact with *Fiddler on the Roof* through official church publications (over 10 million people and over 1,500 congregations)." The church trumpeted the effort, sending a news release to more than sixteen hundred newspapers and trade papers. In addition to recounting Stein's Japan story, the Lutherans urged clergy to tell parishioners to see the movie and offered a series of questions for discussion: the purpose and function of tradition; tradition and change; tradition and personal responsibility; tradition, love, and marriage; tradition, parents, and children; attitudes and prejudice in relation to tradition, Tevye, and God.

America's Catholic church, representing nearly a quarter of the country's population, banged the film's drum, too, after special screenings for Terence Cardinal Cooke, the Archbishop of New York ("he loved it," a United Artists representative reported to Jewison) and priests and nuns around the United States. About a year into its new program for Catholic-Jewish dialogue, instigated by the Second Vatican's pronouncement only a few years earlier that Jews were not collectively guilty for the death of Christ, the church seemed especially eager to show its sensitivity to Jewish culture. The movie itself became a tool of the church's new ecumenism.

A review in the *Catholic Film Newsletter* of November 30, 1971, praised how, "if anything, the film's emphasis is more unabashedly Jewish than that of the stage version," and was quick to add, "Far from limiting this *Fiddler*'s possible audience, however, the very richness of the film's texture that captures so beautifully a whole range of Jewish culture—the custom of family Sabbath prayers, the religious rites and symbols of the synagogue, the ancient Jewish dances and wedding festivities, the respect for family, even the humorous tradition of the marriage broker—only serves to enhance the film's charm and appeal." Of course there was nothing "ancient" about Jerry Robbins's choreography, nor a prevailing convention of comic matchmakers, but the show's gathering aura of authenticity wafted over these representations—and the film, with its realism and reach, fixed them indelibly in the popular imagination as age-old markers of Jewish culture.

In a dutifully latitudinarian reading, the *Catholic Film Newsletter* asserted that the movie's "real universality springs from its boundless faith in the providence of God and the resounding hymn it sings to hope and life and the spirit of man. And the story of Tevye's three oldest daughters, each of whom marries one remove farther outside the expectations of the family's cultural heritage, catches the conflict between change and tradition with a humor and also a poignancy that is as delicate as it is applicable to the cultural crisis of today." (The anonymous writer did not, however, care for Molly Picon's performance, which "smacks a bit too much of the New York Jewish spinster type.")

Audiences came, in droves. Upon opening, *Fiddler* led national movie box-office sales, bringing in nearly six million dollars between November 8 and 14, 1971—one of the highest first-week takes of the year—and it held the number one spot for a healthy five weeks. The figures were all the more impressive in the wake of peevish reviews in the national press.

They irked Jewison. He found Vincent Canby's complaints in the *New York Times*—that the movie "let most of the life out" by setting the action in a real village with real houses, barns, and animals—"condescending and way off track." Jewison suspected that the movie would be "hurt the most" by dismissals from *Newsweek* ("[Topol's] sense of comedy, matched with Jewison's own cement touch, crushes the fun out of every good line") and *Time* ("Gone with barely a trace are warmth, joy, insight, and even the most elementary kind of entertainment"). But United Artists people assured him that the critics hardly mattered. They had no impact on word of mouth in New York, where sales soared, nor as the film opened around the globe—playing to 93 percent capacity crowds in Paris and to 115 percent in Japan.

* * *

When Canby piled on with a Sunday article, comparing the movie unfavorably to Robbins's staging, and accusing Jewison's realism of "overwhelm[ing] not only Aleichem, but the best things about the stage production," Jewison figured that Canby was trying to justify himself in response to Pauline Kael's defense of the film. In her typically quirky and querulous *New Yorker* review, she handed over a socko, marquee-worthy quote: *Fiddler* is "the most *powerful* movie musical ever made" (never mind that this follows the disclaimers that "it is not especially sensitive, it is far from delicate, and it isn't even particularly imaginative"). But it is a peculiar review, as bold as it is infelicitous in its discussion of Jews. In Kael's judgment, the movie succeeds by virtue of not being too Jewish: Topol's "brute vitality" helped to "clear away the sticky folk stuff"; the Gentile director was able to avoid "slip[ping] into chummy Jewish sentimentality." Rather than offering Tevye's story as "a public certificate of past suffering" and pandering, like most Jewish comedy, to "the mixed-up masochism of Jewish audiences," the film offered "vitality, sweetness and gaiety." Much to Kael's relief, "the movie is not a celebration of Jewishness; is a celebration of the sensual pleasures of staying alive."

Jewison didn't seem to see Kael's queasiness about Jews in these remarks, which on their own might have offended him. After all, from his standpoint, it was his thorough commitment to Jewish spirit and specificity—exemplified in the assiduous construction of the shul—that should have given the film its particularity and allure. But Kael's general enthusiasm for this "absolutely smashing movie," appreciated on its own terms—she admits to never having seen the Broadway show—seemed to offer a vindication. Jewison resented Canby's use of the stage production as a bludgeon for battering the movie. "Since when did film ever have anything to do with the theatre?" he fumed. He wanted the *Times* to commission a rebuttal by an "important writer," but United Artists' press team had a better plan: they piped letters to the editor over the names of non-showbiz friends who did appreciate the movie, excoriating Canby for his "elitist" prejudices and failure to understand the differences between a film and a play. Meanwhile, as "part of our campaign to strike back at the negative critics," the PR office encouraged admiring critics like Frances Taylor of the *Long Island Press* (with "considerable syndication") to take Canby's arguments on directly: "One critic complains that 'Fiddler' on the stage moves him but the movie doesn't. He can't explain why."

Jewison and the United Artists team reckoned that Canby and other disdainful critics would be shown up when the Academy Awards rolled around. The picture was nominated in eight categories—including best picture and best leading actors—and they expected to win big. To that end, they mounted a vigorous campaign—far from unusual even then, but taken on with fervor. United Artists spent $75,000, "a lot of money," Walter Mirisch allowed, "but we all agreed that we should make a great effort to win as many of the awards as we possibly can." To lead off they published two-page ads filled with gushing quotes from critics. They assembled a set of quotes to send to all the Academy members and hosted special screenings.

Jewison arrived at the Dorothy Chandler Pavilion in Los Angeles on April 10 for the 44th Academy Awards trying to keep some room in his imagination for the possibility of disappointment. He ardently wanted *Fiddler* to win and believed it deserved to. Becoming the top-grossing movie of the year had its concrete satisfactions, but beyond any ego-driven craving, Jewison wanted his profession to acknowledge the momentousness of the movie. A best-picture win would be a win for *Fiddler*'s values. As the evening wore on, that mental space for dejection had to widen. Delighted as he was about the awards snagged by John Williams for score adaptation, Oswald Morris for cinematography, and David Hildyard and Gordon McCallum for sound mixing, the more high-profile prizes for art direction (Robert Boyle) and acting (Topol, Leonard Frey), eluded them. Jewison watched impassively as William Friedkin claimed the best director statue for *The French Connection* and was stunned to hear that same title called out at the evening's climactic end. "It was a tough night" for him, but Jewison consoled himself: "I knew in my heart that *Fiddler* would become a classic and remain on the screens of the world and in people's minds long after *The French Connection* had faded away."

* * *

The cop thriller hasn't exactly disappeared, but Jewison knew he was making a safe prediction about *Fiddler*. Promotional materials for the film noted that the show had played onstage for thirty-five million people in thirty-two countries before the picture opened and, as movies can, Jewison's *Fiddler* rapidly multiplied those numbers exponentially.

If the critics were right that the movie was heavier than the play—and Jewison himself admitted that he had tamped down the humor—its temper befit the topic and the times. Sure, the film delivered the pleasures of lavish, colorful numbers featuring beloved songs, but without the frivolity and fakery of the failing movie musicals that had so quickly fallen out of fashion. Its grandness and gravity seemed proper for portraying the Jews of the Pale and for the American moment as it reassuringly responded to the "cultural crisis" that alarmed the writers at the Catholic newsletter.

Terms like "generation gap," "counterculture," and "sexism," which had not been part of general parlance when the play debuted, had become the stuff of headlines by the time Topol bellowed "Tradition" on the screen seven stormy years later. And *Fiddler*'s on-the-one-hand, on-the-other-hand disposition gave viewers on either side of these issues a foothold for identification. The film sided with young women defying the demands of the patriarch, but only within the parameters of marriage. It depicted the rift in outlook between parents and children, but showed it from the mystified father's point of view. It waved the countercultural banner against wealth and dog-eat-dog individualism, but by harking back to a bucolic past. (The shtetl "resembles a kind of hippie commune that you find in upstate New York or California," the actor Leonard Frey, the movie's Motel, told a journalist visiting the shoot in Yugoslavia, "with people totally needing each other, depending on each other.") All in all, it imparted a reassuring sense that the current chaos had been weathered before.

Topol's tough Tevye could also be seen in America as a harbinger and a hero of emergent white ethnic pride. The immigration law signed by President Lyndon Johnson toward the end of 1965, abolishing long-standing national quotas that had favored Europeans, was beginning to have an impact, as America's gates opened to Africans, Asians, and Latin Americans. In the wake of these changes and the rise of Black Power, the notion of "Ellis Island whiteness"—as Matthew Frye Jacobson calls it, an ethnic whiteness distinct from WASPdom—was forged and the "ethnic revival" launched. In 1970, Congress had begun to consider a bill calling for an Ethnic Heritage Studies Program, enabling America's children to learn "about the rich traditions of their forefathers ... and the many ways in which these past generations have contributed to American life and culture" as well as increase their "awareness and appreciation of the multiethnic composition of our society." It became law in 1972. In the meantime, when *Fiddler* was in post-production, the Catholic philosopher Michael Novak wrote his high-profile polemic, *The Rise of the Unmeltable Ethnics*, decrying WASP supremacy and, in the name of Poles, Italians, Greeks, and Slavs, demanding the inclusion and special attention he saw Blacks accorded. "People uncertain of their own identity are not wholly free," he wrote. They needed their "historical memory, real or imaginary ... a set of stories for individuals—and for the people as a whole—to live out."

The new ethnicity declared itself in particularly masculinist terms: Novak pugnaciously voiced blue-collar resentment; Meir Kahane and the Jewish Defense League upped the ante on their aggressive theatrics, brandishing baseball bats and lead pipes in a photo for a full-page ad in the *New York Times* with text proposing that "Jewish boys should not be that nice" lest they "build their own road to Auschwitz." "Self-defense" activists in Italian communities—Newark, New Jersey's, city council member Anthony "Tough Tony" Imperiale, for one—wielded serious weapons and turf-war rhetoric, too. In part, they were parroting the macho posing of the Black Panthers. They were also putting themselves forward as the arbiters of ethnic realness, in contrast to their mainstream leaders—wimps, they sniped, who would not stand up and fight for their brethren.

The Tevye of Jewison's movie strode comfortably on this terrain. He could be read both as the lovable, rustic old papa and as the chest-thumping champion of ethnic survival—and these images did not necessarily contradict each other. The "unmeltables" characterized themselves as climbing up from a past of hardship to become responsible, striving Americans, and Topol portrayed a Tevye who, supported by the cohesion of family and ethnic group, did not falter on that paradigmatic path. Jewison had been drawn to the character's humanism, the modern Jew-as-metaphor, but now, here was a *Fiddler* teetering upon a gabled point between assailed liberalism and the coming neoconservatism. The Jewish establishment worried at the time that the postwar "golden age" for Jews had played itself out, according to a cover story in *Newsweek* that was published in March 1971, some eight months before *Fiddler* opened in movie houses all over the country. Titled "The American Jew: New Pride, New Problems," it reported that Jewish communal leaders (in contrast to blustering Meir Kahane, against whom the story pitted them) believed that "an era of unparalleled security and achievement for American Jews may be coming to an end."

Those anxious Jews must have felt so good watching Topol's sumptuous, emphatic arrival on the screen, looming so large in close-ups when he considers his daughter's defiance that viewers are practically in his nostrils. Here was a reassuring rejoinder to the era's disquietude and the community's self-doubt: the reminder of how far they'd come. This was not shtetl nostalgia so much as bootstrap nostalgia. The image countermanded, too, the brash new depictions of neurotic Jewish masculinity that became prominent between 1967 and 1973: Woody Allen, Richard Benjamin, Elliott Gould, Dustin Hoffman, George Segal—the fellows who slinked and slobbered onto the screen in movies like *The Graduate*,

Bye Bye Braverman, Goodbye Columbus, Where's Poppa?, Move, Who Is Harry Kellerman and Why Is He Saying Those Terrible Things About Me?, and all the Woody Allen pictures. J. Hoberman aptly calls them the "nice Jewish bad boys." (Among women in the movies, it was only Barbra Streisand who flaunted her Jewish otherness in this period.) These young men—Tevye's spoiled grandsons—made no effort to "blend in," like the generation before them. But their display, unlike Tevye's out-and-proud self-assertion, was insolent and crude.

* * *

For returning dignity to mass culture's depiction of the Jewish male, Jewison was praised in a *Jerusalem Post* article as "one of the few film-makers left anywhere who still believes a hero can be a good guy, and not necessarily a dope addict, drop-out, sadist, or at best, a loveable lunatic." He seemed to be the only Hollywood director who respected "those old-fashioned virtues movie-makers have discarded, family, love, religion, and humor."

Perhaps that's why some people wanted to bring *Fiddler* home, where images of Anatevka might proclaim those very values. Before the advent of videocassette and DVD releases—and at a time when consumer culture was growing as a form of identification—*Fiddler* moved into living rooms through various lines of domestic tchotchkes.

Ceramic figurines of the characters went on sale, suitable for the display case or shaped to the needs of a host serving snacks: Tevye and the Fiddler as salt and pepper shakers, the house with chickens in the yard and violinist on the rooftop formed into a teapot, even Tevye and his cart as a chip-and-dip set. Chadwick Miller, one of the companies that produced *Fiddler objets*—in a factory in Japan—made music boxes related to any number of popular entertainments. Little porcelain replicas of Ryan O'Neal and Ali MacGraw from *Love Story*, for example, sit atop a green pedestal, as if at a picnic, and when wound up, the music box beneath them plays the theme from the movie. A six-inch ceramic Tevye produced in 1972, arms up, fingers snapping, twirls to "If I Were a Rich Man" as his tune tinkles. But unlike the tragic lovers, he is more than a souvenir for an admirer of the film. Sold through distributors of Judaica, such collectibles allow the purchaser to participate in an American form of home decorating, but with a Jewish twist. Much like items

To Life, To Life... _L'Chaim!_

DAVID M. BARREDA

The Tevye chip and dip set brings *Fiddler* into the home.

from Israel, the objects confer and express a sense of group attachment through what the sociologist Herbert Gans calls "symbolic ethnicity" or, when people buy ritual objects for decorative purposes, "symbolic religiosity."

And there are loads of the latter, for sale to this day: *Fiddler* Hanukkah menorahs (arms aloft as in the "Tradition" number serve as candle holders), spice boxes (used in the Sabbath-ending Havdalah ritual) in the shape of Tevye's house, complete with fiddler on top; even mezuzah covers with Tevye and Anatevka painted on wood or a fiddler molded from metal. The music boxes or tableware might mark a nonobservant home as ethnically Jewish, and so do the ritual items, but as much by dint of their *Fiddler* designs as by their religious functions. The ceremonial *Fiddler* articles are sanctified decor, the figurine Judaized and made functional—for identity-building if not religious practice.

The generation of Jews—and Americans—who would display such items was skewered in a January 1973 spoof of the movie in *Mad Magazine*—another means by which the *Fiddler* film seeped into the general culture. The seven-page spread, "Antennae on the Roof," promised to update the "famous musical about the problems of people who had *nothing*" with a version "about the problems of people who have *everything.*" In this patriarch's house, even the dog kennel has an antenna on its roof. Why? "Because here in the suburbs, a family is measured by one yardstick—POSSESSIONS!" To the family psychiatrist—a dead ringer for Freud himself—the family sings (to the tune of "Matchmaker"), "Headshrinker, headshrinker" about how much they hate their lives. Tevye dreams of being a poor man, singing, "I'd simply sign my name and draw unemployment . . ." As for the daughters, one runs off with a rock band to romp naked in the woods, the second leaves with a fellow dope-fiend, the third gives up her violent commitment to the revolution to elope with her girlfriend.

The panels are packed with cartoonist Mort Drucker's extraordinarily witty and detailed drawings—the house and a pool, Princess phones, golf clubs, televisions, antique car, yacht. He rendered the Tevye figure as Zero Mostel, whose stamp remained on the role, his eyes rolling in one frame, staring maniacally in another, squinting with delight in a third, and in all the frames, a stringy, desperate comb-over stretched across his pate. Topol appears only at the end: as Tevye's ancestor, coming to haunt the suburban man and wife in their unsettling dreams with the other Anatevkans—caricatures of the movie's principals, twisting their mouths into scowls and shaking their bony fingers in accusation. To the rhythm of "Miracle of Miracles," they deride modern humanity for what they take to be its excesses: industrial pollution, labor activism, Yippies, head-busting hard-hats. "But though God's made imbeciles great and small," they sing, "the one that bothers us most of all / Is that we fear that God may make a fuss / And . . . some . . . how . . . blame . . . you . . . on . . . us!"

What's surprising here, and different from the typical *Mad* movie spoof, is that the cartoon doesn't really make fun of the film. Rather, it uses *Fiddler* as a tool of critique, to lampoon materialistic success and its attendant hypocrisies. The repressed shtetl ancestors return to haunt the new generation, which cowers in its suburban brass bed. The comic reversal, where the past disavows the present—a gesture equally conservative and countercultural—suggests that late-twentieth-century American Jews (and by extension, Americans in general) had lost sight of the pure values that once bound them as a community and guided their actions. The familiar romantic shtetl is implied, despite Drucker's grotesque exaggerations of its characters, and ethnic mixing made suspect: "God made a modern Camelot," they sing of America. "Now that we've seen that / Mess you've made / We're afraid / God wants back his melting pot!"

* * *

It's hard to sustain a parody of the movie given its somber turn, harder still to make it the center of an evening of levity. Still, in recent years, the film has been called on to do important iconic duty on the most ironic Jewish celebration each year: Christmas. If "Chinese and a movie" has been a time-honored way for Jews to spend the day when nearly everyone else is otherwise engaged, increasingly that movie has been *Fiddler*, in coordinated events where people come for the express purpose, as cultural scholar Jeffrey Shandler has put it, of enacting their Jewishness. Synagogues, Jewish community centers, and clubs meant to attract young Jews program *Fiddler* sing-alongs as a means for multiple forms of such enactment.

But one doesn't have to make a point of countercelebrating Christmas to sing along to *Fiddler*. At all times of the year, Jewish film festivals from Boston to Seattle have invited moviegoers to dress up as Anatevkans, shimmy their shoulders to "Tradition" and belt out the tunes along with the film's cast. (The lyrics and dialogue are displayed in closed captions, for those too young to have memorized the songs in their suburban dens in the seventies.) In 2006, Bet Shira Congregation in Miami hosted a sing-along on Tu b'Shvat. The synagogue's president, Ron Rosengarten, put on an old vest and a short-brimmed cap. Rabbi Micah Caplan pasted a long gray beard to his chin. And congregant Martin Applebaum donned a puffy-sleeved peasant shirt and stuffed his pants cuffs into the top of his socks. Applebaum also brought twenty rubber chickens to distribute among the audience so they could throw them into the air on the appropriate cue.

More than two hundred synagogue members came to join in the merriment. Children fiddled along with the overture and the babushka-clad sisterhood assembled near the screen to croon "Sabbath Prayer." The twenty chickens were hurled when Lazar Wolf, toasting Tzeitel and Motel, said, "I am giving the newlyweds five chickens." And chocolate

A *Fiddler on the Roof* sing-along: projecting the desire for a usable past.

Hanukkah *gelt* was flung toward the ceiling during "If I Were a Rich Man." Synagogue member Barry Blum kazatzked during the wedding dance scene with a plastic seltzer bottle glued to his felt top hat.

Some ninety minutes into the occasion, the high spirits deflated. How could it be otherwise after the pogrom in Act 1 and the bleaker and bleaker mood as Chava becomes dead to Tevye and Hodel departs for Siberia? Once the Anatevkans receive their expulsion edict and they pack up against a gray, desolate landscape in the pitiful scene the sing-along became dead to participants. The mirthful energy cannot be sustained in the face of such darkness.

But up until that point, participants frequently left their seats to ham it up in front of the larger-than-life images of Tevye and his family, often standing in the path of the projector's flickering light stream so that their own shadows danced into Anatevka. The metaphor was hard to miss:

Fiddler continues to provide American Jews a screen onto which to project their desire for a usable past.

Outside America, and in places with few Jews, *Fiddler* has served as a screen, too, for making visible the shadows of history. Nowhere did this happen as powerfully as in Poland.

CHAPTER 9

Skrzypek na Dachu: Poland

THE TRAIN WAS DUE AT 8:00 P.M. THE CROWD WAITING FOR IT at the station listened for the clatter of wheels on the old, narrow-gauge tracks as it approached, trundling through the San River valley. Soon they could make out the lively beat of a *freylekhs*, a catchy dance tune, being played by a klezmer band in an open boxcar. And quickly, like the couple dozen passengers on the train, they started to clap along. Next stop: Anatevka.

Or so their town had become, it seemed, to residents of Dynów, Poland, who had assembled at the long-abandoned station one July night in 2006 for an open-air performance of *Fiddler on the Roof*. The show would start when the train pulled in with the band playing. The director, Magdalena Miklasz, wanted the spectators to feel like villagers greeting the musicians' arrival. She wanted them to blend in with the world of the play. The old train station was the perfect locale for creating such a mood, she and the designer, Ewa Woźniak, had decided. The station house with its weathered wooden planks would serve beautifully as the inn where Tevye and Lazar Wolf drink *l'chaim*. A rustic old shed would be Tevye's home. The pines and lindens framing the playing space between the buildings, and the terraced fields beyond, would evoke the landscape Tevye traverses with his milk wagon every day. Never mind the wide sight lines. With the audience seated on the tracks and atop old train cars, and the actors playing on the scrubby ground, the layout was ideal.

Everything would feel so close, so immediate, so *real*. The traditional barrier between actor and spectator would dissolve, just as Miklasz wanted,
and the people of Dynów would imagine that they were living alongside
Tevye and his family.

Once upon a time, they had. At least figuratively, as Miklasz saw it.
Before the Holocaust, which snuffed out three million—90 percent—of
Poland's Jews, half of Dynów's population was Jewish. Bakers, barbers,
tailors, shoemakers, city council members, orchestra players, sports club
competitors, recipe-swapping and kid-minding neighbors—Jews were
woven fully into the fabric of life in the town, whose residents numbered
about 3,700 on the eve of the Nazi invasion. Born in 1983 and 1984,
respectively, Miklasz and Woźniak are barely old enough to remember
Poland's Communist times, much less the period before the Second
World War when Catholic Poles, Jews, Ukrainians, and Russians lived
together in inescapable if uneasy propinquity. Yet they wanted to present
Fiddler as a way of recalling Dynów's multicultural past—and as a way of
looking toward Poland's European future.

Miklasz's great-grandparents had lived in Dynów since before the war
in a squat stone house about a mile from the town square. As a young girl
growing up in Kraków, Miklasz spent her summers in the town, visiting
her great-grandmother. Here, in the countryside, she could pick cherries
right from a tree behind the house, sing by the campfires they built in the
rambling backyard, swim in the San. Sometimes she crawled into the
dank concrete root cellar and tried to imagine what it had been like for
her great-grandmother's Jewish neighbors, the Koch family, who hid
there in September 1939 while Nazi soldiers scoured Dynów of its Jews.

How could it have happened? Miklasz wondered. And who *were* these
Jews who once made up such a large portion of her country but had been
decimated long before she could have encountered them directly? Could
they really have left no traces in Dynów? What could that history mean
for her generation now? Miklasz and Woźniak wanted to find out, and as
young theater artists—especially in Poland, where theater traditionally
has played a significant role in progressive movements—their best means
of exploration was to make a play.

In the Bialystok Puppet Division of the National Theater School of
Poland, where Miklasz and Woźniak met in 2004, they worked on a
production of *Memorial Prayer*, an adaptation of Sholem-Aleichem's

Tevye stories with some bits of *Fiddler* woven in, written by the Russian playwright Grigory Gorin in 1989. More rustic and sardonic than the Broadway musical, Gorin's play draws from the same four Tevye stories—"Modern Children," "Hodl," "Khave," and "Get Thee Out"—but adds Menachem Mendel as the matchmaker. Gorin's Tevye was the crowning role for Russia's great comic actor Yevgeny Leonov until his death in 1994, hours before he was to go onstage in the part. Reading the play, Miklasz couldn't believe how familiar the characters seemed. Golde was just like her great-grandmother, she marveled. The beleaguered sense of humor, the folksy aphorisms, the affectionate, jokey antagonism between husbands and wives—it all echoed her girlhood summers in Dynów. Surely this communal temperament was more regional than ethnic. After all, Sholem-Aleichem's imagined Anatevka lay just across the San, which came to mark the boundary between Poland and Ukraine only through the Hitler-Stalin pact. While the national borders slicing up Galicia could mean the difference between life and death for Jews escaping into Soviet territory during the Nazi occupation of Poland, in cultural terms the frontier was arbitrary, meaningless—and not only among Jews.

Miklasz knew that Dynów was part of Galicia, once the most diverse region of the Austro-Hungarian Empire, with its multilingual mix of Jews, Poles, Ukrainians, Russians, Germans, Roma, Czechs, Slovaks, Hungarians, and others. On day trips to nearby Przemysl, a larger town some thirty miles straight east across a narrow, farm-lined road through the San River basin, she and Woźniak noticed how an Orthodox church, a Roman Catholic church, and the remains of a synagogue (now a library) stood within a stone's throw of one another. What clearer sign could there be that different peoples mingled in the public square—and, at least in some instances, beyond? They didn't have to squint hard to envision Tevye pulling his wagon along this lush valley, conjure the Jewish homes where everything came to a tranquil halt for the Sabbath, and see how easily Chava and Fyedka could meet and fall in love.

In the first two summers that Miklasz put on shows in Dynów, the troupe—incorporating under the town-echoing name De-Novo—presented *A Midsummer Night's Dream* and *Puss in Boots*: ambitious and enjoyable projects that gave the locals as much to gloat about as did their pristine views of the Carpathian foothills. The mayor, Zygmunt Frańczak, held high hopes for De-Novo's helping to build tourism and thus to boost the depressed economy of the town, where unemployment climbed to 12 percent in 2008. "If people know where Dynów is, it's because of these performances," said Mayor Frańczak, who granted 2,000 zlotys (about $550) to the company despite his meager municipal coffers. While the town gets some traffic from travelers on their way to the mountains, Dynów is an international destination only for small bands of Hasidic men who make an annual pilgrimage to the grave site of Rebbe Tzvi Elimelekh Shapiro (1783–1841) and his sons. The rebbe's acolytes maintain a small tomb in Dynów's otherwise long-neglected, weed-entangled Jewish cemetery and make a startling spectacle for local residents when they tread through town in their black cloaks and broad hats.

If the mayor saw De-Novo as an engine of economic development, Miklasz and Woźniak were driven by less measurable but perhaps loftier goals. By mixing professional actors, theater students, and local amateurs (adults as well as children), they wanted to hold up high aesthetic standards based on skill, serious preparation, and an uncompromising work ethic. The payoff was not only a solid production but a profound act of community building: everyone had a stake. The people of Dynów voluntarily fed the troupe during their three-week rehearsal period. The bakery doled out bread, local farmers contributed eggs and cheese for lunches, the nursing home served the company dinner five days a week. Parents of children in the production—De-Novo draws a number of them each year given the absence of any day camps or other summer programs—often showed up at the end of a workday with homemade cakes and sweets for everyone. The actors brought in from out of town slept in the public school.

In the 1930s, the area had been famous for its community orchestras, singing groups, and theater clubs, but all that was ground out by the upheaval of the war—and later by the arrival of a television in every home. Miklasz wanted to return that source of pleasure and accomplishment to Dynów. "In a small town like this where there's not much money and not many opportunities, our work shows people how much they can achieve if they have an idea, believe in the idea, and work for it," she said.

By the time she returned to theater school in the fall of 2005 and began thinking about the next summer's project, Miklasz sensed the community was ready to dig deeper. The *Memorial Prayer* production still gripped her imagination. Meanwhile, she felt an unarticulated but palpable queasiness at the narrow nationalistic rhetoric unleashed in the Polish elections that fall, which brought to power the right-wing Law and Justice Party. Then her "crazy uncle Bogdan"—so regarded by the family because of his frequent off-color, vaguely antisemitic, and otherwise inappropriate quips—suggested that De-Novo put on *Fiddler on the Roof* because it was one of his favorite movies. If *Fiddler* could speak to her uncle, Miklasz thought, if it could touch a sensitive place even in him, then it could reach Dynów. All impulses pointed toward Tevye.

* * *

Miklasz and Woźniak had seen *Fiddler on the Roof* on TV as girls. The film is shown on the Polish state channel every now and then. But that was not always the case. Far from it. For all intents and purposes, *Fiddler* was banned in Poland until the years Miklasz and Woźniak were born, two decades after the play's New York premiere.

From shortly after the end of World War II until the openings forced by the Solidarity movement some thirty-five years later, Poland suppressed public discussion and representation of Jewish themes (with the notable exception of the State Yiddish Theater, led by the internationally beloved actor Ida Kaminska). At precisely the moment *Fiddler* was setting out into the wide world of international productions—even to other Soviet satellites—Poland was ever more aggressively smothering what little breath of Jewish expression the country had left. As early as 1966, the legendary opera director Walter Felsenstein was making arrangements to bring the show to his Komische Oper in East Berlin. (Robbins was to have directed but he bowed out, leaving Felsenstein to direct it himself. The production finally went on in 1971, with just a few adjustments personally recommended by the Soviet ambassador: excising the words "pogrom," "America," and "Kiev" and any phrases referring to Jews being forced to leave their homes.) Czechoslovakia opened *Fiddler* in its capital with the first breezes of the Prague Spring in February 1968. By the time the show went up in the western city of Pilsen eighteen months later, the movement had been crushed and its democratic reforms reversed; audiences booed the Russians who burst violently into the wedding scene at the end of the first act as if they were Soviet occupiers.

But there could be no *Fiddler on the Roof*, no *Skrzypek na Dachu*, while Poland was cracking down on its small remnant of Jews. Following the Six-Day War in the summer of 1967, a battle for control within Poland's Communist Party expressed itself in virulent anti-Israel rhetoric that cast the country's 40,000 Jews—in the infamous words of Prime Minister Władysław Gomułka—as a potential "fifth column." The vast majority of these Jews were highly assimilated and regarded themselves as thoroughly Polish, many of them properly anti-Zionist Party faithful. Nonetheless, they found themselves suddenly suspect. Eight months later, when student protests erupted in Warsaw (triggered by the authorities censoring a play) and then spread through the country, the Party blamed the Jews. Right away, Jews were purged from government, academic, and other posts and from the country itself. Some 20,000 were forced to emigrate. When they departed Poland—most for Scandinavia and Europe, not many for Israel—they were required to denounce their Polish citizenship. Ida Kaminska and most of her troupe were among them. Only a few months before their departure, her husband, the theater's manager, had written to Joe Stein expressing interest in presenting *Fiddler* at the State Yiddish Theater. Some of the troupe had seen the Broadway production when they toured the United States in the fall of 1967 with *Mother Courage* and *Mirele Efros*, Yankev Gordin's "Jewish Queen Lear." Now Kaminska was leaving Poland for good, settling in New York with grand—and, it turned out, vain—hopes of opening a Yiddish theater there.

For more than a decade after the events of 1968, the subject of Jews was officially closed in Poland, though no pronouncements were necessary to enforce the ban. Theater artists simply understood that they ought not include *Fiddler on the Roof* on the roster of planned productions that they had to submit for state approval every season. Movie theaters didn't book the film, either. By the late 1970s, it had been commercially screened in Iran, Lebanon, and Turkey, among many other countries. But not in Poland.

That didn't stop the literary critic and translator Antoni Marianowicz from rendering the script and lyrics into Polish. A Jew who had escaped from the Warsaw Ghetto and spent the war years hiding in a glass factory, Marianowicz knew as well as anyone that "staging the play was entirely unthinkable." But he became enthralled by the show when he saw a performance on a visit to New York in the mid-1960s and he prepared the text anyway—for when, he had no idea. It wasn't just the taboo on Jewish subjects that stood in the way. Poland's relationship with the United States had curdled so bitterly that pursuing a standard licensing contract was just as hard to conceive of as broaching the topic of exiled Jews. Marianowicz recalled a Polish propaganda campaign that blamed America for the sudden, mysterious death of the country's chickens during this period and wondered: "How was I supposed to go about getting the rights to stage the play, when telephone calls were being controlled, negotiations with the poultry murderers bordered on treason, and contacting workers from the U.S. Embassy was considered spying?"

Around the same time, the highly successful Polish TV director Jerzy Gruza made a trip to New York and watched an interview with Zero Mostel on his hotel room TV. Gruza laughed so hard he worried that the people in the next room would complain. He didn't have a chance to see Mostel onstage, but the televised bits from the show planted in him the desire to direct the musical someday. He knew exactly who should play Tevye in a Polish *Fiddler*: the Jewish actor Juliusz Berger, whom Gruza had seen in the 1950s as Perchik in Sholom-Aleichem's *Tevye der milkhiker* at the Polish State Yiddish Theater. (The production toured to London in 1957 and again in the summer of 1964, just as *Fiddler* was on its way to Detroit.) Gruza filed the idea in the back of his mind.

Poles had a lot of practice in the Communist era at quietly filing away officially disavowed knowledge—most famously, the knowledge that Soviets had massacred Polish officers at Katyn in 1940, though the official version blamed the Nazis. In 1980, when the Solidarity movement triumphed in Gdańsk, the strikers met to assess their victory and discuss how to organize their new union. Top on their agenda was how to produce a new, truthful history. As Robert Darnton reported in a *New York Review of Books* essay at the time, "The hunger for history, 'true history' as opposed to the official version, stands out as clearly as the bread lines in Poland today." The main newspaper in Kraków started a daily column called "Blank Spaces in the History of Poland." The editor explained to Darnton that Poles needed to repossess their past in order—as the Solidarity slogan demanded—for Poland to be Poland. They needed to know what "actually happened."

Coming to terms with what actually happened to Poland's Jews—in the Holocaust as well as in 1968—was not the immediate concern of the

Solidarity movement, which was heavily connected to the Church and its imagery. But Poles did start to look into Jewish history. A core of the few thousand Jews who remained in Poland started organizing so as to study their heritage—people like the mathematician and philosopher Stanisław Krajewski, whose parents were kicked out of the Party in 1968, while he was in college and active in the student movement. The expulsions had a strange effect: "they reminded us we were Jewish." Krajewski and some colleagues created underground avenues for learning about what that abandoned identity might mean—a "flying university" of study groups, as well as projects to locate and mark traces of Jewish existence. Monika Krajewska, an artist (and Stanisław's wife), began to document Jewish tombstones with photographs. In 1982, she published an album of the pictures, one of the first postwar Jewish books in Poland. Tentatively, Jewishness was moving out of the closet into public discourse. *Fiddler on the Roof* would become a major vehicle.

By the time Krajewska's book was in the works, martial law was attempting to stamp out Solidarity and other opposition movements. But there was no way to put the lid back on popular discussion. On the contrary, Wojciech Jaruzelski's regime needed to persuade the West that it was not crushing democracy with its repressive actions but simply restoring order; one way to do so was by pointing to its easing of the old censorship measures. That's why—both Marianowicz and Gruza surmised—*Fiddler* was approved for production while Poland was still under martial law.

But mounting a production of *Fiddler* would take more than a little sudden state leniency. For several years, Poland had lacked hard cash. The economy was in a chronic state of collapse and the weakness of the zloty proved as censorious as state power in restricting the musical repertoire. How could a Polish theater possibly afford America's licensing fees? And even if the fees were waived, converting the royalties to dollars would have required mountains of money, and even if such money miraculously could have been found, the government would not allow any cash to leave the country.

Marianowicz came up with a plan. In the spring of 1981, he proposed it to Joe Stein. "As you probably know, we in Poland are now involved in a struggle against all forms of political and moral oppression," he explained in a letter. "One of them is antisemitism, and one of the reasons it may still exist is a total ignorance of Jewish history and culture." *Fiddler* would be an important political and artistic intervention, he argued, but the lack of Western currency made normal arrangements impossible. "This is the reason I allow myself to suggest a payment in Polish zlotys, with an appointment to Jewish philanthropic purposes—e.g. to a committee, raising funds for the reconstruction and renovation of famous Jewish cemeteries in Poland."

The *Fiddler* team accepted the proposition—though Robbins would have preferred the proceeds to go to *living* Jews rather than to cemeteries— and Stein replied to Marianowicz two weeks later: "If our show can have some small effect in helping the Polish people in their struggle for political liberty and against antisemitism, we will be most gratified."

Thus *Fiddler* entered the Polish repertoire as a document of Jewish history, bound up with the emerging project of commemoration. As in Jaffa and in Brooklyn, but in yet a different way, *Fiddler* in Poland would be more than just another show. In generating funds for the upkeep of Jewish cemeteries, the Broadway musical would stand in for the slaughtered generations unable to perform the ritual of *geyn af keyver oves*— visiting the ancestral graves. It would also stand in for the ancestors, offering the postwar generation its first contact with a Jewish world and, as Marianowicz observed, reminding older Poles of "the people who once lived in our land" but "after whom nothing remains, like Atlantis after the ocean swallowed it up."

Marianowicz well knew that the swallowed Atlantis was more varied than the one *Fiddler* represented. He himself came from a highly assimilated bourgeois family in Warsaw, which had been a vibrant center of urban Jewish life for more than half a century. It's where Sholem-Aleichem's *Tsezeyt un tseshpreyt* met with success in the spring of 1905, sparking his dreams of the American theater. Soon after, when the czarist ban on Yiddish was lifted, it's where "modern mass Jewish culture," as the scholar Michael Steinlauf has written, "sprang into being virtually overnight." That culture flourished through the interwar years as Jews (and Poles) became increasingly urbanized. On the eve of Hitler's invasion, a majority of Poland's Jews lived in cities. That still left more than a million residing in shtetls, but they were not the norm. Marianowicz could see how the musicalized mythic shtetl might serve as a point of entry for Polish audiences of the 1980s, gently inviting a peek into a distant past that was removed from more raw and recent trauma.

The first production opened at the Musical Theater of Łódź in May 1983. The theater's artistic director had come to love the music after a student of his from America had brought the original cast album with her to Poland in the late 1970s. He was lucky that the local Party dignitary in charge of approving the repertoire had seen the show on a trip to New York and, as Marianowicz put it, "made it his point of honor to bring it to the Łódź stage." By all accounts, this premiere was weak—badly sung, clumsily staged, barely coherent. But it did break the ice—deep, long-frozen ice. Such was the case, too, with Poland's second production, eight months later, at the Grand Theater in Poznań, where the staging was stiffly operatic. Jerzy Gruza's production in November 1984—the biggest hit the Musical Theater of Gdynia had ever seen—shook the state. The opening-night ovation lasted twenty minutes.

Gdynia is the sister city to Gdańsk in the northern port area of the country, and it shared in the role as epicenter of Solidarity activism. The tenacious spirit of resistance that charged the local air energized audiences, who received *Fiddler* and its brave new subject as a continuation of the democracy movement in a highly entertaining form. Gruza was an exuberant showman—"The social task of musical theater is to give entertainment to tired, overworked people," he mischievously maintained—and he made extravagant use of the Communist-style arts subsidies his theater enjoyed, even in tight times. To this day, Gruza boasts of the sheer size and lavishness of the production: a hundred people in the company, another hundred in the orchestra.

Juliusz Berger, veteran of the Yiddish stage, did play the role of Tevye, with warmth and soft-edged stoicism. Gruza's assistant director was Jan Szurmiej—the son of Golda Tencer and Szymon Szurmiej, members of the Yiddish theater who had taken over Ida Kaminska's post. Gruza counted on Berger and Szurmiej to bring "authenticity" to the production by telling the cast about Jewish culture and customs. The subject, for all of them, was a vast blank.

Gruza watched spectators sobbing at the show night after night. "The production raised in them a strong sense of tolerance," he concluded. His good friend Marianowicz couldn't help but hear how "the final scenes of the musical, when the exiled Jews leave Anatevka, resounded in our country." No one could say what happened to emotion spilled in the theater once the curtain came down. But whether roused or stunned or safely and briefly entertained, spectators encountered language and imagery that had been closed to them for decades.

Reviews raved about the heartwarming story and, more, about the grand spectacle of the staging—and the consequent sense that Poland was for the first time living up to the demands of a big Broadway musical. And most of the critics took the opportunity—assisted by materials provided by the theater—to tell readers who Sholem-Aleichem was. While they made no direct comments about Poland's eliminated Jews, these articles were among the first in a long while in the Polish press to use the word "Jew" in anything other than accusatory mode.

The production was invited to play for four nights in Warsaw in a

Poland's first billboard advertises Gruza's production
on Parade Square.

1,500-seat house at the mammoth Palace of Culture and Sciences (where Jerry Robbins presented his Ballets: USA twenty-five years earlier). By far the city's tallest building, it loomed on the skyline as a blunt reminder of Soviet domination. Not only did a Jewish story unfold on the stage at the very heart of Communist officialdom, but outside on the plaza a big, brash banner promoted the show. Sławomir Kitowski, Gruza's "publicity director"—an unusual job title in Poland in the 1980s—had erected Poland's first billboard: a striking twenty-foot by thirty-foot poster showing a hollow-eyed fiddler perched amid a dozen dark rooftops that receded into a red sky. As the humble Jew looked out over wide Marszałkowska Street toward a new horizon, down below on Parade Square emerging capitalists plied their trade on a site more typically used for state propaganda pageants: scalpers sold *Fiddler* tickets at hugely inflated prices, accepting American dollars only.

Fiddler was cemented in the national repertoire as the production toured as Poland's representative to European festivals. Only Szymon Szurmiej at the State Yiddish Theater resisted its seductions. He detested its "falsification" of the great *folkshrayber*.

As the Communist regime tottered through the 1980s, new productions cropped up and pirated videotapes of the film circulated underground, screened at private parties of youngsters looking, with an extra spur of teenage dissidence, to American pop cultural forms. After Solidarity's victory in 1989 and the Soviet Union's collapse shortly thereafter, the lid that had been loosened earlier flew off entirely. Public programs, college courses, commemorative events, and journals by and about Jews proliferated, especially as money started pouring in from Israel and the United States. *Fiddler* was revived with an increasing sense of mission.

Mounting *Fiddler* became an occasion to delve into the history of a town's Jews, as Lublin's theater did when it added the show to its repertoire in 1994 (one of Poland's last municipal theaters to do so). The elaborate program booklet included an essay on the lost Jews of Lublin, a map and photographs of their long-vanished quarter, sepia portraits of bearded old men, a first-person reminiscence, even recipes for cholent and tzimmes. Elsewhere, the acclaimed opera director Marek Weiss, who staged *Fiddler* several times, found in it "medicine for the special Polish illness" of antisemitism. He directed a production in Wrocław at the 4,000-seat People's Hall, a building where Hitler and Goebbels conducted infamous meetings when, as Breslau, the city belonged to Germany. Audiences understood, Weiss maintained, that "in the same place where they planned the destruction, we built Anatevka again, speaking against the total war that they made here."

For more than two decades the show has been presented in a professional production somewhere in Poland every year, and since at least 1988 it has been broadcast on television from time to time. "If I Were a Rich Man" has long held a spot on the standard wedding playlist as a song of good luck, and bands big and small strike it up to welcome a Jewish person or theme to any stage or civic function. A local distillery put out a luxury potato vodka called Fiddler. The milky glass bottle has a black hat for its screw top and features images of dancing men, a violinist on the rooftop above them. A music box that comes with the 40 percent spirit plays a few bars of "If I Were a Rich Man."

Fiddler has become a central reference point for Jewishness itself, one piece of *Yiddishkayt* that everyone can be counted on to know. Even Szurmiej bowed to the signifying power of *Fiddler* and allowed it to be added to the Yiddish Theater's repertoire in 2002, under the deft, straightforward direction of his son Jan. Played on alternate nights in Yiddish and Polish, it sells out the auditorium's four hundred seats to old and young Poles—and international tourists—paying tribute to the persistent Yiddish landmark.

By 2004, when Magdalena Miklasz and Ewa Woźniak met at theater school, Jewish cultural memory, thanks in part to *Fiddler*, was an institution in Poland—in some places, even an industry. Miklasz grew up aware of it, coming as she did from Kraków. There, the Jewish Cultural Festival rocks the streets of Kazimierz, the former Jewish quarter, every June or July with outdoor klezmer concerts and other performances and numerous workshops in Jewish music and history. From a modest start in 1988, the festival has bloomed into a nine-day event featuring international musicians, artists, and scholars and drawing about 20,000 participants, most of them Poles. Though Miklasz never attended the festival—she was always in Dynów in the summer—she couldn't help knowing about it. And countless times she hung around in Kazimierz. The famous quarter that thrived from the fourteenth century until the Holocaust and then served as Kraków's garbage dump for years started to see renovation in the late 1980s—and Jewish tourists started to come, most spending an evening in the neighborhood after their grim, obligatory visit to Auschwitz, a ninety-minute drive away. On the surface, the area looks like an Ashkenazi theme park. "Jewish style" restaurants use signage that evokes Hebrew lettering and serve up dishes like matzo ball soup and stuffed cabbage (occasionally containing pork). In some, waiters don caps and vests or babushkas that look like they've been pulled from the costume rack of a *Fiddler* production. One of the restaurants on the main square is named after the musical's setting: "Anatewka." (At its sister establishment in Łódź, a violinist serenades the patrons from a seat in the rafters.)

For all the apparent kitschiness, the redevelopment of Kazimierz created Jewish public space where exploration was encouraged and more thoughtful enterprises could take root—art exhibitions, historical museums, a cultural center, and indeed the summer festival, among them. Such institutions—and others like them in other cities—served as essential resources for Miklasz and Woźniak when they started to work on *Fiddler*. In a small bookstore in Kazimierz, Woźniak found volumes of Chagall paintings that inspired the dominant blues and greens in her costumes and set.

But availability of information, essential as it is, does not make a scarring or shameful subject any easier to confront emotionally. And especially in small towns that did not participate in the complicated revival of interest in—and even vogue for—Jewish culture, the topic was still sensitive at the dawn of the twenty-first century.

Poland had joined the European Union in 2004 and—revisiting on a new platform deep divisions that go back at least as far as the interwar period—the country was starkly split between those who embraced the wider cultural, economic, and social exchange offered by participation in the EU and those who preferred to tighten a nationalistic grip on a narrowly defined Polishness against what they regarded as European encroachment on their values. The klezmer fad among young people and the more general interest in Jewish culture belonged to—and symbolized—the attitudes of the former. For the most part, Dynów lined up on the other side. Three-quarters of its voters chose Lech Kaczyński, the victorious conservative candidate, in the fall 2005 presidential election. Some residents of Dynów warned Miklasz that *Fiddler* would not play in that particular Polish Peoria.

* * *

At six on a rainy evening the following July, Miklasz opened the first company meeting for De-Novo's production of *Fiddler*. Some two dozen community members and out-of-town theater school friends crammed into a room at the Miklasz house that the director's mother had turned into a gallery. For most of the year, Jolanta Pyś-Miklasz shows her own portraits in oil as well as works by other regional artists in the cool, cement-floor room. But when her daughter arrives in Dynów for the summer, the sculptures are placed in corners, the paintings removed from the brick walls, and the contemplative space metamorphoses into the noisy meeting room, business office, design planning center, and general hangout for everyone involved in the current play.

Sitting side by side, Miklasz and Woźniak looked out at the group, seated around the room's perimeter on narrow wooden benches. They exchanged a glance and, in unison, took a deep breath. After months of preparation, they were about to launch the real work on *Fiddler*. As in any other show's first company meeting, much of the discussion addressed logistics: Does anyone have a car for picking up set materials tomorrow? Who volunteers to help in fund-raising? Anybody know anything about sound systems? Hands went up, tasks got assigned. Here's the rehearsal schedule. Does everyone have the script? The text was a mash-up of Miklasz's devising, combining elements from the Gorin play with songs and scenes from *Fiddler*.

All through the meeting, the company members tried to outdo one another's jokes—puns at every opening, witty rejoinders, anecdotes whenever a person could claim the floor long enough to tell one. Miklasz basked in the good humor. First rehearsals are always as much about the group's bonding as about getting things done. All that laughter promised that the team would cohere nicely.

But an uncharacteristic hush swept over the room when Miklasz came around to the play itself. "This is a very special show," she told them. "It is about a subject that is difficult for some people around here. It's about our history. It's about a family of Jews." Justyna Pinczer, the Dynów high school student cast as Chava, felt a little shudder, like a cold current of energy, race through her body. She didn't know anything at all about Jewish culture. The subject excited her. Nobody asked any questions.

The group piled into cars and headed toward the square to Dynów's only hotel, the Oberja, a four-room, one-star inn whose primary

PIOTR PYRCZ

Golde and her daughters in Dynów.

attraction is the town's largest flat-screen TV. It hangs from the low wooden ceiling over the hotel's dark lounge, outshining the lit-up Tyskie beer signs and upstaging the vaguely S-and-M oil paintings of women in harnesses that decorate the walls. Miklasz handed the bartender a DVD. Crowded onto leather couches, the troupe sat transfixed through all 181 minutes of Norman Jewison's *Fiddler* movie. Many had seen it on TV as kids, but now they watched with laser attention. They knew what roles they'd be playing and treated the screening as a chance to measure their ideas of character against another actor's. More than that, they focused on the actions that marked the family's Jewishness. Not just the costumes but the way the characters spoke and the mysterious things they did: Golde circling her wrists after lighting the Sabbath candles, Tevye tapping something on the doorpost and then kissing his fingers, Tzeitel walking round and round Motel under the wedding canopy, the rabbi wrapping and cradling the Torah he was taking into exile, and so much more. Jewison had demanded realism—he conducted extensive research, consulted experts, and shot in a location as close to the Ukraine as he could get. Now, just a few hundred miles due west of Sholem-Aleichem's birthplace, the film from Hollywood served as the authoritative source on Jewish customs and ritual in the Pale.

The usually voluble group watched silently, except when shouts and applause burst out of them after the dance scenes at the inn and at the wedding and when sobs escaped from a few as the film turned bleaker and bleaker. Justyna bawled when Tevye disowned Chava. She wondered how she would get through such an emotional scene as an actor.

As the company began the scene work the next day, Ewa Woźniak continued to assemble materials for the set. Collecting them from the residents of Dynów became part of the process of conjuring the town's history and of involving the community in the work. Woźniak walked from house to house, knocking on doors. At the first, a thin old woman answered. "Hello, I'm Ewa. If I'm not interrupting anything, I'd like to talk with you." The woman invited her in—she hadn't had a visitor in ages—and Woźniak blinked as she left the blazing July sun for the curtained living room. The woman put out plates of bread and butter. "Do you know the story of *Fiddler on the Roof*?" The woman shook her head. Woźniak gave her a summary—the Jewish milkman with three daughters that are old enough to marry—and explained she was looking for objects for Tevye's house, the inn, and other parts of the set as well as for an exhibition that would be an adjunct to the production, an exhibition that would recall the Jewish life that had once permeated Dynów. "I think that objects have souls," the designer said. "They contain stories."

The woman stood up. "I have something to show you." She disappeared into another room and returned with a small wooden suitcase. "My father made it for me because when I was very, very young I went to school on the other side of the river. I went there with other children from Dynów, including Jewish children and Ukrainian children."

"Was that normal? For Poles, Jews, and Ukrainian kids to be together?"

"Oh, yes. Of course. We were all friends. We had loads of fun together. We were children. Maybe someone's mother might say, 'Don't play with that one, she's Ukrainian,' but children don't care about things like that. Let me show you something else."

Now she brought out an album from the 1930s, brittle pages of faded pastel drawings she'd made as a girl: primitive landscapes of the river and fields.

Album under her arm, Woźniak knocked at the next house. Another woman in her seventies showed off her first communion certificate. At another, a man recalled climbing up into a plum tree as a boy to watch a Jewish wedding. "I could see everything," he recounted. "A Jewish man asked me what I was doing. 'Just looking,' I told him. So he said, 'Well, come on, then. Join us on the men's side. And I went there and danced." Woźniak based the chuppah she made for Tzeitel and Motel's marriage on his recollection of a white canopy painted with bright designs.

And so Woźniak went for about a week, visiting about ten houses each day. Baby cradle, clothes cabinet, linens, rakes, tables, milk cans, even Tevye's wagon: the pieces emerged from the attics and sheds of Dynów. It wasn't always easy. In one house Woźniak related the story of *Fiddler* to the old woman who invited her in. Then she said, "You live in a place where Jewish culture once thrived. What do you remember?"

"Yes. We lived with these people, I know, but I don't remember. I don't remember anything. I was very young. There was the war. The shooting. The fire." She broke off, crying. "Maybe I don't want to remember."

Jews were preparing for Rosh Hashanah when the Nazis occupied Dynów on September 13, 1939. The holiday was to begin that evening. The SS troops, which arrived from the north, had no plans to deport the Jews. They would simply kill them.

Accounts differ on whether it was on the first or second of the High Holy Days, but either way the Jews gathered at the synagogue, a two-story brick building with large windows, built in the eighteenth century after the community had outgrown the old wooden shul, which still stood nearby. Inside, the synagogue was painted with frescoes: a series of animals represented the Talmudic passage "Be strong as a tiger, light as an eagle, fast as a deer, and heroic as a lion in fulfillment of the commandments"; a rendering of the ancient Temple's stone eastern wall shone under a blue Jerusalem sky. A zodiac circled the ceiling. The ranks of the worshippers were swollen by scores of people who had streamed into town from the west a week earlier, fleeing the Nazi invasion. Through the morning service, soldiers stood at the door.

In the afternoon, families went home, only to be torn from their holiday meals by trucks roaring through the streets and soldiers bursting into houses demanding that Jewish men assemble in the schoolyard. There, they were frisked for watches and other valuables, then packed into the trucks and driven half a mile to the edge of town. Soldiers gave about a hundred men shovels and orders; machine-gun fire catapulted them into the fresh ditches they'd dug. Another half mile away, at Zurawiec forest, the same fate befell another two hundred men. Back in town, the soldiers returned to the synagogue where the fifty refugees sought sanctuary. They doused it with gasoline and set it aflame; everyone inside perished.

The work was not done. About two weeks later, all the remaining Jews—1,500 or so women, children, and elderly men—were ordered to the square with whatever they could carry. A brass band accompanied their forced march to the banks of the San. The soldiers offered two options: cross the river into Soviet territory or be shot. Many drowned.

By the first of October, Polish residents awoke to a Dynów stripped of half its population. Quickly and irredeemably, the Jews were dead or gone.

Whether—or how—their possessions ended up in the hands of the Poles left behind, Woźniak didn't inquire. That was not the point. Rather, she wanted to evoke absence in the installation she created from the objects she'd gathered. She called it "People of Dynów's Past"; the "people" appeared only, but powerfully, by implication.

The designer created and furnished a couple of rooms inside an abandoned shed near the old train station. Stepping into the warehouselike space was like entering a home in 1939, with its lace tablecloth, silk lampshade, and wooden wardrobe. Framed family photos hung on the wall—lent by Dynów's one-man historical society, Grzegorz Szajnik, who has amassed a collection of more than a thousand. A half-filled bound journal lay open on a writing table, along with letters and postcards from the period and a handsome art deco radio. Woźniak wanted visitors simultaneously to "touch history" and to feel a sense of immediacy. In one room she placed on a very old table a bowl of very fresh fruit; on another, in a seventy-five-year-old cup, coffee recently enough poured to give off an alluring smell. This was a lived-in space whose residents had left in a hurry, leaving an open book, an unfinished drink. Woźniak often thought about the rich Jewish culture wiped out in the Nazi genocide. In Dynów, she wanted to imagine individual people in the concrete detail of their ordinariness and to create a space where others might do so, too.

* * *

The warnings murmured to Miklasz when she had announced *Fiddler* as De-Novo's 2006 show were not materializing into real opposition as the three-week rehearsal period raced by. Now and then, someone would privately mention that some *other* people might not appreciate De-Novo's dredging up the past, but no one tried to get in the way. The outpouring of communal support was as generous as ever. That didn't mean there wasn't some anxiety passing occasionally like the summer rain clouds over the valley. But Miklasz and Woźniak knew that whatever justification the project had was in the doing of it and, through the doing of it, the community's taking ownership of it. A professional tour of *Fiddler* stopping in Dynów might not have sold a lot of tickets. Who could say? But De-Novo was not simply presenting a ready-made spectacle to an anonymous audience.

"This is it!" Miklasz told the company backstage on opening night. She wasn't inclined to say more. And anyway, she didn't have time. Playing the role of the fiddler—she's a first-rate violinist—she had to assume her position atop the high station house roof, where she would remain for the entire show. Everyone understood this was their only chance to make Anatevka come alive. The entire run was just the one night.

The train bearing the band, a group called Membra Solo from the nearby larger city of Rzeszów, chugged in right on schedule. They had played a klezmer concert as a preview at the other end of the ten-minute train ride. As the musicians debarked and found their places, spectators scrambled for seats. In a town with a population of 6,200, about 2,500 people had come to the show.

Justyna paced behind the shed, repeating her lines to herself; Mateusz Mikoś, the student playing Motel, felt his mind go blank, as if someone had unscrewed his personal hard drive. The stage manager signaled Miklasz, who adjusted the bowler hat on her head and drew out those two notes that begin the opening theme.

The "narrator"—an elder from the Dynów community—walked out and welcomed the crowd with the introduction to Gorin's *Memorial Prayer* (assigned in his script to Tevye). "In Anatevka, Russians, Ukrainians, and Jews lived together since the beginning of time," the speech begins, as apt for Dynów as for the fictional shtetl. "They lived together, worked together, and only died separately in their respective cemeteries. That was the tradition." Unlike *Fiddler*, which built on the postwar

American desire to remember the shtetl as an all-Jewish idyll, the perestroika-era *Memorial Prayer* had an interest in restoring Jewish presence to the multiculti mix of the Soviet republics. More than that, it propounds the closeness of the communities, seeking to minimize (rather than celebrate) ethnic difference. Gorin's Tevye—and De-Novo's—comes on pulling his cart and presenting himself to the audience: "Jewish people call me Tevye; Russians, Tevel. I have five daughters, two cows, and one horse so old it can only take the wagon downhill. When the road goes uphill, I take it myself, and then I take off my hat so it won't stick to my head. And then nobody can tell if I'm a Russian or a Jew. And honestly, what's the difference?"

The play goes on to show how little difference there is. Yes, he celebrates the Sabbath in a particular manner and sees his daughter married under a chuppah, but the beleaguered Tevye of Gorin's play struggles entirely against poverty and antisemitism (which is forthrightly addressed in the text, with the constable, for example, accusing Tevye of a blood libel, a slander still granted great credence in a region to the north of Dynów). The internal challenges to Tevye's faith don't much register in Gorin. Thus, there's no dramaturgical reason to take pains to establish his piety and devout practice. Those exotic behaviors the De-Novo company observed in the Jewison film at the Oberja aren't significant in Gorin and were not employed in Dynów (though the company was treated to a presentation about the Jews of Dynów by Szajnik). If Jerry Robbins had been hounding Gorin to tell him what his play was about, the Russian would not have put "the breakdown of tradition" on his list of answers; he might have said, "the barbarity of narrow nationalism."

But "tradition" still mattered to Miklasz, as a concept and as a musical number. While the attenuation of the daughters' (and, presumably, grandchildren's) ties to Tevye's observance had little resonance in Dynów, that he stood for something did. With only three weeks of rehearsal and only three professionals among a cast of fifty, Miklasz selected only a few *Fiddler* songs for her show—"If I Were a Rich Man," "Sunrise, Sunset," "Anatevka," and, most powerfully, "Tradition." (In place of "Sabbath Prayer," the vocalist for Membra Solo hauntingly sang, as actors lit candles, the Hebrew hymn "*Shalom aleichem, malachei ha-sharet*," which ritually welcomes the Sabbath.)

As in *Fiddler*, the chorus came on singing "Tradition" at the end of

Anatevka materializes in Dynów: "Tradition."

Tevye's self-introduction. At first they could be heard in the distance, but not seen, as they intoned the melody with "boy-boy-boy" syllables in place of the lyrics. The sound grew closer and fuller, and the company began to come into partial view behind the buildings, like fragments of a dream rising into consciousness. Soon, they filed into the playing area and, with their transformation from invisible specters into flesh-and-blood presences, they converted the very ground into the shtetl of old. The Jews had returned. No matter how well anyone acted or sang (it varied) or whether tech ran smoothly (it didn't), this moment of theatrical alchemy could not be reversed.

At the show's end, the chorus dematerialized as they went off singing "Anatevka," as if going back to a shadowy realm where they had been hidden for decades. The audience applauded for fifteen minutes and showered the company with flowers.

Miklasz and Woźniak decided to do *Fiddler* again for 2007, this time for two nights. It wasn't just that Miklasz was disappointed by a brief microphone malfunction during "Rich Man" (with a Tevye played by an admired professional, Maciej Ferlak). She also wanted more music and a longer rehearsal schedule. This time the company would sing "Sabbath Prayer," as she had hoped to have them do the first time. And she felt they could go still deeper with the material. Playing over two consecutive evenings in 2007, the show drew audiences of nearly 2,000 each night.

Could Miklasz and Woźniak determine their show's cumulative effect? They hadn't expected *Fiddler* to change anything, not in any conventionally understood didactic way. That kind of thinking had disappeared, they were happy to note, with the demise of the People's Republic of Poland, whose artists were always too unruly and disgruntled for the cheery heroics the Soviets prescribed, anyway. If De-Novo's work was affecting people in any deep sense, Miklasz and Woźniak understood the impact phenomenologically: it had meaning not by virtue of *referring* to something else but by *being* something else, something the spectators were part of making.

That involvement far exceeded the usual imaginative participation theater demands of an audience. De-Novo's public recognized pieces of their own lives in the show—their household wares, their neighbors, their children—and watched from a space barely separated from the playing area in the open air. There were few boundaries between themselves and the world of Anatevka. They understood it was a fiction; that's why it could be so true. And Tevye's cart left real track marks in the ground.

But for all its evocation of the Jews who once shared their town, De-Novo's *Fiddler* was not primarily salvage work that looked back for the sake of nostalgia or to fulfill the duty that propelled so many in the generation that preceded them—to fill in the huge gaps in the historical record. That work was being ably done all over the country by scholars, curators, and artists. Miklasz and Woźniak were—and are—looking behind in order to look ahead. Miklasz said that in working on *Fiddler* she sometimes felt like she was raising up ghosts. She was. Because her generation needs them to point the way forward.

FIDDLING WITH TRADITION

IN THE MIDDLE OF A FASHIONABLE LOS ANGELES BAR MITZVAH luncheon, a man bursts into the hall. Dressed in a long black caftan and wide-brimmed hat and sporting a beard that straggles onto his sternum, he looks around, bewildered. Clearly, this is not the Orthodox or Hasidic milieu in which his garb would not stand out. At this party, few of the men wear yarmulkes. They sit comfortably with women whose skirts barely brush their knees. The interloper stumbles around, poking his nose into the group at one table, then another, asking for particular people. Finally, he addresses the whole room, loudly. "This isn't the Shapiro-Goldfarb wedding?" he asks, acting as confused as Lieutenant Columbo. "It's Jonathan's bar mitzvah? Oh my goodness, what a coincidence! This is my kinda people, I gotta tell ya! Where's Aunt Frieda?" He names a few more of the family and honored guests and then calls for Jonathan to make his entrance: "Shmuley, Nachum, Avrum, Moyshe, bring him in!"

Half a dozen men in similar Hasidic dress bear the bar mitzvah boy on their shoulders while the band strikes up *Fiddler*'s opening number, "Tradition." These are the Amazing Bottle Dancers, a performance troupe of fake Hasidim for hire. More borscht belt than Borough Park, they also entertain at weddings, birthday parties, and other events all over the country, including the Jewish Heritage Celebration produced each year at a Philadelphia Phillies game.

With their paste-on *payess* bouncing in time to the music, the men deliver the bar mitzvah boy to a seat at the central table. Then the tune shifts and the men perform their showy number: a section of Jerry Robbins's "Bottle Dance" from the wedding scene in *Fiddler*, shatterproof bottles nestled securely into holes cut into the tops of their hats. (The original Broadway dancers enjoyed no such assistance.) In a line facing the honored family, they clasp hands at shoulder height and take a step leftward with the left foot, then cross the right foot in front of the left. Off they go, executing the moves of Robbins's exacting choreography, including the climactic knee slides. Finally, rising to a standing position, they let the bottles drop into their hands, then swerve and bend to the music, eventually forming a circle and inviting all the bar mitzvah guests to join in a mass hora. The routine, according to Michael Pasternak, a Los Angeles–based actor and the founder of the Amazing Bottle Dancers, offers "a way of adding a touch of tradition into the event." As if the bar mitzvah itself were not sufficient to the purpose.

These are fine, athletic dancers and the performance is meant to be good fun (and, as a video advertisement for the group promises, "You don't even have to be Jewish to appreciate the humor"). Whether one finds it amusing, affecting, or appalling, or a wacky combination of all three, this twenty-first-century entertainment reveals how deeply and indelibly *Fiddler on the Roof* has saturated Jewish culture in America and how it has gathered authority. The entertainment depends on a telling transmutation: Robbins absorbed some elements of presumed folk culture from weddings he attended as research, and he remade them into an elaborate composition for a work of the theater. Several decades later, his artistic creation came out of the show intact and returned to the realm of ritual celebration to bestow authenticity on the proceedings. In other words, a Broadway showstopper turned into folklore. Just as Sholem-Aleichem's literary craftsmanship gave way to the idea that he was (in Maurice Samuel's phrase) the "'anonymous' of Jewish self-expression," Robbins's calculated choreography became, in the words of the Amazing Bottle Dancers' promotional video, an "age-old magnificent dance."

When the troupe performed in 2008 on the annual Chabad telethon—the nationally broadcast fund-raising extravaganza of Lubavitch Hasidim—it opened a return lane on the bridge Robbins had built between Old World practice (as he and his collaborators imagined it) and popular entertainment. The "Bottle Dance" helped the image-savvy Lubavitchers remove the aura of strangeness around them by placing them within a familiar comfort zone. It was as if the two-minute performance, which opened the broadcast, was telling viewers: "Hey, you know us! We might look odd with our cloaks and beards and hats. But you've seen us in *Fiddler on the Roof!*"

The show about tradition has become tradition. And in the twenty-first century, that is still a fraught concept even though—or maybe precisely because—in the five decades since *Fiddler* premiered (as long a stretch of time as between Sholem-Aleichem's original stories and their Broadway incarnation) we have learned that tradition is "invented," along with other postmodern lessons that can help illuminate why the show can be invoked both to confer Jewish bona fides on bar mitzvahs and to invite American rapport with Hasidim. We know, too, that, in the words of scholar Barbara Kirshenblatt-Gimblett, heritage "is a mode of cultural production in the present" and that identity is fluid, fragmented, contingent, "performative"—not an innate given but brought into being through the living of it. *Fiddler* has become part of the material out of which a new generation, applying those lessons, is self-consciously fashioning contemporary Jewish culture and forging a usable past for a new era. The show is never far from arguments, artworks, public proclamations, material objects, communal gatherings, celebrations, and ritual practices through which current debates over Jewish authenticity are joined. Even as old orders explode and the Jewish community fragments, Tevye, along with the imagined world he represents, holds firm as a primary figure to whom artists, ideologues, and folks with products to peddle turn to consider—and often just glibly to indicate—both the unacceptable loss and the irrefutable promise of change. He trudges on within—and as—a storm of contradictions.

Tevye's twenty-first century began, on the one hand, with the Yiddish literary critic Ruth Wisse's continuing the scholarly sport of condemning *Fiddler* for degrading Sholem-Aleichem—and, through its positive portrayal of Fyedka, as she sees it, for far worse. "If a Jewish work can only enter American culture by forfeiting its moral authority and its commitment to group survival," she sneers in *The Modern Jewish Canon*, "one has to wonder about the bargain that destroys the Jews with its applause." On the other hand, also in 2000, Jerry Bock and Sheldon Harnick were honored with a Special Cultural Arts Award by the venerable Yiddish center, the YIVO Institute for Jewish Research; the fund-raising gala included a "poignant musical tribute that included a medley of their songs." *Fiddler on the Roof*: cultural *génocidaire* or cultural hero? Nowadays, the Yiddishists themselves are divided.

So are the Israelis. A right-wing ultra-Orthodox settler, Tzvi Fishman, self-published a 580-page novel called *Tevye in the Promised Land* that brings the hero and his family to Palestine after the expulsion from Anatevka and reads like a kosher version of the evangelical Christian *Left Behind* series as it transforms the old dairyman into a swamp-clearing, Turk-battling, messianic Zionist. Meanwhile, Dan Almagor decided that the most fitting way to use royalties on his Hebrew translation of *Fiddler* was to purchase violins for Palestinian children in a music program in the Israeli-occupied West Bank town of Jenin.

In a video supporting a Rabbis for Human Rights campaign against Israeli displacement of Bedouins in the Negev, Theodore Bikel, a

Fiddler as shorthand for the cheeky Anti-Semitic
Cartoons Contest.

long-beloved Tevye, invokes the character he has played more than two thousand times, to decry the eviction and how "the very people who are telling them to get out are the descendants of the people of Anatevka." And he dons Tevye's costume in a magazine advertisement for a Jewish funeral provider, ballyhooing Dignity Memorial for "working for generations to preserve Jewish traditions." At the same time, the show's authority can be called on to confront Jewish anxieties: Aron Katz summoned it for his prizewinning entry in the Israeli "Anti-Semitic Cartoons Contest," cheekily launched in the wake of the controversy over Muhammad cartoons in a Danish paper and the subsequent call by an Iranian publication for Holocaust cartoons. In Katz's image, which referred to conspiracy theories that Jews masterminded the September 11, 2001, attacks on the United States, a silhouetted male figure in caftan and wide-brimmed hat fiddles atop the Brooklyn Bridge while in the distance the World Trade Center towers burn. Nothing so efficiently supplies the means for reassuring and for ruffling Jewish sensibilities as *Fiddler on the Roof.*

What's striking about these deployments of *Fiddler* and so many more—a progressive fair-tax lobbying campaign called the "If I Were a Rich Man Tour"; the assertion by disgraced Washington lobbyist Jack Abramoff that he decided to become religiously observant upon watching the *Fiddler* movie; Stephen Colbert's joking that after Christians properly reclaim Rosh Hashanah they will stage *Fiddler* with Tevye played by Mel Gibson—is their self-conscious sincerity. All take seriously *Fiddler*'s status as a luminous icon capable of projecting echt Jewish luster, even if it's only a show.

To some degree, that's simply a function of pop culture's reign and reach in general. But the frequency and undiminished pungency of *Fiddler* references after all these years speak to the unusually abundant and various entry points the show continues to provide for people of all persuasions. Today, it plays an even larger role in the new Jewish cultural sphere, where it has been embraced by artists who once disparaged it. The klezmer violinist Alicia Svigals remembers heading to gigs in the 1980s dreading that someone might ask her to play "Sunrise, Sunset." But by the turn of the new century, some of the most serious klezmer players happily took part in the pathbreaking (if highly uneven) album *Knitting on the Roof*, produced by the label attached to the original Knitting Factory venue in Manhattan, which specialized in musical experiment and was a deliberate breeding ground for "new Jewish culture." The album features a range of contemporary musicians, each interpreting—or deconstructing—a song from the show. A similar framework organized the kickoff for the Oy!hoo Festival at Manhattan's 92nd Street Y in 2007: each performer in a lineup of leading Jewish music makers covered one of the Bock and Harnick tunes, responding to them with hip-hop, Sephardic, indie rock, klezmer, and other soulful styles.

Projects like these served to lift the curse of kitsch off *Fiddler*. They could do so for two reasons. First, the musicians' own work over the years: artists like Svigals joined the nascent klezmer revival movement in the 1980s shortly after it was earnestly under way, and they began learning from old LPs and from aging Yiddish musicians who still played for weddings and bar and bat mitzvahs. What they picked up about tough, complex rhythms they did not discern in the Broadway show; in place of sophisticated approaches to the phrasing they were studying, they heard in *Fiddler* glissandos and vibrato—"all that slipping, sliding stuff," Svigals calls it—that does not properly belong to the genre. But as the wave of klezmer and of other new Jewish sounds rose, the Bock and Harnick score was swept from its unsought place as prime exemplar of Jewish music. Svigals and her colleagues began to see that dismissing those songs from the klezmer canon was like complaining that Mozart's "Rondo alla Turca" is lousy Turkish music. *Fiddler* never intended to be there in the first place. Svigals could finally recognize the score for what it is—great show tunes—and even publicly admit to having played the original cast album to death in her adolescence. More than that, the score introduced the wider culture to some Jewish sounds—passages in the *freylekhs* mode, melodic reliance on the all-important interval of the fourth— effectively keeping a foot in the door that the new generation could come along and kick open. And as the foil to the seekers of counternostalgic "authentic" Yiddish music, it could even be said that it made the klezmer explosion possible.

Second, by the twenty-first century, when the generation after Svigals was expanding the repertoire of new Jewish music, culture was coming to the fore as a primary means of Jewish expression and identity making. In contrast to the Broadway songsmiths who happily "just happened to be Jewish," the younger artists needed to make their Jewishness happen publicly. They were inventing new ways of proclaiming their belonging and determining its meaning. More dissociated from Jewish institutions than any generation yet, they have been coming of age in the "postidentity" era, when affiliation and self-naming still matter but have become more playful and open, less bound to politics, and less deferential to policing authorities. A "Heebster" or "New Jew" or "post-Halakhic Jew"—as younger Jews have been called—might in a single gesture reject and assert Jewish connection: violating Jewish law against bodily desecration by tattooing a Jewish star on her or his body.

In a pop culture landscape in which Jon Stewart's bemusement and Sarah Silverman's sassiness have supplanted Woody Allen's angst and Gilda Radner's send-up of stereotypes, Jewish outsiderness is no longer an issue—and thus, Jewish striving to fit into the mainstream no longer defines the community. Hardly exiled to the margins of power, American Jews boast high rates of academic achievement (55 percent of Jews graduate from college, compared with 28 percent of the general population), economic success (the median income of a Jewish household is $54,000—compared with $42,000 in general), and political muscle (12 percent of the current U.S. Senate is Jewish, compared with some 2 percent of the population). They take aim at Jewish insiderness by restoring a countercultural flicker of Jewish difference to their self-making. And they share it with the tools of that project—including *Fiddler*.

Projects like the Oy!hoo concert or the album of *Fiddler* songs by the Australian punk band Yidcore, *Fiddlin' on Ya Roof*, with its snarled delivery, racing tempos, and assaulting guitar chords, neither reject *Fiddler* nor make fun of it; they *incorporate* it into their own, larger cultural enterprise. Remaking the work in their own idiom, they put a generational stamp on it that oddly Judaizes it. Theirs is the opposite of the universalizing gesture of albums like Joe Quijano's *"Fiddler on the Roof" Goes Latin* or Cannonball Adderley's jazz covers of the score of the 1960s. Suspicious of claims of universalism, the current generation of artists gleefully adds to, and takes from, a multiculti smorgasbord of raw materials but keeps the identifying tags on the items that they own and those that they borrow. In this view, *Fiddler*'s Jewishness does not dissolve by virtue of its being absorbed into someone else's work. In place of the satisfied marvel that attended the Japanese embrace of *Fiddler* in the late 1960s, reactions today to non-Western productions, especially, express amusement. A link to a YouTube video of a Japanese troupe rehearsing the "Tradition" number—"Shikitari" in Japanese—made e-mail rounds in 2006, introduced by remarks about how "hilarious" and "unbelievable" it was. A 2008 production of *Fiddler* in Hindi translation in Delhi merited a report in the *Forward* as a man-bites-dog sort of story. These productions differed little from foreign versions in the 1970s, but the Jewish American discourse around them had changed.

The reclaiming or highlighting of *Fiddler*'s Jewishness has also helped make the show available to parallel projects with their own ethnic claims. Lin-Manuel Miranda has frequently said that *In the Heights*, his 2008 Tony-winning hip-hop musical about a changing Dominican neighborhood, blatantly borrowed structure and thematic development from *Fiddler*. The Bollywood director Rajiv Menon has been dreaming for several years about translating *Fiddler* into the local cinematic idiom. He wants to set the story in Kashmir in the 1980s, portraying Tevye as a Hindu Pandit farmer who is ethnically cleansed from the valley and lives in a refugee camp in Jammu; he'd add an act that follows Tevye back to his native village.

* * *

All these revampings extend Fiddler's scope and significance, but they don't replace the show itself, which unswervingly maintains an insistent power and popularity. Even Ruth Wisse has to admit that, much as she despises it, *Fiddler* is "in many respects, an adaptation of genius." The licensing agency Music Theatre International counted several hundred amateur and professional productions in 2012, from Panama City to Klaipeda. In the form in which it has long been known and loved, *Fiddler* still packs the house. Topol toured the show through Australia and New Zealand in 2005 and 2007 to wide acclaim and then, beginning in January 2009, at age seventy-three, headlined a "farewell tour" across North America (which he left after ten months because of a shoulder injury; he was replaced by Harvey Fierstein). Huge houses sold out from Jersey City to San Francisco.

Topol did not, however, star in the production mounted in 2008 at Tel Aviv's leading repertory theater, the Cameri, as part of his native Israel's sixtieth-anniversary celebration; the role went to a younger, rough-hewn charmer with sly humor and a strong singing voice, Nathan Datner. The unexpected casting served the anniversary goal of honoring one strong strain of national roots with a fresh take on the past. The director, Moshe Kepten, thirty-seven, knew he'd have a hard time retrieving the play from the common view that the old classic had been gathering barnacles in its several revivals since the Godik production at the Alhambra. Two generations after *Fiddler* helped sabras approach a once-reviled past, it seemed to have nothing more to say. Young actors hesitated to accept roles Kepten offered until he described, at length, the robust new approach he and his set designer, Roni Toren, had in mind. If he and Toren could not—or did not want to—entirely undo the mechanism whereby an origin myth supplies a justification for the present, they could add a strain of critique. They could strip away any shtetl romance.

That meant finding a visual idiom whose fabulist quality did not rely on the cliché of Chagall and whose sense of real stakes did not depend on spelling out every domestic detail. Toren fashioned a more abstract and open playing space. The show began with a roof freely suspended, like an island floating over the stage, and the fiddler—lithe and clad all in white—initially standing astride it. As Tevye introduced the community and summoned them with those foot stomps and the call of "Tradition," the roof tilted into a vertical position to become a mizrach—a beautifully painted eastern wall of a traditional synagogue—and to reveal the Anatevkans singing before it. Immediately the production established its new terms: magical, historical, self-consciously theatrical. In short, operatic.

Most significant, the proscenium arch was lined with sepia portraits of folks from the Old Country. Kepten and Toren wanted the audience to feel they were entering the story as if paging through a family photo album—no matter if their families had come from Poland or Yemen or Spain or Iraq. Some of the photos came from Toren's own family (his father, from Bessarabia, wrote fiction set in the shtetl); some were pictures of the cast members made to look as if they'd been taken a century earlier. The images were meant to work in several ways: first, to give spectators a sense of a personal link as part of a nation of immigrants (among Jews) and, second, literally to put a frame around the action that might produce some critical distance and reveal historical parallels—specifically, Kepten hoped, with the ongoing dispossession of Palestinians. Though Kepten said that in postperformance discussions some playgoers freely brought up the analogy, it was not noted by the major critics and certainly not mentioned in the Cameri's promotional materials. The third reason for the photos made more sense within the institutional choice of *Fiddler* for the state's anniversary celebration: to commemorate the end of the civilization the show depicts. To say, "This is the past," as Toren put it. "This world is finished and we are looking backwards into the story." At the play's close—when the departing, singing Anatevkans pause in their choreographic arm movements to hold up their hands in a gesture of surrender that perfectly mimics the young boy in a cloth cap in the famous Warsaw Ghetto photograph—flames light up beneath each of those proscenium portraits: memorial candles.

At three hours, the show clocked in at nearly twice the length of most Cameri productions, and at 8 million shekels (about $2 million) nearly twice the usual budget. The theater had to extend the run repeatedly, more than doubling the initially planned sixty performances. Typically stingy with standing ovations, Israeli audiences rose to their feet night after night. Kepten, Toren, and their colleagues had given them not only a new look at *Fiddler* but also one made specifically for them. Earlier productions, overseen by American directors, had replicated the original Robbins staging (as the licensing typically requires), but in 2008 the Cameri addressed its own Jewish public directly through the bedecked proscenium. "The dramaturgical main premise," said Toren, "is that we look backwards to our history via the gate of personal family." The production hailed its Jewish audiences and—more self-consciously than the Israeli flag and national anthem, which refer to Jewish symbols without concern for non-Jewish citizens—reaffirmed their national myth.

* * *

A visual revamping of the show in New York in 2004 had an opposite effect on some Jewish spectators.

Invoking the commonplace, seemingly unobjectionable notion that theater is not a museum but a living dynamic form, Bock, Harnick, and Stein began to yearn for a "new look" to *Fiddler*. (Robbins died in 1998.) Talk of a fortieth-anniversary Broadway revival was brewing—there had already been three (in 1976, starring Mostel, in 1981 with Herschel Bernardi, and in 1990 with Topol)—and recent, revelatory new takes on *Carousel* and *Cabaret* suggested, as Bock put it, that *Fiddler* could benefit from "a fresh, exciting approach." Should the show ever return to New

York, the authors wanted it to be "a production that will not only stir memory, but create the kind of excitement as if the audience were seeing it for the first time."

Up to a point. They rejected a director who wanted to break for intermission after the scene where Tevye concocts the Grandma Tzeitel dream, present the wedding after the intermission, and cut the rest of the act down considerably. Robbins's choreography was also nonnegotiable: preserving it was written into the licensing agreement for any future productions. That, they all agreed, was as it should be. Who could possibly improve on those dances? Still, there was plenty of room to create what Bock called a "renewal, not revival."

The person who did get the job, the British director David Leveaux, thought one way would be to include a new song. Yente could use one, he suggested—even though Bock and Harnick hadn't collaborated since 1970, when they differed over the firing of the director of their show *The Rothschilds*. In the original *Fiddler*, before the utterly downward arc of Hodel's departure, Chava's elopement, and the community's eviction, Yente started a light number called "The Rumor": passing one another as they rush along in front of the curtain, the Anatevkans share news of Perchik's arrest, each twisting the information, like in a game of telephone, into a string of increasingly absurd catastrophes. In addition to adding a little levity, the song's primary function was to cover a scene change. Norman Jewison did not use it in the film—he had the jump cut at his disposal— and many productions since had found ways to do without it. Leveaux figured there was still room in that moment for Yente to inject some humor into act 2, but in a way that made a stronger thematic link. The matchmaker's role was dwindling—a complaint the original Efrayim makes in Sholem-Aleichem's "Tevye Leaves for the Land of Israel"—and Yente could comment on how tradition was breaking down for her, too.

The production was already in its second week of rehearsal, so the songwriters had to work fast. Bock relished the chance to put some klezmer into the score—by 2004, the more traditional Jewish sound had shed the mawkishness associated with it in the 1960s, thanks to the inventive music of bands like the Klezmatics, who blasted onto the scene like a Yiddish Led Zeppelin in the late 1980s. Harnick focused on keeping energy and vitality in the number, despite his worries that there might not be anything Yente could say that the audience didn't already grasp.

The two came up with "Topsy-Turvy," in which Yente expresses her bewilderment over young people seeking wedded bliss—a spry but, still, incidental song that in Harnick's view didn't work as well as "The Rumor" in front of an audience.

The change to Yente that satisfied him more was a tweak he and Stein gave to her lines that went unremarked in the press but suggests more about *Fiddler*'s relationship to a changing context. In the departure scene, she originally tells Golde that she is heading to "the Holy Land" (an unlikely locution warranted by the impossibility of her saying on a New York stage in 1964 what a character in 1905 actually would have said: "Palestine"). Yente says she will continue her work as a matchmaker and "help our people be fruitful and multiply." By 2004, the authors didn't like the ring of those lines in relation to the Israeli-Palestinian conflict: they may have sounded like an endorsement of the idea of a "demographic war." Stein replaced them. "I just want to go where our foremothers lived and where they're all buried," she now says. "That's where I want to be buried—if there's room."

Leveaux's eagerness to "take that musical and strip it of the schtick that has become attached to it" mostly took a visual form. Theatrical language had changed in four decades and that meant the set could be "more evocative rather than representational." He and the scenic designer, Tom Pye, started from scratch—no Aronson turntables, painted drops, folding house. They covered the orchestra pit to move the action closer to the audience in the cold and distant Minskoff Theater—and placed the orchestra on the stage. They played the scenes on a raked wooden platform that helped to delimit the space. And they surrounded it all with pretty silver birch trees and scattered leaves. Above them twinkled dozens of lanterns that resembled the oil lamps of synagogues. Leveaux restaged the dream scene with clear homage to Chagall—Tzeitel and Motel flew over the scene as floating bride and groom—and tilted the platform until it was nearly vertical, so that the audience seemed to be watching the expressionistic dream from a bird's-eye perspective.

No question, it all looked gorgeous. But whether gorgeous is how *Fiddler* ought to look became part of a savage critical debate, one in which it was sometimes hard to distinguish between legitimate disagreements and a bizarre form of critical jingoism. Leveaux steered Alfred Molina into playing an excessively mellow Tevye, deliberately damping him down in rehearsals when emotions surged forth. Apparently he wanted to surrender Tevye's centrality and have him blend into the ensemble; that just doesn't work for the character through whom the audience sees everything. (This balance shifted for the better when Harvey Fierstein took over the role after about a year and led the production for the next thirteen months; Leveaux had thawed by then or simply let Fierstein do what he wished, and his Tevye generated great warmth.) On the other hand, some critics experienced a form of collective hysteria, ascribing the production's faults to a shortage of Jews. The accusations began while the show was still in previews, ignited by an instantly infamous essay in the *Los Angeles Times* by Thane Rosenbaum and immediately enflamed by the *New York Post*'s mischievous theater columnist Michael Riedel. On top of Rosenbaum's complaints that the production "tastes great and looks Jewish but isn't entirely kosher," Riedel declared it "de-Jewed" (flimsily attributing the phrase to anonymous "Broadway insiders"). A rumor spread charging that Leveaux had conducted callback auditions on Yom Kippur. (A "ludicrous joke," Leveaux said.)

In reviews, claims to ethnic authenticity, which had not been the currency of theater discourse forty years earlier when *Fiddler* originally opened, dominated the discussion. Much of the tribal rancor was reserved for Molina—the actor "has many inventive skills," Peter Marks declared in his *Washington Post* review, "but infusing Tevye with an ebullient Jewishness is not one of them"—although the cavil extended to the rest of the cast. Riedel had suggested that something was amiss when actors playing the three daughters were named Kelly, Murphy, and Paoluccio, and in a review for the *New York Sun*, Jeremy McCarter picked up on the very point: one shouldn't expect such performers, he said, "to abound in Russian-Jewish authenticity." Months later, when Harvey Fierstein took over for Molina, the critic for the website Theatermania.com kept the meme going, praising Fierstein's "personal and touching" performance and, bizarrely surprised, declaring Broadway's gay godfather convincing as a paternal figure "even if his daughters seem a couple of gene pools removed from his own." In 1964, no one had any problem accepting Tanya Everett and Julia Migenes—and Joanna Merlin, who, though Jewish, was a Midwesterner not well-steeped in *Yiddishkayt*—as Tevye's children. They were *acting*, after all.

Tom Pye's set model for a fresh take on *Fiddler.*

Audiences generally accepted Leveaux's *Fiddler*—it played 781 performances over nearly two years, running considerably longer than any other Broadway revival thus far—but reviewers from publications large and small piled on. The "Jewish problem" remained the primary frame through which the Leveaux production was critically seen. In the *New York Times*, Ben Brantley devoted an entire paragraph to describing how "a nickname for the revival had already started circulating among theater insiders: 'Goyim on the Roof.'" The satirical revue *Forbidden Broadway*, Gerard Alessandrini's regular send-up of the season, covered the production with a sketch called "Fiddler with No Jew."

As fiercely as Irving Howe and Robert Brustein and Cynthia Ozick had once tried to defend Sholem-Aleichem from what they considered the vulgarities of Broadway, the new generation of theater critics now wanted to safeguard their *Fiddler* from the vulgar misapprehensions of a bold Brit. For these writers, "new look" was another name for "goyish." The show its authors once feared was *too* Jewish now wasn't Jewish enough.

It could be that the objection stemmed, in part, from the fully calcified idea of the shtetl from *Life Is with People*, Maurice Samuel's books, and the other postwar works of "popular ethnography." The solid but false idea of the hermetic enclave clashed with the birch trees, which looked so *Russian*, like they belonged to a drama by Chekhov (Sholem-Aleichem's favorite playwright). Rosenbaum said as much in an interview at the time: the production, in his view, improperly elevated the universal themes "without the truer feelings of that old, vanished shtetl life."

There's more to it. Where Howe and his compatriots decried the oversimplification and exploitation of a whole Yiddish civilization, the critics crying foul about the Leveaux production lamented the lost world of the 1960s and 1970s of their childhoods, when they listened to LP's of *Fiddler* and sang "tradition, tradition" in the car. Peter Marks admitted as much in the first sentence of his *Washington Post* review: "In the secular Jewish home of my childhood, about the closest we ever came to spiritual sustenance was *Fiddler on the Roof*." Jewish critics, at least, seemed to expect the new revival to reweave their frayed Jewish connection; they didn't know where else to look.

Their furious disappointment betrayed two kinds of nostalgia: for a Jewish identification that makes only sentimental demands and for the big-story musical, of which *Fiddler* was one of the last. Sholem-Aleichem's Tevye stories addressed the anxiety of generational loss; a century later, critics in New York acted out over their own recursive confrontation of this theme.

In the 1960s, *Fiddler on the Roof* served as an engine of Jewish acculturation in America. For the next generation of assimilated Jews, it became a sacred repository of Jewishness itself. And for the next generation still, it became part of a multivalent legacy, available as a source of further exploration for those who wish to follow Tevye as he wanders on.

* * *

Perhaps it's fitting that Sholem-Aleichem's Tevye stories never came to a full conclusion. His writing of "Get Thee Out" in 1914, after publishing the earlier Tevye stories in a single volume in 1911, gave him the opportunity to bring Khave back into the picture and to keep Tevye in history. But "Get Thee Out" doesn't properly end so much as peter out. Scholars think that a fragment Sholem-Aleichem wrote later in 1914 was a stab at closing the Tevye cycle properly, but the author didn't finish it before his death. Even though he permitted its publication, translators often drop it altogether or append its last paragraphs, the only part that isn't redundant, to the end of "Get Thee Out." In this sutured finale, Tevye is not sure where he is going. Addressing Sholem-Aleichem, as usual, he wonders if they might some day meet on a train, "or in Odessa, or in Warsaw, or maybe even in America." In all those places, and far beyond, the world has met—and embraced—him. He belongs nowhere. Which is to say, everywhere.

Notes

ARCHIVES—ABBREVIATIONS

Box and folder information follows the abbreviation in the notes where appropriate. For example, JRPP1:2 would mean Jerome Robbins Personal Papers, Box 1, Folder 2. The Arnold Perl Papers include some clipping materials on microfilm reels; APPmicro2 would mean reel 2 of the microfilm in the Perl Papers.

AJC The New York Public Library–American Jewish Committee Oral History Collection, Dorot Jewish Division, New York Public Library, Astor, Lenox and Tilden Foundations.

APP Arnold Perl Papers 1947–1964, U.S. Mss 65AN, Wisconsin Historical Society Archives/ Wisconsin Center for Film and Theater Research.

BAP Boris Aronson Papers and Designs, *T-VIM 1987–012, Billy Rose Theatre Division, New York Public Library for the Performing Arts.

BSA-TA Beth Sholem Aleichem, Tel Aviv. *"Tevye der milkhiker/Tuvia ha-kholev"* files.

CLIPS Clipping and Program Files at the New York Public Library for the Performing Arts: Music Division, Jerome Robbins Dance Division, Billy Rose Theatre Division.

EPP-B Edmond Pauker Papers. General Collection, Beinecke Rare Book and Manuscript Library, Yale University.

EPP-42 Edmond Pauker Papers 1923–1959, MssCol2354, New York Public Library.

EPP-PA Edmond Pauker Papers, *T-Mss 1960-001, Billy Rose Theatre Division, New York Public Library for the Performing Arts.

FCP Fred Coe Papers 1949–1975, U.S. Mss 198AN, Wisconsin Historical Society Archives/ Wisconsin Center for Film and Theater Research.

FSG Farrar, Straus & Giroux, Inc. records (Noonday Press), Manuscripts and Archives Division, New York Public Library.

HPP Harold Prince Papers, Billy Rose Theatre Division, New York Public Library for the Performing Arts.

ITA-TA Israeli Theater Archives, Tel Aviv University.

JBP Jerry Bock Papers, JPB 02-10, Music Division, New York Public Library for the Performing Arts.

JRP Jerome Robbins Papers, (S) *MGZMD 130, Jerome Robbins Dance Division, New York Public Library for the Performing Arts.

JRPP Jerome Robbins Personal Papers, (S) *MGZMD 182, Jerome Robbins Dance Division, New York Public Library for the Performing Arts (with thanks for access and permission to the Jerome Robbins Trust).

JSP-NY Joseph Stein Papers and Scripts, Performing Arts Research Collections, New York Public Library for the Performing Arts.

JSP-W Joseph Stein Papers 1942–1969, U.S. Mss 33AN, Wisconsin Historical Society Archives/Wisconsin Center for Film and Theater Research.

LHP Leland Hayward Papers, Collection ID *T-Mss 1971-002, Billy Rose Theatre Division, New York Public Library for the Performing Arts.

MCNY-P Museum of the City of New York, program and photo collections, *Fiddler on the Roof*, Yiddish Theater.

MS Maurice Schwartz collection, RG 498, YIVO, Center for Jewish History, New York.

ND New Dramatists, Inc., Archive, Yale Collection of American Literature, Beinecke Rare Book and Manuscript Library.

NJAB National Jewish Archive of Broadcasting of the Jewish Museum, New York.

NJP Norman Jewison Papers, U.S. Mss 122AN, Wisconsin Historical Society Archives/Wisconsin Center for Film and Theater Research.

NYPL-PA New York Public Library for the Performing Arts.

PZP Patricia Zipprodt Papers and Designs, *T-Vim 1999-001, Billy Rose Theatre Division, New York Public Library for the Performing Arts.

RHA The Rodgers and Hammerstein Archives of Recorded Sound, New York Public Library for the Performing Arts.

RRP Richard Rodgers Papers, *T Mss 1987-006, Billy Rose Theatre Collection, New York Public Library for the Performing Arts.

SHP Sheldon Harnick Papers 1937–1968, U.S. Mss 104AN, Wisconsin Historical Society Archives/Wisconsin Center for Film and Theater Research.

SHP-NYPL Sheldon Harnick Papers, JPB 04-11, New York Public Library for the Performing Arts.

TOFT Theater on Film and Tape Archive, New York Public Library for the Performing Arts.

Z&KMP Zero and Kate Mostel Papers, *T-Mss 1993-007, Billy Rose Theatre Division, New York Public Library for the Performing Arts.

ZRT Zbigniew Raszewski Theater Institute Archives, Warsaw.

Cinematheque Archives, Tel Aviv.

Library of Congress, Special Collections (National Theater programs), Washington, DC.

World Jewish Newspapers & Periodicals on Microfilm, Dorot Jewish Division, New York Public Library.

Yizkor (Holocaust Memorial) Books, Dorot Jewish Division, New York Public Library.

INTERVIEWS

With enormous thanks, I acknowledge the scores of artists, administrators, relatives, colleagues, and other relevant parties, who shared their memories and insights with me in lengthy conversations—sometimes several of them—and then in follow-up calls and e-mails:

All interviews took place in person and in New York City unless otherwise noted.

Robert Aberdeen (working under the name Robert Berdeen during *Fiddler*, Nov. 21,

2009); Dan Almagor (Tel Aviv, Jan. 7, 2009); Bruce Ampolsky (by phone, June 4, 2009); Lisa Jalowetz Aronson (Nyack, NY, Jan. 9, 2010); Marc Aronson (Dec. 28, 2009); Tanya Everett Bagot (June 11, 2010); Sammy Bayes (Dec. 1, 2009); Anna Vita Berger (July 19, 2010); Eleanor Bergman (Warsaw, July 2, 2008); Olga Berlozecka (Warsaw, July 2, 2008); Bruce Birnel (by phone, June 23, 2009); Duane Bodin (Aug. 11, 2010); Frances Brown (Aug. 11, 2010); Janice Cabon (April 12, 2010); Mariusz Choma (Dynów, July 8, 2008); Olga Carter Dais (Sept. 9, 2009); Natan Datner (Tel Aviv, Jan. 5, 2009); Merle Debuskey (New Milford, CT, Aug. 2, 2010); Robert DeCormier (by phone, Aug. 10, 2010); Ruby Dee (by phone, Aug. 5, 2010); Beverley Cannon Dorsey (Albany, NY, June 14, 2009); Howard Enders (New Rochelle, NY, June 17, 2008); Margo Feiden (Nov. 24, 2009); Joanne Felcher Gibson (Aug. 11, 2009); Harvey Fierstein (by phone, June 16, 2011); Mayor Zygmunt Frańczak (Dynów, July 9, 2008); Rachel Perl Garson (by phone, Aug. 20, 2010); Joe Gilford (Oct. 17, 2010); Sidney Gluck (May 16, 2008); Eli Gorenstein (Tel Aviv, Jan. 5, 2010); Jerzy Gruza (Warsaw, July 1, 2008); Mirosław Haponiuk (Lublin, July 12, 2008); Sheldon Harnick (Aug. 1, 2006; June 18, 2008; Sept. 22, 2010; and Jan. 9, 2012); Sheila Haskins (Somerset, NJ, Dec. 13, 2010); Michael Hausman (by phone, March 24, 2010); Stephan Hirsch (Aug. 23, 2009); Charlie Isaacs (Newburgh, NY, June 21, 2010); Hans Jenny (by phone, April 3, 2008); Norman Jewison (by phone, May 27, 2011); Marian Josicz (Lublin, July 12, 2008); Bel Kaufman (May 27, 2010); Sandra Kazan (April 11, 2011); Moshe Kepten (Holon, Israel, Jan. 6, 2009); Emily Perl Kingsley (by phone, Aug. 4, 2010); Tomek Kitlinski (Lublin, July 12 and 13, 2008); Sławomir Kitowski (by phone from Warsaw, July 1, 2008); Stanley Koor (Aug. 19, 2010); Maciej Kosłowski (Kraków, July 4, 2008); Stanisław Krajewski (Kraków, July 5, 2008); Ken Le Roy (by phone, July 12, 2010); Pawel Leszkowicz (Lublin, July 12 and 13, 2008); David Leveaux (Jan. 5, 2004); Janusz Makuk (Kraków, July 6, 2008); Carolyn Maxwell (June 29, 2010); Duane McCullers (July 23, 2009); Joanna Merlin (Nov. 26, 2008); Janusz Miklasz (Dynów, July 7, 2008); Magdalena Miklasz (Dynów, July 7, 8, 9, and 10, 2008); Mateusz Mikoś (Dynów, July 7, 2008); Alan Miller (July 27, 2009); Peff Modelski (by phone, July 23, 2009); Joshua Mostel (Feb. 8, 2011); Tobias Mostel (by phone, Sept. 6, 2010); Patrick Palmer (by phone, Feb. 13, 2013); Michael Pasternak (by phone, April 11, 2008); Austin Pendleton (April 3, 2008); Adam Perl (by phone, Aug. 5 and 9, 2010); Nancy Perl and Mick Benderoth (East Hampton, NY, Aug. 17, 2010); Rebecca Perl (by phone, Aug. 16, 2010); Dominik Piejko (Dynów, July 7, 2008); Justyna Pinczer (Dynów, July 7 and 8, 2008); Richard Piro (deceased, San Francisco, March 16 and 18, 2009); Joe Ponazecki (July 22, 2009); Harold Prince (Dec. 3, 2008); Rivka Raz (Nov. 12, 2008); Maurice Reid (June 23, 2010); Maritza Figueroa Reynolds (June 23, 2010); Frank Rich (Aug. 9, 2010); Shirley Romaine (by phone, July 12, 2010); Alan Rosenberg (by phone, July 26, 2010); Julius Rubin (by phone, June 9, 2009); Malgorzata Semil (Warsaw, July 2, 2008); Roberta Senn (Great Neck, NY, Aug. 18, 2010); Joe Sicari (June 8, 2009); Ewa Sikora (Dynów, July 7, 2008); Orna Smorgonski (Tel Aviv, Jan. 8, 2009); Albert Stankowski (Warsaw, June 30, 2008); Harry Stein (by phone, Feb. 15, 2012); Joseph Stein (deceased, June 27, 2007); Alicia Svigals (Feb. 10, 2010); Grzegorz Szajnik (Dynów, July 8, 2008); Jan Szurmiej (Warsaw, June 29, 2008); Szymon Szurmiej (Warsaw, July 2, 2008); Chaim Topol (Jan. 24, 2009); Roni Toren (Tel Aviv, Jan. 8, 2009); Marek Weiss (Warsaw, June 30, 2008.); Jitu Weusi (June 23, 2010); Ewa Woźniak (Dynów, July 7, 9, and 10, 2008).

I'm also grateful to those who, while not sitting for full-fledged interviews, provided answers to (sometimes multiple) queries on various details by phone and/or e-mail: Don Aslan; Maya Benton, curator, Roman Vishniac Collection, International Center of Photography; Ronald Blanche; Jerry Bock (deceased); Louis Botto; Jim Brochu; Joseph Butwin; Lee

Grant; Mary Rodgers Guettel; Deborah Jowitt; Vladimir Levin, Acting Director, Center for Jewish Art, Hebrew University of Jerusalem; Branko Lustig; Rajiv Menon, Mumbai; Jeff Ovall, Lead Research Specialist, FOIA/Privacy Act Office, Securities and Exchange Commission; Richard Patterson and John Prignano, Music Theatre International; Barry Rosenberg, Contract Associate for Production at Actors' Equity; Elisa Shevitz, Director of Communications, The Broadway League Inc.; Elisa Stein; Richard Ticktin; Amanda Vaill; Cynthia Young, curator, Robert and Cornell Capa Archives, International Center of Photography; Gilda Zwerman.

I regret that some artists central to the productions here declined to be interviewed—among them Jerry Bock, Gino Conforti, Bernie Gersten, and Julia Migenes—but I respect their wishes.

And I especially regret that despite a couple of years of scheduling efforts, interviews could never be arranged with some artists—among them, Theodore Bikel and Pia Zadora—who generously agreed in principle to speak with me.

Of course there are many more who could not be located or who chose not to respond to queries that may have reached them. Regardless of their level of involvement with this project, I hope everyone finds events they were part of accurately represented.

INTRODUCTION: A LITTLE BIT OF THIS, A LITTLE BIT OF THAT

1 **Glenn Beck** See "Courage, Tears and *Fiddler on the Roof* at Glenn Beck's Israel Rally," Jill Rayfield, Talking Points Memo, August 24, 2011, http://tpmdc.talkingpointsmemo.com /2011/08/courage-tears-and-fiddler-on-the-roof-at-glenn-becks-israel-rally.php; and "Live Blog: Glenn Beck's 'Restoring Courage' Rally in East Jerusalem," Sara Miller and Morten Berthelsen, *Haaretz*, http:///www.haaretz.com/news/national/live-blog-glenn-beck-s -restoring-courage-rally-in-east-jerusalem-1.380474, published 16:46, August 24, 2011; last update, 20:36, August 24, 2011.

1 **"worse than Robespierre"** Beck radio show, October 10, 2011; video embedded on Huffington Post, "Glenn Beck: Occupy Wall Street Protesters Will 'Kill Everybody,'" Jack Mirkinson, October 10, 2011, http://www.huffingtonpost.com/2011/10/10/glenn -beck-occupy-wall-street-kill-everybody_n_1004016.html.

2 **two hundred schools across the country put it on each year** listings of licensing agency, Music Theater International.

2 **"Now, I know I haven't been the best Jew"** "Homer's Triple Bypass," Season 4, Episode 11, of *The Simpsons*, first aired December 17, 1992.

2 **Pinochet banned *Fiddler*** "Chilean Leader Tells Jews Why 'Fiddler' Is Out," *Jewish Week* (Washington, DC), September 19, 1974.

3 **Chavez defunded the orchestra** Hausman (director of production) interview.

4 **"What shall I write you about yesterday's triumph?"** Sholem-Aleichem letter to his daughter, Tissi, April 14, 1905, Berkowitz, *Sholem-aleichem bukh*, 62.

CHAPTER 1: TEVYE'S LONG JOURNEY TO THE NEW YORK STAGE
Unless otherwise noted, translations from Yiddish are my own.

9 **Sholem-Aleichem . . . thought about the New York theater** Berkowitz, *Sholem-aleykhem bukh*, 207; Waife-Goldberg, *My Father*, 211–13; Sholem-Aleichem letters to Fishberg, cited below.

13 **"Just like it says in the Bible"** Sholem-Aleichem, *Tevye the Milkman*, 3.

13 **"Have you heard any news about the cholera in Odessa"** ibid., 69.

14 **"as a vulgar comedian who pandered"** Miron, "Darkside," 42.

15 **asked Fishberg to bring this surefire hit** Sholem-Aleichem letter to Fishberg, September 13, 1905, Berkowitz, *Sholem-aleykhem bukh*, 208.

15 **"should have told you this before"** Sholem-Aleichem letter to Fishberg, October 8, 1905, ibid., 209.

15 **"with trembling hands"** Sholem-Aleichem to Fishberg, October 24, 1905, ibid.

15 **At first he took heart in seeing armed soldiers** ibid. Pogrom report also quoted, in English, in the *Aberdeen Daily News*, November 27, 1905.

16 **"sit out these evil times"** Sholem-Aleichem letter to Fishberg, October 24, 1905, Berkowitz, *Sholem-aleykhem bukh*, 209.

16 **"I send you the fifth act of *Stempenyu*"** Sholem-Aleichem letter to Fishberg, October 26, 1905, ibid.

16 **In this fraught period** This phase of Sholem-Aleichem's life and work is discussed in detail in Litvak, "Khave and her Sisters," a significant influence on my reading.

16 **"Don't make a book out of this"** Sholem-Aleichem, *Tevye the Milkman*, 82.

17 **"the king of the Yiddish actors"** Berkowitz, *Undzere* v2, 137.

17 **"Reb Yankev Gordin, he who translates and improves Shakespeare"** Sholem-Aleichem letter to Berkowitz, Berkowitz, *Undzere* v2, 141.

18 **He had despised *Der meturef* . . . bound all thirty copies of *David ben David*** Berkowitz, *Undzere* v2, ch. 95, "David ben David," 137ff.

18 **Sholem-Aleichem . . . read his new play . . . Adler . . . "fidgeted and nodded his head"** Israel Cohen, "On the Horizon: Sholem Aleichem in Exile," *Commentary* 8 (1949): 584.

19 **"nothing can dispel the despondency and the gnawing in the heart"** Sholem-Aleichem ship diary/letter to family, October 19, 1906, Berkowitz, *Sholem-aleykhem bukh*, 81; quoted and trans. in Waife-Goldberg, *My Father*, 184.

19 **"The occasion could not be more exultant" . . . "it seems a new era is dawning on our horizon, full of success, luck, and happiness"** Sholem-Aleichem letter to Tissi, October 21, 1906, Berkowitz, *Sholem-aleykhem bukh*, 82.

20 **"make up for [Sholem-Aleichem's] lack of ability as a dramatist"** "The Season of Yiddish Drama: Plays and Players," *Menorah*, September 1905, 153.

20 **fans packed all three tiers** "Aleichem Welcomed," *New York Times*, November 1, 1906.

20 **"The Jewish quarter might have shown some unity"** *Chronicler*, November 2, 1906, quoted in YIVO, "Sholem Aleichem in America," 11.

21 **Educational Alliance . . . charter** quoted in Sachar, *A History*, 157.

21 **"I am the American Sholem-Aleichem"** an oft-quoted and likely apocryphal remark, recounted, among other places, in Waife-Goldberg, *My Father*, 187.

21 **"great literary personality"** cited in Waife-Goldberg, *My Father*, 187.

21 **humiliated and angry . . . request the money** Berkowitz, *Undzere* v2, 164.

22 **"with only a hard chill"** ibid., 169.

22 **two years' wages** *Bulletin of the Bureau of Labor*, issue 71 (Government Printing Office, 1908), 35: Pressers averaged $0.21/hour, working a fifty-four-hour week, amounting to about $590 a year if the presser does not take a single day off.

22 **"When girls objected"** Abe Cahan, "Introduction," in Thomashefsky, *Mayn lebens geshikhte*, ii.

23 **"like poor patches on a rich garment"** Berkowitz, *Undzere* v2, 187.

23 **"The audiences seemed happy to me"** Sholem-Aleichem letter to his family, February 9, 1907, Berkowitz, *Sholem-aleykhem bukh*, 84.

23 **ideological fault lines** Nina Warnke offers the full political analysis of Sholem-Aleichem's reception in America in "Of Plays and Politics."

23 **"new page in Yiddish theater"** Sholem-Aleichem's speech described in Berkowitz, *Undzere* v2, 188–89, and essentially reiterated in the *Tageblat*'s anonymous review of February 11, 1907, quoted in Schulman, "*Sholem-aleykhems stzenisher debyut.*"

23 **"new winds blowing"** Sholem-Aleichem speech quoted in Schulman, "*Sholem-aleykhems stzenisher debyut.*"

24 **didn't hesitate to crank out some potboilers** See Joel Berkowitz, "Jacob Gordin, Man and Myth," *Forward*, May 30, 2008.

24 **"a new epoch"** *Morgn zhurnal*; "no true Yiddish theater," *Tageblat*, February 11, 1907; "This is simply scandalous," "whenever a flash," *Varhayt*; Entin in *Yidisher kempfer*—all quoted in Schulman, "*Sholem-aleykhems stzenisher debyut.*"

25 **"brought to an end Sholem-Aleichem's career as a playwright"** B. Goren, *Di geshikhte fun yidishn teatr*, 181.

25 **"the figures"** Abe Cahan, *Forverts*, February 19, 1907, quoted in Schulman, "*Sholem-aleykhems stzenisher debyut.*"

25 **"Once Sholem-Aleichem played a great role"** ibid.

27 **"Do you think she complained? Do you think she cried even once?"** Sholem-Aleichem, *Tevye the Milkman*, 96.

27 **the entire 1906–07 season bombed at the People's and Kalish theaters** B. Goren, "*Der sakh hakol fun fergangenem yidishn teatr sezon,*" "*Der bankrut fun yidishn teatr,*" *Der amerikaner*, May 24 and 31, 1907. See also Thissen, "Reconsidering."

28 **"genuinely Jewish comedy"** Sholem-Aleichem letter to Jacob Adler, quoted in Berkowitz, *Undzere* v3, 91.

28 **"Watch the impression"** ibid., 90.

28 **"My good friend and great artist Adler!"** ibid.

28 **Adler complained that the play piled up** ibid., 96.

29 **the preferred amusement** On the decline of the theaters, see Thissen, "Reconsidering."

29 **mawkish musical melodramas** For discussion of the "*harts, neshome, pintele*" plays, see B. Goren, *Geshikhte* v2, 203–31; Thissen, "Reconsidering."

30 **they were pressing to have "Hebrew" removed** See Goldstein, *Price of Whiteness*, 102–3.

30 **"great new continent that could melt up all race differences"** Zangwill, *Melting Pot*, 179.

31 **unleashed a national debate** For discussion of the success and impact of *The Melting Pot*, see Edna Nahshon's "Introduction" to her *Ghetto to Melting Pot*.

31 **sold his lease for the Grand Theater** Thissen, "Reconsidering," 192.

32 **"What's the point of the whole circus"** Sholem-Aleichem, *Tevye the Milkman*, 99.

32 **"where all the old Jews like you go to die"** ibid., 110.

32 **"To tell you the truth, when I think the matter over"** ibid., 100.

33 **a spate of Beilis plays** See Joel Berkowitz, "The 'Mendel Beilis Epidemic' on the Yiddish Stage," *Jewish Social Studies* 8:1 (Fall 2001): 199–225.

33 **Sholem-Aleichem followed the Beilis case** Roskies makes this point in *Jewish Search for a Usable Past*, 11.

34 **"a hysterical shaking"** Berkowitz, *Undzere* v5, 93.

34 **In the last scene—the most touching** Sholem-Aleichem letter to Olga Rabinowitz, February 25, 1914, Berkowitz, *Sholem-aleykhem bukh*, 117.

35 **"We ought to be counting our blessings"** Sholem-Aleichem, *Tevye the Milkman*, 126.

35 **"the crown of my creation"** Sholem-Aleichem letter to David Pinski, February 16, 1914, Berkowitz, *Sholem-aleykhem bukh*, 250.

35 **"the audience loves him all the more"** Sholem-Aleichem letter to Pinski, February 16, 1914, ibid., 251.

35 **"Although a hard man to do business with"** Sholem-Aleichem letter to Pinski, February 16, 1914, ibid., 250.

35 **"great artist and master of the Yiddish stage"** Sholem-Aleichem letter to Jacob Adler, January 20, 1914, ibid., 249.

36 **the author never even sent the letter** So claims Berkowitz in the *Sholem-aleykhem bukh*, 249; and Zylbercweig in *Leksikon* v4, 3404 (dating it to 1913); Rosenfeld, *Bright Star*, claims otherwise: 321–22.

36 **directors there no longer believed in the potential** Berkowitz, *Undzere* v5, 98.

38 **Sholem-Aleichem burst out with a bitter laugh** ibid., 170.

38 **Sholem-Aleichem felt more alienated than ever** ibid., 174.

38 **"I hope to have it produced in the fall by Adler or Thomashefsky"** Sholem-Aleichem letter to Emma and Misha, July 7, 1915, Berkowitz, *Sholem-aleykhem bukh*, 125.

39 **Kessler nodded off** Berkowitz, *Undzere* v5, 197.

39 **in Europe things were even worse** Sholem-Aleichem letter to family, quoted in Berkowitz, *Undzere* v5, 210.

39 **His funeral—including a stately procession** For discussion of the spectacle and politics of Sholem-Aleichem's funeral that makes the case for the way it unified Jewish factions, see Kellman, "Sholem-Aleichem's Funeral"; also A. Goren, "Sacred and Secular: The Place of Public Funerals in the Immigrant Life of American Jews," *Jewish History* 8:1–2 (1994): 269–305.

40 **"a microcosm of the Jewish people"** Yehoash, eulogy for Sholem-Aleichem delivered at the Educational Alliance on May 15, 1916, and excerpted in *Groyser kundes*, May 19, 1916; quoted in YIVO, "Sholem-Aleichem in America," 21.

41 **"not a 'folk writer,' not even 'the folk writer'"** Yosef Haim Brenner, "On Sholem Aleichem (The Writer and the Folk)," trans. David Roskies, *Prooftexts* 6:1 (January 1996): 17.

41 **Berkowitz added the village priest** Berkowitz, *Undzere* v5, 99; Weitzner, *Sholem-Aleichem in the Theater*, 80.

42 **"What more can the stage say"** M. Grim quoted in Zylbercweig, *Yiddish Art Theater in America*, 148.

42 **Others mocked Schwartz's penchant** *Tevye der milkhiker* reviews by Vladek, Goren, Frumkin, others quoted in Zylbercweig, *Yiddish Art Theater in America*, 134–46.

42 **Schwartz's "wholehearted" and "realistic" performance** Cahan quoted in Zylbercweig, *Yiddish Art Theater in America*, 140ff.

43 **"an unstrained style" . . . "to downright slapstick"** Jacob Copper, "Yiddish Art Players in Debut Here," *Los Angeles Times*, July 19, 1929, A9.

43 **"It was hard to tell if Schwartz created Tevye or Tevye created Schwartz"** Gersten quoted in Zylbercweig, *Leksikon* v4, 3411–12.

44 **"the whole Jewish people is in danger"** Vladek quoted in Zylbercweig, *Yiddish Art Theater in America*, 136–37.

45 **GOSET belonged to** See Veidlinger, *Moscow State Yiddish Theater*.

46 **Chagall "hated real objects"** Avrom Efros quoted in Harshav, *Moscow Yiddish Theater*, 69.

46 **"fossilized patriarchal . . . dead dogma"** Shloyme Mikhoels, "Sholem-Aleichem's Hero," *Jewish Currents* (January 1998): 22–24, translated from the Yiddish by Lyber Katz.

47 **Schwartz said it looked just like the Ukrainian countryside** "Studio and Screen: Ambassador's Film—A Jewish Humorist," *Manchester Guardian*, August 11, 1939; and Martha Drieblatt, "Poland in Jersey, Ukraine on Long Island," *New York Herald Tribune*, February 25, 1940, E3.

47 **While filming, the company heard** recounted in Hoberman, *Bridge of Light*, 307–9.

47 **"There sits upon Tevya's shoulders"** Mae Tinee, "Praises Acting in Yiddish Film of Famed Play," *Chicago Daily Tribune*, May 6, 1940, 22.

48 **"a triumphant rebuke"** Hoberman, *Bridge of Light*, 309.

48 **"does not at all agree with the spirit and essence"** N. Buchwald, *Morgn frayhayt*, quoted in Zylbercweig, *Leksikon* v4, 3419, and in Hoberman, *Bridge of Light*, 309.

48 **"Merely a shadow"** L. Fogelman, "Tevye the Milkman in a Movie," *Forverts*, December 25, 1939, quoted in Zylbercweig, *Leksikon* v4, 3318, and in Hoberman, *Bridge of Light*, 309.

CHAPTER 2: BETWEEN TWO WORLDS OF SHOLEM-ALEICHEM

50 **"the leading spokesman of Jewish rejuvenation"** Emanuel Goldsmith, "Maurice Samuel," in Kessner, *Other New York*, 228.

50 **"dogma" and "intellectual bullying"** Samuel, *Little Did I Know* (henceforth, *LDIK*), 42.

51 **"gateway into Jewish life"** ibid., 136.

51 **"as if the pogroms had been two-sided"** ibid., 244.

51 **"defined themselves Jewishly"** Kessner, *Other New York*, 3.

51 **"to help Jews acquire an interest in Jewish knowledge"** Samuel, *LDIK*, 286.

52 **"The man who does not see in the prophets"** Samuel, *Gentleman*, 168.

52 **"the mirror of Russian Jewry"** Samuel, *World*, 6.

52 **"the first American newspaper reports"** Hecht, *Child of the Century*, 539–40.

53 **"It was a principle of Russian law"** Samuel, *World*, 5.

53 **"transmitted rather than translated"** Samuel, *LDIK*, 271–72.

53 **The resulting work** For discussion of Samuel's approach to Sholem-Aleichem, see, especially, Kirshenblatt-Gimblett, "Imagining Europe," and Shandler, "Reading Sholem-Aleichem from Left to Right," both of whom influenced my reading.

53 **"the common people in utterance"** Samuel, *World*, 6.

53 **"an exercise in necromancy"** ibid., 3.

53 **"We could write a Middletown"** ibid., 6–7.

53 **"best known and best loved . . . big dark jungle of history"** ibid., 14.

54 **"very real hatred" of women** Samuel letter to Eugenia Shafran, likely 1924, quoted in Kessner, *Marie Syrkin*, 169.

54 **"without equal at handing out a dinner of curses and a supper of slaps"** Samuel, *World*, 10. (*Life is with People* also supported the stereotype of the oversolicitous and husband-nagging Jewish mother; see Antler, *You Never Call*, 73–82.)

54 **"the greatest single invention"** Roskies, *Jewish Search for a Usable Past*, 41.

55 **"a remarkable civilization"** Samuel, *World*, 5.

55 **"prosperity was spiritual rather than material"** ibid.

55 **"forever frozen in utter piety and utter poverty"** Davidowicz, *Golden Tradition*, 6.

55 **as the antisuburb** Shapiro, *Time for Healing*, 151.

55 **"one great portrait of a life abjectly poor"** Heschel, "Preface" to Vishniac, *Polish Jews*, 5.

56 **Vishniac's project** On the history of Vishniac's project and the changing cultural function and valuation of images over time, see Shandler, "The Time of Vishniac"; on the discovery and meaning of Vishniac's more extensive archive, see Alana Newhouse, "A Closer Reading of Vishniac," *New York Times Magazine*, April 4, 2010, 36–43. On the exhibit and the response to Heschel's speech, see Kirshenblatt-Gimblett, "Imagining Europe" and also "Introduction" to *Life is with People*. The discussion here is indebted to their research and insights.

56 **"salvage ethnography"** The phrase is Kirshenblatt-Gimblett's in "Imagining"—an influential source for this discussion. See also Zipperstein, *Imagining Russian Jewry*.

56 **"a composite portrait"** Kirshenblatt-Gimblett, "Folklore, Ethnology, and Anthropology," *The Yivo Encyclopedia of Jews in Eastern Europe*, http://www.yivoencyclopedia .org/article.aspx/Folklore_Ethnography_and_Anthropology.

57 **"more than a book"** Ben Hecht, "Tales of Capering, Rueful Laughter," *New York Times*, July 7, 1946.

57 **"fine, juicy humor"** display ad, *Chicago Daily Tribune*, June 23, 1946.

57 **"scattered" among pieces from other Sholem-Aleichem series** Frances Butwin, "Preface" to Sholem-Aleichem, *Tevye's Daughters*, x.

57 **Richard Rodgers and Oscar Hammerstein** In the *New York Times*, show business columnist Sam Zolotow followed their interest: November 18, 1949 (noting their acquisition of the option), January 18, 1950 (reporting that Menashe Skulnik was gunning for the role of Tevye), July 10, 1950 (casting doubt that the Tevye play would happen in the coming season), and August 28, 1950 (reporting that R&H had let their option lapse and that Michael Todd had bought it). More detailed, inside discussion of R&H's initial and then waning interest, and then Todd's involvement, can be found in Hammerstein's correspondence with Edmund Pauker, agent to Irving Elman, EPP-B, EPP-PA.

57 **they felt the Tevye script needed a huge amount of work** Hammerstein letter to Edmond Pauker, July 24, 1950, EPP-PA15:11.

58 **"folk play with music"** Pauker letter to Judah Bleich, November 28, 1955, EPP-B22:470.

58 **"you need to take out all the animals"** producer Michael Ellis to Pauker, February 20, 1953, EPP-B22:477.

58 **"feels so unwieldy as to be almost unmanageable"** ibid.

58 **"sprawling, undramatic"** José Ferrer—who suggested the play to R&H—to Pauker, August 15, 1949, EPP-PA15:11.

58 **"too Jewish and too folkish"** Eddie Blatt to Pauker, September 8, 1949, EPP-PA15:11.

58 not **"commercial enough"** Jed Harris's view as reported by Pauker to Elman, October 6, 1949, EPP-PA15:11.

59 **the tercentenary celebration . . . Kallen complained** See A. Goren, *Politics and Public Culture*, ch. 9, "The 'Golden Decade' 1945–1955," 186–204.

59 **Elman's play** In the early 1960s, Elman tried to mount the play again, this time under the title *As Long as You're Healthy* and later as *Sweet and Sour*, but by then Bock, Harnick, and Stein had secured the rights to the material and Elman's effort to claim fair use of the Yiddish originals did not fly. See: "2 Musicals Due" and "Coe Planning Musicals" in Sam Zolotow's columns, *New York Times*, September 26, 1962, and August 6, 1963.

60 **"not in a postwar effort"** Butwin, "Tevye on King Street," 132.

60 **"remarkable acts of memory and invention"** ibid., 134.

60 **shaped American culture well into the Cold War** See Denning, *The Cultural Front*.

60 **"great friend, mentor, and comrade" . . . "country" books** Butwin, "Tevye on King Street," 155.

60 **"lacking food, clothing, money"** Robert Cromier, *Chicago Daily Tribune*, June 30, 1946.

61 **Sophie Maslow** . . . *The Village I Knew* videotape, NYPL for the Performing Arts; see also Naomi Jackson "Choreographer Draws on Her Jewish Heritage for Inspiration," interview with Maslow by Laura Bleiberg, *Orange County Register*, Santa Ana, CA, April 19, 1992, F26.

61 **mainstream Jewish organizations were purging leftists** See Shapiro, *A Time for Healing*, 37ff.

62 **Butwins saw [Da Silva]** . . . **in** . . . *Oklahoma!* author correspondence with Joseph Butwin, January 29, 2012.

62 **Taylor** . . . **"he always seems to have"** Navasky, *Naming Names*, 79.

62 **Da Silva was sworn in** transcript, "Communist Infiltration of Hollywood Motion Picture Industry—Part 1," March 21, 1951. On Da Silva's actions at the hearing—shouting, testiness, etc.—see "Larry Parks Says He Was Red; Gives Other Hollywood Names; Two Other Film Figures Won't Talk at House Hearing, " UP, March 21, 1951, and *Los Angeles Times*, March 22, 1951; "Parks Admits He Was a Red But 2 Other Actors Balk at House Prober's Queries," *Baltimore Sun*, March 22, 1951; Murrey Marder, "Screen Star Admits He Was a Red," *Washington Post*, March 22, 1951, 1.

63 **Arnold Perl was never called before HUAC** Perl FBI file, generously shared by Rebecca Perl.

63 **"I have gotten radio detectives"** Perl quoted in Joseph Liss, ed., *Radio's Best Plays*. New York: Greenberg, 1947: 122.

63 **specifically when he entered Dachau** Perl quoted in interview with Dr. N. Sverdlin in *Der tog*, September 5, 1957, APPmicro3.

64 **"mutual impulse"** Perl letter to Mary Ann Jensen, November 4, 1969, APP2:5.

64 **share this culture** Da Silva letter to Oscar Lewenstein, January 3, 1954, APP2:8.

64 **if they didn't know Yiddish** Perl interviewed by Sverdlin, *Der tog*, September 5, 1957, APPmicro3.

64 **"Sholom-Aleichem's gentle but firm plea"** *Theater Arts* feature, July 1953: Aimee Scheff, "Art on a Shoestring," n.p., clipping, APP3:7.

64 **paid barely over minimum wage** Perl letter to Mary Ann Jensen, November 4, 1969, APP2:5.

65 **"reminding people of where they come from"** Perl letter to B. Z. Goldberg, May 25, 1953, APP2:5.

65 **The press agent, Merle Debuskey, had to insist** Debuskey interview.

65 **about 500 fixed seats and a small proscenium** Debuskey interview.

66 **some of them too fearful of guilt by association to go backstage to greet the company** Debuskey, Dee interviews.

66 **"fine theater and splendid humanity"** Brooks Atkinson, "At the Theatre," *New York Times*, September 12, 1953.

66 **"Human warmth, generosity"** Walter Kerr, "Sholom Aleichem' Full of Sympathy and Good Theater," *Los Angeles Times*, September 20, 1953, D2.

66 **"shows how theater-wise imagination"** Vernon Rice, *New York Post*, n.d., APPmicro3.

66 **Eleanor Roosevelt** *Chicago Sun-Times*, January 29, 1954, APPmicro4.

67 **composer who went uncredited** Robert de Cormier interview.

67 **torn from a packing crate** Perl letter to Ida Nasatir, October 16, 1953, APP2:6.

67 **avoid "over-detailed naturalism"** Da Silva letter to Sam Wanamaker, November 26, 1954, APP2:8.

68 **working from** . . . **"The Golden Peacock"** DeCormier interview.

68 **"obscure chapbook"** . . . **deliberately aimed to mimic the style of a folk narrative** Roskies, *Bridge of Longing*, 160–66.

68 **"If we have succeeded in moving from fantasy"** "Production Notes," Perl, *The World of Sholom Aleichem* script, 51.

69 **"This is the dawn of a new day"** *The World of Sholom Aleichem* script, 46.

69 **"very real interest on the part of the left"** Perl letter to Da Silva, March 9, 1956, APP2:5.

69 **"continuous emphasis on the most negative virtues"** letter from Katya and Bert (Gilden) to Perl, March 10, 1953, APP2:4.

69 **"increasingly aware that simply presenting"** Ring Lardner letter to Da Silva, October 20, 1953, APP2:4.

70 *Counterattack* **obsessively chased the play** In addition to the lengthy report on September 25, 1953, warnings about the show appeared in issues on October 9, 1953; March 26, 1954; July 30, 1954; and October 15, 1954.

70 **Perl boasted** Perl letter to Oscar Lewenstein, March 30, 1956, APP2:8.

70 **"stir up, however gently, the social consciences"** Cecil Williams quoted in a letter from Lewenstein to Perl, March 15, 1956, APP2:8.

70 **performances had to take a hiatus while a coup overthrew Juan Perón** letters from Ben-Ami to Perl, July 26 and September 21, 1955, APP3:4.

70 **"in a manner designed to promote Moscow's line"** *Counterattack*, March 26, 1954.

70 **vodka straight-up and Pall Malls without filters** Rebecca Perl interview.

71 **Jewish Welfare Board . . . [urged] JCCs . . . not to allow radicals** Shapiro, *A Time for Healing*, 37.

71 **helped to arrange a tour** letter from Perl to D. Fogel, November 21, 1955, APP2:5.

71 **"lox and bagels rash"** J. I. Fishbein, "A House with Only Fish," *Sentinel*, January 1, 1954, APPmicro4.

71 **"humor smelt of dead herring"** Rabbi Jacob J. Weinstein, *National Jewish Post*, February 12, 1954, APPmicro5.

71 **"slanted toward the lowest human denominator"** *Greenwich Hebrew Institute Bulletin*, October 7, 1953, APPmicro5.

71 **"Goebbels-like mockery"** B. Z. Goldberg review of *The World of Sholom Aleichem* for *Der tog*, May 6, 1953; typescript of English translation, APP3:5.

71 **"the finest and best"** J. I. Fishbein, "A House with Only Fish," *Sentinel*, January 21, 1954, APPmicro4.

71 **"surprising to see European Jewish life"** *Commentator*, Yeshiva College, n.d., APPmicro3.

71 **"what had hitherto been termed unachievable"** Maurice M. Shudofsky, *Jewish Frontier*, no. 12 (December 1953).

71 **"Let's have Jewish plays in English"** Shudofsky review.

71 **Rabbis endorsed the play** For example, letter from Rabbi Jacob K. Shankman to Perl, December 9, 1953, APP2:4; reviews cited above by Rabbi Jacob J. Weinstein and rabbi's column in Greenwich Hebrew Institute bulletin.

71 **Zionist Organization of America found in it "particular meaning"** letter from Jacob Dinnes of ZOA–Long Island to Perl, May 21, 1954, APP2:4.

71 **Midge Decter wrote to the *New York Times*** appeared on January 31, 1954; see also "On the Horizon: Belittling Sholom Aleichem's Jews," *Commentary* (January–June 1954): 389–92.

72 **Fishbein . . . "May this herald"** *Sentinel*, January 21, 1954, APPmicro4.

72 **"with the limited Center audiences in mind"** Perl letter to Lewenstein, March 30, 1956, APP2:8.

72 **The promotional materials for *Holiday*** February 5, 1956, APP1:5.

72 **"I have violated"** Perl letter to Lewenstein, March 30, 1956, APP2:8.

73 **"Here are the beginnings"** Patterson Greene, "Aleichem in New Sketches," *Los Angeles Examiner*, March 21, 1957.

73 **announced the New York premiere of *Tevya and His Daughters*** Lewis Funke, "Gossip of the Rialto," *New York Times*, July 14, 1957, 77.

73 **"a new and vital theatre center"** Perl's "rough notes on Banner productions," n.d., APP1:1.

73 **"he is Don Quixote"** . . . **taking the "same care"** promotional material, n.d., APP1:8.

73 **the show had taken in $28,000** press release by Debuskey, September 16, 1957, APP1:8.

73 **budgeted production costs of $19,644** Perl notes on *Tevya*, n.d., APP1:8.

74 **avoid any shred of shrewishness** Anna Vita Berger interview.

74 **avoid exaggeration** Berger interview; parallels Da Silva's notes on *The World of Sholom Aleichem*, letter to Sam Wanamaker, November 26, 1954, APP2:8.

74 **"Rich she'll be"** . . . **"My enemies"** Perl, *Tevya* 10, 38.

74 **"A woman is like a melon"** . . . **"Work is noble"** ibid., 19, 31.

75 **"this is the way God made"** . . . **"If you will it"** ibid., 32, 44.

75 **"He'll serve his time"** . . . **"My Chava, my next"** ibid., 46, 47.

76 **"it is theater that is missing"** Brooks Atkinson, "Theatre: Tevya's Family," *New York Times*, September 17, 1957, 38.

76 **"This is not *our* Tevya"** review by Dr. N. Sverdlin, *Forverts*, September 19, 1957.

76 **"cast, director, playwright"** "Found in the Drama Mailbag," *New York Times*, October 13, 1957, 123.

77 **"plea for racial tolerance"** So Bernstein wrote across the top of the *Romeo and Juliet* text from which he was working on the initial idea that became *West Side Story*; Library of Congress online exhibit, "*West Side Story*: Birth of a Classic," http://www.loc.gov/exhibits/westsidestory/introduction/.

77 **made up some 70 percent of Broadway audiences** *Encylopaedia Judaica*, in its entry on New York City culture, states that "one rough estimate placed Jews at 70 percent of the city's concert and theater audience during the 1950s." Vol. 12, p. 119. Jerusalem Keter Publishing House, 1971; first printing, New York: Macmillan.

78 **"all syrup," "too sweet," and "languid"** Reviews: Walter Kerr, *New York Herald Tribune*; Richard Watts, "Two on the Aisle" column, *New York Post*; Thomas Dash, *Women's Wear Daily*: all September 17, 1957.

78 **"a beginning of a thaw"** Perl letter to Lewenstein, July 7, 1955, APP2:8.

78 **"And yet, my friend"** Perl letter to Ben-Ami, August (n.d.) 1955, APP3:4.

79 **Susskind and . . . Landau, who derided the work as "too Jewish"** Henry Weinstein interview by Alan H. Rosenberg, n.d. I am grateful to Rosenberg for generously sharing his research notes with me. Other material in this chapter about Weinstein's decisions comes from that interview.

79 **Richardson (born Melvin Schwartz) . . . despite Susskind's anxiety** Don Richardson letter to Mrs. Schreibman, National Jewish Archives of Broadcasting, August 14, 1984; from files at NJAB. Thanks to Andrew Ingall for making this material available. Richardson's account of the rehearsals and shooting method come from this letter.

79 **Richardson soon excluded his former student from rehearsals** Weinstein interview with Rosenberg.

80 **"highlight of the show"** "The Play of the Week," *Variety*, December 16, 1959.

80 **"stunning production" of "three one-acters"** reviews: Nick Kenny, "Sholem Aleichem's 'World' a TV Gem," *New York Mirror*, December 15, 1959; Kay Gardella, "Ch. 13's 'Play of Week' a Stunning Production," *Daily News*, December 16, 1959; Jack Gould, "TV:

Aleichem's 'World': Play of the Week Offers 3 One-Acters of Beauty, Compassion, and Protest," *New York Times*, December 15, 1959, 79.

81 **"a victory just to get something"** Lee Grant, phone message for author, July 26, 2010.

81 **Perl credited *World*'s success on *Play of the Week*** Adam Perl interview; Arnold Perl had, in fact, found named writing gigs earlier—he refers to the first in a letter to Lewenstein on July 7, 1955, but he deemed the material "worthless" (APP2:8); *The World of Sholom Aleichem* was one to be proud of.

81 **Jews . . . voted for John F. Kennedy** Shapiro, *A Time for Healing*, 218.

81 **Where one American in five told pollsters** ibid., 39.

82 **"the transcendent place of the 'destruction and renewal' theme"** A. Goren, *Politics*, 190.

82 **advance sale of $1.6 million** Silver, *Our Exodus*, 204.

82 **"the fighting Jew who won't take shit"** Uris letter to his father, June 25, 1956, quoted in Silver, *Our Exodus*, 1.

82 **"They are Jews who fight, who die"** Frank Cantor, "A Second Look at *Exodus*," *Jewish Currents* (November 1959): 20.

82 **Historians . . . point repeatedly to *Exodus*** See, for example, Shapiro, *A Time for Healing*; Silver, *Our Exodus*; and Bartov, *The "Jew" in Cinema: From The Golem to Don't Touch My Holocaust* (Bloomington: Indiana University Press, 2005); Andrew Furman, *Israel through the Jewish-American Imagination* (Albany: SUNY Press, 1997, esp. 39–58); Michelle Mart, *Eye on Israel: How America Came to View Israel as an Ally* (Albany: SUNY Press, 2006, esp. 169–76).

84 **"Since Tevya had the worst of everything"** Brooks Atkinson, "Fun with Words: Tevya Has a Phrase to Solve Anything," *New York Times*, September 29, 1957, 117.

CHAPTER 3: TEVYE LEAVES FOR THE LAND OF BROADWAY

87 **cost of nearly $250,000** cited in Jowitt, *Jerome Robbins*, 304.

88 **"There have been brilliant successes before"** "Tour Analysis," July 3 to November 4, 1959, quoted in Vaill, *Somewhere*, 318, and in Jowitt, *Jerome Robbins*, 310.

88 **"Sir, all my works have been acclaimed"** Robbins testimony, Investigation of Communist Activities in the New York City Area, Part 2, Hearing before the Committee on Un-American Activities, House of Representatives, May 5, 1953, United States Government Printing Office, 1324.

88 **"to even put more"** Doyle, Robbins HUAC testimony, 1325.

88 **"I didn't want to be a Jew"** notes, September 8, 1976, JRPP19:6.

89 **"I affect a discipline over my body & take on another language"** notes, January 23 (no year), JRPP19:4.

89 **"I betrayed them to HUAC"** notes, October 6, 1976, JRPP2:18.

89 **Robbins himself never confirmed the conventional wisdom** See Navasky, *Naming Names*, 75, and letters, Navasky to Robbins, December 26, 1979, and Robbins to Navasky, January 4, 1980, JRPP92:15.

89 **"a display of 100 per cent Americana of 1959"** *Daily Telegraph*, September 8, 1959, in clippings folder, JR124:1.

90 **episode of *This Is Your Life*** See Shandler, *While America Watches*, 30–40.

90 **"Auschwitz with its three million dead!"** Uris, *Exodus*, 85.

90 **Robbins hated it and couldn't wait to leave** Robbins's diary from the trip, JRPP:136.

90 **four full days in town** trip itinerary and Robbins passport, JRPP26:29.

90 **On a chilly morning, they headed east** recounted in Vaill, *Somewhere*, 319.

91 **Rozhanka was neglected** *Yizkerbukh*, "Community of Rozanka."

91 **"tiny town with dirt streets and kerosene lamps"** notes, January 12, 1975, JRPP1:7.

91 **"It was my home, that I belonged to"** notes, January 12, 1975, JRPP1:7.

91 **On the tape, he chokes back a sob** Jowitt, *Jerome Robbins*, 11.

91 **began with a German incursion** *Yizkerbukh*, "Community of Rozanka."

92 **he would have needed a Soviet visa** phone interviews and e-mail exchanges with: Hui Hua Chua, Michigan State University Library, Government Information Online for the US State Department; Terri Miller, Michigan State University Slavic Librarian; Rob Davis, Columbia University Slavic Librarian, August 2 and 3, 2011; and Steven Corssin, curator, Dorot Jewish Division, NYPL, August 4 and 6, 2011. (All concur.)

92 **Robbins's companion didn't recall one** as described by Amanda Vaill; I am grateful to Vaill for discussing her research with me. (Jamie Bauer did not return letters or phone calls requesting an interview.)

92 **"everything was a void"** Kugelmass and Boyarin, *From a Ruined Garden*, 221.

93 **"Oh, Rozhanka, my shtetl, so prized"** *Yizkerbukh*, "Community of Rozanka," 446.

93 **"The 'Anatevka' of our youth"** *Sefer yizkor le-yehudei rudki v-ha-seviva*, 317, quoted in Kugelmass and Boyarin, *From a Ruined Garden*, 9.

93 **the fictional setting in stories by Sholem-Aleichem** A real town called Anatevka (sometimes Anatouka or Hanativka) lay west of Kiev, but except in name, it had no known relation to Sholem-Aleichem's invention.

93 **"a new life on the stage"** Harnick-1 interview.

94 **Bock, born in New Haven** For Bock's biographical background, see Lambert, *To Broadway*, 7–16; Bock, interviewed by Flender, AJC; Ewen, *Composers*, 23ff; Prideaux, *American Musicals: Bock and Harnick*; news clips.

94 **"The turkey has"** Harnick's Thanksgiving poem, "'Fiorello!' and Harnick," Gilbert Millstein, *New York Times*, December 27, 1959; for Harnick's biographical background, see also Bryer and Davison, *Art of the American Musical*, 73–94; interviewed by Flender, AJC; Prideaux, *American Musicals: Bock and Harnick*; author interviews.

94 **"bowled over"** Harnick quoted in Bryer and Davison, *Art of the American Musical*, 76.

95 **"I thought it was extraordinary"** Harnick-1 interview.

97 **"Why don't you write that up?"** Stein interview.

98 **bankrolled by a Philadelphia department store owner** Stein interview.

98 **planted a tape recorder mic among the celery** Murray Schumach, "The Amish and Music," *New York Times*, January 23, 1955, X1.

99 **criticized for failing to find** See Richard P. Cooke, "The Theater: O'Casey to Music," *Wall Street Journal*, March 11, 1959; Brooks Atkinson, "Musical 'Juno,'" *New York Times*, March 15, 1959; Brooks Atkinson, "Theatre: A Musical 'Juno' Arrives," *New York Times*, March 10, 1959.

99 **Stein didn't have either musical consciously in mind** Stein interview.

100 **Harnick loved it** Interviews: Harnick-1; Stein.

100 **"a succession of insufficiently fused fragments"** "Actors' Odyssey Told in 'Roaming Stars'" (no author cited), *New York Times,* January 25, 1930, 7.

100 **But where to find the stories** Stein interview.

100 **In March 1961, Bock, Harnick, and Stein met formally** Diary, JBP23:11.

101 **"wrote them off"** Harnick-1 interview.

101 **"so warm"** Harnick-1 interview.

101 **"Over and above"** unidentified program note or newsletter article, SHP, 3:5.

101 **"It never entered our minds"** Harnick interview.

101 **"happened to be Jewish"** Stein interview.

101 **"never very involved in religion"** Stein interview.

101 **ethnic "juices"** quoted in Altman and Kaufman, *Making of a Musical*, 35.

101 **"I'll go through the motions"** Stein interview.

102 **"Who would be interested"** Stein interview.

102 **"It was pure speculation"** Stein quoted in Leonard Harris, "'Fiddler' on the Concourse," *New York Herald Tribune*, December 28, 1964, 20.

102 **"the next day they were engaged"** Sholem-Aleichem, *Tevye's Daughters*, 37.

102 **vital need to narrate himself through every situation** See Roskies, *Bridge of Longing*, 157ff.

103 **"I wasn't worried about God so much"** Sholem-Aleichem, *Tevye's Daughters*, 160.

104 **numbering sections with a light pencil** Stein showed me the volume during our interview.

104 **"I'm not a stenographer"** Stein interview.

104 **"With pogrom threatening"** Outline, "Old Country II," n.d., SHP3:6.

104 **even Shprintze's suicide** variant "Old Country" outline, n.d. (in which the character based on Sholem-Aleichem's Shprintze is called Leah), SHP3:6.

104 **"light and humorous treatment"** "Suggestions for Chava Sequence," JSP-W29:1.

105 **too dark for the show** Harnick interview-3.

105 **just "felt right"** Stein interview.

105 **less "exotic" names like Rachel and Sarah** "Old Country" outline, n.d., JSP29:1.

105 **"Does Tevye live in Boiberik?"** JBP21:3.

106 **"Move! March, you foolish animal!"** *Tevye* draft, October, 17, 1961, JSP26:1 and JBP21:1.

106 **"pure, unadulterated exposition"** Bock and Harnick note to Stein, n.d., SHP3:6.

107 **Stein's father died** Bock diary, JBP23:11; Harry Stein interview.

108 **"musical guesses"** Stein quoted by Lambert, *To Broadway*, 50.

108 **"Sheldon, here's a little gay folk thing"** London Original Cast Recording bonus track.

108 **"let your daughter take my place, live in my house, carry my keys, wear my clothes"** Sholem-Aleichem, *Tevye's Daughters*, 36.

108 **Harnick quickly affixed the words** Harnick interview-1.

109 **He "felt it was inside me"** quoted in Altman and Kaufman, *Making of a Musical*, 34.

109 **"opportunity to now express myself"** Bock interviewed by Terry Gross on NPR's *Fresh Air*, "Jerry Bock and Shelton Harnick Discuss Writing Music for 'Fiddler on the Roof,'" June 21, 2004.

109 **Bikel maintains . . . Bock siphoned some tunes** Bikel quoted in Margo Lemberger, "A Musical Milkman's Multi-Culti Appeal: 'Sunrise, Sunset' Glows in El Paso as 'Fiddler' Heads Back to Broadway," *Forward*, January 5, 2001, 17. For analytical musical comparison, see Lambert, *To Broadway*, 166–69.

109 **"a certain Yiddish-Russian quality"** London Original Cast Recording bonus track.

109 **Words . . . "crystallized" on the music** Harnick-1 interview.

110 **Negotiations . . . expected a contract** Bock diary, JBP23:11.

110 **he secured exclusive rights** interviews with Nancy Perl and attorney Don Aslan; "Prospectus" for *Tevye* (as *Fiddler* was first called), which describes Perl's prior deal, JRP15:1.

110 **Perl's family would maintain . . . Stein claimed** interviews with Nancy Perl, Rebecca Perl, Adam Perl, Stein.

110 **8.2 percent royalty** Contract, HPP105:4.

110 **The deal was done in July 1962** Bock diary, JBP23:11.

110 **"What will we do when we've run out of Hadassah groups?"** Harnick-1 interview; also Stein interview and many public interviews the authors gave over the years; they loved to tell this story.

110 **Tyrone Guthrie** preface to Kohansky, *Hebrew Theatre*, v.

110 **coded Jewish sensibility** See Andrea Most's pioneering study, *Making Americans*.

111 **"those shows weren't Jewish"** Harnick-2 interview.

111 **"something overall that bothers me"** Prince letter to Bock, July 27, 1962, JBP20:11.

112 **"as foreign to the shtetl"** Prince interview.

112 **"being simply an ethnic folk tale"** Prince interviewed by James Cook for *Forbes*, typed transcript, November 30, 1971, kindly provided by Karen Cook; article, "Making a Business of Show Business," appeared in *Forbes*, February 1, 1972.

112 **"He knew Sholem-Aleichem better than we did"** Harnick-1 interview.

112 **the film director and producer Arthur Penn** In addition to Bock's diary note on August 8, 1962 (JBP23:11), Bock discussed his interest in Landmark symposium, 16.

113 **"side splitting," "uproarious," "marvelously funny"** Howard Taubman review of *Enter Laughing*, *New York Times*, March 1, 1963.

113 **"three snappy numbers"** "New Bil and Cora Baird Puppet Show, 'Man in the Moon,' offered at Biltmore Theater." *New York Times*, April 12, 1963, 29.

114 **"Also, have you read *Another Country*** Robbins to Bernstein, July 25, 1963, JRPP72:14.

114 **On August 15, Bock and Harnick came** Robbins 1963 appointment book, JRPP567:3.

114 **On the twentieth, his lawyer called** message from Bill Fitelson, Robbins phone log, JRPP567:5.

114 **"something I feel deeply related to"** Robbins to Rodgers and Leland Hayward, August 27, 1963, JRP510:25.

114 **The next day he heard back** August 28, 1963, JRPP113:6.

114 **"I'm going to do a musical"** Robbins cable to Ruth Mitchell, August 23, 1963, displayed in "New York Story: Jerome Robbins and His World" exhibit at the New York Public Library for the Performing Arts, curated by Lynn Garafola, March 25 to June 28, 2008.

114 **"a musical which should really star my father"** Robbins letter to Nancy Keith, August 27, 1963, JRPP97:12.

115 **"He becomes obsessed by his demons"** Harnick-1 interview.

117 **"nought about the religion"** Robbins notes, JRPP23:5.

117 **books Robbins bought** inventory, JRP5:1.

117 **Robbins had already put in some calls** phone logs, JRPP567:5.

117 *Hebrew Lesson* appears in the background of a portrait of Robbins at his desk, taken by Henri Cartier-Bresson for a *Queen* magazine photo essay feature, August 2, 1961, Robbins clipping file, JRP4:12.

117 **"old wizened, decrepit"** Robbins notes for the "Poppa piece," January 1975, JRPP107:12.

118 **"The play must celebrate"** JRP13:10.

119 **"our guide and our Bible"** Robbins quoted by Jerry Tallmer, "Tokyo-Bound Robbins Bones Up on Far East," *New York Post*, December 13, 1964.

119 **purchased at least six copies** Robbins's assistant placed orders with the *Forward* for copies on February 3, 6, and 11, 1964, JRP16:1.

119 **"falsifying the world of Sholem Aleichem"** Brustein, *Seasons of Discontent*, 169.

119 **"being in love with the material"** Robbins notes, September 4, 1963, JRP13:10.

119 **"keep the guts"** JRP13:10.

120 **As "wonderful"** Robbins correspondence with Stravinsky quoted in Vaill, *Somewhere*, 363.

120 **Chagall had talked** Marc Chagall, *"Mayn ershte bagegenish mit shloyme mikhoels,"* *Yidish kultur*, January 1, 1944; also Waife-Goldberg, *My Father*, 157–58.

120 **"fantasy & poetry"** Robbins draft letter to Harold Clurman, n.d., JRP16:43.

120 **"In his fantasy atmosphere, particulars"** JRP13:10.

120 **"We would be very honored"** . . . **"MERCI VOTRE"** JRP5:4.

121 **The painter was not simply making an excuse . . . his annoyance** See letters from Chagall to Bernard and Becky Rels, October 12, 1963, describing his disappointment that he could not accept Robbins's invitation and his irked amazement that Robbins would use Chagall's drawings against his will, in Harshav, *Marc Chagall and His Times*, 894–95.

121 **The fiddler sawing out a sound track** Boris Aronson notes from conversation with Robbins, October 16, 1963, BAP37:5.

121 **Prince kept his word** contract dated October 15, 1963, HPP105:4.

121 **Boris Aronson was waiting** interview with Lisa Aronson.

121 **The call came** Robbins phone message log, JRP:567:3.

121 **Aronson was born** first draft of "A Designer's Notebook," n.d., BAP9:1. See also Rich and Aronson, *Theater Art of Boris Aronson*, 3–30.

121 **designers "must be reborn with each show"** "Notes on Designing Musicals," typescript, August 16, 1974, BAP9:14.

122 **"By the time I was fourteen"** quoted in Rich and Aronson, *Theater Art*, 5; also BAP9:1.

122 **"home-sweet-home calendar art"** quoted in Rich and Aronson, *Theater Art of Boris Aronson*, 8.

122 **"contemporary Jewish graphic art"** "Imaginary Interview of Aronson by Aronson," typescript, BAP9:13.

122 **"tonal juiciness"** typescript translation of Aronson's monograph on Chagall, BAP9:6.

122 **Aronson named his son Marc, after the artist** Marc Aronson interview.

122 **"with awkward baggage, crowded emotions"** BAP9:10.

123 **When he met the big, solemn man** Robbins appointment calendar, JRPP567:3.

123 **Prince was unsure** Lisa Aronson interview; Harnick-3 interview.

123 **the Storm King Art Center** the trip was described in interviews with Lisa Aronson, Hal Prince, and Frank Rich.

123 **"a traveling circus"** Aronson notes on *J.B.*, n.d., BAP9:5.

123 **Marxist parable at the ARTEF (Arbeter Teatr Farband), *Jim Kooperkop*** See Edna Nahshon, *Yiddish Proletarian Theatre*.

123 **But it was his design** Lisa Aronson interview. She and others remembered this set piece from *Stempenyu*, but it was a house Aronson had made for another Schwartz production, *Tenth Commandment* (1926), that had a house that opened up more like the one in *Fiddler*. Neither is listed on the Storm King program for the exhibit, which showed work from 1930 forward, but perhaps some were there or the team saw these designs at Aronson's studio and conflated that display with the exhibit.

124 **"to become men and women"** Manumit School early brochure, n.d. http://manumitschool.com/ManumitDocs/Brochures/pagebrochure.htm.

124 **"was how to walk into a chicken house"** Rosenthal, *Magic of Light*, 12.

124 **"used courtesy"** ibid., 34.

124 **"Dancers live in light"** ibid., 117.

124 **"the play—the playwright's play"** ibid., 59.

125 **Aronson, who resented her at first** ibid., 34, and Lisa Aronson interview.

125 **"technician and dreamer"** Boris Aronson quoted in Rosenthal, *Magic of Light*, 72.

125 **"Bring six to half, darling"** Winthrop Sargeant profile of Rosenthal, "Please, Darling, Bring Three to Seven," *New Yorker*, February 4, 1956, 33–59.

125 **lined her up on September 12** Robbins phone log message: "Jean Rosenthal is set— she's delighted to do the show," JRPP567:3.

125 **"all black and my hair in a bun"** Ellen Lampert-Gréaux, "Patricia Zipprodt: One of

Our Greatest Costume Designers, Reflects on an Astonishingly Varied Career," *Entertainment Design*, March 1994, 30–35.

125 **"I saw them as pure painting with fabric"** Laurel Graeber, "Stage Presence: A Costume Designer for 30 Years, Patricia Zipprodt has Moved Aggressively from One Stage to the Next. Now She has Broadway All Sewn Up," *DNR the Magazine*, May 1986, 20.

125 **"It wasn't like I was seeing yellow"** quoted in Lampert-Gréaux, "Patricia Zipprodt," 31.

125 **The effect "swept me away"** quoted in Graeber, 20.

126 **"how to create the structure for anything"** quoted in Lampert-Gréaux, "Patricia Zipprodt," 31.

126 **"gone over eight thousand reds"** quoted in Lawrence, *Dance with Demons*, 304.

127 **"shook him until his hat fell off"** ibid.

127 **She was to read the Sholem-Aleichem stories** Zipprodt notes, PZP10:6.

128 **Rothbort had traveled** For Rothbort's background with work samples and news clips, see www.samuelrothbort.com; Cabon (Rothbort granddaughter) interview.

128 **"Don't romanticize the characters"** Robbins's notes to Zipprodt, JR13:11.

129 **"the guts and toughness of the people"** Robbins's "notes on the score," JRP5:4.

129 **"a rural unsophisticated area"** JRP13:11.

129 **"combine elements of fantasy and reality"** BAP35:5.

130 **together they made up less than 10 percent** There are no direct figures for 1963. Estimates range from 4 percent (Charles Liebman, "Orthodoxy in American Jewish Life," in *The American Jewish Yearbook*, 1965) to 11 percent by 1970 after a resurgence, according to *The American Jewish Yearbook* of 1971.

130 **Hasidism represented a radical challenge** This idea is argued by Samuel C. Heilman in *Defenders of the Faith* and his Foreword to Beclove-Shalin, *New World Hasidim*, xi–xv. See also Jack Kugelmass, "Jewish Icons: Envisioning the Self in Images of the Other," in *Jews and Other Differences: The New Jewish Cultural Studies*, ed. D. Boyarin and J. Boyarin (Minneapolis: University of Minnesota Press, 1997), 30–53.

130 **Lapson took Zipprodt** Lapson expenses list, July 13, 1964, HPP113:7.

131 **"with best wishes"** Lapson offprints, JPR13:2.

131 **Robbins headed across town** Robbins phone message and appointment books, JRP567:2,3.

131 **Their dancing came as a revelation** Harnick-1 interview.

131 **Robbins sent Lapson a big bouquet of flowers** Lapson thank-you message, phone log, JRP567:3.

132 **"I am a friend of the Rabbinical families"** Lapson letter to Rabbi Tennenbaum, October 21, 1963, JRP5:3.

132 **"virile ferocity"** Robbins draft letter to Clurman, JRP16:43.

132 **she'd call with reminders** Robbins phone message log, JRP567:3.

132 **For a fee of $500** Lapson expenses list, HPP113:7.

132 **"My great wonder"** Robbins draft letter to Clurman, JRP16:43.

133 **"the man balances a bottle"** Lapson, "Jewish Dances of Eastern and Central Europe," *International Folk Music Journal* (n.d.): 59; offprint in JRP13:1.

133 **"Mr. Redbeard"** Lapson phone message, Robbins log, JRP568:1.

133 **"intense research"** Robbins letter to Mary Hunter Wolf, October 22, 1963, JRPP122:6.

133 **Stein felt his own family background** Stein interview.

134 **"Money is the world's curse"** Samuel, *World*, 172.

134 **"You want some Jewish customs"** letters to Harnick from his mother and from his aunt Chone, n.d., SHP3:5.

134 **"feel more Jewish"** Harnick-3 interview.

134 **"I knew who I was"** quoted in Altman and Kaufman, *Making of a Musical*, 25.

134 **"feel my father's feelings so strongly"** Robbins notes, JRPP19:4.

134 **"juggling and bending"** Robbins notes, JRPP2:18.

135 **"both awed and scornful"** Robbins notes, JRPP19:5.

135 **"laid open for me"** Robbins notes, JRPP19:6.

135 **Stein had restored** This draft can be found in JSP-W26:6.

136 **Robbins had complaints** Harnick-2 interview.

136 **"a race with time"** Zborowski and Herzog, *Life is with People*, 39.

137 **"We've Never Missed a Sabbath Yet"** unused lyrics folder generously provided by Sheldon Harnick; and bonus track on London cast recording.

137 **"darts from broom to oven"** *Life is with People*, 39.

138 **"What is this show about?"** . . . **like a district attorney** Harnick-1 interview.

138 **"That's 'The Previous Adventures'"** Harnick, Stein interviews.

139 **"a pair of comfortable old shoes"** "The Goldbergs March On," *Life*, April 25, 1949, 59.

139 **"about the dissolution of a way of life"** Harnick interview; Bock tells this story on the *Fresh Air* interview and the authors repeated it on many occasions.

139 **"quiet, growling presence"** Prince interview.

139 **Right away, an image took shape** . . . **"I'll begin it with"** Harnick-2 interview.

140 **"Shtetl means my community"** JRP13:10.

CHAPTER 4: IT TAKES A SHTETL

141 **Pendleton auditioned seven times** Pendleton interview.

142 **October to January, Robbins saw hundreds of actors** audition sheets, SHP2:8, JRP13:3, 4, 5.

143 **"Golde: wife of Tevye"** "cast breakdowns," n.d., HP108:1.

143 **he might attend a voice lesson** Merlin, Aberdeen interviews.

143 **Stuart Damon** Altman and Kaufman, *Making of a Musical*, 79.

143 **a Baptist who had gone to a Catholic boarding school** Tanya Everett interview.

144 **"Marvelous. Sings well"** SHP2:8.

144 **audition on Friday, November 22** Merlin interview; audition sheets, JRP13:3.

144 **Jackie Kennedy . . . told *Life*'s Theodore H. White** "For President Kennedy: An Epilogue," *Life*, December 6, 1963, 158–59.

145 **Plymouth Rock to Ellis Island** Jacobson, *Roots Too*.

145 **the Anti-Defamation League** "Kennedy Will Get Award by League," *New York Times*, October 21, 1962.

145 **auditions resumed on November 26** Robbins calendar, JRP567:3.

146 **Jackie Kennedy came to see *Fiddler*** message from her theater companion, Kitty Hart; Robbins phone message log, November 25, 1964, JR568:1. See also an item about Kennedy's attendance in Leonard Lyons's column, "The Lyons Den," *New York Post*, November 24, 1964.

146 **"ordinary" quality** Harnick-2 interview; Robbins quoted in Robert Kotlowitz, "Corsets, Corned Beef and Choreography," *Show*, December 1964.

146 **arrangement with the Hebrew Actors' Union** phone message log, JRP567; audition sheets, JRP5:2.

146 **"lovable schnooks"** annotated script, JRP10:1.

146 **since "the part is written very Jewish"** Stein letter to Prince, HPP101:6.

146 **jottings on audition sheets** SHP2:8, JRP5:2.

147 **"Don't use your conscious past"** Stella Adler quoted in *New York Times* obit, December 22, 1992.

147 **Robbins's undated notes from the Adler sessions** JRPP1:10.

147 **combine the blustery certitude** See Altman and Kaufman, *Making of a Musical*, 78.

147 **scores of eager young men** audition schedules, JRP567:3.

147 **Fielding had decided** Prince message to Robbins, March 9, 1964, JRP368:1.

148 **"insisted on examining"** Stein interview.

148 **Bock and Harnick had also seen him in** *The World of Sholom Aleichem* Harnick-2 interview.

148 **Da Silva's "natural voice"** Harnick-3 interview.

149 **the actor never auditioned for Robbins** audition sheets and Harnick-3 interview.

149 **The actor's family recounts** The Mostel biographies (citing the same or no source) all say Stein brought Mostel the script while he was in *Forum*; his sons Josh and Tobias Mostel affirmed this in interviews; Stein denied it in an interview.

149 **"roar with laughter"** quoted in Brown, *Zero Mostel*, 7.

149 **"Would somebody tell Zero that this show will be good for him?"** Pendleton, Aberdeen interviews.

149 **authors played the score for Mostel** Harnick-3 interview; Bock, interviewed by Nancy Hamburger Sureck, videotape.

149 **by the sixteenth** Robbins phone log, JRP567:3.

150 **the mink coat** Tobias Mostel interview.

150 **Friends, though, remember Mostel's excitement** Debuskey interview.

150 **"greatest Yiddish character"** Mostel quoted in Richard Christiansen, "Mostel in Excelsis Enlivens a Blossoming Hit," *Chicago Daily News*, August 7, 1964, 4.

150 **$4,000 a week against 10 percent** *Tevye* prospectus, JRP15:1; in *Contradictions*, Prince says the payroll for the cast, including Mostel, was $15,000 per week; 107.

150 **"I'm sorry that it hasn't worked out"** HPP108:5.

151 **might object to his number one fix-it man** Mostel and Gilford, *170 Years*, 9; Prince, *Contradictions*, 94–95; Prince interview.

151 **"Naming names . . . is not Jewish"** quoted in Brown, *Zero Mostel*, 126.

152 **"crude, vulgar, but healthy and satisfied"** Robbins notes, October 8, 1976, JRPP2:18.

152 **roguishly buttered a roll** legendary incident referred to in Dora Jane Hamblin, "Zero," *Life*, December 4, 1964, 108–18.

152 **"Could you imagine my father"** quoted in Brown, *Zero Mostel*, 4.

153 **Harvard lecture** transcript of "The Art of Comedy," delivered May 21, 1962, Z&KMP9:10.

154 **one Broadway reporter** The story appeared in an article by Ernio Hernandez in *Playbill* (February 26, 2004) on the occasion of the 2004 Broadway revival of *Fiddler*; it quotes *Playbill* archivist Louis Botto saying Robbins practically had to drag Mostel into the theater. The story was picked up from there and retold in Jim Brochu's one-man show, *Zero Hour*. In interviews, Josh Mostel, Harnick, and Prince expressed enormous doubt about the plausibility of this story. In a phone interview, Botto did not remember his source for it; he simply said it had been "in all the papers." A search of New York dailies and *Variety* did not produce any trace of it.

154 **"He has a mother?"** Josh Mostel interview.

154 **Mostel sustained a lifelong grudge** Josh Mostel interview.

154 **his father praying privately** Tobias Mostel interview; Josh Mostel said he never saw this.

155 **his name derived from Tevye** Tobias Mostel interview.

155 **Fred Coe had neglected to raise** Harnick-1, Prince interviews; Krampner, *The Man in the Shadows*.

156 **cut back to 12 percent** contract, June 23, 1964, HPP105:4.

156 **"preliminary prospectus"** copies in JRP15:1; HPP106:4.

156 **"opera, play & ballet"** Robbins notes, September 14, 1963, JRP13:10.

156 **the prospectus was completed** JRP15:1, HP106:4.

157 **nearly 150 investors** JRP15:1, HPP106:4.

157 **"The resolution is the decision . . . move on to the new world"** April 16, 1964, prospectus, 6; see Wolitz, "The Americanization of Tevye."

158 **Robbins met Aronson and Zipprodt frequently—often several times a week—and separately** phone message and appointment books for 1964, JRP568:1, 2, 3; Lisa Aronson interview.

158 **She called Aronson . . . "intuitively related in style"** Lisa Aronson interview.

159 **"Colors bump into one another"** Zipprodt quoted in Tom Topor, "Confessions of a Costume Designer," *New York Post*, October 15, 1978.

160 **the evocation of the master's painterly style** Aronson, "Notes on Designing Musicals," BAP9:14; Lisa Aronson interview.

160 **Robbins couldn't decide . . . "height of the house isn't right"** Lisa Aronson, Prince interviews.

161 **more weddings, more reading, more poring over pictures . . . Vishniac's book** Robbins phone message logs and appointment books for 1964, JRP568:1.

161 **leaving messages every day or two** Robbins phone message logs, JRP568.

161 **"mess around with"** Robbins letter to Nancy Keith, January 15, 1964, JRPP97:12.

161 **return flight was due in New York at 1:55** Friday, January 31, 1964, in appointment book, JRP568:2, 3.

161 **"The drama of the play"** JRP13:10.

162 **"Underlying all his actions"** JRP13:10.

162 **"Her performances astound"** "Barbra: Some Notes," December 22, 1965, JRPP24:14.

163 **March 18 read-through of *Tevye* at the Hellinger Theater** Robbins appointment calendar, JRP568:2, 3.

163 **"not written within the time and tempo"** Robbins letter to Stein, April 3, 1964, JRP13:11.

163 **About twenty actors** memo from Hal Prince office, March 16, 1964, HPP105:7.

163 **"Good evening. My name is Tevye"** script dated November 17, 1963, in JSP-W27 and n.d. in JBP21:5. (There is no dated script in the archives between this one and the rehearsal script.)

163 **writers felt pleased. Robbins said little** Harnick-3 interview.

163 **"treasure of the season"** Robbins, "Production Notes on *Fiddler on the Roof* and Letters to Friends and Associates," audio recording, *MGZTL 4-3119 JRP, NYPL-PA. Transcript, amended by Robbins, in JRP13:11.

163 **"book changes"** and subsequent quotations from this document and cover letter, JRP13:11.

163 **"notes on the score"** and subsequent quotations from this document and cover letter, JRP5:4.

166 **"Please, Reb Robbins"** letter from Bock and Harnick to Robbins, n.d., JRP5:4.

166 **cut an amusing song for Lazar about "a butcher's soul"** compare spring 1964 script; Harnick-3 interview.

166 **composer, Albert Hague, had boasted** Stein interview.

167 **Holding tryouts in town** Richard F. Shepard, "'Café Crown' Opens on April 17 after Presenting 30 Previews," *New York Times*, April 9, 1964.

167 **more than 42 percent of America's Jews still lived in the New York metropolitan area** *American Jewish Yearbook* 65 (1964), 3.

167 **fumbling their lines . . . failing to keep his wig on straight** review of *Café Crown* in *Life*, May 15, 1964.

167 **"harmonious interfaith relations"** Jack Gould, "3 Faiths Discuss 'Deputy' with TV: Leaders Concerned over Coverage of Play's Opening," *New York Times*, February 20, 1964.

168 **he offered the role of Golde** Harnick-2, Prince interviews; Altman and Kaufman, *Making of a Musical*, 82.

168 **Harnick thought she was "great"** audition notes, SHP2:8; Harnick-2 interview.

169 **too American** Harnick-2 interview; Altman and Kaufman, *Making of a Musical*, 80.

169 **He took a chance on young Leonard Frey** letter from Frey to Robbins, October 15, 1963, JRP5:5.

169 **Robbins didn't want Perchik to be "too handsome"** Altman and Kaufman, *Making of a Musical*, 78.

170 **some came dressed** Senn interview.

170 **"The Russians are coming"** Bodin interview.

170 **these were poor Jewish folk** Aberdeen, Bodin, Kazan, Modelski, Senn interviews.

170 **"You've never seen such a motley crew"** Prince interview.

170 **"Don't ever ask me"** telegrams exchanged between Robbins and Prince, May 18, 1964, HPP105:6.

170 **Prince coolly replied** Prince interview.

171 **Prince urged Robbins . . . hurried to see the drawings** Robbins phone message log and appointment books, JRP568:1, 2, 3.

171 **what was the show** JRP13:11; JSP-W27, 29:2.

171 **Prince scanned the list** Harnick-3, Prince, Stein interviews.

CHAPTER 5: RAISING THE ROOF

172 **circulation of 7.5 million** Nielsen Media Service stats quoted in Peter Bart, "Publisher Drops Nielsen Service," *New York Times*, April 12, 1963.

172 **"The Vanishing American Jew"** Thomas B. Morgan, *Look*, May 1964, 43–46.

172 **"the vitality"** "Vanishing," *Look*, 43.

172 **third-generation** *American Jewish Year Book*, October 1963.

173 **"The liberalism of the Jewish parent"** Sklare, "Intermarriage and the Jewish Future," *Commentary*, April 1964, 52.

174 **the contemporary parallels Robbins found** in an interview with the *New York Herald Tribune*, June 11, 1964. Also, Prince interview.

174 **He started the work** Aberdeen, Everett, Prince interviews.

175 **"What the hell does all this have to do"** Aberdeen interview.

175 **"Nobody ever complained to Jerry"** Prince interview.

175 **"make a shtetl out of them"** Robbins quoted in Kotlowitz, "Corsets," 91.

175 **"like one of those figures"** Pendleton interview.

175 **"You didn't do"** Merlin interview.

176 **He'd blurt out Actors Studio words** Lonne Elder report.

176 **he helps her lay down a tablecloth** Merlin, Pendleton interviews.

177 **"A couple of weddings"** Pendleton interview.

178 **"two degrees below hostile"** Stein interview.

178 **"Mostel likes to test you"** Robbins quoted in Kotlowitz, "Corsets," 91.

178 **Mostel touched the doorpost** Tobias Mostel, Harnick-3 interviews; oft-repeated lore.

178 **When Bock and Harnick wrote** Harnick-1 interview, Bock and Harnick interview by Terry Gross on *Fresh Air*, June 21, 2004.

179 **"little hoard" . . . "a large house with a tin roof"** Sholem-Aleichem, *Tevye's Daughters*, 6, 9.

180 **"dream-tasting spiral"** Richard Gilman, "Hail the Conquering Zero," *Newsweek*, October 19, 1964, 95.

180 **"He can do the same thing four ways"** Stein quoted in Gilman, "Hail," 95.

181 **"bagful of water"** Robbins quoted in Kotlowitz, "Corsets," 91.

181 **simply a song** Harnick-1 interview.

181 **"the butchest dancers"** Aberdeen interview.

181 **those playing Jews** Aberdeen, Bayes interviews; *Fiddler on the Roof Choreographic Manual.*

182 **Robbins clapped his hands** Pendleton, Modelski, Senn interviews; *Fiddler on the Roof Choreographic Manual*, 224.

184 **"accumulated" . . . "kept rolling"** Bock in Landmark Symposium, 19.

185 **"are not 'characters'"** Robbins notes on costumes for Zipprodt, JRP13:11.

185 **vegetable graters, wood rasps** Zipprodt notes, "Principles of Ageing," PZP53:1.

185 **"bleach and overdye"** Zipprodt notes in "Costume Bible," PZP53:2.

186 **outrageous cost of $9,000 . . . "biggest monsters"** memo from Prince office objecting to ten trailers at $896.90 each, July 30, 1964, HPP105:9.

186 **"those very mild pickups"** Robbins phone message, JRP568:1.

186 **Fisher Theater's lush lobby** Luzenski and Levin, *Fisher Theatre*; Lynn, *National Trust Guide*, 105–7; "Fisher Building Interior," June 2, 2009, Detroitfunk, http://detroitfunk.com/?p=1849; and "Fisher Building Damage," June 3, 2009, http://detroitfunk.com/?p=1852.

187 **"milk towns"** Robbins office note, July 16, 2004, JRP568:1.

187 **"The subscription in Detroit is hefty"** Prince letter to Robbins, February 6, 1964, HPP108:1.

188 **"we could die in Detroit"** Harnick-1 interview.

188 **"You should see this ladies' room!"** Elder, "Observer's Report," 12.

188 **"easy to assume"** Harrington, *Other America*, 4.

189 **"What are you going to do" . . . "Whatever it is"** Elder, "Observer's Report," 17.

190 **"They were inching out backwards"** Harnick-2 interview.

190 **"Well, *we* like it"** Stein interview.

190 **"we got through"** Duane Bodin interview.

190 **"Dear, Sweet Sewing Machine"** lyrics provided by Harnick; Harnick-1, Pendleton interviews.

191 **"a feeling that we might have something very special"** Stein quoted in William Glover, "Fiddler on the Roof on Top the Longest," *The Record*, July 12, 1971.

191 **"Everything is ordinary"** Tew, "Legit Tryout: Fiddler on the Roof," *Variety*, July 28, 1964, 2.

191 **"uncommonly fine musical"** Jay Carr quoted in Prince letter to investors, July 28, 1964, HPP120:4.

191 **upbeat letter to investors** July 28, 1964, HPP120:4.

192 **"receiving good response"** "Detroit Responding to 'Fiddler on the Roof,'" *New York Times*, August 8, 1964, 10.

193 **"agonizingly long" . . . "hell to go to"** Bodin, Kazan interviews.

194 **innocent, even pretty** Everett, Aberdeen, Ponazecki interviews.

194 **"that 'golly–oh gee shucks' business"** Elder, "Observer's Report," 15.

194 **"You are not going to Coney Island"** ibid., 23.

195 **"Are you out of your mind?"** Harnick-1 interview.

195 **"what a lot of fun it is"** Prince letter to Robbins, June 18, 1964, HPP105:6.

196 **"his world begins to tilt"** Robbins notes, n.d., JRP13:10.

197 **"the show died"** Stein in Landmark Symposium, 23.

197 **"If he takes it out altogether"** Harnick-1, 2 interviews.

197 **"It was a mistake"** Harnick-2 interview.

198 **Mostel was channeling** Tobias Mostel interview.

198 **five minutes' worth of lazzo** Harnick-2 interview.

199 **threw new pages** Elder, "Observer's Report," 22.

199 **"The man is a genius"** Pendleton, Everett interviews.

199 *Fiddler* **pulled its first hint of profit** HPP120:6 and Prince interview.

199 **"Suddenly all the composition"** Pendleton interview.

200 **Robbins was faring even worse** Kazan, Pendleton, Bodin, Harnick interviews.

200 **"bête noire number 2"** title on set of unused lyrics supplied by Harnick and Harnick–2 interview.

201 **"Give me klutzy!"** Bodin interview.

201 **Attle, was knocked out** Bayes, Aberdeen, Everett, Pendleton interviews.

202 **he filled out the quitting notice** Bodin interview.

202 **"unsophisticated audience" . . . "electrifying"** Rich interview.

202 **"Joy, there is such joy"** Leo Sullivan, " 'Fiddler on the Roof,' Is a New Musical to 'Enjoy, Enjoy,' " *Washington Post*, August 28, 1964.

203 **His understudy, Paul Lipson** Aberdeen, Bodin, Everett, Kazan, Prince interviews.

203 **people in the lobby** Elder, "Observer's Report," 28.

203 **Lipson . . . played the role more than two thousand times** Paul Lipson obituary, *New York Times*, May 5, 1996.

203 **"you may just not be able to find"** "National's 'Fiddler' a Winner," *Star*, August 28, 1964.

204 **"Last night during the wedding scene"** Pendleton interview.

205 **Convy had lobbied . . . "Miracle of Miracles" fitting** Pendleton, Harnick-2, Prince interviews.

205 **"What's the problem, Austin?"** Pendleton interview.

206 **"over here a few"** "When Messiah Comes" unused lyrics from Harnick, and bonus track on *Fiddler* Broadway Deluxe Collector's Edition.

206 **"From the stage he couldn't see"** Harnick-2 interview.

206 **doctrinal difference** S. A. Lewis made this point in a letter in response to an article of mine about *Fiddler* in the *Forward*, "Letters," September 15, 2006.

207 **"without any constructing elements"** Robbins draft letter to Clurman, JRP16:43.

207 **"The wedding scene is going to be wonderful"** Robbins, notes on Tevye, JRP13:11.

208 **What are Tevye and Golde** *doing?* Harnick-1 interview.

209 **"This is the dance"** Bayes, Aberdeen, Bodin, Prince interviews; *Fiddler on the Roof Choreographic Manual.*

209 **"You're working yourself into a state of joy"** Bayes interview.

210 **when choreographing "The Small House of Uncle Thomas"** Eileen Blumenthal, "In the Wings, 'Noh, Noh, Nanette?' " *New York Times*, April 26, 1987, H5; and Eileen Blumenthal, "How Thai Is It?," *American Theater*, July–August 1996, 6–7.

211 **"Any man who can do that"** Aronson quoted in Altman and Kaufman, *Making of a Musical*, 68.

213 **a new generation of Pilgrims** Wolitz, "Americanization of Tevye."

214 **"swirling away"** Everett Bagot interview.

214 **"some real excitement . . . enormous"** ibid.

215 **"We're not going to put it in"** Pendleton interview.

215 **"gamboling on the green"** Prince interview.

216 **"For the only time in my life"** Harnick-2 interview.

216 **"serene quietness"** Elder, "Observer's Report," 31.

216 **"We came to love our village"** Modelski interview.

216 **break-a-leg telegrams** JRP5:7,8,9; SHP5:14; JBP20:7.

216 **gifts they exchanged** JRP545:14; SHP5:14; Lisa Aronson, Harnick-2 interviews.

217 **troupe gave Robbins a white yarmulke** JRP13:19.

217 **Mostel . . . opened his mouth** Merlin, Modelski interviews.

217 **"like somebody tiptoeing"** Modelski interview.

218 **He had never been so certain** Prince interview.

218 **Robbins was startled** Altman and Kaufman, *Making of a Musical*, 106.

219 **"a picturesque twist session"** "Frank Farrell's New York by Day: The Play Was the Thing, Dinner's Forced to Wait," *New York World Telegram*, September 23, 1964.

219 **Kate Mostel . . . jitterbug with John C. Attle** Tobias Mostel interview.

219 **her husband whirled around the floor** Joanne Stang, "At Home with Tevye, Tevye at Home," *New York Times*, October 4, 1964, X1.

219 **Kerr accused the creators** *New York Herald Tribune*, September 23, 1964; *Fiddler* clips, NYPL-PA.

219 **Prince took the mic** Prince, Pendleton interviews.

219 **"didn't want to see Jerry"** Pendleton interview.

219 **Taubman declared** *New York Times,* September 23, 1964, 56; *Fiddler* clips, NYPL-PA.

219 **Roberta Senn wrote to her parents** Senn interview; Senn letter to parents, n.d., generously shared from her personal files.

219 **"There was something in this show"** Harnick interview.

219 **By February, Prince was sending distributions to investors** box office report, February 20, 1965, notes $45,000 in distributions made with the report, JRP16:6.

221 **Joe Stein loved to tell** Harnick maintains that the story of the Japanese producer is apocryphal but acquired the force of gospel. E-mail correspondence with author.

221 **"as you must know"** Dolan letter to Robbins, September 26, 1964, JRP5:29.

221 **"Broadwayized"** N. Sverdlin, *"Sholem-aleykems 'helden' in brodvey musikal,"* *Der Tog Morgen Zhurnal*, September 25, 1964.

221 **"Jewish America's most beautiful"** Chaim Ehrenreich, *"Sholem-aleykhems 'Tevye der milkhiker' af brodvey,"* *Forverts*, September 26, 1964.

221 **"laid open"** Robbins, autobiographical notes, JRPP19:6.

222 **"a glory for my father"** Robbins, autobiographical notes, JRPP1:18.

222 **"This is the first seder"** Spiro to Prince, April 12, 1968, HPP109:1.

222 **Fiersteins** Fierstein interview.

223 **"The play was the life of my grandparents"** Belle Miller to Paul Lipson, August 30, 1966, HPP109:3.

223 **"just such a little town in Russia"** Schwartz to Prince, November 30, 1964, HPP109:4.

223 **how an actor should properly pronounce "Kiev"** letters to Prince, 1964ff., HPP109:3, 4.

223 **900th New York performance . . . profit of 352 percent** press release of November 22, 1966, Sol Jacobson and Lewis Harmon, clippings, "*Fiddler*."

224 *Newsweek* **. . . paid circulation 1.6 million** Number cited in "Relinquishing of Editorial Control at Time, Inc., by Henry Luce Marks End of Era," John Lee, *New York Times*, April 17, 1964, 55; and in a display ad for *Newsweek* in the *New York Times*, March 30, 1964, 46.

224 **wedding bands . . . expected** Hans Jenny (bandleader/booker) interview.

224 **"funny kind of tenderness" his old teacher** Robbins notes, JRP542:8.

224 **letters objected** HPP109:2, 3, 4.

224 **Maurice Samuel issued a public protest** described in a letter from Stein to Robbins, November 28, 1966, displayed in "New York Story: Jerome Robbins and His World," exhibit at the New York Public Library for the Performing Arts, curated by Lynn Garafola, March 25–June 28, 2008.

224 **"The real intention"** Prince letters to complainants, HRP109:2.

225 **"simple, gentle man" . . ."for the sake of the show"** Stein letter to Prince, displayed in "New York Story" exhibit.

225 **"that rabbi problem again"** Robbins letter to Sandor, December 9, 1966, displayed in "New York Story" exhibit.

226 **"strong and appealing"** Prince letter to Robbins, May 26, 1965, JRP5:16.

226 **"It makes me especially angry"** Prince letter to Robbins, September 19, 1966, JRP5:16.

226 **"It is true that I am an actress"** Marisse letter to Robbins, JRP5:16.

226 **Marisse complained to Actors' Equity** Douglas Watt, "Actress to Take Jewish Holiday Case to Board," *Los Angeles Times*, October 6, 1966, D16.

226 **"of all things"** "'Fiddler' Drops Girl Absent on Holy Days," *New York Post*, n.d., clippings.

227 **Lyons ran a brief item** *New York Post*, n.d., *Fiddler* clippings.

227 **Letters to Prince's office** HPP109:3.

227 **"The Imperial is not a Temple"** Prince letter to Lyons, September 29, 1965, HPP109:3.

227 **southpaw's refusal to pitch** For discussion of Koufax's contract, likely activity that Yom Kippur, and impact, see Jane Leavy, *Sandy Koufax: A Lefty's Legacy* (New York: HarperCollins, 2002).

228 **affiliation with synagogues . . . from 30 percent . . . to nearly 60 percent** Shapiro, *A Time for Healing*, 148.

229 **standing ovations eight times a week** Le Roy interview.

229 **"cutest shtetl"** Irving Howe, "Tevye on Broadway," *Commentary*, November 1964, 74.

230 **"I am enormously gratified"** Stein program note for first Israel production, ITA-TA.

CHAPTER 6: THE OLD COUNTRY IN THE OLD-NEW LAND

233 **Almagor . . . received an urgent call** Almagor interview. All quotes from Almagor below from interview unless otherwise indicated.

233 **not until Godik came along** See *Waiting for Godik*.

234 **A mural and poem** See Emily Alice Katz, "It's the Real World After All: The American-Israel Pavilion-Jordan Pavilion Controversy at the New York World's Fair, 1964–1965," *American Jewish History* 91:1 (March 2003): 129–55.

235 **the new "muscle Jews"** so named in 1898 by the early Zionist activist Max Nordau. For this concept and for discussion of the rejection of Diaspora, see Segev, *Seventh Million*; Naomi Seidman, *A Marriage Made in Heaven: The Sexual Politics of Hebrew and Yiddish* (Berkeley: University of California Press, 1997); Daniel Boyarin, *Unheroic Conduct: The Rise of Heterosexuality and the Invention of the Jewish Man* (Berkeley: University of California Press, 1997).

236 **"empty glasses and full ashtrays"** Almagor, "The Fiddler Who Went on the Roof," *Ma'ariv*, September 11, 1964, trans. Elik Elhanan.

238 **"as if greeting an old friend"** Topol, *Topol by Topol*, 98.

238 ***Sallah* rose to classic status** See Shohat, *Israeli Cinema*, 138–55.

238 **"fled from the theater"** Topol, *Topol by Topol*, 1.

238   "one felt the whole of the Russian Jewish experience" ibid., 100.

238   By mid-November . . . the deal was done Godik letter to Prince, November 16, 1964, HPP11:6.

239   "tragically distorted and twisted" Natan Altman, quoted in Vladislav Ivanov, "Habima and Biblical Theater," in Susan Tumarkin Goodman, ed., *Chagall and the Artists of the Russian Jewish Theater* (New York: Jewish Museum; New Haven, CT: Yale University Press, 2008), 31.

239   "mostly melodramatic adaptations" Freddie Rokem, "Hebrew Theater from 1889 to 1948," in Ben-Zvi, *Theater in Israel*, 73. See also Kohansky, *Hebrew Theatre*.

239   "drew Kasrilevke not with ink but with poison" Michael Ohad, "With Powder and Lipstick," 1965, *Haaretz*, June 19, 1965, trans. Elhanan, clipping, BSA-TA.

240   "diluted, abridged, fragmentary" Miron, "Literary Image of the Shtetl," 187.

240   blew up a local Yiddish press See A. Pilowsky, "Yiddish Alongside the Revival of Hebrew: Public Polemics on the Status of Yiddish in Eretz Israel, 1907–1929," in Joshua Fishman, ed., *Readings in the Sociology of Jewish Languages* (Leiden: E. J. Brill, 1985), 123.

240   Berkowitz offered a hero besieged See Weitzner, *Sholem Aleichem in the Theater*, and also plot summary in program in 1943 Habima program booklet, ITA-TA.

241   "A sacrilege" quoted in *Waiting for Godik*.

242   false set of expectations See Altman and Kaufman, *Making of a Musical*, 122–33.

243   Berkowitz admitted to changing Tevye's puns and distortions See Benny Mer, "The Fall and Rise of Tevye," Haaretz.com, May 12, 2009.

243   "only country where they played around with the script" Stein interview.

243   "It's been constant arguments" Altman letter to Robbins, May 25, 1965, JRP6:28.

243   "inefficiency here is stupendous" Altman letter to Robbins, June 3, 1965, JRP6:28.

244   "They all are responding to our directions" Abbott letter to Robbins, May 3, 1965, JRP6:28.

244–45 "Everyone—but everyone" Altman letter to Robbins, May 6, 1965, JRP6:28.

245   "he read the more serious scenes very well" Altman letter to Robbins, April 20, 1965, JRP6:28.

245   "has the equipment" Stein letter to Robbins, n.d., JRP6:28.

245   "shockingly lazy" . . . "audiences absolutely love him" Altman letter to Robbins, June 3, 1965, JRP6:28.

245   "My Tevye doesn't groan, weep, wail" Zur quoted in Moshe Brilliant, "Tevye Stirs Up a Storm," *New York Times*, August 15, 1965, X2.

245   "What makes you think we would be interested" Stein interview.

246   "cheap, empty, and hollow" Dr. Emil Feuerstein, "Fiddler on the Roof at the Godik Theater," *Ha'tzoffe*, June 11, 1967, trans. Elhanan, clippings, BSA-TA.

246   "saccharine water with rose petals made of cellophane" Chaim Glickstein, unidentified, n.d., trans. Elhanan, clippings, BSA-TA.

246   "*Yiddishkayt* drowning in shmaltz" Gamzu, "Last Night in the Theater," *Haaretz*, June 8, 1965, trans. Elhanan, clippings, BSA-TA.

246   "not even fresh shmaltz" Michael Ohad, "Lipstick."

246   Tevye as "a warmhearted human being" Zur quoted in Brilliant, "Tevye Stirs Up a Storm."

246   "never knew what an exilic Jew is" Feuerstein, *Ha'tzoffe*.

246   "he was the least Jewish" Glickstein.

246   "more goy than Sholem-Aleichem-like" . . . "grace and charm" Gamzu, "Last Night in the Theater."

246 **"miscast as Tevye"** . . . **"and not entertain"** Mendel Kohansky, "Tevye via Broadway," *Jerusalem Post*, June 11, 1965.

246 **attorney general, Gideon Hausner, vowed to pronounce the indictment** quoted in Segev, *Seventh Million*, 347. For further discussion of the Eichmann trial, see also Arendt, *Eichmann*, and Cesarani, *Becoming Eichmann*.

247 **"marked the beginning of a dramatic shift"** Segev, *Seventh Million*, 361.

247 **"The Diaspora is returning to us"** Ohad, "Lipstick."

248 **more than one-quarter** Prince office press release, August 25, 1966; *Fiddler* clips, NYPL-PA, "1966."

248 **"5,760-mile Off-Broadway production"** leaflet in HPP111:6.

248 **"He filled that character with human warmth"** "A Great Actor of Small People," obituary for Shmuel Rodensky by Amnon Nevot, n.p., n.d., trans. Elhanan, clippings, BSA-TA.

248 **"It shows how rooted and mature"** "A Yidl mitn Fidl," *Ma'ariv*, September 1965, trans. Elhanan, clippings, BSA-TA.

249 **"give the show a particularly Jewish reputation"** Prince letter to Hutto, October 21, 1965, HPP111:6.

249 **the Israeli ambassador in Bonn** Kohansky, "Fiddlers on All Roofs," *Australian Jewish News*, September 19, 1969.

249 **"the greatest Tevye ever"** . . . **"tore my heart"** Topol interview.

250 **"There will be virtually no competition"** Pilbrow letter to Prince, September 30, 1966, HPP114:4.

250 **"wild" about [McKern]** Pilbrow letter to Prince, August 5, 1966, HPP114:1.

250 **there was "no other Englishman"** Pilbrow letter to Prince, August 17, 1966, HPP114:1.

250 **out of their minds** Pilbrow letter to Prince, August 19, 1966, HPP114:1.

250 **"If he should turn us down"** Prince to *Fiddler* authors, September 12, 1966, JRPP6:1.

250 **Mostel demanded 10 percent** Fisher (Prince office) letter to Pilbrow, September 22, 1966, HPP114:4.

250 **London would go no higher than 7.5** telegram from Pilbrow office to Prince, September 19, 1966, HPP114:4.

250 **"when the authors are off in Boston"** Prince letter to Pilbrow, September 23, 1966, HPP114:4.

251 **"You must deliver"** telegram from P. Littler (Pilbrow office), September 21, 1966, HPP114:4.

251 **"being produced in fourteen languages"** Prince letter to Toby Rolwands (Pilbrow office), October 3, 1966, HPP114:4.

251 **"Hal would like to know"** Annette Meyers letter to Pilbrow, August 14, 1966, HPP114:5.

251 **"CHYAM POPAL"** telegram from Pilbrow to Prince, October 4, 1966, HPP114:4.

251 **"Somebody totally unknown"** Pilbrow letter to Prince, October 6, 1966, HPP114:1.

251 **Topol . . . thought the invitation was a joke** Topol, *Topol by Topol*, 2–3.

252 **"far more exciting than we ever dared to hope"** Pilbrow letter to Prince, October 31, 1966, HPP14:1.

252 **Altman worried** Altman and Kaufman, *Making of a Musical*, 140.

252 **"doing everything correct"** quoted in background essay in *Playbill* for 1990 production of *Fiddler* at the Gershwin, starring Topol, JBP22:6; Topol interview.

252 **by March the show was fully booked until the following Christmas** Topol, *Topol by Topol*, 114.

252 **nearly 600 percent profit** press release from Sol Jacobson-Lewis Harmon stamped "rec'd May 22, 1967," *Fiddler* clippings, "1967."

252 **the Six-Day War** See Sachar, *A History of Israel*, 615–66; Segev, *1967*.

253 **Topol traveled up and down** Topol, *Topol by Topol*, 120–24, and Topol interview.

253 **the threat of extermination** Segev, *Seventh Million*, 392.

253 **He had left London as a star** Altman and Kaufman, *Making of a Musical*, 167; Pilbrow, *A Theatre Project*, 157.

254 **Robbins "should come over . . . and try to save the show"** Topol letter to Robbins, October 2, 1967, JRP6:1.

254 **"extremely good shape"** Pilbrow letter to Robbins, October 5, 1967, JRP6:1.

254 **"since the rest of his behavior"** Prince letter to Robbins, October 19, 1967, JRP6:1.

254 **"actually the worst offender"** Bock note to Robbins, November 8, 1967, JRP5:12.

254 **"history repeats itself"** Prince letter to Robbins, n.d. (enclosing Alfie Bass reviews), JRP6:5.

254 **When Mirisch saw a notice** Mirisch, *I Thought*, 306; Jewison, *This Terrible Business*, 178–79; Jewison interview.

254 **Jewison hadn't liked [Mostel]** Jewison interview.

255 **"must be rooted in truth"** Jewison letter to Mirisch, September 8, 1969, NJP32:14.

255 **Tevye had to feel like a Russian Jew** Jewison interview.

255 **"I identified very strongly with Israel"** *Fiddler* post-screening Q&A, Film Society of Lincoln Center, Norman Jewison Retrospective, May 29, 2011.

256 **"you could see him stiffen"** Lincoln Center Q&A.

256 **"My grandfather was a sort of Tevye"** Topol quoted in McCandlish Phillips, "Topol, Film Tevye, Looks Back at Role," *New York Times*, November 3, 1971, 38.

257 **"collective incarnation of a new ethnic heroism"** Sachar, *A History of the Jews in America*, 713; see also S. Rosenthal, *Waning*.

257 **"wondered if they had not neglected"** Sachar, *A History of the Jews in America*, 818.

CHAPTER 7: *FIDDLER* WHILE BROOKLYN BURNS

258 **"We were in show business"** Piro-1 interview.

259 **"where Jews can live as in the Old Country"** Sachar, *A History of the Jews in America*, 214.

259 **rapidly deteriorating subdivided houses** See Podair, *Strike*, and Pritchett, *Brownsville*.

260 **"notoriously, a place that measured"** Kazin, *Walker*, 12.

261 **threatened to boycott** See Ravitch, *Great School Wars*, 270ff., and "Schools to Seek Rights Panel Aid," *New York Times*, August 27, 1963.

261 **surrounded by community protesters** Rubin interview.

262 **"taste excellence"** Piro-1 and Rubin interviews.

262 **"With your scores"** Piro-1 interview.

262 **"We are not martyrs"** Piro, "Teaching the Disadvantaged," letter to *Music Educators Journal* 54:4 (December 1967): 16.

262 **"For Mr. Piro"** Beverly Cannon Dorsey interview.

263 **"the only place you could feel free"** Haskins interview.

263 **Stephan Hirsch . . . found refuge there** Hirsch interview.

263 **"time to get down to business"** McCullers interview.

263 **"a big brother and father figure"** Maritza Figueroa Reynolds interview.

263 **"don't do assembly-type"** Piro, *Black Fiddler* (henceforth, *BF*), 18.

263 **Bruce Birnel had just seen** Birnel interview.

263 **"Maybe Black Power is what"** Clive Barnes, "Theater: All-Negro 'Hello, Dolly!' Has Its Premiere," *New York Times*, November 13, 1967.

265 **When they reopened, some 350 UFT teachers . . . stayed home** *New York Times* coverage: "Admit Teachers, M'Coy Is Ordered," May 24, 1968; "Classes Go On Despite District Woes," June 11, 1968; "Donavan Says Schools in Ocean Hill–Brownsville District Will Remain Open," June 17, 1968; "Ocean Hill Unit 'Dismisses' 350," June 21, 1968.

265 **"If community control . . . becomes a fact"** Shanker quoted in Rossner, *Year Without Autumn*, 39, and in Sol Stern, " 'Scab' Teachers," *Ramparts*, November 17, 1966, 21.

265 **"coming into the ghetto to cripple"** letter to Shanker from parent/community negotiating committee for IS 201, quoted in Ravitch, *Great School Wars*, 306.

265 **"educational genocide"** Reverend C. Herbert Oliver, quoted in Martin Mayer, "The Full and Sometimes Very Surprising Story of Ocean Hill, the Teachers' Union and the Teacher Strike of 1968," *New York Times*, February 2, 1969.

265 **"hoodlum element" . . . "mob rule"** Shanker quoted in *New York Times*, " 'Hoodlum Element' Said to Run Schools," February 12, 1968, and, for example, UFT full-page *New York Times* ad for a "rally to protest mob rule and save our schools," September 13, 1968.

265 **"a white motherfucking Jew bastard"** Piro-1 interview, and Piro, *BF*, 27.

266 **"Can't you do *Guys and Dolls*?" . . . "unsettled" . . . "sensitive time"** Rubin interview.

266 **a "queer old auntie"** quoted in Samantha Ellis, "Lionel Bart's Oliver!, June 1960," *Guardian*, June 18, 2003, http://www.guardian.co.uk/stage/2003/jun/18/theatre.samanthaellis.

267 **James Baldwin** "Negroes Are Anti-Semitic Because They Are Anti-White," *New York Times Magazine*, April 9, 1967.

267 **"It's called *Fiddler on the Roof*"** Piro, *BF*, 28.

268 **help Teddy "keep it together"** Dorsey interview.

269 **"Gestapo tactics" . . . "Fuck you"** quoted in Gitlin, *Sixties*, 334.

269 **Only a year earlier, the Anti-Defamation League** The ADL commissioned Gary T. Marx to conduct the study. He published it as *Protest and Prejudice: A Study of Belief in the Black Community* (New York: Harper & Row, 1967).

270 ***Variety* joked in September** clipping and note from Prince's assistant, September 16, 1968, HPP109:1.

270 **"Commie fascists," "Black Nazi lovers," and "nigger lovers"** quoted in Leonard Buder, "Parents Smash Windows, Doors to Open Schools," *New York Times*, October 19, 1968, 1.

270 **"racist pigs"** Leonard Buder, "Brooklyn Inquiry Begun on Threats in JHS 271 Crisis," *New York Times*, October 16, 1968.

270 **leaflet filled with Jew-hating invective** The leaflets are reproduced—and their use analyzed—in Fred Ferretti, "New York's Black Anti-Semitism Scare," *Columbia Journalism Review* 8:3 (Fall 1969): 18–28.

270 **temperate terms of the ADL** quoted in Bill Kovach, "Racist and Anti-Semite Charges Strain Old Negro-Jewish Ties," *New York Times*, October 23, 1968, 1.

271 **"perpetrated multiple fraud"** New York Civil Liberties Union report quoted in Ferretti, "New York's Black Anti-Semitism Scare," 18.

271 **shocked to find himself jeered** Kovach, "Racist and Anti-Semite Charges," 1.

271 **Piro had voted with his union to strike** Piro-1 interview.

271 **"a professional theater schedule"** Piro-2 interview.

271 **"it looked like a drag queen"** Piro-2 interview.

272 **Sheila found quick identification** Haskins interview.

272 **Olga thought about** Olga Carter Dais interview.

272 **"Tevye—he's a poor milkman"** Teddy quoted in Richard Schoenstein, "Kiddie Afro Fiddler Brownsville Smash," *New York Magazine*, April 7, 1969, 44.

272 **"all about getting into character"** Dais interview.

272 **The afternoon work turned technical** Reynolds, Haskins, Dorsey, Dais, McCullers, Piro, Sicari interviews.

272 **"I'm not going to do it like that"** Piro-1 interview.

273 **"living and breathing your words"** Hirsch interview.

274 **They called themselves the Maccabees** Piro, "Black Fiddler," *Music Educators Journal* 58:3 (November 1971): 54.

275 **personal secrets blazoned** Piro, *BF*, 130.

275 **threatened to kill him** unpublished manuscript submitted to the *New York Times* in 1971 by colleague Dan O'Neil: "I was with Piro in the teacher's cafeteria when one Jewish teacher threatened to kill him if the play went on." Piro personal files, kindly shared.

275 **On the day of the assembly** Piro, *BF*, 85–90; Piro-1, Birnel, Dorsey interviews.

276 **"It was real"** Dorsey interview.

276 **"This show has been canceled"** **"those fucking Jews"** Piro, *BF*, 99, and McCullers interview.

276 **"The girl giving me freedom"** Haskins interview.

276 **That night, Olga's mother** Piro, *BF*, 101; Dais interview; interview with Lillian Carter in Enders, *Black Fiddler*.

277 **"That's a good show"** Brown interview and Piro, *BF*, 107–10.

277 **trying to "scratch out a simple tune"** Piro-2 interview.

277 **"We urgently request"** council letter quoted in Piro, *BF*, 128, and Brown interview.

278 **with fury and dread** Rubin interview.

278 **It was Birnel** Birnel, Piro interviews.

278 **It took Bock, Harnick, and Stein less than five minutes** Harnick-2 interview.

278 **Robbins was away at the time** memo from Floria Lasky to Robbins, March 6, 1969, JRP8:8.

278 **"embarrassing"** Harnick-2 interview.

278 **"Hamlet can only be played"** Stein interview.

278 **"quite a marvelous thing"** Stein quoted in WCBS report, Jean Parr.

278 **had realized a profit of 1,300 percent** Betty Flynn, "Boy Were those critics wrong!" *Chicago Daily News*, February 22, 1969, 3.

278 **the issue was a poem** Lester, *Lovesong*, and Ferretti, "New York's Black Anti-Semitism Scare"; also Weusi interview.

279 **Metropolitan Museum of Art was just opening** Schoener, *Harlem on My Mind*. For discussion and analysis of the exhibit and the protests, see Steven C. Dubin, "Crossing 125th Street: *Harlem on My Mind* Revisited," in *Displays of Power: Memory and Amnesia in the American Museum* (New York: New York University Press, 1999), and Bridget R. Cooke, "Black Artists and Activism: *Harlem on My Mind* (1969)," *American Studies* 48:1 (Spring 2007): 5–40.

279 **"anti-Jewish feeling is a natural result"** Van Ellison, "Introduction," in Schoener, *Harlem on My Mind*, 13–14. A further controversy erupted when it became clear that some of the inflammatory assertions were Van Ellison's paraphrases from Glazer and Moynihan that went uncredited because Schoener had taken out the footnotes.

280 **six o'clock news** *Jeanne Parr Report*, WCBS-NY, aired January 30, 1969.

280 ***60 Minutes*** Jane Nicholl, "Fiddler in the Ghetto," aired June 10, 1969.

280 **Enders's hour-long film, *Black Fiddler: Prejudice and the Negro*** broadcast on ABC, August 7, 1969.

280 **Campbell's cultural nationalism had been fostered** Weusi interview.

280 **"the equivalent of an African griot"** Weusi interview.

280 **Frances Brown's enthusiasm** Brown interview.

281 **"ensemble playing in the finest sense"** Piro, *BF*, 172.

281 **That night he wrote the cast** Piro, *BF*, 172–74.

281 **foraging trips along Pitkin and Belmont** Ampolsky interview.

281 **birch trees to project** Birnel interview, video footage.

282 **Mayor Lindsay assembled** James P. Sterba, "Mayor Names 13 to Calm Schools," *New York Times*, March 13, 1969, 1.

282 **"demonstrations, rampages"** Martin Arnold, "Public-School Violence Spreads; 24 Students, 5 Adults Arrested," *New York Times*, April 25, 1969, 1.

282 **set upon and suffered a broken nose** Hirsch interview.

282 **Beverly tried to organize** Dorsey interview; Piro, *BF*, 192–93.

282 **"battle-zone atmosphere"** Piro, *BF*, 195.

283 **two hundred high school kids broke twenty-five . . . windows** Michael T. Kaufman, "School Battered by Band of Youths," *New York Times*, May 1, 1969, 38.

283 **"That's some way to attract an audience"** Piro, *BF*, 203.

284 **from "optimistic universalism"** Rieder, *Canarsie*, 27.

284 **"the Jewish passage"** Podair, *Strike*, 144.

284 **breaking another twenty windows** "Brooklyn School Stoned by Youths," *New York Times*, May 2, 1969, 28.

285 **Rubin was out there talking to police brass** Rubin interview.

285 **even Beverly's mother** Dorsey interview.

285 **"dedication to the idea"** *Fiddler* program at Eiseman, *Fiddler* clips, New York Public Library.

285 **Piro gave the kids the requisite backstage pep talk . . . wept openly** Dorsey, McCullers, Hirsch, Haskins, Reynolds, Dais, Piro, Birnel interviews.

287 **"The one word which keeps knocking"** Piro memo; Piro, *BF*, 226.

287 **"It helped me to embrace"** Reynolds interview.

287 **"all in vain"** Piro-1 interview.

289 **A special screening was arranged** "Black Students React to New 'Fiddler' Film," Jewish Telegraphic Agency, *Jewish Press* (Omaha, NE), November 18, 1971, clippings, BSA-TA.

289 **film being shot with pieces of stocking** "Dialogue with Norman Jewison," *Hollywood Reporter*, February 13, 2003.

CHAPTER 8: ANATEVKA IN TECHNICOLOR

291 **"the most important film"** Jewison letter to publicity team in Toronto (Mick Langston), July 20, 1971, NJP32:15.

291 **the first Harry Belafonte special** Jewison, *This Terrible Business*, 49.

291 **"my life was being wasted"** Jewison, *This Terrible Business*, 92–93.

291 **Jewison wiggled out of his contract** See Mark Harris, *Pictures at a Revolution*, 143.

291 **"the movie that made me feel"** Jewison, *This Terrible Business*, 114.

292 **"wanted to make films about political problems"** Jewison interview.

292 **summoned to the office of United Artists** Jewison interview. In *This Terrible Business*, Jewison dates this meeting to 1969, clearly an error. He and Mirisch traveled to London to consider Topol for the role before mid-February 1968; correspondence between Jerry Robbins and his lawyer as well as Hal Prince in March and April 1968 refer to Jewison's having been signed for the film; Mirisch, in *I Thought We Were Making*, says he's the

one who offered the position to Jewison at his "first opportunity" (p. 305) after a summer 1967 meeting with United Artists.

292 **"never a big fan"** "Norman Jewison, the Man Behind Fiddler on the Roof, Talks to John Williams," news clipping from unidentified publication; n.d., NJP33:4.

292 **"Studios Again Mining Gold with Lavish Film Musicals"** by Howard Thompson, *New York Times*, October 26, 1968, 39.

293 **United Artists went after it** memos to Jerry Robbins JRP8:27.

293 **Kramer put in a bid** Memo from Floria Lasky to Robbins, April 22, 1965, JRP8:27.

293 **"memorandum of terms"** HPP115:8 and JRP8:27.

293–94 **he stood to receive $100,000 . . . "exact a high price"** Floria Lasky memo to Robbins, March 16, 1966, JRP8:29. Also see meeting summary memo, March 11, 1966, HPP115:8.

294 **Perl demanded $250,000** Memo from Floria Lasky to Robbins, March 23, 1966, JRP8:28.

294 **He got $75,000** Letter from Jerome Talbert to George Litto (Perl representative), April 4, 1966, JRP8:28.

294 **a last-minute, $2.5 million bid** "Minutes of meeting re: 'Fiddler on the Roof'— United Artists," October 24, 1966; letter from Allen Klein to Edward Colto, Esq., November 17, 1966. JRP8:28

294 **$2.75 million** Mirisch, *I Thought We Were Making*, 305.

294 **Hollywood, like the rest of America, had been rocked by change** For a thorough discussion of these changes, see Harris, *Pictures at a Revolution*.

295 **the leader of the bloody slave revolt** See Jewison, *This Terrible Business*, 153–56; also see Christopher Sieving, *Soul Searching: Black-Themed Cinema from the March on Washington to the Rise of Blaxploitation* (Middletown, CT: Wesleyan University Press, 2011), esp. 83–117.

295 **Jewison assertively told the press** Wayne Warga, "Civil Rights and a Producer's Dilemma: Rights Challenge for Jewison," *Los Angeles Times*, April 14, 1968, N1.

295 **Jewison had been feeling discouraged . . . "grief and disappointment"** Jewison, *This Terrible Business*, 175–77. Also, Jewison interview.

295 **"to bring it into the big money"** clipping from *Variety*, July 14, 1971, NJP33:4.

296 **"What would you say if"** Jewison, *This Terrible Business*, 12–13. Also, Jewison interview and Lincoln Center Q&A, May 29, 2011.

296 **"He covered so beautifully"** Jewison, Lincoln Center Q&A, May 29, 2011.

296 **"He could make a film free of complexes"** "G. Yitur talks to Chaim Topol," *Olam Hakolnoa*, December 16, 1971, trans. from Hebrew, Elik Elhanan, clipping, BSA-TA.

296 **"hey Jewboy" bullying** Jewison, *This Terrible Business*, 11–15.

296 **"we need to feel how 'the other' "** ibid., 216.

296 **"I'm not a cerebral filmmaker"** *Norman Jewison, Film maker*, documentary produced and directed by Doug Jackson, "special feature" on *Fiddler on the Roof* DVD, 2-Disc Collector's Edition.

296 **37 books** List of books purchased and forwarded from London to Los Angeles, November 6, 1969, NJP30:16.

296 **copies** *of Life Is with People* memo from Jewison's assistant, December 16, 1969. NJP 31:7.

296 **whirlwind five-day trip to Israel** letter from Moshe Davis to Jewison, September 1, 1969; and draft itinerary, proposed schedule change, October 15, 1969, NJP30:15.

297 **old immigrants** Jewison, *This Terrible Business*, 178, and notes from interview, NJP30:15.

297 **he also spent an afternoon** Jewison letter to Vishniac, September 30, 1971, NJP31:7.

297 **"dear old Roman Vishniac"** Jewison letter to Dan Smolen, UA, September 30, 1971, NJP32:15.

297 **"the look of the people"** Jewison interview.

297 **"casting breakdown" notes** Jewison notes, December 8, 1969, NJP30:6.

297 **"in a dignified manner"** letter to Jewison from Rabbi Israel Klavan, Executive Vice President of the Rabbinical Council of America, March 9, 1970, NJP31:4.

297 **"direct connection" with Sholem-Aleichem** Jewison interview.

298 **The incident "devastated" Jewison** Jewison interview.

298 **"MADAME CHAGALL SAYS"** Western Union telegram from Saul Cooper to Norman Jewison, March 12, 1970, NJP30:8.

298 **Cooper updated Jewison** letter, June 11, 1970, NJP30:8.

298 **"where there are animals"** Jewison interview.

298 **"That's when I turned to Tito"** Jewison interview.

298 **"almost as much as he loved hard currency"** Jewison, *This Terrible Business*, 178.

299 **forty-five minutes' drive** "General Information re Yugoslavia from Mirisch Films Limited," July 13, 1970, NJP10:12.

299 **"All we had to do was build a synagogue"** Jewison in "The 'Fiddler' Meets the Yugoslavs" by Frederick M. Winship, UP (dateline: New York), *The Record*, November 23, 1971.

299 **Decades before wide interest** In 2004, the Handshouse Studio, a U.S.-based nonprofit fostering hands-on educational projects, began building, piece by piece, a replica of a magnificently painted wooden synagogue built in 1731 and burned down during the Holocaust in Gwoździec (Ukraine); in 2011, the nascent Museum of the History of Polish Jews entered into a collaboration with Handshouse to build and raise the synagogue replica at the museum, on the site of the former Warsaw Ghetto. It will stand as "a symbol of the vitality of Jewish culture in Poland," Handshouse declares. They had no trouble raising nearly $57,000 from 441 donors through a Kickstarter campaign to document the project by film.

299 **building it from the timber** Robert Boyle, "Set in Reality: Production Design," featurette, Disc 2, *Fiddler on the Roof*, 2-Disc Collector's Edition, MGM.

300 **visited whatever standing synagogues** Jewison interview.

300 **In Targu Neamt . . . even tried to purchase** Jewison interview and Mirisch Productions letter from associate producer Patrick Palmer, to Bucharest (National Cinema Center) March 19, 1970, NJP30:12.

300 **The request was denied** Patrick Palmer interview.

300 **re-creating pastel murals** Among the books Jewison and Boyle consulted was David Davidovits, *Tsiyure-kir be-veit-kenesset be-Polin* (Jerusalem: Mosad Byalik, 1968). Books Purchased—and Forwarded from London to Los Angeles, November 1969, NJP30:16.

302 **"I wanted audiences to feel the racial hatred"** Jewison, *This Terrible Business*, 178.

303 **Though not so thoroughly ignored** See Hasia Diner, *We Remember with Reverence*.

303 **in an image inspired by Vishniac** Jewison interview.

304 **"the only wooden period replica"** Jewison letter to Marvin Mirisch, May 24, 1972, NJP32:9.

304 **to the dismantling and rebuilding costs** letter to Jewison from Meir Meyer (Israel Museum) who reports on presenting the matter of the synagogue to Dr. Z. Warhaftig, minister of religious affairs, January 2, 1971, NJP32:8.

304 **"I think Jerusalem has enough"** Kollek letter to Meyer Weisgal, Weizmann Institute, June 14, 1972, forwarded by Weisgal to Jewison, July 4, 1972, NJP32:8.

304 **the minister of religion was reported** letter from Meir Meyer to Jewison saying that the minister of religious affairs "wants the synagogue very much," May 8, 1972, NJP32:8.

304 **shul had been torn down** Jewison letter to Arthur N. Greenberg, December 18, 1972, NJP32:8.

304 **advertising budget of more than $3.3 million** "Basic Starting Roadshow Advertising and Exploitation Budget for Fiddler on the Roof covering advance and opening through February 26, 1972: $1,440,024," and letter from Jewison to United Artists approving the revised advertising budget of $3,360,451, June 20, 1972, NJP33:4.

304 **"We must not merchandise a Winston Diamond"** Jewison letter to Walter Mirisch, October 6, 1971, NJP32:14.

305 **"logged the largest group sales advance"** *Variety*, July 14, 1971; clip in JRP33:4.

305 **advertising director didn't think it was necessary** letter to Jewison from Donald Smolen, United Artists director of advertising, February 12, 1971, NJP33:4.

305 **"strong initial ethnic pull"** Jewison letter to Gabe Sumner, United Artists, September 4, 1971, NJP33:4.

305 **"avoid stressing its Jewishness"** letter from Quinn Donoghue (United Artists, UK) to Hy Smith (United Artists, NY), cc'd to Jewison, June 11, 1970, NJP33:2.

305 **"the 1971 UNICEF film"** letter from Quinn Donoghue to Mirisch Co., cc'd to Jewison, June 11, 1970, NJP33:2.

305 **Jewison repeated the anecdote** United Artists press kit, clippings, "Fiddler on the Roof" folder 1966, NYPL-PA. Also, Jewison is quoted in several preview stories telling this story.

305 **"90 percent of Lutheranism"** Jewison letter to Fred Goldberg, United Artists, December 15, 1971, NJP33:2.

306 **urged clergy to tell** NJP33:2.

306 **"he loved it"** letter to Jewison from Mike Hunter, United Artists, December 16, 1971, NJP33:2.

306 *Catholic Film Newsletter* November 30, 1971, copy in NJP33:2.

307 **"let most of the life out"** Vincent Canby review of *Fiddler, New York Times*, November 4, 1971.

307 **"condescending and way off track . . . hurt the most"** Jewison letter to Gabe Sumner, United Artists, December 9, 1971, NJP33:2.

307 **"[Topol's] sense of comedy"** Paul D. Zimmerman review of *Fiddler, Newsweek*, November 15, 1971.

307 **"Gone with barely a trace are warmth"** "Last of the Dinosaurs," Jay Cocks, *Time*, November 22, 1971.

307 **playing to 93 percent capacity crowds in Paris** Gabe Sumner letter to Jewison, December 7, 1971, NJP33:3.

307 **"overwhelm[ing] not only Aleichem"** Vincent Canby, "Is 'Fiddler' More DeMille Than Sholem Aleichem?" *New York Times*, November 28, 1971.

307 **"the most *powerful* movie musical ever made"** Pauline Kael, "The Current Cinema: A Bagel with a Bite out of It," *New Yorker*, November 13, 1971, 133–39.

308 **"Since when did film ever have anything to do with the theatre?"** Jewison letter to Gabe Sumner, December 9, 1971, NJP33:2.

308 **"elitist" prejudices** Denton Stein, "Movie Mailbag: 'Elitist: Did Bogdanovich Go to School?" *New York Times*, December 26, 1971. See also John Vitale, "Letter to the Editor 6," *New York Times*, January 9, 1972. In letters to Jewison, United Artists staff Gabe Sumner (January 6, 1972) and Fred Goldberg (January 7, 1972) admit to having written these. NJP33:3.

308 **"part of our campaign"** Fred Goldberg letter to Jewison, January 14, 1972, NJP33:3.

308 **"One critic complains"** Frances Taylor column, "Fiddler's Appeal Snares Some Critics," December 5, 1971, *Long Island Press* clipping, NJP33:3.

308 **"a lot of money"** Walter Mirisch letter to Jewison, March 28, 1972, NJP33:4.

308 **To lead off they published** Gabe Sumner letter to Jewison, December 7, 1971, NJP33:3.

309 **"It was a tough night"** Jewison, *This Terrible Business*, 183.

309 **played onstage for thirty-five million** press materials in NJP and quoted, for example, in "Tevye on Film," Sight and Sound, *Hadassah Magazine*, December 1971.

309 **Jewison himself admitted that he had tamped down** Jewison quoted in Joyce Haber, "The Genesis of Jewison's *Fiddler on the Roof*," *Los Angeles Times*, January 9, 1972, VII.

310 **"resembles a kind of hippie commune"** Leonard Frey quoted in Bernard Weinraub, "Tevye's Suffering Enacted for Movie," *New York Times*, January 4, 1971.

310 **"Ellis Island whiteness"** Jacobson, *Roots*, 7ff.

310 **"about the rich traditions of their forefathers"** Roman Pucinski (D-Ill.) opening speech of the hearing on H.R. 14910: U.S. Congress. House Committee on Education and Labor. Ethnic Heritage Studies Centers: Hearings before the General Subcommittee on Education. 91st Cong., 2nd Sess., February 19, 1970, 1.

310 **In the meantime** Introduction to the 1996 Transaction edition of *The Rise of the Unmeltable Ethnics*. See more at: http://www.firstthings.com/onthesquare/2006/08/novak-the-rise-of-unmeltable-e#sthash.iuh44aj8.dpuf.

310 **"People uncertain of their own identity"** Novak, *Unmeltable*, 271.

310 **"historical memory, real or imaginary"** ibid., 47–48.

310 **particulary masculinist terms** Feminists reached back to recover the histories and creations of the forgotten women, often within their ethnic groups, but early on, the dominant mode of the new ethnicity played as score-settling for dissed manhood. Even as the tribal demagoguery settled down and claims for "heritage" found more genteel forms of expression, it long sustained a male cast. Irving Howe's 1976 blockbusting book about Yiddish life on the Lower East Side was told, indeed, as a *World of Our Fathers*.

311 **"Jewish boys should not be that nice"** Jewish Defense League display ad, *New York Times*, June 24, 1969, 31. For a discussion of JDL, see Michael Staub, *Torn at the Roots: The Crisis of Jewish Liberalism in Postwar America* (New York: Columbia University Press, 2002; Robert I. Friedman, *The False Prophet: Rabbi Meir Kahane from FBI Informant to Knesset Member*, New York: Lawrence Hill Books, 1990. Janet Dolgin, *The JDL and Jewish Identity* (Princeton, NJ: Princeton University Press, 1977); Meir Kahane, *The Story of the Jewish Defense League* (Radnor, PA: Chilton, 1975).

311 **council member Anthony "Tough Tony" Imperiale** photographed for and interviewed in "In Politics, It's the New Populism," *Newsweek*, October 6, 1969.

312 **"nice Jewish bad boys"** J. Hoberman, "Flaunting It: The Rise and Fall of Hollywood's 'Nice' Jewish (Bad) Boys," in Hoberman and Shandler, *Entertaining America: Jews, Movies, and Broadcasting*, Princeton, NJ; Princeton University Press, and New York: Jewish Museum, 2005, 220–43.

312 **"one of the few filmmakers left"** "Fiddler on the Screen," *Jerusalem Post Magazine*, February 12, 1971, no byline, BSA-TA clippings.

313 **"symbolic ethnicity," "symbolic religiosity"** Herbert Gans, "Symbolic Ethnicity and Symbolic Religiosity: Towards a Comparison of Ethnic and Religious Acculturation," *Ethnic and Racial Studies* 17:4 (1994): 577–92.

313 **"about the problems of people who have"** Drucker and Jacobs, "Antennae on the Roof," *Mad Magazine* 1:156, January 1972, 4.

314 **"But though God's made imbeciles"** Drucker and Jacobs, "Antennae," 10.

315 **"God made a modern Camelot"** ibid.

315 **enacting their Jewishness** Jeffrey Shandler, *Jews, God, and Videotape*, esp. 185–229.

315 **In 2006, Bet Shira Congregation** This discussion was first developed for my two-part essay in *The Forward*: "How *Fiddler* Became Folklore," September 1, 2006, and "Tevye, Today and Beyond," September 8, 2006.

CHAPTER 9: *SKRZYPEK NA DACHU*: POLAND

318 **The director, Magdalena Miklasz, wanted the spectators** All quotes and ideas attributed to Miklasz from interviews.

318 **the designer, Ewa Woźniak, had decided** All quotes and ideas attributed to Woźniak from interviews.

321 **"If people know where Dynów is"** Mayor Zygmunt Frańczak interview.

322 **As early as 1966** letter from Walter Felsenstein to Jerry Robbins, May 4, 1966, JRP5:17.

322 **Robbins was to have directed** Donal Henahan, "Sing Along with Felsenstein?" *New York Times*, May 30, 1971, D13.

322 **with just a few adjustments** letter from Johannes Felsenstein to Hal Prince, January 2, 1971, HPP111:5.

322 **audiences booed the Russians** "*Sholem-aleykhems 'fidlr afn dakh' regt on di tshekhn tzum vidershtand kegn der okupatziye*," *Haynt*, July 24, 1969; *Fiddler* clippings, BSA-TA.

323 **interest in presenting** *Fiddler* **at the State Yiddish Theater** letter from Meir Melman to Ed Khouri, representing Stein at William Morris, March 1, 1966, JSP-NY "Fiddler-foreign-misc."

323 **Theater artists simply understood** Gruza, Weiss interviews.

323 **it had been commercially screened** United Artists financial statement, November 25, 1978, JRP16:37.

323 **"staging the play was entirely unthinkable"** "Droga Skrzypka do Polski" ("The Fiddler's Road to Poland")—Antoni Marianowicz, program note for Gruza's production, program, Gdynia, 1984; trans. Agnieszka Sablinska. ZRT programs.

324 **Jerzy Gruza made a trip to New York** Gruza interview.

324 **Robert Darnton** "Poland Rewrites History," *New York Review of Books*, July 16, 1981.

325 **"they reminded us"** Krajewski interview.

325 **"As you probably know"** letter from Antoni Marianowicz to Joe Stein, April 1, 1981, JRP7:13.

326 **Robbins would have preferred** Robbins note on memo about Marianowicz's request: "yes—but not for cemeteries but for *living* people," April 15, 1981, JRP7:13.

326 **"If our show can have"** Stein letter to Marianowicz, April 15, 1981, JRP7:13.

326 **"the people who once lived in our land"** Marianowicz, "Droga Skrzypka do Polski."

326 **"modern mass Jewish culture"** Michael Steinlauf, "Yiddish Theater," *YIVO Encyclopedia of Jews in Eastern Europe*.

327 **had come to love the music** Rajmund Ambroziak (director of the Musical Theater of Łódź) interview for *Dziennik Lodzski*, April 21, 1983, trans. Agnieszka Sablinska, ZRT clippings.

327 **and . . . "made it his point of honor"** Marianowicz, "Droga Skrzypka do Polski."

327 **"The social task of musical theater"** Gruza interviewed by Andrzej Ibis-Wróblewski, *Radar* 17:484 (1984), trans. Helena Chmielewska-Szlajfer, ZRT clippings.

327 **"The production raised"** Gruza interview.

327 **"the final scenes"** Marianowicz, "Droga Skrzypka do Polski."

328 **Reviews raved** clippings, ZRT; trans. Helena Chmielewska-Szlajfer and Agnieszka Sablinska.

329 **striking twenty-foot by thirty-foot poster** Kitlowski interview and images kindly supplied by e-mail.

329 **He detested its "falsification"** Szymon Szurmiej interview.

329 **screened at private parties** Kitliński, Leszkowicz, Haponiuk interviews.

329 **Lublin's theater** Marian Josicz (actor who played Tevye) interview; and program booklet, Teatr Muzycyny, Lublin, 1994, ZRT programs, trans. Agnieszka Sablinska.

329 **elaborate program booklet** from Lublin: ZRT programs, trans. Agnieszka Sablinska.

329 **"medicine"** Marek Weiss, interview.

330 **deft, straightforward direction** production viewed in Warsaw on June 29, 2008.

331 **Three-quarters of its voters** National Electoral Commission, Republic of Poland, Presidential Election Voting Results, October 23, 2005, http://www.prezydent2005.pkw .gov.pl/PZT/EN/WYN/W/181600.htm.

332 **felt a little shudder** Pinczer interview.

332 **The group piled into cars** descriptions of seeing the film and subsequent descriptions of rehearsals and performances from interviews with cast members.

334 **Woźniak walked from house to house** Woźniak interviews and interviews with neighbors in Dynów.

335 **Nazi invasion** See Krasnopolski and Szajnik, *Dynów*; Moritz, *"Khurban"*; Wenig, *From Nazi Inferno*; Virtual Shtetl, http://www.sztetl.org.pl/en/; and Szajnik interview.

337 **The "narrator" . . . walked out** production description based on video of performance kindly supplied by Miklasz, and interviews with Miklasz, Woźniak, and a dozen cast members.

338 **a slander still granted great credence** Tokarska-Bakir, "Sandomierz Blood-Libel Myths," manuscript generously shared by its author.

EPILOGUE: FIDDLING WITH TRADITION

341 **a man bursts into the hall** description of the performance from Pasternak interview; see also promotional video of their performances at bottledancers.com.

341 **Amazing Bottle Dancers** This section was excerpted for my article "Balancing Act," *TDR* 55:3 (T211) (Fall 2011): 21–30.

342 **"a way of adding a touch of tradition"** Pasternak interview.

342 **"age-old magnificent dance"** Amazing Bottle Dancers promotional video.

342 **Chabad telethon** April 6, 2008, http://youtube/AwOzf8dvFNU.

343 **"a mode of cultural production"** Kirshenblatt-Gimblett, *Destination Culture*, 7.

343 **"If a Jewish work . . ."** Ruth Wisse, *Modern Jewish Canon*, 65.

344 **"poignant musical tribute"** *YIVO News*, no. 190 (Summer 2000): 3.

344 **royalties on his Hebrew translation of** *Fiddler* Almagor interview; Isabel Kershner, "Palestinians Serenade Survivors in Israel," *New York Times*, March 26, 2009, A10.

345 **"the very people who are telling"** "Theodor Bikel: It Hurts that the Descendants of Anatevka Expel Israeli Bedouin," posted May 31, 2013. http://www.youtube.com/watch ?v=fLeWQ470G6.

345 **"working for generations"** *David Magazine*, Las Vegas, NV, n.d., clipping shared by Jack Solomon (deceased).

345 **"Anti-Semitic Cartoons Contest"** http://jewschool.com/2006/02/14/10045/israelis-launch -own-antisemitic-cartoon-contest/.

345 **"If I Were a Rich Man Tour"** a project of Bent Arc, A Jewish Partnership for Justice, in fall 2012; see http://bendthearc.us/campaigns/if-i-were-rich-man-tour/news_items.

345 **Abramoff . . . decided to become religiously observant** Abramoff quoted in Michael Crowley, "A Lobbyist in Full," *New York Times Magazine*, June 24, 2010.

345 **Stephen Colbert's joking that** *The Colbert Report*, Comedy Central, broadcast September 22, 2009.

345 **Alicia Svigals** Interview.

346 **"new Jewish culture"** See, for example, Steven M. Cohen and Ari Y. Kelman, *The Continuity of Discontinuity: How Young Jews Are Connecting, Creating, and Organizing Their Own Jewish Lives* (New York: Andrea and Charles Bronfman Philanthropies, 21/64, 2007), http://www.bjpa.org/Publications/details.cfm?PublicationID=327; Steven M. Cohen and Ari Y. Kelman, *Uncoupled: How Our Singles Are Reshaping Jewish Engagement*, Jewish Identity Project of Reboot, 2008, http://www.bjpa.org/Publications/details.cfm?PublicationID=332; Barbara Kirshenblatt-Gimblett, "The New Jews."

347 **high rates of academic achievement** This figure and others cited come from the National Jewish Population Survey 2000–2001. While the survey's methodology generated controversy and its findings are now more than a decade old, it remains the most comprehensive picture we have.

348 *In the Heights* Miranda interviewed on "Chasing Broadway Dreams," PBS, May 27, 2009; see also Miranda's wedding surprise for his bride, posted on YouTube: A rendition of "L'Chaim" led by him and his new father-in-law, http://youtube/KgZ4ZTTfKO8.

348 **Rajiv Menon has been dreaming** e-mail correspondence with Menon, September 12, 2008.

348 **"in many respects, an adaptation of genius"** Wisse, *Modern Jewish Canon*, 63.

349 **the roof tilted into** Cameri production viewed in Tel Aviv, January 5, 2009; interviews with Datner, Kepten, Smorgonski, Toren.

350 **"fresh, exciting approach"** Bock letter to Theodore Bikel, February 1, 2001, JBP20:8.

351 **They rejected** Harnick-3 interview.

351 **"renewal, not revival"** Bock speaking on *Fresh Air*, June 21, 2004.

351 **Leveaux figured there was still room** Leveaux interview.

351 **Bock relished the chance** Bock speaking on *Fresh Air*, June 21, 2004.

351 **Harnick focused on** Harnick-3 interview.

352 **"Topsy Turvy" . . . didn't work as well** Harnick-3 interview.

352 **authors didn't like the ring of those lines** Harnick-3 interview.

352 **"take that musical and strip it of the schtick"** Leveaux interviewed by Mark Shenton, *What's on Stage*, June 16, 2003.

353 **damping him down in rehearsals** Harnick e-mail.

353 **"tastes great and looks Jewish"** Thane Rosenbaum, "A Legacy Cut Loose," *Los Angeles Times*, February 15, 2004.

353 **"de-Jewed"** Michael Riedel, "Shtetl Shock—L.A. Times Hits Roof; Actress Hits the Road," *New York Post*, February 18, 2004.

353 **"ludicrous joke"** Leveaux interview.

353 **"has many inventive skills"** Peter Marks, "A 'Fiddler on the Roof' Hopelessly Out of Tune," *Washington Post*, February 27, 2004.

353 **"to abound in Russian-Jewish"** Jeremy McCarter, "The Musical to Start All Musicals," *New York Sun*, February 27, 2004.

353 **"personal and touching"** Marc Miller, "Fiddler on the Roof," January 21, 2005, the atermania.com/story/5558?.

354 **reviewers from publications large and small** See, for instance, Linda Winer, "Fiddler on the Roof," *Newsday*, lamenting that Molina's "biddy biddy bums" in "Rich Man"

"sound more like a Bing Crosby croon than a playful Talmudic approximation," *Newsday*, February 27, 2004.

354 **Ben Brantley devoted an entire paragraph** "A Cozy Little McShtetl," *New York Times*, February 27, 2004.

354 **"Fiddler with No Jew"** *Forbidden Broadway: Special Victims Unit*, by Gerard Alessandrini, opened on Broadway at the Douglas Fairbanks Theater, December 16, 2004. Original cast album released April 26, 2005, on DRG.

355 **"without the truer feelings"** Rosenbaum quoted in Riedel, "Shtetl Shock."

355 **"In the secular Jewish home"** Peter Marks, "A 'Fiddler on the Roof' Hopelessly out of Tune," *Washington Post*, February 27, 2004.

Selected Bibliography

————

PRINT/TEXT

Adler, Jacob. *A Life on the Stage: A Memoir.* Translated by Lulla Rosenfeld. New York: Applause, 2001.

Altman, Richard, and Mervyn D. Kaufman. *The Making of a Musical: Fiddler on the Roof.* New York: Crown, 1971.

American Jewish Yearbook. American Jewish Committee and Jewish Publication Society, 1899–2008. http://www.ajcarchives.org/main.php?GroupingH=40.

Antler, Joyce, *You Never Call! You Never Write!: A History of the Jewish Mother.* New York: Oxford University Press, 2007.

Arendt, Hannah. *Eichmann in Jerusalem: A Report on the Banality of Evil.* New York: Penguin Books, USA, 1994 (first published in the U.S. by The Viking Press, 1963).

Ascherson, Neal. *The Polish August: The Self-Limiting Revolution.* Middlesex, England; New York: Penguin Books, 1981, 1982.

Ausubel, Nathan. *A Treasury of Jewish Folklore.* New York: Crown, 1948.

Back, Adina, Jack Salzman, and Gretchen Sullivan Sorin. *Bridges and Boundaries: African Americans and American Jews.* New York: George Braziller, 1992.

Belcove-Shalin, Janet. *New World Hasidim: Ethnographic Studies of Hasidic Jews in America.* Albany: State University of New York Press, 1995.

Ben-Zvi, Linda, ed. *Theater in Israel.* Ann Arbor: University of Michigan Press, 1996.

Berkowitz, Y. D., ed. *Dos Sholem-aleykhem bukh.* New York: Farlag ikuf/Prompt Printing Press, 1926 and 1958.

———. *Undzere rishoynim: zokhroynes-dertzeylungen vegn sholem-aleichem un zayn dor,* vols. 1–5. Tel Aviv: Farlag hamnorah, 1966.

Berube, Maurice, and Marilyn Gittell, eds. *Confrontation at Ocean Hill–Brownsville.* New York: Praeger, 1969.

Bezmozgis, David. *The Free World.* New York: Farrar, Straus and Giroux, 2011.

Bialin, A. H. *Moris shvartz un der yidisher kunst teater.* New York: Farlag biderman, 1934; Amherst, MA: National Yiddish Book Center, Steven Spielberg Digital Yiddish Library No. 06217.

Bikel, Theodore. *Theo: The Autobiography of Theodore Bikel.* New York: HarperCollins, 1994.

Boris, Martin. "Once a Kingdom: Maurice Schwartz and the Yiddish Art Theatre." The Museum of Family History, http://www.museumoffamilyhistory.com/mschwartz-ok.htm.

Brown, Jared. *Zero Mostel: A Biography.* New York: Atheneum, 1989.

Brustein, Robert. *Seasons of Discontent: Dramatic Opinions, 1959–1965.* New York: Simon and Schuster, 1965.

Bryer, Jackson, and Richard A. Davison. *The Art of the American Musical: Conversations with the Creators.* Piscataway, NJ: Rutgers University Press, 2005.

Buhle, Paul, and David Wagner. *Hide in Plain Sight: The Hollywood Blacklistees in Film and Television, 1950–2002.* New York: Palgrave Macmillan, 2005.

Butwin, Joseph. "Tevye on King Street: Charleston and the Translation of Sholem Aleichem." *American Jewish History* 93:2 (2007): 129–56.

Cala, Alina. *The Image of the Jew in Polish Folk Culture.* Jerusalem: Magnes Press, 1995.

Cesarani, David. *Becoming Eichmann: Rethinking the Life, Crimes, and Trial of a "Desk Murderer."* Cambridge, MA: Da Capo Press, 2006.

Chagall, Bella. *Burning Lights.* New York: Schocken, 1946.

Counterattack: Facts to Combat Communism. New York: American Business Consultants.

Dash Moore, Deborah. *To the Golden Cities: Pursuing the American Jewish Dream in Miami and L.A.* New York: Free Press, 1994.

Davidowicz, Lucy. *The Golden Tradition: Jewish Life and Thought in Eastern Europe.* Syracuse, NY: Syracuse University Press, 1996; originally published 1967.

Davies, Norman. *Heart of Europe: The Past in Poland's Present.* Oxford, UK: Oxford Paperbacks, updated edition, 2001.

Denning, Michael. *The Cultural Front: The Laboring of American Culture in the Twentieth Century.* New York: Verso, 1997.

Diner, Hasia R. *We Remember with Reverence and Love: American Jews and the Myth of Silence after the Holocaust, 1945–1962.* New York: New York University Press, 2009.

Dylewski, Adam. *Where the Tailor Was a Poet: Polish Jews and Their Culture.* Translated by W. Graniczewski and R. Shindler. Bielsko-Biala: Pascal, 2002.

Ewen, David. *Composers for the American Musical Theater.* New York: Dodd, Mead, 1968.

Feingold, Henry L. *Bearing Witness: How America and Its Jews Responded to the Holocaust.* Syracuse, NY: Syracuse University Press, 1999.

——. *Jewish People in America.* Vol. 4: *A Time for Searching: Entering the Mainstream, 1920–1945.* Baltimore: Johns Hopkins University Press, 1992.

Fishman, Zvi. *Tevye in the Promised Land.* Jerusalem: Shorashim, 2011.

Frieden, Ken. "A Century in the Life of Sholem Aleichem's Tevye." B. G. Rudolph Lecture in Judaic Studies. Syracuse, NY: Syracuse University Press, 1997.

Gebert, Konstanty. *Living in the Land of Ashes.* Krakow: Austeria Publishing House, 2008.

Gitlin, Todd. *The Sixties: Years of Hope, Days of Rage.* New York: Bantam Books, 1987.

Goldsmith, Emanuel S. "Maurice Samuel," in Carole S. Kessner, ed., *The Other New York Jewish Intellectuals* (New York: New York University Press, 1994), 228–45.

Goldstein, Eric L. *The Price of Whiteness: Jews, Race, and American Identity*. Princeton, NJ: Princeton University Press, 2006.

Gordon, Jane Anna. *Why They Couldn't Wait: A Critique of the Black-Jewish Conflict over Community Control in Ocean Hill–Brownsville, 1967–1971*. New York: Routledge, 2001.

Goren, Arthur A. *The Politics and Public Culture of American Jews*. Bloomington: Indiana University Press, 1999.

Goren, B. *Di geshikhte fun yidishn teatr*. New York: Literarisher farlag, 1918.

Gorin, Grigory. *Memorial Prayer*. Unpublished play-text translated from the Russian by Lina Zeldovich, 2012.

Greenberg, Cheryl Lynn. *Troubling the Waters: Black-Jewish Relations in the American Century*. Princeton, NJ: Princeton University Press, 2006.

Grossman, Samuel. "Five Years of the Jewish Art Theatre." *Menorah Journal*, (August 1923): 202–14.

Gruber, Ruth Ellen. *Virtually Jewish: Reinventing Jewish Culture in Europe*. Berkeley: University of California Press, 2002.

Gushteyn, A. *Sholem-aleykhem: Zayn lebn un shafn*. Moscow: Melukhe-farlag der emes, 1946.

Halberstam, David. *The Fifties*. New York: Random House, 1993.

Harrington, Michael. *The Other America: Poverty in the United States*. Baltimore: Penguin Books, 1962; reprinted 1966.

Harris, Louis, and Bert E. Swanson. *Black-Jewish Relations in New York City*. New York: Praeger Publications, 1970.

Harris, Mark. *Pictures at a Revolution: Five Movies and the Birth of the New Hollywood*. New York: Penguin Books, 2008.

Harshav, Benjamin. *Marc Chagall and His Times: A Documentary Narrative*. Stanford, CA: Stanford University Press, 2004.

———. *The Moscow Yiddish Theater: Art on Stage in the Time of Revolution*. New Haven, CT: Yale University Press, 2008.

Hecht, Ben. *A Child of the Century*. New York: Simon and Schuster, 1954.

———. *A Flag Is Born*. New York: American League for a Free Palestine, 1946.

———. *We Will Never Die*. New York: Committee for a Jewish Army of Stateless and Palestinian Jews, 1943.

Heilman, Samuel C. *Defenders of the Faith: Inside Ultra-Orthodox Jewry*. Berkeley and Los Angeles: University of California Press, 1992.

Heinze, Andrew R. *Adapting to Abundance: Jewish Immigrants, Mass Consumption, and the Search for American Identity*. New York: Columbia University Press, 1992.

Herberg, Will. *Protestant, Catholic, Jew: An Essay in American Religious Sociology*. Chicago: University of Chicago Press, 1955; 1983 edition, published by arrangement with Doubleday.

Heschel, Abraham Joshua. *The Earth Is the Lord's: The Inner World of the Jew in East Europe*. New York: H. Schuman, 1950.

Hirsch, Foster. *Harold Prince and the American Musical Theatre*. Cambridge: Cambridge University Press, 1989.

Hoberman, J. *Bridge of Light: Yiddish Film between Two Worlds.* New York: Museum of Modern Art and Schocken Books, 1991.

Ilson, Carol. *Harold Prince: A Director's Journey.* New York: Limelight Editions, 2000.

Isaacs, Charlie. Unpublished memoir about teaching in the Ocean Hill "experimental district" in Brooklyn in 1968–69. Manuscript generously shared by the author.

Jackson, Naomi. *Converging Movements: Modern Dance and Jewish Culture at the 92nd Street Y.* Middletown, CT: Wesleyan University Press, 2000.

Jacobson, Matthew Frye. *Roots Too: White Ethnic Revival in Post–Civil Rights America.* Cambridge, MA: Harvard University Press, 2006.

Jewison, Norman. *This Terrible Business Has Been Good to Me: An Autobiography.* New York: Thomas Dunne Books, 2005.

Jowitt, Deborah. *Jerome Robbins: His Life, His Theater, His Dance.* New York: Simon and Schuster, 2004.

Kalman, Nadia. *The Cosmopolitans.* Livingston: Livingston Press, University of West Alabama, 2010.

Kaminska, Ida. *My Life, My Theater.* New York: Macmillan, 1973.

Kaufman, Jonathan. *Broken Alliance: The Turbulent Times between Blacks and Jews in America.* New York: Scribner, 1988.

Kazin, Alfred. *A Walker in the City.* New York: Harcourt, 1951.

Kellman, Ellen. "Sholem Aleichem's Funeral (New York, 1916): The Making of a National Pageant." In Deborah Dash Moore, ed., *YIVO Annual* 20 (Evanston, IL: Northwestern University Press and the YIVO Institute for Jewish Research, 1991), 277–305.

Kessner, Carole S. *Marie Syrkin: Values beyond the Self.* Lebanon, NH: Brandeis University Press, 2008.

———, ed. *The Other New York Jewish Intellectuals.* New York: New York University Press, 1994.

Kirshenblatt-Gimblett, Barbara. *Destination Culture: Tourism, Museums, and Heritage.* Berkeley and Los Angeles: University of California Press, 1998.

———. "Imagining Europe: The Popular Arts of American Jewish Ethnography." In Deborah Dash Moore and Ilan Troen, eds., *Divergent Centers: Shaping Jewish Cultures in Israel and America* (New Haven, CT: Yale University Press, 2001), 155–91.

———. "Introduction." In Mark Zborowski and Elizabeth Herzog, *Life Is with People* (New York: Schocken Books, 1995), ix–xlviii.

———. "The New Jews: Reflections on Emerging Cultural Practices." Conference presentation for Re-Thinking Jewish Communities and Networks in an Age of Looser Connections, December 2005, http://www.nyu.edu/classes/bkg/web/yeshiva.pdf.

———. "Sounds of Sensibility." *Judaism* 47:1 (Winter 1998): 49–78.

———. "Theorizing Heritage." *Ethnomusicology* 39:3 (Autumn 1995): 367–80.

Kohansky, Mendel. *The Hebrew Theatre: Its First Fifty Years.* New York: Ktav, 1969.

Krajewski, Stanisław. *Poland and the Jews: Reflections of a Polish Jew.* Kraków: Austeria, 2005.

Krampner, Jon. *The Man in the Shadows: Fred Coe and the Golden Age of Television.* New Brunswick, NJ: Rutgers University Press, 1997.

Krasnopolski, Mieczysław, and Grzegorz Szajnik. *Dynów w okresie drugiej wojny światowej.* Kraków: CLICO, 2006, unpublished translation, "Dynów during the Second World War," by Ursula Kudelski.

Kugelmass, Jack, and Jonathan Boyarin, eds. and trans. *From a Ruined Garden: The Memorial Books of Polish Jewry*. New York: Schocken Books, 1983.

Lambert, Philip. *To Broadway, To Life!: The Musical Theater of Bock and Harnick*. New York: Oxford University Press, 2011.

Landmark Symposium: *Fiddler on the Roof*, Peter Stone, Moderator; Jerry Bock, Sheldon Harnick, Joseph Stein in conversation. Transcript in *The Dramatists Guild Quarterly*, 20:1 (Spring 1983): 10–29.

Lapson, Dvora. *Dances of the Jewish People*. New York: Jewish Education Committee, 1954.

———. *Folk Dances for Jewish Festivals*. New York: Jewish Education Committee, 1961.

Lawrence, Greg. *Dance with Demons: The Life of Jerome Robbins*. New York: Berkley Books, 2001.

Lester, Julius. *Lovesong: Becoming a Jew*. New York: Arcade, 1988, especially chapter 6.

Litvak, Olga. "Khave and Her Sisters: Sholem-Aleichem and the Lost Girls of 1905," *Jewish Social Studies: History, Culture, Society* 15:3 (Spring/Summer 2009): 1–38.

Luzenski, Jim, and Steve Levin. *Fisher Theatre, Detroit, Michigan: Graven & Mayger, Architects*. Elmhurst, IL: Theatrical Society of America, ca. 2004.

Lynn, Karyl Charna. *The National Trust Guide to Great Opera Houses in America*. New York: Wiley, 1996.

Marianowicz, Antoni. *Life Strictly Forbidden*. Translated by Alicia Nitecki. Portland, OR: Valentine Mitchell, 2004.

Marmor, Kalmon. *"Sholem-aleykhems ershter bazukh in amerike." In Yidishe kultur*, vol. 6. (New York: 1939), 23–27.

Mestel, Yankev. *Undzer teatr*. New York: YCUF, 1943.

Millstein, Gilbert. *"Fiorello!* and Harnick: The Latter's Lyrics Bite Like La Guardia, but Bark Much Less." *New York Times*, December 27, 1959, SM18.

Mirisch, Walter. *I Thought We Were Making Movies, Not History*. Madison: University of Wisconsin Press, 2009.

Miron, Dan. "The Dark Side of Sholem-Aleichem's Laughter." Derekh Judaica Urbinatensia, January 2003. Central and Eastern European Online Library.

———. *From Continuity to Contiguity: Toward a New Jewish Literary Thinking*, especially chapter 11: "How Kafka and Sholem Aleichem Are Contiguous," 351–402. Stanford, CA: Stanford Studies in Jewish History and Culture, Stanford University Press, 2010.

———. *The Image of the Shtetl and Other Studies of Modern Jewish Literary Imagination*. Syracuse, NY: Syracuse University Press, 2000.

———. "The Literary Image of the Shtetl." *Jewish Social Studies*, n.s., 1:3 (Spring 1995): 1–43.

———. *A Traveler Disguised: The Rise of Modern Yiddish Fiction in the Nineteenth Century*. Syracuse, NY: Syracuse University Press, 1996.

Moritz, David. *"Khurbn dynow, sonik, dibetsk"* ("The Destruction of Dynów, Sanok, and Dubieck"). *Yizkerbukh* 1949/50. Translated for JewishGen, Inc. and the Yizkor Book Project, http://jewishgen.org/yizkor/dynow/Dynow.html.

Most, Andrea. *Making Americans: Jews and the Broadway Musical*. Cambridge, MA: Harvard University Press, 2004.

Mostel, Kate, and Madeline Gilford. *170 Years of Show Business*. New York: Random House, 1978.

Mukdoni, A. "*Sholem-aleykhem—a teatr far zikh.*" *Yidish Kultur* no. 6 (New York, 1939), 9–17.

Nahshon, Edna. *From the Ghetto to the Melting Pot: Israel Zangwill's Jewish Plays.* Detroit, MI: Wayne State University Press, 2006.

———. *Yiddish Proletarian Theatre: The Art and Politics of the Artef, 1925–1940.* Westport, CT: Greenwood Press, 1998.

Nasaw, David. *Going Out: The Rise and Fall of Public Amusements.* Cambridge, MA: Harvard University Press, 1999.

Navasky, Victor. *Naming Names.* New York: Viking Press, 1980.

Novak, Michael. *The Rise of the Unmeltable Ethnics: Politics and Culture in the Seventies.* New York: Macmillan, 1972.

Peiss, Kathy. *Cheap Amusements: Working Women and Leisure in Turn-of-the-Century New York.* Pittsburgh: Temple University Press, 1986.

Perl, Arnold. "The Empty Noose." *Hollywood Quarterly* 2:2 (January 1947): 145–52.

———. *Tevya and His Daughters.* New York: Dramatists Play Service, 1958.

———. "To Secure These Rights." *Hollywood Quarterly* 3:3 (April 1948): 267–77.

———. *The World of Sholem Aleichem.* New York: Dramatists Play Service, 1953.

Pilbrow, Richard. *A Theatre Project: An Autobiographical Story.* With David Collison. New York: PLASA Media, 2011, digital edition.

Piro, Richard. *Black Fiddler.* New York: William Morrow, 1971.

Podair, Jerald E. *The Strike That Changed New York: Blacks, Whites and the Ocean Hill–Brownsville Crisis.* New Haven, CT: Yale University Press, 2002.

Popkin, Henry. "The Vanishing Jew of Our Popular Culture." *Commentary* 14:1 (July 1952): 46–55.

Prideaux, Tom. *American Musicals: Bock and Harnick.* Notes to Time-Life Records, 4TL-AM14, Alexandria, VA, 1982.

Prince, Harold. *Contradictions: Notes on Twenty-Six Years in the Theatre.* New York: Dodd, Mead, 1974.

Pritchett, Wendell. *Brownsville, Brooklyn: Blacks, Jews, and the Changing Face of the Ghetto.* Chicago: University of Chicago Press, 2002.

Ravitch, Diane. *The Great School Wars: A History of the New York City Public Schools.* Baltimore and London: Johns Hopkins University Press, 2000.

Rich, Frank. *Ghost Light: A Memoir.* New York: Random House, 2001.

Rich, Frank, and Lisa Aronson. *The Theater Art of Boris Aronson.* New York: Alfred A. Knopf, 1987.

Rieder, Jonathan. *Canarsie: The Jews and Italians of Brooklyn against Liberalism.* Cambridge, MA: Harvard University Press, 1985.

Rosenfeld, Lulla Adler. *Bright Star of Exile: Jacob Adler and the Yiddish Theatre.* New York: Thomas Y. Crowell Company, 1977.

Rosenthal, Jean. *The Magic of Light.* New York: Little, Brown, 1972.

Rosenthal, Steven T. *Irreconcilable Differences?: The Waning of the American Jewish Love Affair with Israel.* Brandeis Series in American Jewish History, Culture and Life. Hanover, NH: Brandeis University Press, 2001.

Roskies, David. *Against the Apocalypse: Responses to Catastrophe in Modern Jewish Culture.* Cambridge, MA: Harvard University Press, 1984.

———. *Bridge of Longing: The Lost Art of Yiddish Storytelling.* Cambridge, MA: Harvard University Press, 1996.

———. *The Jewish Search for a Usable Past.* Bloomington: Indiana University Press, 1999.

———. "Sholem Aleichem: Mythologist of the Mundane." *AJS Review* 13:1/2 (Autumn 1988): 27–46.

Rossner, Robert. *The Year without Autumn: Portrait of a School in Crisis.* New York: R. W. Baron, 1969.

Ryan, William. *Blaming the Victim.* New York: Pantheon, 1971.

Sachar, Howard M. *A History of Israel: From the Rise of Zionism to Our Time.* New York: Alfred A. Knopf, 1989.

———. *A History of the Jews in America.* New York: Vintage Books/Random House, 1993.

Sainer, Arthur. *Zero Dances: A Biography of Zero Mostel.* New York: Limelight Editions, 1998.

Samuel, Maurice. *Blood Accusation: The Strange History of the Beiliss Case.* New York: Alfred A. Knopf, 1966.

———. *The Gentleman and the Jew.* New York: Alfred A. Knopf, 1950.

———. *I, the Jew.* New York: Harcourt Brace, 1927.

———. *Little Did I Know.* New York: Alfred A. Knopf, 1963.

———. *Prince of the Ghetto.* New York: Alfred A. Knopf, 1948.

———. *The World of Sholom Aleichem.* New York: Alfred A. Knopf, 1945.

———. *The Worlds of Maurice Samuel: Selected Writings.* Edited by Milton Hindus. Philadelphia: Jewish Publication Society of America, 1977.

Sandrow, Nahma. *Vagabond Stars: A World History of Yiddish Theater.* New York: Harper and Row, 1977.

Sarna, Jonathan D., ed. *The American Jewish Experience.* 2nd ed. New York: Holmes and Meier, 1997.

Schoener, Allon, ed. *Harlem on My Mind: Cultural Capital of Black America, 1900–1968.* New York: Random House, 1968.

Schulman, Elihu. "*Sholem-aleykhems stzenisher debyut in amerike.*" *Yivo bleter* 4 (August–December 1923): 419–31.

Schwartz, Maurice. "Is New York Ready for a New Yiddish Theater?" *Forverts*, March 2, 1918 (translated by Adrienne Cooper and Jenny Romaine).

Sefer-zikaron li-khehilot shts'uts'in, vasilishki, ostrin, novidvor, roz'anke / ha-'orekh, l. losh. Rozhanka section (in Yiddish) edited by Avraham Lis. Tel Aviv: Hotsa'ah meshutefet shel yots'e ha-kehilot ha-n.l. be-yiśra'el, 1966. Rozhanka portion translated into English as "Community of Rozhanka" by William Cohen for jewishgen.org, http://www.jewishgen.org/yizkor/szczuczyn-belarus/szc435.html.

Segel, Harold B. *Stranger in Our Midst: Images of the Jew in Polish Literature.* Ithaca, NY: Cornell University Press, 1996.

Segev, Tom. *1967: Israel, the War, and the Year That Transformed the Middle East.* Translated by Jessica Cohen. New York: Metropolitan Books, 2007.

———. *The Seventh Million: The Israelis and the Holocaust.* Translated by Haim Watzman. New York: Hill and Wang, 1993.

Shandler, Jeffrey. *Jews, God and Videotape: Religion and Media in America.* New York: New York University Press, 2009.

———. "Reading Sholem Aleichem from Left to Right." In Deborah Dash Moore, ed., *YIVO Annual* 20 (Evanston, IL: Northwestern University Press and the YIVO Institute for Jewish Research, 1991), 305–32.

———. "'The Time of Vishniac': Photographs of Pre-War East European Jewry in Post-War Contexts." In Michael Steinlauf and Anthony Polansky, eds., *Polin: Studies in Polish Jewry*, vol. 16 (Oxford, UK, and Portland, OR: Littman Library of Jewish Civilization, 2003), 313–33.

———. *While America Watches: Televising the Holocaust*. New York: Oxford University Press, 2000.

Shapiro, Edward S. *The Jewish People in America*. Vol. 5: *A Time for Healing: American Jewry since World War II*. Baltimore: Johns Hopkins University Press, 1992.

Shmeruk, Khone. "Sholem Aleichem and America." In Deborah Dash Moore, ed., *YIVO Annual* 20 (Evanston, IL: Northwestern University Press and the YIVO Institute for Jewish Research, 1991), 211–38.

Shohat, Ella. *Israeli Cinema: East/West and the Politics of Representation*. Austin: University of Texas Press, 1989.

Sholem-Aleichem. *The Bloody Hoax*. Translated by Aliza Sherrin. Bloomington: Indiana University Press, 1991.

———. *Briv fun sholem-aleichem 1879–1916* . Tel Aviv: Y. L. Perets farlag, 1995.

———. *Funem yarid*. Warsaw: Yidishbukh, 1966; National Yiddish Book Center electronic edition, Steven Spielberg Digital Yiddish Library, No. 10435.

———. *Gantz tevye der milkhiker, ale verk fun sholem-aleykhem* 8. New York: Sholem-aleykhem foksfond oysgabe, 1925.

———. *The Great Fair: Scenes from My Childhood*. Translated by Tamara Kahana. New York: Noonday Press, 1955.

———. *It's Hard to Be a Jew*. Translated by Mark Schweid, in *Sholem Aleichem Panorama*, ed. Melech Grafstein. London, ON: Jewish Observer, 1948.

———. *The Old Country*. Translated by Frances and Julius Butwin. New York: Crown, 1946.

———. *Oysgeveylte briv*. Edited by I. Mitlman and Khatski Nadel. Moscow: 1941.

———. *Stempenyu*. The play script used by Thomashefsky can be found in the Boris Thomashefsky papers at YIVO: a handwritten bound notebook titled *Yidishe tekhter oder Stempenyu*, transcribed February 3, 1907.

———. *Stempenyu: A Jewish Romance*. Translated by Hannah Berman. Hoboken, NJ: Melville House, 2007.

———. *Tevye der milkhiker: A drame*. In *Ale verk fun sholem-aleykhem*, xxv: 167–235. New York: Sholem-aleykem folksfont oysgabe, 1923.

———. *Tevye the Dairyman and Motl the Cantor's Son*. Translated by Aliza Shevrin. New York: Penguin classics, 2009.

———. *Tevye the Milkman and the Railroad Stories*. Translated by Hillel Halkin. New York: Schocken Books, 1987. All quotations from the Tevye stories come from this volume.

———. *Tevye's Daughters*. Translated by Frances Butwin. New York: Crown, 1949.

———. *Tsezeyt un tseshpreyt, ale verk fun sholem-aleykehm*. Vol. 4: *Dramatishe shriftn*. New York: Sholem-aleykhem foksfond oysgabe, 1925.

———. *Wandering Stars*. Translated by Aliza Shevrin. New York: Viking, 2009.

———. *Di yudishe folks-bibliotek: A bukh fir literatur, kritik un vissenshaft*. Kiev: Sholem-Aleichem, 1888; National Yiddish Book Center electronic edition, Steven Spielberg Digital Yiddish Library, No. 02379.

Silver, M. M. *Our Exodus: Leon Uris and the Americanization of Israel's Founding Story*. Detroit, MI: Wayne State University Press, 2010.

Simonson, Robert. *The Gentleman Press Agent: Fifty Years in the Theatrical Trenches with Merle Debuskey*. New York: Applause Theatre and Cinema Books, 2010.

Sklare, Marshall. *Jewish Identity on the Suburban Frontier: A Study of Group Survival in the Open Society*. New York: Basic Books, 1967.

———. *Observing America's Jews*. Edited and with a foreword by Jonathan D. Sarna. Hanover, NH: Brandeis University Press, 1993.

Sleeper, Jim. *Closest of Strangers: Liberalism and the Politics of Race in New York*. New York: Norton, 1990.

Sorin, Gerald. *The Jewish People in America*, Vol. 3: *A Time for Building: The Third Migration, 1880–1920*. Baltimore and London: Johns Hopkins University Press, 1992.

Sponberg, Arvid F. *Broadway Talks: What Professionals Think about Commercial Theater in America*. Westport, CT: Greenwood Press, 1991.

Staub, Michael E., ed. *The Jewish 1960s: An American Sourcebook*. Lebanon, NH: Brandeis University Press, 2004.

Stein, Joseph. *Juno*. New York: Samuel French, 1959.

Stein, Joseph, Jerry Bock, and Sheldon Harnick. *Fiddler on the Roof*. New York: Limelight Editions, 2002. Tenth printing. Originally published by Crown, 1964. Music and lyrics © Sunbeam Music Corp.

Stein, Joseph, and Will Glickman, with lyrics by Arnold B. Horwitt and music by Albert Hague. *Plain and Fancy*. New York: Random House, 1955.

Steinlauf, Michael. *Bondage to the Dead: Poland and the Memory of the Holocaust*. Syracuse, NY: Syracuse University Press, 1996.

———. "Jewish Theater in Poland." In Michael Steinlauf and Anthony Polansky, eds., *Polin: Studies in Polish Jewry*, vol. 16 (Oxford, UK, and Portland, OR: Littman Library of Jewish Civilization, 2003), 71–91.

Steinlauf, Michael, and Antony Polansky, eds. *Polin: Studies in Polish Jewry*. Vol. 16: *Focusing on Jewish Popular Culture in Poland and Its Afterlife*. Oxford, UK, and Portland, OR: Littman Library of Jewish Civilization, 2003.

Swain, Joseph B. *The Broadway Musical: A Critical and Musical Survey*. New York: Oxford University Press, 1990.

Szajnik, Grzegorz. *Stosunki polsko—ukrainsko—zydowskie w miescie I gminie Dynow*. Dubiecko: Przedsiebiorstwo Budowlano, 2008. ("Polish, Ukrainian, Jewish Communities in the Municipality of Dynów"). Unpublished translation: Ursula Kudelski.

Taylor, Clarence. *Knocking at Our Own Door: Milton A. Galamison and the Struggle to Integrate New York City Schools*. Lanham, MD: Rowman and Littlefield, 2001.

Thissen, Judith. "Reconsidering the Decline of the New York Yiddish Theatre in the Early 1900s." *Theatre Survey* 44:2 (November 2003): 173–97.

Thomashefsky, Boris. *Mayn lebens geshikhte*. New York: Trio Press, 1937.

Tokarska-Bakir, Joanna. "Sandomierz Blood-Libel Myths: Final Report 2006." Unpublished manuscript kindly shared by the author.

Topol. *Topol by Topol*. London: Weidenfeld and Nicolson, 1981.

Uris, Leon. *Exodus*. Garden City, NY: Doubleday, 1958.

Urofsky, Melvin I. *American Zionism from Herzl to the Holocaust*. Lincoln: University of Nebraska Press, Bison Book Edition, 1995; previously published Garden City, NY: Anchor Press/Doubleday, 1975.

Vaill, Amanda. *Somewhere: The Life of Jerome Robbins*. New York: Broadway Books, 2006.

Veidlinger, Jeffrey. *The Moscow State Yiddish Theater: Jewish Culture on the Soviet Stage*. Bloomington: Indiana University Press, 2000.

Vishniac, Roman. *Di farshvundene velt—The Vanished World*. Edited by Raphael Abramovitch. New York: Forward Association, 1947.

————. *Polish Jews: A Pictorial Record*. New York: Schocken Books, 1988; originally published 1947.

Waife-Goldberg, Marie. *My Father, Sholom Aleichem*. New York: Simon and Schuster, 1968.

Warnke, Nina. "Immigrant Popular Culture as Contested Sphere: Yiddish Music Halls, the Yiddish Press, and the Processes of Americanization, 1900–1910." *Theatre Journal* 48:3 (1996): 321–35.

————. "Of Plays and Politics: Sholem Aleichem's First Visit to America." In Deborah Dash Moore, ed., *YIVO Annual* 20 (Evanston, IL: Northwestern University Press and the YIVO Institute for Jewish Research, 1991), 239–76.

Wasserstein, Bernard. *Vanishing Diaspora: The Jews in Europe since 1945*. Cambridge, MA: Harvard University Press, 1996.

Weidman, Jerome, George Abbott, Jerry Bock, and Sheldon Harnick. *Fiorello!* New York: Random House, 1960.

Weitzner, Jacob. *Sholem Aleichem in the Theater*. Madison, NJ: Fairleigh Dickinson University Press, 1994.

Wenig, Larry. *From Nazi Inferno to Soviet Hell*. Hoboken, NJ: Ktav Publishing House, 2000. Memoir, beginning in Dynów.

Whitfield, Stephen J. *The Culture of the Cold War*. Baltimore: Johns Hopkins University Press, 1991, 1996.

Wishengrad, Morton. *The Eternal Light: Twenty-Six Radio Plays*. New York: Crown, 1947.

Wisse, Ruth. *The Modern Jewish Canon: A Journey through Language and Culture*. Chicago: University of Chicago Press, 2000.

Wolitz, Seth L. "The Americanization of Tevye, or Boarding the Jewish Mayflower." *American Quarterly* 40:4 (1988): 514–36.

YIVO Institute for Jewish Research. "Sholem Aleichem in America: The Story of a Culture Hero." Catalog for exhibition at YIVO, May 17, 1990–March 15, 1991. My thanks to curator Jeffrey Shandler for sharing source materials from this catalog with me.

Zangwill, Israel. *The Melting Pot*. New York: Macmillan, 1914.

Zborowski, Mark, and Elizabeth Herzog. *Life Is with People: The Culture of the Shtetl*. New York: Schocken Books, 1995; originally published by International Universities Press in 1952.

Zipperstein, Steven J. *Imagining Russian Jewry: Memory, History, Identity*. Seattle: University of Washington Press, 1999.

————. "Underground Man: The Curious Case of Mark Zborowski and the Writing of a Modern Jewish Classic." *Jewish Review of Books*, no. 2 (Summer 2010): 38–42.

Zylbercweig, Zalmen. *Leksikon fun yidishn teatr*. 6 volumes, published over the period 1931 to 1969 in New York, Mexico, and Warsaw. National Yiddish Book Center electronic edition, Steven Spielberg Digital Yiddish Library, numbers 01089 to 01094.

Most of the material on Sholem-Aleichem can be found in volume 4: 3309 to 3578. This extraordinary compendium of biographical material, plot summaries, production descriptions, and quotations from reviews has been rendered userfriendly by the librarian Faith Jones, who indexed it at the Dorot Jewish Division at the New York Public Library.

————. *Yidisher kunst-teatr in amerike*. At the time of his death in 1972, Zylbercweig was working on a book about Maurice Schwartz's Yiddish Art Theater and on a seventh volume of the *Leksikon fun yidishn teatr*. The latter, including a 371-page section on Schwartz, covering the Yiddish Art Theater from 1918 to 1924, was in galleys that were never published, until, that is, 2011, when Steve Lasky of the Museum of Family History digitized and posted it online at http://www.museu moffamilyhistory.com/yt/yata.htm.

ARCHIVAL AUDIO/VIDEO

Jerry Bock collection of audiovisual recordings. *L (Special) 03-01. Rodgers and Hammerstein Archive, New York Public Library.

Jerry Bock and Sheldon Harnick Dialogue. Videotaped by the New York Public Library's Theatre on Film and Tape Archive at the New York Public Library for the Performing Arts, New York, NY, May 12, 1975.

Fiddler on the Roof. Videotape of performance starring Zero Mostel. *1976.* TOFT. Thank you to the Jerome Robbins Trust for permission to view it.

Fresh Air: Jerry Bock and Sheldon Harnick interviewed by Terry Gross, National Public Radio. n.d. 1988 and June 21, 2004.

Maslow, Sophie. *The Village I Knew.* Videotape of performance by the Sophie Maslow Dance Company. Filmed onstage at the Theater of Riverside Church, New York, New York, May 1977. NY Public Library for the Performing Arts, Dance Collection.

Music Division Oral History Project, New York Public Library for the Performing Arts. Nancy Hamburger Sureck interview: Jerry Bock, November 12, 2002; Sheldon Harnick, January 16, 2003.

Jerry Robbins. "Production Notes on Fiddler on the Roof." *MGZTL 4-3119, JRPP.

Joseph Stein in dialogue with Morton Gottlieb. Videotaped by the New York Public Library's Theatre on Film and Tape Archive at the New York Public Library for the Performing Arts, New York, NY, December 18, 1973.

Weekend Edition Sunday. Jerry Bock and Sheldon Harnick interviewed by Liane Hansen, National Public Radio, May 7, 2000.

RADIO AND COMMERCIAL AUDIO RECORDINGS

Adderley, Cannonball. *Cannonball Adderley's Fiddler on the Roof.* Original release: Capitol ST-2116, 1964. Reissue: Capitol 14309, 1991. CD.

Bikel, Theodore. *Theodore Bikel Sings Jewish Folk Songs.* Elektra, 1958. LP.

———. *Theodore Bikel Sings More Jewish Folk Songs.* Elektra, 1959. LP.

The Eternal Light

"The Daughters of Tevye," adapted from Sholem-Aleichem by Joseph Liss; broadcast August 10, 1947. Newton, CT: RadioGoldindex. CD 71689.

"The Fiddle," adapted from the Sholem-Aleichem story by Arnold Perl; broadcast May 4, 1947. Howell, MI: Audio Classics Archive. CD020798 #134.

"The Great Purim Scandal," adapted from Sholem-Aleichem by Morton Wishengrad; broadcast March 17, 1946. Howell, MI: Audio Classics Archive. CD020769 #72.

"A Passover Guest," adapted from Sholem-Aleichem by Arnold Perl; broadcast August 31, 1947. Newton, CT: RadioGoldindex. CD 75757.

"The Town of the Little People," adapted from Sholem-Aleichem by Joseph Mindel; broadcast October 6, 1946. Howell, MI: Audio Classics Archive. CD020784 #101.

"The World of Sholom Aleichem," adapted from Maurice Samuel by Morton Wishengred; broadcast March 4, 1945. Newton, CT: RadioGoldindex. CD 15993.

Fiddler on the Roof
Original Cast Recording. RCA Victor LOC-1093, 1964. LP.
Broadway Deluxe Collector's Edition. RCA Victor, 2003. CD.
New Broadway Cast Recording. PS Classics, PS240, 2004. CD.
Original London Cast Recording. Columbia Masterworks SX-30742, 1971. CD.

A fidlr afn dakh. Yiddish recording made in Israel. CBS Records 70020. LP.
Knitting on the Roof. Knitting Factory Records. KFW-260, 1999. CD.
Perl, Arnold. *Tevya and His Daughters*, Columbia Masterworks, 1957. LP.
———. *The World of Sholom Aleichem.* Tikva Records, T-28, 1953. LP.
Quijano, Joe. *Fiddler on the Roof Goes Latin.* MGM Records, E/SE 4283, 1965. LP.
Schlamme, Martha. *Martha Schlamme Sings Jewish Folk Songs.* Vanguard Classics, 1957. LP
Tales from the Old Country as told by Howard Da Silva. DECCA Album no. DU5, 1948. LP. (Thanks to Lorin Sklamberg, sound archivist at YIVO, for providing this.)

FILM, TV, VIDEO/DVD, WEB
Black Fiddler: Prejudice and the American Negro. Howard Enders, WABC-TV NY, August 7, 1969.
Exodus. Directed by Otto Preminger. DVD. United Artists, 1960.
Fiddler on the Roof. Directed by Norman Jewison. DVD. Two-Disc Collector's Edition. MGM, 1976/2001.
Footnote. Written and directed by Joseph Cedar. United King Films and Movie Plus, 2011.
Ghetto Pillow. Directed by Harriet Semegram, paintings by Samuel Rothbort, 1960. (Reissued as *Memories of the Shtetl*, 1989).
Jerome Robbins: Something to Dance About. Produced and directed by Judy Kinberg, written by Amanda Vaill. American Masters. Kulture DVD, 2009.
Laughter Through Tears. Directed by Grigori Gricher-Cherikover. VUFKU 1928; Waltham, MA: National Center for Jewish Film, 2006. DVD.
Memorial Prayer by Grigori Gorin, televised version of the Lenkom Theater production directed by Mark Zaharov and starring Yevgeny Leonov, viewable at: http://art-sluza.info/2009/02/10/pom/ In Russian. (Thanks to Olga Gershenson for simultaneous translation.)
Sallah Shabati. Directed by Ephraim Kishon, a Sallah Limited Production, Israel, 1964.
Sholem Aleichem's Tevye der milkhiker. Film starring and directed by Maurice Schwartz, 1939; videocassette. Waltham, MA: National Center for Jewish Films, 1979.
Sixty Minutes. Jane Nicholl, "Fiddler in the Ghetto," CBS, June 10, 1969.
Tevye and His Seven Daughters. Directed by Menachem Golan. Viewed at Cinematek, Tel Aviv, January 11, 2009.
Waiting for Godik. Lama Films, 2007. My gratitude to Ari Davidovich, director, for enabling me to see it online.
WCBS-NY. 6 O'clock News. Jeanne Parr report on *Fiddler* at Eiseman Junior High, January 30, 1969.

The World of Sholom Aleichem. Television version, originally broadcast December 14, 1959. My gratitude to Alan Rosenberg for a copy of the videotape along with his generously shared research material on the production; it has since been issued on DVD by the Archive of American Television, Entertainment One B0057O6IFU.

REPORTS, TRANSCRIPTS, GOVERNMENT DOCUMENTS

American Jewish Committee Oral History Collection, New York Public Library. Jerry Bock interviewed by Harold Flender, February 4 and 11, 1971. Sheldon Harnick interviewed by Harold Flender, February 22, March 1 and 4, 1971.

Cook, James. Harold Prince interviewed for *Forbes*, February 1, 1972. Unpublished transcript kindly provided by Karen Cook.

Elder, Lonne III. "Observer's Report: *Fiddler on the Roof,*" 1964. Thanks to New Dramatists and Judy Ann Elder for making this available.

Fiddler on the Roof Choreographic Manual. Jerome Robbins's choreography diagrammed and described. New York: Music Theatre International.

Investigation of Communist Activities, New York Area—Part VI (Entertainment). Hearings Before the Committee on Un-American Activities, United States House of Representatives, Eighty-Fourth Congress, August 15 and 16, 1955. Government Printing Office, 1955. (Includes testimony of Sarah Cunningham and Madeline Lee.)

Zero Mostel testimony. Investigation of Communist Activities, New York Area—Part VIII (Entertainment), United States House of Representatives, Subcommittee of the Committee on Un-American Activities, *Congressional Record.* October 14, 1955: 2489–509.

Jerome Robbins testimony before the House Committee on Un-American Activities Investigation of Communist Activities, New York City area: Hearing before the Committee on Un-American Activities, House of Representatives, Eighty-Third Congress, first session, Part 2. May 5, 1953. Congressional Record, 1315–25.

Howard Da Silva testimony before the House Committee on Un-American Activities: Transcript of Hearings before the Committee on Un-American Activities, House of Representatives, Eighty-Second Congress, "Communist Infiltration of Hollywood Motion Picture Industry"—Parts 1 and 2. March 21, 1951. Washington, DC: Government Printing Office, March 21, 1951: 112–21.

FBI Files

Zero Mostel. FOIA No. 1151480-000. WFO FILE 100-28145.
Arnold Perl. FOIPA No. 1071473 generously shared by Rebecca Perl.
Jerome Robbins. FOIPA No. 1151493-000.

ACKNOWLEDGMENTS

———

The large number of people who deserve my thanks is a tribute both to their generosity and to the abiding power of *Fiddler on the Roof.* Many friends, relatives, and colleagues shared stories about seeing the show or performing in school or summer camp productions, pointed me to references, forwarded YouTube links, spread enthusiasm. And they did so with delight born of the material itself. I'd have to list nearly my entire contacts file to name everyone touched by *Fiddler* who helped out in this way and thus must express my heartfelt gratitude with this general shout-out: A blessing on all your heads!

Professional curators, archivists, and librarians were no less magnanimous, whether digging out dusty or digital files, answering queries, or arranging special access. Thanks to each of the many wonderful people— too numerous to name individually—working in the archives and collections in the United States and abroad that are listed in the notes section.

What luck that I reside in the same city as the New York Public Library for the Performing Arts—in fact, I practically resided in its Special Collections area for a couple of years. I'm grateful to everyone there, from coat-checkers to curators to copiers, among them: John Calhoun, Danielle Castronovo, Temma Hecht, Tanisha Jones, Tom Lisanti, Louise Martzinek, Jeremy Megraw, Karen Nickeson, Charles Perrier, Amy Schwegel, Alice Standin, Annmarie van Roessel. And how fitting that Jerome Robbins's royalties from *Fiddler* fund the dance film archive there.

Jeffrey Shandler and Alan Rosenberg shared their personal research files with me—an exceptionally generous gesture that I deeply appreciate. Jeffrey was also one of the kind souls—along with David Hajdu, Erika Munk, and Jordan Schildcrout—who read some or all of the manuscript and offered invaluable feedback.

Over the years, I was lucky to have the opportunity to write about *Fiddler* and to share my developing ideas in talks and conferences. This book benefits from the insights of the editors of the articles, Charles McNulty, then at the *Village Voice* (where the idea began) and Alana Newhouse, then at the *Forward,* and of the conveners and interlocutors of the presentations: Barbara Kirshenblatt-Gimblett and Jeffrey Shandler and the seminar participants at New York University's Working Group on Jews, Media and Religion, and the Objects of Affection: The Wedding in Jewish Culture conference at the Center for Jewish History; Henry Bial at the University of Kansas; Joel Berkowitz then at the Center for Jewish Studies, the University at Albany; my sister Debby Simon and her chavurah in Overland Park, Kansas; Warren Hoffman, Jewish cultural studies panel at the Modern Language Association; Edna Nahshon and the Jews/ Theater/Performance in an Intercultural World conference, Jewish Theological Seminary; Yael Zerubavel and the Beyond Eastern Europe: Jewish Cultures in Israel conference at Rutgers University; Jill Dolan and Stacy Wolf and the Good for the Jews? conference at Princeton (who also published an article based on my talk in a special issue of *TDR*); and Jenna Weissman Joselit of George Washington University, who honored me with the invitation to give the Frieda Kobernick Fleischman Lecture in Judaic Studies, George Washington University, and to the Washington, D.C., JCC, Ari Roth and the staff at Theater J who hosted it.

In traveling for research, I enjoyed the warm hospitality of Ron and Deb Shattil in San Francisco; Sinai and Timna Peter, Lilka Peter, Udi Aloni and Sarah Kamens, and Ruthie and Dani Toker, in Israel; and Tomek Kitlinksi and Pawel Leszkowicz in Lublin. Tomek and Pawel also kindly provided on-the-spot translation in Lublin; Ewa Zielińska and Piotr Domalewski did so in Dynów.

For translating clippings and other relevant finds, my thanks to: Elik Elhanan (Hebrew); Helena Chmielewska-Szlajfer, Ursula Kudelski, and Agnieszka Sablinksa (Polish); Olga Gernshenson, Lina Zeldovich (Russian); Jenny Romaine with input from Adrienne Cooper (z"l) (Yiddish columns by Maurice Schwartz). For locating some of those finds: Anna Brenner. And for assisting with photo research and licensing, Roberta Newman.

I'm delighted to have such beautiful and powerful images as illustrations. Photographers and relevant archives or agencies are gratefully noted alongside them. I want to add special thanks to people who were particularly generous in helping me acquire them: Lisa Jawoletz Aronson, Eileen Darby Images, Joseph Dorman, Zeev Godik, Aron Katz, Sławomir Kitowski, Tom Pye, Daniel Sieradski, Ewa Wozniak, Ewa Zielińska, Milo Zonka.

I humbly acknowledge the artists, without whom *Fiddler* and its proliferating versions would not have been. I feel fortunate to have met with Joseph Stein and to have corresponded with Jerry Bock before they both died in 2010 and to have spent several days with Richard Piro, who died in 2012. I'm grateful to have been granted access to the Jerome Robbins Personal Papers by the Jerome Robbins Trust and for the cheerful assistance of Christopher Pennington. I hope this book honors in its modest way the considerable legacy of each of those artists.

Sheldon Harnick graciously met with me on many occasions and patiently answered e-mail queries on many more, always with a welcoming, buoyant spirit; he also read the final manuscript with careful attention. Deep thanks, too, to the many cast members, musicians, designers, writers, directors, artists' relatives, and scholars who granted me interviews and/or corresponded with me. (They are listed in the notes section.)

And thanks to those (not already mentioned elsewhere) who helped open doors to those interviewees, provided useful suggestions or materials, shared ideas, cheered me on, and/or helped keep me whole: Joyce Antler, Deirdre Baker, Mark Bandy, David Barreda, Eileen Blumenthal, Jonathan Boyarin, Aseem Chhabra, Karen Cook, Ari Davidovich, Carolyn Dinshaw, Judyann Elder, Monika Fabianksa, Sharon Feiman-Nemser, Elinor Fuchs, Mark Gevisser, Bob Gibbs, Sheila Goloborotko, Agata Grenda, Mark Harris, Andrew Hsiao, Andrew Ingall, Melanie Joseph, Jonathan Kalb, Carla Kaplan, Josh Kun, Gideon Lester, Vladimir Levin, Alan Levine, Todd London, Marget Long, Rivka Meshulach, Framji Minwalla, Kaicho T. Nakamura, Nidaime A. Nakamura, Joanna Nawrocka, Victor Navasky, Donna Nevel, Debra (Khinke) Olin, Robert M. Prince, Gordon Rogoff,

Elissa Sampson, Stuart Schear, Gary Shapiro, Bob Simon, Lorin Sklamberg, Anna Deavere Smith, Carolyn Solomon, Mike Solomon, Rena Solomon, Sree Sreenivasan, Nyssa Tang, Evan Zelermyer, David Zellnik.

I'm incalculably fortunate to have a job that I love, with students who teach me new things every day and colleagues who inspire me with their own work and their camaraderie. Every one of my colleagues at the Columbia School of Journalism has encouraged and supported me and I am grateful to them all. Deans Nicholas Lemann and Bill Grueskin, and my partner in the Arts & Culture MA concentration, David Hajdu, also made it possible for me to have some time off from teaching to write—a most precious gift. Sam Freedman and Michael Shapiro offered essential advice in just the right doses. Marguerite Holloway shared every step of the process with me as she worked on her beautiful book, *The Measure of Manhattan*: she is the finest writer and the finest friend.

My comrades in the radio-show collective for "Beyond the Pale" did extra work so that I could be AWOL from the program for ages: Marissa Brostoff, Kiera Feldman, Adam Horowitz, Alex Kane, Esther Kaplan, Lizzy Ratner, Jenny Romaine, Eve Sicular.

I was fortunate to receive a George A. and Elizabeth Gardner Howard Foundation Fellowship in Theater Studies early on to support research travel.

Metropolitan Books has been a perfect match, arranged by my savvy and sensitive agent Scott Moyers, and sustained with enthusiasm and smarts by Adam Eaglin when Scott moved to Penguin Press. It has truly been a wonder of wonders to work under the guiding brilliance of both Sara Bershtel and my editor Riva Hocherman, who combines a keen mind and perfect ear with good humor and tender care. The whole team—in copyediting, art, and promotion—has been a pleasure to work with.

This undertaking has been overdetermined in myriad ways, beginning with the influences of my parents. My mother, Josephine Kleiman Solomon, a professional Jewish educator, instilled my love of *Yiddishkayt* as a living source of insight and pleasure, as well as my passion for music and theater. My father, Jack Solomon, who loved American culture and popular forms, was especially enthusiastic about this project, and took great pleasure in passing along tips. I read him a chapter of the just-completed first draft on our last visit. He was weak and sometimes out of it—he died only two weeks later—but his mind was sharp as ever and he shared zeal and suggestions, only the last of his many gifts.

It would take dozens of pages to thank my partner, Marilyn Kleinberg Neimark, for all the ways she has helped make this book—and my happiness—possible. So I dedicate it to her, my *beshert*.

Index

Page numbers in *italics* refer to illustrations.

About the Author

Alisa Solomon teaches at Columbia University's Graduate School of Journalism, where she directs the Arts & Culture concentration in the MA program. A theater critic and general reporter for the *Village Voice* from 1983 to 2004, she has also contributed to the *New York Times*, *The Nation*, *Tablet*, *The Forward*, and other publications. Her first book, *Re-Dressing the Canon: Essays on Theater and Gender*, won the George Jean Nathan Award for Dramatic Criticism. She lives in New York City.